Psychology for Professional Groups

PSYCHOLOGY FOR TEACHERS

Psychology for Professional Groups

Series editors: Antony J. Chapman and Anthony Gale

Psychology for Professional Groups is a well-established textbook series providing the full range of current scientific expertise on the psychology available to professionals, whether practising or in training for qualifying examinations.

Psychology for Professional Groups

PSYCHOLOGY FOR TEACHERS

Second Edition

David Fontana

Reader in Educational Psychology
University College Cardiff

Published by
The British Psychological Society
in association with
Macmillan Publishers Ltd.

Published by The British Psychological Society, St Andrews House,
48 Princess Road East, Leicester, LE1 7DR, UK, in association
with Macmillan Publishers Ltd, Basingstoke.

First published 1981 by
THE MACMILLAN PRESS LTD
Houndmills, Basingstoke, Hampshire RG21 2XS
and London
Companies and representatives
throughout the world

ISBN 0–333–46124–X hardcover
ISBN 0–333–46125–8 paperback

A catalogue record for this book is available
from the British Library.

Printed in Hong Kong

Reprinted 1982, 1983, 1985, 1986
Second edition 1988
Reprinted 1989, 1991, 1991, 1993

Contents

Contents

Contents

PART IV   SOCIAL INTERACTION, TEACHER–CHILD RELATIONS AND TEACHER PERSONALITY

11   Social Behaviour and Social Skills   259

Contents

Introduction to First Edition

The purpose of this book is to acquaint the reader with those areas of psychology of most practical value to the teacher. It deals, therefore, not only with matters relating directly to the classroom, but with matters pertaining to the child's background outside school and to his or her own self-perceptions and self-concepts. The teacher's task can only be clarified if he or she has a knowledge of children as complete persons rather than simply as individuals who spend the hours from nine o'clock until four sitting in classrooms. The child's personality, ability to learn, motivation, social behaviour, and attitudes towards school are all formed as a consequence of a complex set of interrelated factors which begin at birth (and even before) and extend throughout each moment of waking life. By the time you have finished this book you should have a clear idea of what these factors are, and of how they influence child behaviour. You should also have a clear idea of the part you as teacher can play in the determination of this behaviour, and of how you can best help children to benefit from the learning opportunities that school has to offer.

The application of psychology to education has a long and honoured history, and stretches back to the first occasion when adults tried to influence the behaviour of the young. But it is only in comparatively recent years that the association between the two subjects has been given a firmly scientific basis. By this I mean that it is only during the last 60 years or so that psychology has developed the precision and methodology that allow it to make accurate generalizations about child behaviour, and to provide the teacher with the kind of information necessary if he or she is to make objective professional decisions and judgements. Without such information, the teacher can only fall back upon the sort of anecdotal evidence that we often hear when people are discussing children. We hear, for example, that children are supposed to be basically honest (or dishonest), that they like (or do not like) firm discipline, that they have (or have not) a sense of fair play, that they learn best in informal (or in formal) teaching environments, that they are influenced (or not influenced) by what they see on television and so on. One school of thought has it that children's behaviour is the result of conditioning, another that they have the freedom to decide for themselves. We are told on the one hand that abilities such as intelligence are largely inherited, and on the other that they are largely the result of environmental influences. Small wonder that faced with such conflicting statements inexperienced teachers often feel confused, and decide in the end that they must make up their own minds on these and other important matters.

It would be wrong to suggest that modern psychology has final answers to all the questions that face us in education. Children (and teachers) are individuals, and often must be studied as individuals before detailed guidance on particular problems can be given. And, in any case, there are still large gaps in our knowledge that remain to be filled. Human behaviour is very complex and its measurement and assessment fraught with many difficulties. It is in fact this very complexity that gives the study of psychology much of its fascination. But psychology helps teachers recognize the factors that influence child behaviour and learning, and assists them in developing strategies to cope with the tasks that must be faced in the classroom. Furthermore, it helps the teacher to examine his or her own general professional behaviour, and to identify areas where this behaviour may itself have contributed towards particular problems that may have arisen. As is stressed repeatedly throughout the book, psychology shows us that no child's behaviour can be fully understood unless we study also the behaviour of others – teachers, parents, school friends – towards that child. Each individual stands at the centre of a complex matrix of interrelated influences, each of which must be taken into account if we are to comprehend the way in which the individual lives his or her life. In the case of the child this matrix is of particular importance. Still at an early formative stage in development, the child is very much dependent upon other people's behaviour. When the teacher, for example, speaks critically of the child's performance in a particular subject, the child may get the impression that this indicates he or she lacks ability in it, and that future performance may deteriorate even further. If we are to help that child improve his or her standards we must look therefore not only at the gaps in their knowledge but at the way in which the teacher, albeit unwittingly, has been undermining the child's confidence in his or her own potential.

Psychology also helps us answer some of the questions on the origins of individual differences. Are we born different, or do we simply become different as the result of experience? Put another way, are individual differences genetically or environmentally determined? By individual differences we mean not only intelligence but also such things as personality, creativity and motor skills. As we shall see, these answers are of critical importance for the teacher since they indicate some of the limits to the influence which education can have upon our lives. If individual differences are largely inherited then there is little that education can do beyond developing what is already there. If, on the other hand, these differences are mainly the result of environment, then education has an enormous potential to redress and alter the consequences of early disadvantage and to help all children achieve the same high standards.

The book deals with children from an early age through into adolescence and the end of compulsory schooling, but this does not mean that you should pick out only those sections that apply to the ages you plan to teach or are actually teaching. For a full understanding of older children the secondary school teacher needs to know something of the formative influences that have been at work during the early part of their lives, while the primary school teacher needs to know something of the problems that may lie ahead of children in their care in order to play a full part in helping them develop the skills and strategies necessary to cope with such problems. The book is designed for both serving teachers and students in training, and the emphasis throughout is upon the practicalities of the teacher's task. Thus theoretical areas of psychology that may be of interest in themselves but that have little real application for what the teacher actually does with children are avoided. A high premium is also placed upon clarity, so that the non-specialist should be able to read the book without experiencing undue difficulties in understanding any of the points raised. Finally, the book can be read as a whole or dipped into, depending upon the needs of the reader. The important thing is that it should be of some use.

The plan of the book

The plan of the book is simple. In Part I we look at early influences upon the child such as parent–child relationships, family size, and social class. Part II then examines cognitive factors (i.e. mental factors to do with thinking, intelligence and learning) while Part III looks at affective factors (i.e. emotional factors to do with personality, attitudes and values). Part IV looks at social factors: that is, at the factors involved in the child's relationships with the teacher and with the classroom group, and at the teacher him or herself, at what is known about the qualities that make the successful teacher and at the ways in which we study interaction between the teacher and the class.

Each chapter outlines current knowledge in the areas concerned and discusses practical implications for the teacher. At the end of each chapter there are suggestions for further reading, together with a list of questions and discussion points. These questions are not designed so much to test your factual knowledge as to draw attention to some of the most important issues discussed in the chapter and to start you thinking creatively about them.

David Fontana
University College Cardiff, 1981

Introduction to Second Edition

A number of extensive alterations to the material contained in the first edition have been made. Some of this material, in keeping with the policy for the *Psychology for Professional Groups* series of which this book is a part, was by authors other than myself. These contributions do not appear in the new edition, as I have rewritten the topics covered by them with teacher education exclusively in mind. The convention in the first edition of dividing the theoretical content of each chapter from the practical content has also been changed in the new edition with the result that each chapter now links theory and practice closely together throughout.

Opportunity has also been taken in the new edition to amalgamate the two chapters on personality, since this further helps the linkage of theory and practice. Across a wide area of subjects new sections have also been added, for example on early attachment, ethnic groups, neglected children, the home–school conflict, language and the school, teacher language, approaches to personality, personality states, measuring the self, social status, social roles, social skills and teacher stress. In addition, each part of the book has been thoroughly revised and updated, in the light both of current developments within the field of educational psychology and the feedback to the first edition obtained from students, practitioners and book reviewers. It is the hope of the publishers, the series editors and myself that these extensive alterations will further strengthen the book's usefulness both to student and to serving teachers.

David Fontana
University College Cardiff, 1988

Part one

The Early Years

Introduction — The child's social life begins in the home. Throughout the formative years the child spends more waking hours in and around the home than in school. For a five year old the ratio is approximately 5:3 in favour of the home, and for an adolescent it rises to about 2:1. Our closest relationships are usually formed within the home, and the child also locates there most of his or her physical possessions and leisure interests. Not surprisingly, therefore, the influence of the home is of critical importance in a child's psychological development. In particular, it helps determine how individual abilities are used, how attitudes and opinions are formed, and how motivation towards school and towards one's future develops.

Part One

The Early Years

1

Early Social Development

Human beings are social creatures. The relative defenceless-ness of the individual, particularly in early childhood, has helped ensure over the millions of years of human evolution that people stick together. We live and work in social groups, and there is evidence that isolating the individual from others can lead to severe cognitive and emotional problems. We have become programmed, if you like, to be gregarious. And so pervasive is this programming that the way in which we experience our own lives is very much determined for us by the way in which we think other people see us. Not content with simply living together in our social groups, we need the esteem and support of the group if we are to develop into happy and well-adjusted people.

The child's first social group is of course the family, and for the majority of children this remains the most important group throughout childhood. But a close second in many ways is the school, and the teachers and the circle of friends a child meets there. As we shall see shortly, problems arise for many children when the pattern of social behaviour (and the values and standards that go with it) taught in one of these groups differs markedly from that taught in the other. A home–school conflict of this kind can not only leave a child confused and resentful but can materially hinder his or her progress in formal learning.

The child in the home
A young child's first social relationship is with his or her mother or mother substitute (the *caregiver*). The caregiver's voice (at around two months) and face (at around three months) are amongst the first things the baby recognizes, along with the special way he or she has of handling the infant. In view of the closeness of this relationship and of its obvious importance in socializing the child, it has come in for a great deal of study by child psychologists. The term used for this early social bonding between the child and his or her principal caregiver is *attachment*. The signs that a baby is developing attachment for a particular adult are that the baby:

3

- is more readily comforted by the caregiver when dis-
  tressed than by anyone else
- is less upset by the unfamiliar when with the caregiver
  than when with others
- shows more pleasure when the caregiver appears and
  makes more movements towards him or her than towards
  others.

In families where both parents have close ties with the children, attachment may develop equally to both mother and
father. But one interesting finding is that children who are
kept at home and treated more restrictively by their caregiver
show more attachment behaviour than children who attend
pre-school playgroup and generally have more freedom
(Kagan, 1984). This indicates that attachment *per se* is no
absolute indication of satisfactory social and personal development in these early years. A child who is made to feel
nervous and anxious by parents may attach strongly to them
because they represent the only security in an otherwise
insecure world.

This probably explains why some children, from very difficult deprived homes where they are neglected or cruelly
treated, nevertheless show strong links with their parents, at
least in the early years. The emotional damage done to these
children may be grave and lasting, yet attachment appears to
take place. It would seem that nature has programmed the
human infant, for survival reasons, to attach to whoever is
providing him or her with care, however minimal that care
may be. Some authorities (e.g. Sluckin, Herbert and Sluckin,
1983) suggest this may be analogous to imprinting in animals, the innate mechanism that prompts the young of some
species to form a lasting bond with whatever moving object
they see during the critical early hours of life. But there are
certain dangers in extrapolating lessons for human behaviour
from observations on animals, who develop physically much
more rapidly in infancy than we do. So the important issues
from the psychologist's point of view are simply that in
humans:

- attachment appears to be a necessary phase in early child
  development
- attachment takes place principally between the child and
  his or her most significant caregiver, (whether that caregiver be the natural mother or not)
- attachment is the first step in a child's social learning.

The influence of attachment upon later development

I have said that attachment takes place between a child and
even an inadequate parent, provided that parent acts as
principal caregiver. But for satisfactory social development

to take place, it seems vital that the early child–parent relationship be a good one. Clarke and Clarke (1976) present evidence to show that the adverse effects upon children of early neglect or ill-treatment can be remedied to some degree by appropriate compensatory care later in childhood, but nevertheless early experiences have a particularly potent influence upon later development. The work of Harlow and Harlow (1966) show that in rhesus monkeys, deprivation of adequate parental care in the first six months leads to extreme difficulty in forming successful social and sexual relationships at maturity, and to an inability on attaining parenthood to offer proper love and care to offspring. Again we have to be careful about extrapolating lessons for human behaviour from experiments with animals, but rhesus monkeys show many developmental similarities to humans, and it seems reasonable that early neglect and ill-treatment in the first two years of a childs life (analogous to the first six months of a rhesus monkey's life) may interfere with the child's subsequent abilities to relate successfully to others.

This suggests that early childhood may be a *critical period* for social learning. Unless a child receives a generous minimum of adequate care (love, tactile contact, comfort, happy social interaction) during the stage of the first attachment, then the child in turn may find it difficult to love and care for others, either in childhood or in adult life. One tragic confirmation of this is the fact that child batterers frequently have a history of having themselves been battered in childhood. Deprived of love and care during the early years, and subjected to physical abuse, they are all too often handicapped when attempting to raise their own children. Thus the foundations of good parental behaviour may in significant measure lie back in the handling a child receives in the early years.

Research into other aspects of social relationships provides further support for the long-term effects of early attachment experiences. Goldfarb (1955) compared children raised in an institution for the first three years of their life prior to fostering with children fostered at a much earlier age, and found the former to be less mature at adolescence, less emotionally stable, and less capable of giving and receiving affection than the latter. While few authorities question the view that early deprivation has adverse consequences, Goldfarb's work has been challenged in recent years. The challenges are aimed in particular at the view that the consequences of early deprivation are irreversible (Clarke and Clarke, 1976). Certainly, as Tizard (1977) shows, institutional children adopted into good homes even after the age of three seem capable of satisfactory development; but the standard of early care received by the children in her sample was probably much better than that available in the institutions at the time of Goldfarb's studies a quarter of a century earlier. And the point remains that the great majority of children raised in unsatisfactory homes in the first years of life do *not* receive the excellent compensatory care available in adoptive families. In most cases, their early deprivation is followed by continuing deprivation throughout childhood, and the child stands little chance of making up the lost ground. Hence the *cycle of deprivation* so well known to social workers, in which neglecting or battering parents raise children who themselves become neglecting and battering.

ATTACHMENT TO WHOM? I've already made it clear that children attach most strongly in the early years to the adult who serves as their principal caregiver, who may be the mother or father, or grandparents or other relatives, or someone with no blood ties at all. This is an important point. It means that there is nothing magical about blood relationships. A child will attach just as strongly to adoptive parents as to natural ones. It also means that a child who is left with a good childminder while his or her mother goes out to work is unlikely to come to any social harm. Certainly it may mean that the mother has to contend with her own feelings of jealousy when she sees her child attaching to a childminder as strongly as to herself, but provided both she and the childminder relate to the baby in similar ways and have similar ideas on child-rearing, the *child* will cope with things happily enough.

But we must not get the idea that attachment is something that *only* happens during these early years. Consider a young boy developing over the years. As he grows older, so he is able to rationalize more and more about the adults in his life, and to make choices as to whom he likes and dislikes, but he will continue to bond with people who satisfy his basic needs for care and guidance. However, where the child bonds too dependently with adults other than his parents, it may be that his innate drive to form attachments is not being fully satisfied at home. This can be seen at school level for example in the boy who becomes excessively demanding upon his teacher, staying physically close to him or her and showing a high level of emotional involvement. The boy from a secure home in which attachment has taken place satisfactorily will have a good relationship with his teacher, but will indicate clearly enough that he or she takes second place to his family. At the other extreme, the boy who shows withdrawal or major hostility towards adults and other children, and no evidence of bonding, may come from a background in which there have been few opportunities to learn the lessons of attachment, leaving him showing early evidence of the cycle of deprivation just mentioned.

The nature of early social learning

A child brought up with parents who respond with love, understanding, and clear and sensible guidance, stands an excellent chance of learning how to relate successfully to other people. The child learns that other people are nice to be with, that they look after you and provide fun and happiness. But as you grow older, you learn that they have rights and needs too, and that you can in turn study their feelings and bring them happiness. If your parents encourage you to mix freely with others, and to accept and value your own role in these social interactions, you learn to be at ease with other people, to be confident and articulate, and to prize others while at the same time preserving your personal autonomy and independence.

This is a considerable feat of learning, depending strongly upon example as well as upon precept. But their natural drive towards sociability means that children are programmed to learn quickly. Obviously temperamental differences (see Chapter 8) will mean that the strength of this drive varies from child to child. Some children are happy from an early age with their own company, while others are only at their best when they are with other people. But few – perhaps no – children born without mental handicap lack the innate ability to relate well to their fellows. Individuals who grow up excessively shy or cold or hostile or aggressive have been denied the chance to learn that the experience of being with others is a mutually enriching one, enhancing the quality of one's own life and the quality of life of those around one. As Erikson (1950) puts it, perhaps this early social learning can best be summed up in one word, *trust*. If as a child you learn that people close to you can be trusted, that they love you and care for you and behave consistently towards you, then you are free to relate warmly and sensitively back to them, and ultimately to see yourself as a valued and useful member of the community.

Essential to this early lesson of trust is the quality of the communication that takes place between parents (or other caregivers) and children. By touch, gesture, eye contact, tone of voice, parents convey to children their feelings for them, and allow them to experience a sense of safety and security. Soon language also begins to play an important part (see Chapter 4). Once children can understand what is being said to them, and can begin to put their own responses into words, the potential for parent–child communication increases enormously. Through language children are given a much clearer picture of their parents' attitude towards them, and gain an increasingly comprehensive picture of how other people see them and of their social standing within the family and the wider social group. Through language, children build up concepts about themselves and about their relationships with others, and learn how to express personal and social needs.

7

Much of their early development is therefore intricately linked to the proficiency with which they acquire linguistic skills.

Sex roles

Men and women are complex creatures, and no single set of psychological theories can adequately explain all aspects of their social development. Perhaps nowhere is this more true than of sex roles. Men and women have far more similarities than differences, both physically and psychologically, but it is the differences that often attract most of our attention. Physical differences are biologically determined, though we often emphasize them by the way we dress, style our hair, use or do not use make-up, and generally present ourselves to the world. But psychological differences are another matter. Does our biology predestine us to be psychologically distinct? Are men programmed by nature to be the dominant sex, the achievers and the aggressors, the leaders and initiators? And are women programmed to be forever the subservient sex, passive rather than active, followers rather than leaders?

Enough has been written on this topic to make most people familiar with the issues concerned. Suffice it to say that in most mammals the female tends to be less aggressive than the male from the early months of life onwards. This certainly suggests some biological influence on behaviour. On the other hand, each of the human sexes does show the characteristics of the other, albeit to a lesser degree. Which leads us to ask whether, with the appropriate education, females could be taught to behave very much like males, and males taught to behave like females. Or more specifically, can our roles as men and women be modified by the kind of education we receive?

Before discussing the answer to these questions, it is right to point out that blurring the sex role differences between men and women may not necessarily be a good thing, particularly if it is aimed at making women more like men. Arguably it is the qualities associated more closely with maleness, such as dominance, aggression, and violence that have brought the world to the position in which it now finds itself. Useful as these qualities may have been in humankind's long evolution, it is debatable whether they can be safely accommodated in a world which has the means for self-destruction. The pressing need now seems to be for an infusion of those qualities more traditionally associated with femaleness, such as sensitivity, compassion, and peace. The debate should therefore be primarily about how to value females properly in society, and give them equal rights with men, rather than how to turn them into male clones.

Nevertheless it may be that unless women can be more assertive, more confident, more sure of their own status, society will continue to deny them their equality and their due influence over events. Which means that we must take a look at whether social learning plays a part in assigning women (and men) their present roles, and whether it could with suitable modifications play a part in equalizing the imbalances that operate. For there is no doubt that women are consistently assigned the subservient role in western society. In politics, in the higher levels of the civil service, in higher education, in industry and commerce, in the judiciary, in the police, in entertainment and the arts, in sport, (the list is virtually endless) males are dominant. On the other hand, most of the menial and lower-paid jobs in society are held by females. In most western countries average weekly earnings of females are only some two-thirds of those of males. Men own most of the property in society and control most of the wealth.

Some of this inequality can be explained by woman's child-bearing role. It is harder for her to have ambitions outside the home and make a career for herself should she so wish, if periodically she has to absent herself in order to bring new life into the world. But what cannot be explained is society's failure to take woman's maternal role into account, and to ensure that not only is she valued appropriately for it but given the necessary opportunities to compensate for it. Evidence of this failure can be seen not only in society at large but within the home and the school. The discrimination against women starts virtually at birth, and continues throughout childhood. And sadly, it is often women themselves who play a major part in discrimination. It is the mother within the home, and the female teacher at school, who often teach the young girl much of her female role.

We can see this in the research for example of Lewis (1972) which reveals that in early infancy the young girl playing in the park is given less freedom to explore before being called back by her mother than is the young boy. Or in research which shows that women handle girl babies differently from boys, encouraging the former to be quieter and more dependent and the latter more boisterous and self-reliant (see Archer and Lloyd, 1982), or in the long-term studies of Davie, Butler and Goldstein (1972), which show that girls are consistently more orientated by their parents towards home and domestic matters than boys. Or in the school-based research (see e.g. Doyle and Good, 1982) which shows that in the classroom boys are more likely to be praised when producing good work and girls more likely to be praised when producing good behaviour, thus emphasizing academic achievement in the former and social conformity in the latter.

This does not mean that boys in their turn are not discriminated against at times, though in a different way. The emphasis upon a boy being a 'man', upon not showing his feelings, upon 'toughness' and physical strength, forces a boy into a predetermined mould in much the same way as his sister. Such a mould is perhaps equally damaging in terms of personality development and even physical health (the inability to show one's feelings is for instance linked in later life with certain illnesses such as coronary heart-disease). But the point is that, in social terms at least, boys are given many of the advantages that lead to apparent success in later life, while girls are left with the disadvantages. Even in a crucial area like self-esteem (see pp. 236–243) girls are given less chance to value themselves, which may be one explanation for the higher incidence of neurotic and psychotic problems amongst women in adult life.

Finally, I must make it clear that there are no intellectual reasons why boys should be favoured over girls (a point to which I return in Chapter 5). In fact, intellectual differences between the sexes are of relatively minor importance, and of uncertain origin. Girls tend to be more verbal than boys in the early school years, and to show fewer reading difficulties, while boys perform better on mathematical and spatial problems. Whether these differences are due to innate factors or to environmental factors (girls spend more time in the home and are more exposed to language learning; boys spend more time outside the home and are more exposed to spatial experiences) is not known. But in any case, these differences decrease in importance as the child moves through the school. At all ages, boys show more incidence of educational backwardness than girls, and more incidence of outstanding achievement, prompting some experts to suggest that boys are more given to extremes than girls, but this could be due to cultural rather than innate factors. Backward boys may be left by parents and teachers to fend more for themselves than backward girls, while outstanding boys may be given more encouragement than outstanding girls.

Ethnic groups

In a multicultural society, many of the social differences in behaviour between individuals are determined by the particular ethnic groups to which they belong. Differences between ethnic groups in religious beliefs, in customs and traditions, in moral standards, in dress and speech, and in general life style are often very marked, leading to misunderstandings and prejudices and even active hostility. Human beings often find it hard to tolerate divergence from the social norm, so minority groups are particularly at risk from these instances of social discrimination.

At formal school level, little of this dicrimination is deliberate. Yet through simple misunderstanding of the ethnic backgrounds from which their children come, some educators can misinterpret both classroom behaviour and learning difficulties. Detailed examination of these issues belongs to a sociological rather than a psychological text, but children from backgrounds differing significantly from that of the teacher may have been taught ways of relating to authority and of showing respect and friendliness which diverge markedly from those which the latter recognizes as appropriate. Thus although the children may intend no offence, their manner of talking and their use of words may be construed by the teacher as deliberate provocation. Similarly, boisterous exuberant and extravert behaviour, acceptable within the culture from which the children come, may be construed by the teacher as disruptive and challenging.

The same type of problem may emerge when it comes to learning difficulties. The child may appear to understand the teacher, yet show subsequently that he or she has missed the point, not because of unfamiliarity with the words used by the teacher but because within his or her own culture they carry a different meaning. Equally, the child may produce incorrect answers on tests of intelligence and ability not because of a failure to read the questions but because the tests are not *culture-fair*, that is because they are not free of the cultural influences which handicap children from a different background. Thus children from certain ethnic groups may be wrongly diagnosed as of low intelligence, and may be over-represented in remedial streams, simply because of cultural inadequacies in our teaching methods or in our test procedures (see Chapter 5).

With increased understanding and tolerance of cultural differences, the risks of children being wrongly diagnosed as maladjusted or as backward are greatly diminished. One of the obvious needs is for more teachers – and more educational psychologists – to be drawn from these minority groups, and for more opportunities to be given to student teachers to understand fully minority group characteristics. To date, little sustained and co-ordinated effort has been made in this direction. The result is that society at large is still imperfectly educated for life in a multicultural community, and children from minority groups remain subject to discrimination both within the educational system and within the job market. The consequences of this for social divisions and social strife are all too clear.

Social class

Just as children from ethnic groups which differ from that of the teacher can be unintentionally misinterpreted, so can children from certain social groups. Social class is rightly a sensitive issue, and one which carries all kinds of political implications. Discussion of these implications lies outside the

scope of the present text. So indeed does any extended examination of social class. But one way of helping the teacher
understand the implications of the class structure for education is to look at the Classification of Occupations issued
for the United Kingdom (UK) by the Registrar General. This
classification places families in five categories of paternal
occupation, ranging from very 'superior' professions like law
and medicine at the top down to unskilled labourers at the
bottom. The terms Upper Social and Economic Status (USES)
and Lower Social and Economic Status (LSES) are sometimes
used as broad divisions between the top two categories and
the bottom two. Research shows consistently that USES children are much more likely to be successful in school-leaving
examinations and much more likely to go on to higher education than LSES children. Not surprisingly, they also subsequently obtain better jobs and amass more wealth.

If we look for the reasons for this, one of the most obvious
is that LSES children come from more deprived backgrounds,
with much less access to the kind of experiences that lead to
educational success. We must not generalize too extensively.
Many LSES homes are excellent, while many USES are emotionally impoverished. But in the main, when they start school,
LSES children have less knowledge on how to relate to the
teacher, on how to control their own behaviour, and on
patterns of conduct acceptable to the educational system.
They may come from a background in which aggression and
toughness are the only things that bring results, and may find
it hard to learn the lessons of sharing or of waiting their turn.
They may have parents who have little regard for school, are
indifferent towards their school progress, and show no encouragement and support for academic achievement. Small
wonder that such children, in spite of their abilities, make a
poor start to their school careers and continue to drop inexor-
ably behind their more privileged classmates.

In the crucial area of language LSES children may have had
little practice of how to put their thoughts and wishes into
words, or of how to listen and respond to others. Verbal
impoverishment often contributes to cognitive impoverishment (without adequate language we find it harder to develop
our powers of reasoning). Without books and an early introduction to the value of reading, a further linguistic deficit
opens up. Similarly they may be denied early experiences of
the value of numeracy, and thus fail to see the point of
mathematics. Looked at from every angle, the child from an
impoverished background is at a massive disadvantage at the
start of formal education. Schools are geared very much
towards the standards of behaviour and of thinking of USES
groups, and often find difficulty in understanding the world of
the LSES child.

Many teachers and student teachers very laudably dislike

attaching labels to children and assigning them to so-called middle- or working-class groups (or to USES or LSES). They argue that such labelling carries undesirable judgemental implications, and that in any case the use of class-orientated terms only helps to perpetuate social inequalities. Nevertheless, there are for the teacher a number of helpful practical lessons to be learnt from the research that has gone into the effects of social class background upon educational performance. Extended discussion of these lessons belongs more properly to a text on sociology then to one on psychology, but I must emphasize that such research indicates that the poor living conditions, the economic problems, the verbally unstimulating environment, and the lack of cultural and leisure facilities experienced by many lower social and economic status families inevitably act as a powerful handicap to the educational progress of their children. Such children often have nowhere at home where they can read quietly or do homework, are not introduced to books within the family, have limited access to play facilities, to libraries, and to other cultural amenities like museums and theatres. They also find themselves in a social environment that may place little stress upon the importance of education, and which offers them little vocational guidance, and which generally finds itself at odds with the aims and value systems held by the school.

The role of the teacher when working with children from social backgrounds of this kind is a complex one. Teachers must uphold the values of the school, yet at the same time must sympathize with the problems of children, and must not alienate them further by attempts to turn them against the subculture in which they have been raised. It is the job of the teacher to demonstrate to children that the purpose of school is to help them tackle the tasks and difficulties of life. Thus, far from simply being concerned to measure them against academic standards and find them wanting, the school has direct relevance for both their current experiences and for the years that lie ahead. The purpose of schooling is to increase the range of desirable possibilities that face the child in terms of leisure and vocational interests and, whenever a child dismisses school as irrelevant, careful thought must be given to the way in which this purpose is being translated into concrete curricular terms. Detailed discussion of the curriculum would be out of place in the present text, but from a psychological viewpoint I must emphasize that the relationship between teacher and class is very much conditioned by what children suppose the school is able to offer them.

The family

Important as ethnic and socio-economic groups undoubtedly are, the most important unit of all in the social development of the child is undoubtedly the family. Not only is it within the family that the child's first attachments take place, it is within the family that we learn many of our other social roles. Families are naturally influenced by the ethnic and socio-economic groups to which they belong, but even within these groups there are enormous variations in the way in which families behave and treat each of their members. So much so in fact that the professional study of the family is now something of a speciality in its own right, combining elements of psychology, sociology and social administration.

The changing nature of the family

To understand this study, we must distinguish at the outset between the so-called *nuclear* and *extended* families. The nuclear family consists of first-degree relatives (parents and children), while the extended family includes second- and third-degree relatives (grandparents, uncles and aunts, cousins) and even beyond. Both the nuclear and the extended families, as institutions, have undergone important changes in developed countries in recent years. In the case of the nuclear family, these changes are mostly structural. The traditional family unit of father, mother and one to three children is now no longer the universal norm. Family break-up (one quarter of all marriages in the UK are now likely to end in divorce) and the increasing incidence of children conceived outside marriage (one in ten as a national average, and much higher in some parts of the country) have led to a massive increase in the number of single-parent families. And even in two-parent families, the norm of father going out to work and mother staying at home now applies only in a minority of cases. Sixty per cent of mothers of school-age children have paid employment outside the home, and in many families the high unemployment rate of adult males means that if either parent stays at home during the day it is just as likely to be the father as the mother.

In the case of the extended family, the most important change has been its decline in importance. Social mobility means that many young people move from the areas in which they were reared, with the result that they marry and raise children well away from grandparents and other relatives. Social mobility of this kind, leading as it does not only to a break-up of the extended family but also to a disintegration of small tight-knit communities, is often advanced as one reason for the current alleged decline in social restraints and law and order. Brought up within the extended family and the familiar world of neighbours and friends, children were subject to far more pressures towards social conformity then is now the case. Since everybody in the immediate environment knew them, children were likely to be identified if they got up to mischief, and to be sensitive to the disapproval of second- and third-degree relatives. And since these relatives were always on hand, children were less likely to want for parental substitutes if both their parents were away from home during the day or evening.

Neglected children

The changing nature of both nuclear and extended families means in addition that inadequate parents may now have less support than ever, leaving the children of such families increasingly vulnerable to neglect and perhaps cruelty. The increase in reported child neglect, child battering and sexual offences against children would seem to testify to this sad reality. The social services, who increasingly have to take on roles traditionally assumed by the extended family, find it almost impossible to identify and monitor all children at risk.

As indicated earlier when discussing attachment, parents who were themselves badly treated in childhood often seem unable to relate correctly to their own children. This applies not only to the physical aspects of the relationship but also to the emotional. Thus some parents, although apparently taking good care of their children's material needs, provide them with an emotional environment which may contribute to severe neurotic or psychotic problems in childhood or adult life. The family has been blamed for a wide range of such problems, including even schizophrenia, and a parent–child relationship in which parents are excessively cold, demanding, accusing, or inconsistent may be responsible for much disturbed child behaviours.

As a consequence the technique of *family therapy*, in which the therapist works not just with the problem child but with the whole nuclear family, is now attracting considerable attention. In family therapy the family attends the therapy sessions as a unit, allowing the therapist to watch how each member interacts with the others, how tensions develop, how misunderstandings arise, how one family member may be 'victimized' by the others, how much separate identity the family allows each individual, how well the parents know their children and get on with each other, and so on. Thus the therapist can observe how the family has contributed towards the problems faced by the child, and how the child in turn causes problems for the rest of the family.

Family therapy can also be of value where the initial problem is posed by one of the parents rather than by the child. Alcoholism in one parent, or gambling, or violence, or discord between the parents themselves, can often best be understood and treated within the context of the family, and it is only reluctance on the part of some parents to share 'their' problem (or admit to its existence) with their spouse and children that prevents more use from being made of this approach. Drug addiction in children is another problem that can often best be approached in this way. The chances of parents understanding the reasons for a child's addiction, and of their giving the right support to help him or her break the habit for good, are much better if the addiction is treated as a whole family problem rather than as a problem confined to only one of its members.

Finally, where families break up, it is all too often the children who are the ones who suffer most. Children are resilient creatures, and can survive the most disruptive family circumstances provided they are sure of their parents' love and support. There is no evidence for example that children of working mothers do any less well at school or are any more likely to be emotionally disturbed than children whose mothers stay at home. Nor is there evidence that children of single parents are at a marked disadvantage (though they certainly miss the role model provided by the absent parent). But children who are brought up in the insecurity of a unhappy home, where parents are subjecting each other to emotional or physical violence, cannot help but suffer. Not only are they denied the proper attention of their parents, they experience divided loyalties and the constant threat to their emotional security of witnessing angry confrontations. Often the break-up in the family, when it finally comes, may be the best thing for them; but it brings other problems, with each parent vying perhaps for their affections, and using them as weapons against the other. Not surprisingly the scars take a long time to heal, and since they have had no good role model for how partners to a marriage should relate to each other, it comes as no surprise to find that children of a broken home are themselves less likely one day to make happy and lasting marriages than their more fortunate contemporaries.

Family conflict

In view of the major changes that have taken place in the role and composition of both nuclear and extended families, the teacher often needs to revise preconceived notions of the domestic backgrounds from which children come. Having perhaps a happy family life him or herself, the teacher may be unaware of the stress placed upon a child by continual discord (and perhaps physical violence) between parents, or by alcoholism in a father or mother, or by a single-parent home in which the child has to take early responsibility for younger siblings. The teacher may also be unaware of the kind of demands that can be made upon children by domineering or by emotionally unbalanced parents, or of the different kind of stress caused by a parent with chronic depression who is unable to cope with the tasks of domestic life. Once appreciative of these demands, the teacher will find it hardly surprising that children faced with difficulties of this kind within the home often present behaviour problems at school. Such problems may simply be those of physical exhaustion or of lack of motivation, but they may also take the form of withdrawal in that the child, preoccupied with worries at home, is unable to reach out to others and participate in school activities. At their most disruptive they may take the form of extreme demands for teacher attention or of resentment and hostility towards the world in general.

THE NEED FOR TEACHER SYMPATHY. These and other questions relating to behaviour problems are dealt with more fully in Part IV, but my present emphasis is that the teacher should become sensitive to the potent influence upon school conduct of a child's family background. The teacher can, of course, do little to change this background. Teachers are not social workers, and any attempts at interference would probably be resented and counter-productive (though one must be prompt to report to the headteacher and through the headteacher to the social services any instances of physical neglect or abuse). But understanding and sympathy shown towards children in school will help them to live with problems at home. It hardly needs saying that children deeply troubled by such problems must not be further disturbed by an insensitive school environment in which no account is taken of the reasons for their failure to concentrate on classwork or to get homework done or to relate satisfactorily to others. Late arrivals at school, unaccountable absences, unpopularity with other children, sudden displays of violent temper, and general moodiness may all be traced back to difficulties at home, and it is part of the teacher's task to look closely into these difficulties before deciding what action to take. Teachers should also bear in mind that children may often be reluctant to admit to domestic upsets either through a sense of shame or through a sense of loyalty to parents. Further, many children with a background of this kind may also be relatively inarticulate (due to the lack of verbal stimuli to which I have already made reference) and may find it hard to put their problems into words, particularly if they feel they are not assured of a sympathetic hearing.

THE IMPORTANCE OF PARENTAL INVOLVEMENT. Educationally, the importance of the family is not simply restricted to providing the child with a secure domestic background. Parents need also to take an active interest in a child's schooling, since such interest is associated positively with the child's school progress. Through their interest in his or her education, parents show the child both the importance they attach to good school progress and the importance they attach to him or her as a person. Such parental interest also usually leads to offers of help with the schoolwork the child brings home, and means that parents attend school functions and generally become familiar with the school and with its standards and values. It means they get to know the child's teachers and are ready to turn to them for advice, while the teachers also benefit in that they get to know more about the child's background and can discuss learning problems where the parents may be able to help.

Teachers often remark, of course, that the very parents they most want to see are the ones least likely to come anywhere near the school, and this is undoubtedly true; but even where parents never attend parents' evenings or any of the other opportunities given to them to meet the staff, this does not necessarily mean that they take no interest in the child's progress. Indeed, where certain parents consistently fail to attend anything held at school the school needs to ask itself why it has been so unsuccessful in attracting their attention. It may be that the parents in question feel overawed by the school and by its well-spoken and well-educated staff. Or it may be that they know that their child is doing badly and are either ashamed by this or are reluctant to hear even more bad reports of him or her. Or it may be that they are unimpressed by the school and by what it has to offer, and by the essentially middle-class cultural activities (school orchestra and choirs, school plays and so on) that it uses to attract parents into the school.

Some schools have identified this last as a major problem and mount bingo sessions and dances as a way of bringing parents into the school and establishing the kind of informal contacts that will lead to future attendance at parents' evenings. When such attendance does take place, they are also careful to avoid subjecting parents to a disheartening catalogue of their children's inadequacies or, worse still, to a lecture on the contribution the parents themselves have made to these inadequacies. Instead, they adopt a positive line, emphasizing what can be done to help the child, and stressing those areas where the child has performed with more credit. Once parents have learnt to trust the school, and to see the improvements in their child's performance which are linked to the closer interest they are now learning to take in his or her education, their sense of commitment and involvement is likely to increase, to the great benefit of all concerned.

FAMILY SIZE. A further vital point is that family size appears to be inversely correlated with school performance. In their extensive longitudinal study, Davie and his colleagues (Davie, Butler and Goldstein, 1972) found that, irrespective of social class, children from large families tended to do less well in reading, number work, oral skills and creativity than only children or children with one or two siblings. This may well be a direct consequence of the fact that in large families parents normally have less time to spend with individual children, and the latter therefore receive less verbal and other forms of stimuli within the home. Davie also noticed that it appears usually to be the oldest child who suffers most, presumably because they are increasingly left to fend for themselves as younger and more demanding siblings are added to the family. Obviously teachers can do nothing about family size, but it behoves them to be aware of the educational disadvantage often experienced by children with many brothers and sisters, and to see that everything possible is done to compensate for it within school. Children from large families may also prove particularly prone to demand teacher attention to make up for the lack of adult attention within the home, and the teacher who is aware of the reasons for such demands is more likely to respond to them with the sympathy and patience that they warrant.

The home–school conflict

Where children come from a home background which teaches markedly different standards from those taught at school, they experience an almost inevitable conceptual and emotional conflict. This may be apparent if they come from minority ethnic groups or from an LSES group, or from a violent or aggressive family. Schools, in general, teach a European culture and USES values. They emphasize thrift, self-control, ambition, industry, the deferral of immediate satisfaction in the interests of long-term goals, respect for authority, good manners and non-violence. To a child from a background with a different set of values, all this looks very alien. If the child adjusts to it, and carries the school's values back into his or her own home, the child may find that at best they do not seem to work, or at worst that he is or she is actively ridiculed or punished.

On the other hand, if the child carries the values of his or her culture, social group, or family into school, he or she may find the same results. At best these values do not work, and at worst they invite ridicule and punishment. The only way in which the child can resolve the conflict between the different values of home and school is either to adopt double standards, behaving one way at school and another way at home, or to reject either the school or the home. If the child adopts the former course he or she sets up problems of personal identity, and if the latter is adopted the child fares badly in whichever of the two institutions is rejected.

The home–school conflict is not of the child's own making,

and it is vital the school does everything possible to recognize it and lessen its impact. Some schools manage this very successfully. The staff get to know the background from which their children come, avoid imposing on them rules and standards which are clearly incompatible with it, and at the same time initiate them gradually and sensibly into those that are non-negotiable. Other schools insist on imposing behaviour that may have no relevance outside the school, and which are seen by the children simply as an example of how remote authority is from their lives. Similarly, some schools try wherever possible to make the school curriculum meaningful to pupils and related to the life they live outside school, while others impose upon children material which does nothing to help them understand their lives and plan sensibly and realistically for the years to come.

Small wonder then that two schools, close together and drawing upon similar catchment areas, may show wide divergence in the amount of truanting, vandalism and aggressive behaviour adopted by their pupils. In the one case we have a school that sees its children as significant human beings, who come to school to be helped to understand and overcome the disadvantages of their background, while in the other we have a school that seems concerned solely to impose upon them an almost alien culture. The second school may not actually be creating its own problems, but it is certainly making them worse.

Specific classroom issues

In any discussion of the social relationships between the child and parents and teachers it must be stressed that each child is an individual and responds to other people in a unique way. Thus children themselves play a part in determining adult attitudes towards them. A child may, for example, be a contented individual who copes well with minor irritations, and who responds warmly to the affectionate advances of parents. On the other hand he or she may be difficult and restless and apparently struggle hard to avoid these advances. This question of inherited temperament is discussed more fully in Chapter 8, but the point to be emphasized here is that, not surprisingly, most parents relate more readily, from the early weeks of life onwards, to a contented, easy child than to a more difficult, fractious one. And inevitably they convey something of this to their child.

The teacher, of course, also finds it easier to get on with some children than with others, but if we are to understand human relationships we must accept that each relationship is an interactive process. It takes the interaction between two people to make a relationship, and in the course of this interaction each may antagonize the other. Thus in the case of parents and children we may find that sometimes their behav-

iour is mutually antagonistic from the beginning, and becomes increasingly bitter and difficult as the years go by and
the opportunities for discord and misunderstanding multiply.
At their worst, of course, relationships of this kind can lead to
physical abuse of the child and it is important that all teachers
should be alert for the signs of bruises and cuts that provide
evidence of this distressing phenomenon. It is estimated that
some two or three children die each week as a result of
physical assault from parents or parent substitutes, and many
thousands more receive injuries of varying degrees of severity.
The psychological damage inflicted upon these unfortunate
children, who go in constant physical fear within the home, is
incalculable. However, when discussing the causes of baby
battering and child abuse, we must look closely at the child as
well as the parent. Social psychologists recognize that there
are often identifiable characteristics within children, such as
extreme restlessness or dependence, which single them out as
likely victims. Where such children are brought up in poor
economic circumstances, in adverse living conditions, and in
social isolation (which together place added strains upon the
parents) then battering becomes more likely to occur.

   None of this should be taken as an attempt to excuse baby
battering and child abuse, or to place the blame upon the
child. All I am indicating is that factors in the child's own
behaviour, often apparent in the early weeks of life and long
before he or she has had a chance to learn to modify them,
may lead to parental frustration and antagonism. This antagonism upsets the child and intensifies his or her problem
behaviour, which causes increased parental antagonism,
which in turn further upsets the child. The vicious circle
continues until, given the deprived circumstances referred to
earlier, the child is put increasingly at risk. As we have seen,
the risk is further compounded if the parents themselves
experienced loveless childhoods, and were thus denied the
lessons associated with the giving and receiving of affection.
Typically, battering parents, perhaps as a consequence of
their own experiences of early deprivation, also appear to be
lacking in maturity, and therefore perhaps in the ability to
cultivate patience and understanding in their dealings with
their children.

Language and social development

Although much of the early communication between parent
and child takes the form of touch, language quickly esta-
blishes itself as the principal medium of social contact, and
the child who comes from a verbally fluent and expressive
household has enormous advantages over the child whose
home is verbally impoverished. By talking to children, by
encouraging them with verbal praise, by naming the objects

with which they play, and simply by conversing with them even though they are unable to understand at first all that is said, verbally fluent parents quickly help children to build up a working vocabulary. As shown in Chapter 4 when language is discussed in more detail, it is through language that children become able to indulge in complex thinking, to communicate fully with those around them, and to express their specific likes and dislikes. Language therefore seems essential to development of much of the behaviour that we identify as intelligent and, particularly in the early years of schooling, children may be classified by a teacher as generally backward when in fact their main problem may be simply that they come from a verbally unstimulating background. Such children may also sometimes appear physically more aggressive than the norm because they lack the linguistic sophistication to relate to people more appropriately or to express their feelings verbally. In addition, they will seem less well-mannered in social encounters with adults, and will be less ready to pick up language-related skills such as reading and writing.

Clearly the onus is upon the teacher to recognize the social and intellectual inadequacies in a child that stem from a verbally impoverished home life. Such recognition not only allows the teacher to be more patient with the child's problems, but also indicates what sorts of remedial help should be offered. The difficulties faced by verbally impoverished children are often made worse, for example, by the fact that throughout their school career they tend to mix primarily with other children who share their verbal disadvantage. Their lack of verbal skills makes it hard for them to form close friendships with more articulate children, and in group work within the class they often gravitate towards other verbally impoverished pupils. The teacher should see to it, therefore, by general classroom organization, that children in this category are given every chance to take part in the sort of verbal encounters likely to improve their skills. This means encouraging them to play and work with verbally fluent children, and to make their rightful contribution to classroom discussion and debate. It is important that the teacher should take every opportunity to talk to the child, using appropriate language, and should be prepared to listen patiently and encouragingly to their replies. Too often in a busy professional life the teacher does not allow him or herself sufficient time to listen in this manner while a relatively inarticulate child tries to explain something. Either the teacher well-meaningly but misguidedly finishes the child's own sentence, or else he or she conveys to the child by impatient signals that time is too valuable to be taken up in this way. Not surprisingly the child either grows antagonistic towards the teacher, feeling that he or she is not interested, or the child gives up the effort to communicate any but the simplest ideas. Either way, the teacher has failed to help the child redress the balance of early disadvantage.

Gender differences

As we have seen, the greater part of the differences in behaviour between the sexes (sex roles) appears to be learnt, and learnt in particular from within the family. Not only do children identify with the parent of the same sex, they also take over from the parent of the *opposite* sex his or her notion of what is 'manly' or of what is 'feminine'. Thus from both sexes they learn what is expected of them as boys or girls, and tend to adhere increasingly to these stereotypes as they grow older. Even where parents try hard to avoid sex-typing, influences from outside are strong. Television, children's and adolescents' magazines, and adults generally are obvious examples here, but so too are the child's friends. Children are often described as being essentially conformist, and this is true in the sense that they like to feel accepted by their peers, and quickly learn that such acceptance is often dependent upon being like everyone else. In particular, they strenuously avoid acquiring labels such as 'sissy' or 'tomboy', and boys especially come in for a good deal of censure if they are seen to show too much kinship with the opposite sex. Even in adolescence, where a certain amount of pairing off is regarded as appropriate, boys are often still subject to teasing from their friends and are not expected to lose their sense of manly dignity over a mere girl. Poets and troubadours may indeed have been inspired by romantic love, but if an adolescent boy feels similar noble stirrings within, he often finds it is politic to keep quiet about them!

Obviously the teacher cannot change these sexual stereotypes single-handed. Nor would it be right to expect children to engage in unisex behaviour that would hold them up to ridicule outside school. But nevertheless there is much that can be done within the classroom to help children develop more desirable attitudes, and to help girls in particular escape some of the handicaps that sex-typing lays upon them. Most obviously, all school activities should be open equally to both sexes, and there should be no question of boys being channelled, say, towards wood and metalwork while girls are restricted to domestic science, or of boys being given every opportunity to take part in organized games while girls have to make do with the odd game of netball if and when someone can be found who is prepared to take them. Of equal importance, the teacher should avoid all unnecessary polarizations like the ones implied by such instructions (heard in dinner queues, physical education lessons, etc.) as 'girls on one side of the room, boys on the other', or 'girls lead now', or 'girls only now' (to the accompaniment of gentle, melodic music) and 'now the boys' (to the accompaniment of growling, heavy passages). In addition, everything possible should be done to see that girls aim as high as boys, and go for the same range of vocational opportunities. The notion that for girls a career is only something to fill in time until marriage is still too prevalent both within the family and within education. Even where girls take this line themselves, it should be pointed out to them that more and more married women want to take up jobs when their children start school, and that such jobs should be as rewarding and fulfilling as those enjoyed by the male sex.

Ethnic factors

Just as there are limits to how much the teacher can do in changing sexual stereotypes, so there are limits to what can be done in abolishing ethnic differences. Many of these differences are, in any case, of great value, adding a creative variety to society, and introducing new concepts and new forms of cultural expression. But teachers do carry a responsibility for seeing that no child is handicapped by ethnic background, and for ensuring that children do not judge each other on colour or accent or creed. Children have a tendency to be intolerant of individual differences, particularly as they grow older, and the school must play its part in educating children out of these narrow and divisive attitudes.

One way in which this education takes place is through example. If the school staff are seen to value each child equally, irrespective of race, and seen to be sensitive towards the particular problems faced by individuals from minority groups, then many children will take their cue accordingly, as they will from the respect which teachers show towards the beliefs and customs of these groups, even where these involve changes in school routines. But more specific educational strategies, aimed at helping children empathize with ethnic minorities and appreciate fully the feelings of alienation and rejection which they may be experiencing, are also called for. Children who have been fed racially prejudiced views outside school need help in re-examining their attitudes and in assessing the local, national, and international damage that racial hostility can cause.

In addition to these processes of education and re-education, it is vital that the school examine both its assessment procedure and its curriculum to see if these are appropriate for its ethnic minorities. I have already stressed that children from these minorities may be misdiagnosed as learning or behaviour problems simply because of their language difficulties or because of the different behavioural mores within which they have been reared at home. But we can now add to this the fact that many schools present a curriculum which takes insufficient account of the special needs of children with non-European backgrounds. Even where such children were born in the United Kingdom, they are still deeply influenced by the culture of their parents and their own racial group, and a curriculum which fails to recognize this fact cannot help but lack full relevance. Where the curriculum goes directly contrary to this culture (as for example in its teachings on social behaviour and attitudes, on religious observances and beliefs, and on moral values) there is the additional risk of overt home–school conflict.

Closely linked to these cultural issues are the special problems which ethnic minorities face when it comes to employment, or to the prospect of mixed marriages, or choosing where to live and how to protect basic civil liberties. No school can gear its curriculum exclusively towards ethnic minorities. Equal obligations exist towards the rest of the children in the school. But formal education has a duty to foster both social cohesion and the rights of individuals within that cohesion. The duty is not an easy one to discharge, and often involves a careful balancing act in which the rights of one group are never advanced to the detriment of the rights of another. But no school is exempt from this duty, and no teacher exempt from the task of studying each child against the background from which that child comes.

| The home and the school | Enough has been said in this chapter to show that, when dealing with social development, children can only be fully understood if they are viewed within the context of both home and school. As social institutions, both home and school play vital roles in shaping children into effective social beings. The more familiar we are with these roles, the more we can appreciate that children are only partly responsible for the social inadequacies which their behaviour may reveal. Their inadequacies 'belong' less to themselves then to the social environment in which they are being raised. The family therapist recognizes this, and although the school cannot act as a family therapy unit, it is vital that wherever possible a child who is presenting social problems should be interviewed by senior school staff in the company of his or her parents. By observing how the parents react to their child and each other, the teacher can gain an insight into the domestic stresses and pressures with which the child has to contend. At the very least, the school must glean from welfare officers and the social services every piece of information on a child's home background, and must take this information into account in deciding how to handle the child. |

It cannot be stressed too often that a child who already has major problems at home should not have these pressures unnecessarily added to by the school. The school is there to help, and it can only do this if it understands these domestic problems and the impact they are likely to have upon a young impressionable mind. Even where the child has no special difficulties at home, a school which is unfamiliar with a child's background may inadvertently institute a home–school conflict to the detriment of a child's progress. This is particularly possible in the context of those marked social or ethnic differences between home and school which were discussed earlier. The school cannot change its basic standards to accord with those taught in many of the homes from which children come, but it can present these standards in a way which does not excessively divide a child's loyalties. This means, essentially, helping children to see the purpose and the relevance behind the school's standards, and avoiding any attempt to hold their own standards up to ridicule or insensitive comment.

References

Archer, G. and Lloyd, B. (1982) *Sex and Gender*. Harmondsworth: Penguin.

Clarke, A.M. and Clarke, A.D.B. (ed.) (1976) *Early Experience: Myth and Evidence*. London: Longman.

Davie, R., Butler, N. and Goldstein, H. (1972) *From Birth to Seven*. London: Longman.

Doyle, W. and Good, T.L. (ed.) (1982) *Focus on Teaching*. Chicago: University of Chicago Press.

Erikson, E.H. (1950) *Childhood and Society*. New York: Norton.

Goldfarb, W. (1955) Emotional and intellectual consequences of psychological deprivation in infancy; a re-evaluation. In P. Hoch and J. Zubin (ed.) *Psychopathology of Childhood*. New York: Grune.

Harlow, H.F. and Harlow, M.H. (1966) Learning to love. *American Scientist* 54, 3.

Kagan, J. (1984) *The Nature of the Child*. New York: Basic Books.

Lewis, M. (1984) State as an infant–enviroment interaction: an analysis of mother–infant behaviour as a function of sex. *Merrill-Palmer Quarterly in Behavioural Development, 18*.

Sluckin, W., Herbert, M. and Sluckin, A. (1983) *Maternal Bonding*. Oxford: Basil Blackwell.

Tizard, B, (1977) *Adoption: A Second Chance*. London: Open Books.

1. What are the signs that attachment is taking place?

2. Why does a child who is brought up restrictively often show more attachment behaviour then usual?

3. What is the evidence that childhood is a critical period in social learning?

4. What is the 'cycle of deprivation'?

5. If a child bonds too closely with his or her teacher, what may this indicate about the child's home life?

6. Explain the importance of trust in early social development.

7. Are sex roles learnt or innate?

8. List some of the factors which lead to social discrimination against women and girls.

9. Why are children from minority ethnic groups sometimes misdiagnosed in school?

10. Why are the children from LSES homes often at a disadvantage when they start school?

11. Examine reasons for the break-up of the extended family. What are the social consequences of this break-up?

12. How can schools help avoid the creation of home–school conflicts?

Additional Reading

Banks, J.A. (1981) *Multi-Ethnic Education: Theory and Practice.* New York: Allyn & Bacon.
Surveys the major issues surrounding all aspects of multiethnic education.

Booth, T. (1975) *Growing up in Society.* London: Methuen.
A good account of the influence of the social context upon the developing child. Demonstrates the significant extent to which the child is the creation of social forces.

Davie, R. (1984) Social development and social behaviour. In D. Fontana (ed.) *The Education of the Young Child: A handbook for nursery and infant teachers,* 2nd edn. Oxford: Basil Blackwell.
Concise and practical survey of social development in the infant and nursery school years.

Goldenberg, I. and Goldenberg, H. (1980)*Family Therapy: An overview.* New York: Brooks-Cole.
A useful comprehensive text for those who want to know more about family therapy.

Kagan, J. (1984) *The Nature of the Child.* New York: Basic Books.
Good on all aspects of child development, and with a particularly good chapter on the role of the family. (Also recommended for Chapter 3.)

Kaye, K. (1982) *The Mental and Social Life of Babies*. London: Methuen.
Rather minimizes the abilities of babies, but a useful survey of the available evidence.

Kempe, R. and Kempe, E. (1978) *Child Abuse*. London: Fontana/Open Books.
Good account of the distressing phenomena of physical and sexual abuse, with suggestions for prevention and treatment.

Maccoby, E. and Jacklin, C. (1974) *The Psychology of Sex Differences*. Stanford, California: Stanford University Press.
Thorough examination of sex roles and of sex differences in intellectual behaviour.

Mussen, P.H., Conger, J.C. and Kagan, J. (1984) *Child Development and Personality*, 6th edn. New York: Harper & Row.
Excellent on all aspects of child development. A deservedly popular text: highly recommended. (Also recommended for Chapter 3.)

Pringle, K. (1980) *The Needs of Children*, 2nd edn. London: Hutchinson.
Examines children's needs within all areas of their development, and raises many issues which have bearing upon general social policies.

Rutter, M. (1981) *Maternal Deprivation Reassessed*. Harmondsworth: Penguin.
A comprehensive and stimulating review of the research on the influence of maternal deprivation upon the child.

Schaffer. H.R. (1977) *Mothering*. London: Fontana/Open Books.
A concise and sympathetic look at the mother's task, with a good survey of recent evidence and a welcome emphasis upon the reciprocal nature of the mother–child relationship.

2

Play

As will become apparent to the reader, this chapter could as
readily have been included under cognitive development as
under social development. Play appears to have important
implications for all areas of a child's psychological life (see
Smith, 1982, for a review of the extensive literature), and it is
a mistake to see it even in older children as a trivial, time-
wasting activity. On the other hand, it is a mistake to lose
sight of the fact that the purpose of play from the child's point
of view is simple enjoyment (Hutt, 1979). A child does not
consciously engage in play in order to find out how things
work, or to try out adult roles, or to stimulate imagination, or
to do any of the other things that commentators over the
years have claimed to identify in various aspects of this play.
A child plays because it is fun, and the learning that arises out
of play is to him or her quite incidental. Even when engaged in
so-called *structured* play (that is, play organized by the adult
with the express intention of providing desirable learning
experiences) the child still sees it as an essentially non-serious
activity offered for personal diversion.

We should not assume that play is any the worse for this
hedonistic (pleasure-seeking) element. Western society has
placed its major emphasis on work, and activities entered into
for the sake of pleasure have been held to be of little real
worth. For the psychologist, however, anything that contributes toward the psychological health of the individual is of
importance, and in this respect pleasure-orientated activities
may at times be of greater value than those related to work.
For the teacher also, the pleasure aspect of children's play
should not be dismissed too lightly. It is inappropriate for him
or her to see childhood as simply a preparation for adulthood
rather than as a phase of life to be savoured for its own sake.
In childhood, emotions often have a sharper, more intense
quality than they have in later life, and to deny a child the
opportunity to experience delight is to deny experiences that
may never present themselves again in quite the same form.
Delight, in other words, should be seen as a desirable end in
itself, rather then as diverting the child from what are held to

be more long-term and more worthwhile pursuits. Those who hold that such an argument is impossibly frivolous may wish to console themselves with the knowledge that the experience of happiness, which is really what we are talking about, appears to carry desirable physiological as well as psychological benefits for the individual concerned, and this in itself makes it of inestimable value for anyone concerned with the future well-being of others. By learning that play is an experience valued by adults, and one which can be indulged in without constant feelings of guilt for all the other, more serious things to be done, the child is also helped to develop positive attitudes towards the place of leisure in life, attitudes which should stand him or her in good stead in adulthood. We should not forget that one of the shortest but perhaps most satisfactory definitions of psychological health available to us is that the healthy individual is one who can work and play and love (see Allport, 1961).

The nature of play

The young of many species of animals engage in activities which appear to have the non-serious qualities of play (i.e. they do not seem to be directed primarily towards hunting or mating, or the exercise of territorial rights, or the evasion of danger). The higher up the so-called evolutionary scale the species happens to be, the more apparent and purposeful this 'play' becomes. In the case of all animals except humans, however, 'play' involves primarily intense physical movement such as chasing and romping and is usually directed towards peers or other animate objects. Only rarely does it involve inanimate objects, and only rarely does it show obvious development as the animal grows older. In humans, by contrast, play increasingly involves the use of physical objects, many of them standing symbolically for things other than themselves as the infant grows older, and follows a discernible developmental pattern involving ever-increasing complexity. This utilization of physical objects is indicative both of the manipulative skills available to humans through the use of fingers and thumbs, and of the presence of imagination (i.e. of the ability to call to mind situations or objects or processes that are not physically present at that point in time), while the growing complexity of play is indicative of the development of cognitive skills and of the increasing use of language both in communication with others and in thinking.

Piaget, whose work on cognitive development is looked at more closely in Chapter 3, suggests that the emergence of set rules and procedures in children's play as they grow older is further evidence of the development of their powers of thought. Thus the child moves in a few short years from the apparently entirely physical play of the small baby, which is perhaps analogous to the unthinking play of animals to which attention has already been drawn, to play which involves many of the sophisticated mental processes that help to mark humans out as distinct from other species. Piaget also has it that not only do the child's developing powers of thought help in the development of more complex methods of play, but the methods of play help him or her develop more complex ways of thinking. Sadly, the play of mentally handicapped children shows only a limited developmental range, and often remains repetitive and stereotyped.

Socially, play moves from the solitary play of the very small child (solitary in the sense that it is not indulged in reciprocally with other children) to the parallel play of the three year old (where children play side by side and perhaps imitate each other but still function essentially as individuals), to the truly social play of the normal four and five year old where much of the activity depends upon interaction with peers. During each of these stages adults, of course, can initiate or participate in the play activities but, until the stage of social play is reached, the child will respond to or imitate the adult rather than interact with the latter in what might be termed a play partnership.

Categories of play

Various attempts have been made to classify children's play in terms of its content. One of the best known of these is given in a classic early work by Buhler (1935), who suggests four main categories, namely functional, fictional, receptive, and constructive. *Functional* play, which is the first to emerge, involves the practice of a particular function or skill which is usually relatively crude such as kicking or clapping hands, but can involve delicate movements of the hand. *Fictional* play emerges next, usually during the second year of life, and involves fantasy or pretend behaviour in which individuals give themselves or the objects with which they are playing a particular role (e.g. a doll is treated like a real baby). Shortly afterwards or at the same time comes *receptive* play in which the child listens to a story or looks at the events in a picture. By the end of the second year *constructive* play has also usually made an appearance, involving playing with bricks, drawing, and playing with sand and other natural materials. To these four categories is added a fifth, play with rules, which involves the set procedures we normally term *games*, and which usually becomes established by nursery-school age.

Although the other four forms of play tend to reach a peak at the age of seven or eight, and show a subsequent gradual decline, play involving games increases steadily in importance, and under the heading of 'sport' may remain an abiding interest throughout life. Schools foster this interest by offering organized games as part of the curriculum, but such games increasingly include a new element: that of competition. In other words, they are not undertaken simply for the pleasure involved in the activity itself, but in order to produce winners and losers, and the prestige and disappointments associated with these categories. With the advent of competition, play could be said therefore to lose some of its non-serious quality, and consciously to serve psychological functions other than the hedonistic one to which we have already drawn attention. With the increasing professionalization of sport in adult life, and with the increasing emphasis, both social and economic, upon winning, it is doubtful indeed whether organized games as practised at a high level can really any longer be classified as play at all.

As long ago as 1949, Huizinga identified the decline of play in adult life as one of the disturbing elements in western civilization, and this thesis could be further developed now that television and the media generally have turned organized games into a multimillion-pound industry in which even the rules under which teams and individuals compete are altered to suit the convenience of the cameras and of viewing schedules. Psychologists and sociologists are currently showing much interest in the implications of this shift away from play for human behaviour, not only for the kind of behaviour exemplified by soccer hooliganism and by the decline in participation in favour of spectating, but for the general attitudes and values of society. Doubtless sport reflects these values as well as perhaps helping to form them, but the moving force behind much sport currently appears to be something much grimmer than the delightful qualities that define play in childhood. The commercial values exhibited by much organized sport and many professional sportsmen and women may therefore tend to lend credence to the mistaken notion that things should never be undertaken for the pleasure or diversion they bring in themselves but for the extrinsic rewards (usually monetary) they can command.

Play and learning

There is no doubt that children learn through play, just as they learn, consciously and unconsciously, from all forms of experience. In examining the nature of this learning it is important to remember, however, that for the young preschool child there is no real distinction between play and what an adult might think of as work. Helping mother or father in the garden or in the home is a form of play to him or her because, like playing with toys, it is engaged in for non-serious ends. The two and three year old will enjoy making cakes with mother or father in the kitchen not because this will provide something nice to eat for tea, but because the business of mixing in the flour and adding the milk and the other ingredients is enjoyable in itself. The child may in fact have lost all interest in the cakes by the time they make their appearance on the dining-room table, and in any case will see little connection between the neat objects arranged on the plate and the many-coloured, malleable substances he or she had control over a few hours previously in the kitchen. It is only as children grow older and come to associate certain kinds of activity (e.g. helping with the housework) with certain kinds of reward (e.g. parental praise), that they begin to see present behaviour as indulged in less for the sake of immediate gratification than for the sake of long-term benefits. This is partly a function of the strength of the reward or rewards themselves, and partly a function of children's developing cognitive skills which enable them to see more clearly the link between cause and effect.

As was implied in the opening paragraph of this chapter, many commentators over the years have tended to see play as simply representing the child's method of learning. They identify what might be called a *play drive*, and see this drive, along with the hunger drive and other survival-orientated drives, as being the innate mechanism that leads children to interact with their environment (as opposed to lying passively in a cot) and thus to learn the way in which it works. This view is not incompatible with the notion that children engage in play for hedonistic reasons (though it must not make us lose sight of the fact that for the child, the hedonistic reasons are all that matter). Certainly, in the early months of life at least, playing does seem to be an innate rather than a learnt activity, and as such therefore can be classified with other drive mechanisms. It is also quite clearly a strong promoter of activity, and thus puts children in a position in which learning is likely to take place. As Piaget suggests, it may also help them develop more complex forms of thinking as they they strive to reflect upon the way things behave as they interact with them, and may in addition be a stimulator of social learning as children discover what is acceptable, and not acceptable to the people with whom they are playing.

Clearly, the more opportunities a child is offered during the course of play, the more likely it is that new learning will take place. A child growing up in an environment in which there are few objects to manipulate, in which there is little access to materials like sand and clay, in which there are no construction toys like bricks or drawing materials, in which there is a restricted range of textures and colours, and in which there is only limited social interaction, will learn less rapidly than one placed in a more stimulating enviroment. By 'stimulating' in this context I do not necessarily mean a cupboard full of expensive mechanical gadgets that emit coloured lights and sparks, or lifesize dolls that wet themselves at both ends, or plastic machine-guns realistic enough to mount a bank raid; I mean a wealth of natural (though safe) objects that the child can explore and arrange and rearrange and use imaginatively, natural materials that can be mixed and shaped and poured without fear of adult outrage at the ensuing mess and, just as important, a parent who delights in the child's company and actually enjoys getting down on the floor alongside the child and re-entering a once familiar magic world.

Play and the curriculum

Detailed discussion on how best to use play within the school curriculum belongs more to a book on teaching methods than to one on psychology. Clearly, though, it is nursery and primary school teachers who are most likely to be concerned with the first four categories of play mentioned in the main part of the chapter (i.e. functional, fictional, receptive and constructive) while secondary school teachers are more likely to be interested in the fifth category (games). Accordingly, let me make some general comments applicable to teachers of younger children first, and then pass on to the work of teachers of older age groups.

Within the nursery school, play is the major component of the curriculum. This does not mean, as the uninitiated are sometimes prone to suppose, that children are allowed to run riot and do very much as they please under the eye of a teacher whose main concern is to keep them from physical harm. Though nursery (and infant) school teachers are well aware of the pleasurable aspects of play, their purpose is to provide children with the kind of experiences that are likely to lead in addition to desirable forms of learning (both cognitive and social). And since in this they do not differ from teachers of older children, we can say that it is the methods of teaching rather than the aims of teaching that mark nursery and infant off from other schools. In nursery and infant schools, it is the task of the teacher to offer a range of play activities and to help children explore them to the full. Sometimes this involves initiating particular activities with particular children, while at others it entails observing the activities children have chosen for themselves and prompting them to modify and develop these experiences so that they may realize their full learning potential. Importantly, the teacher encourages children to verbalize what they are doing: that is, to describe their actions, to say why they are being undertaken, and to offer suggestions on why certain results follow from these actions. Thus children are helped to develop linguistic and cognitive skills, and to gain confidence in their own ability to command appropriate vocabulary structures, while at the same time extending their knowledge of how the physical world behaves and of the appropriate skills for dealing with this world.

Structuring young children's play

One problem that arises is the degree of structure that the
teacher should impart to children's play; that is, the extent to
which children should be offered set patterns of routine and
guidance in play specifically designed to introduce them to
identifiable skills and techniques. One school of thought has it
that play should remain free and spontaneous with very
young children, and that the task of the teacher is to provide a
range of opportunities from which the child will choose
according to inclination and developmental level. But another
argues that by introducing an element (though not an over-
obtrusive element) of structure into play the teacher renders
children's learning less haphazard and therefore more efficient. This structure may involve setting aside certain blocks
of time for certain definite activities (number games, word
identification games, movement activities, story time, music-
making and so on), or simply the provision of play equipment
designed with the learning of specific skills in mind.

Obviously, as the child grows older and moves from the
nursery school into and through the infant school, the degree
of formalization in the timetable becomes more apparent, and
the emphasis upon play decreases. (Some argue that this is a
bad thing, and that ideally one should throughout life make
little distinction between work and play, deriving the same
pleasure from both; whether such a thing is possible in an
industrialized society where many jobs are dull and repetitive
is another matter.) But even in the nursery school, current
consensus appears to be moving towards an increased degree
of structure, and towards the use of commercially prepared
structured play equipment (such as the Peabody Language
Kit, 1968) aimed at encompassing a wide range of important
early skills. This is doubtless a good thing, as long as we do
not lose sight of the intrinsic value of play as a promoter of
happiness in children, and of the child's need to exercise
choice and initiative in a significant proportion of what he or
she does.

In addition to the learning that comes to the child through
play, the teacher in turn can learn by observing the way in
which the child responds to play experiences. We have already discussed the developmental aspect of play in the preceding sections, and the link between play and cognitive
development. A child who therefore consistently employs
stereotyped and unimaginative play should alert the teacher
to possible signs of retardation. By watching the child at play
the teacher can assess his or her ability to sort and categorize,
to match by colour, size and shape, to recognize familiar
objects and symbols, to identify the links between cause and
effect, to use and modify existing knowledge in the solution of
new problems, and to develop essential manipulative skills

such as using pencils, paintbrushes, scissors and constructional toys. Of equal importance, the teacher can also gain
some insight into the child's personality and social development. A child who consistently plays alone, or who shows
marked destructiveness or aggression, or seems unable to
share or wait for a turn, or constantly demands adult attention, or who cannot tolerate minor frustrations, may be giving
indications of some psychological disturbance. More subtly,
the child's use of roles when involved in domestic play may
give some insight into relationships with parents or brothers
and sisters at home. At all times, the observation of children's
play helps the teacher listen for the child's use of language,
both as a medium for expressing thoughts and as a way of
communicating fluently and responsibly with others.

Older children's play

Turning now to teachers of older age groups, where the
emphasis is upon games rather than upon play, there are
again some general psychological points that offer possibilities for practical help. The first of these is that games do not
involve only what goes on in the gymnasium or on the games
field. There is increasing evidence that games are an aid to
learning in most school subjects, just as it has been found that
they are of value in business and industry, and in particular in
the learning of management skills and techniques. The use of
games in classroom-based learning, and in particular of the
kind of games known as simulation exercises, is covered in
Chapter 7. All we need say at present is that these games can
prove highly enjoyable both to children and teachers, and can
be used to mimic the real-life situations in which children may
one day put their classroom-based knowledge to practical use.
One problem that faces education at all levels is that so much
teaching and learning takes place in the artificial environment
of the classroom: that is, in an environment divorced from the
outside world and therefore from the context to which school
learning really applies. This problem can be partly solved if,
through the use of carefully organized and planned games,
children can be enabled to see the direct practical relevance of
what they are learning for the tasks that may one day face
them in their future careers, or for the tasks that face them in
everyday social life, or for the tasks that face society and
western civilization as a whole. As Chapter 7 stresses, learning is most likely to take place where the learner can see the
immediate relevance of what is being learnt, either by putting
it to practical use or by relating it to problems that he or she
has already identified (or is readily able to identify) as being of
importance.

Sport

Moving on now from the classroom to the games field, we find that great emphasis has been laid over the years on the belief that sport is not only good for physical development and physical fitness but for personality growth as well. We are told that sport develops 'character', that it teaches the value of teamwork and co-operation, that it teaches fair play and all the other good things that come under the heading of 'sportsmanship', that it teaches unselfishness and helps the individual to take knocks in life, and so on. If sport is indeed good for personality growth then this is a strong argument for its inclusion in the school curriculum, since education is concerned with the personal development of the individual as well as with the transmission of knowledge. Unfortunately, there is no consistent evidence that sport does have this desired effect, or that such lessons as it does teach are generalizable to situations occurring off the sports field. Attention has already been drawn to the apparent decline of play in modern society, and to the doubtful values that motivate much organized sport, and it therefore seems fair to suggest that, in any case, even if these values are generalizable their influence may not always be for the good.

It seems possible that the reason why such an extensive mythology has grown up around the educational value of sport is that, in view of the strong emphasis upon work and the relative neglect of play in western society, some justification had to be found when sport was first introduced into the school curriculum. It was not sufficient to put it there because children for the most part enjoyed it, since enjoyment was not seen as a necessary part of education. Nor was it sufficient to lay stress simply upon its physical benefits, since physical development was held at that time to be very much secondary to mental growth and the training of the so-called mental 'faculties'. So in Britain, to take one example from western culture, we have the paradox of a sport-loving nation which yet was reluctant to admit that sport was there for sheer pleasure, and that the experience of such pleasure was sufficient justification in its own right.

With changing patterns of employment in modern society, and with the prospect of an extensive addition in leisure time for most of us, it may be that games will come increasingly to be seen as conferring social benefit. They have the potential to occupy the individual's time pleasantly and to give physical exercise, thus promoting both bodily and psychological health. They can also be a way of bringing people together, and of providing opportunities for co-operation and mutual support. It may be that when these benefits are fully appreciated, the value of play will be recognized not only for small children but for adolescents and adults as well. One hopes, too, that individuals with no great aptitude for sport will perhaps be less likely to be turned against games during their school careers if this happens, since the criteria under which they take part would then become not how they compare with the standards of their peers but how much pleasure they actually derive from the experience themselves.

References

Allport, G.W. (1961) *Pattern and Growth in Personality.* New York: Holt, Rinehart & Winston.

Buhler, C. (1935) *From Birth to Maturity.* London: Kegan Paul.

Dunn, L.M., Horton, K.B. and Smith, J.O. (ed.) (1968) The Peabody Language Development Kit. Circle Pines, Minnesota: American Service Inc.

Huizinga, J. (1949) *Homo Ludens: A study of the play element in culture.* London: Routledge & Kegan Paul.

Hutt, C. (1979) Play in the under-fives: form, development and function. In J.G. Howells (ed.) *Modern Perspectives in the Psychiatry of Infancy.* New York: Brunner/Mazel.

Smith, P.K. (1982) Does play matter? Functional and evolutionary aspects of animal and human play. *Behavioural and Brain Sciences, 5,* 139–184.

SOME QUESTIONS

1. Why could this chapter on play have been 'as readily . . . included . . . under cognitive development as under social development'?

2. Do you agree with the statement that western society has placed a major emphasis upon work? What are the reasons for your answer?

3. What do we mean by hedonistic?

4. Why should 'delight . . . be seen as a desirable end in itself'?

5. How can the adult best help the child to 'develop positive attitudes towards the place of leisure in life'? How would you define and recognize these attitudes (i) in children and (ii) in adults?

6. Attempt a definition of 'play' that holds good for both children and adults.

7. List the major differences in play as indulged in by children and play as indulged in by animals. What do these differences tell us about the psychological skills of the two groups concerned?

8. What are the differences between solitary, parallel, and social play?

9. What are the categories of play identified by Buhler? Can you suggest alternative categories which you consider may be more helpful for the teacher?

10. Suggest ways in which play can be structured for children in the nursery–infant age range to facilitate learning. Are there any possible dangers behind structuring in this way?

11. What are the major differences between play and games?

12. What do you consider are the major implications of the shift of western society away from play? Can you suggest ways in which this shift can be counteracted?

13. Suggest some of the reasons why children come to make an increasing distinction between play and work as they grow older.

14. From your own experience, however limited, of babies and small children, do you think those psychologists who talk of an innate 'play drive' are justified?

15. List some of the qualities that you think good play equipment should possess (i) for children of nursery school age and (ii) for children in the infant school.

Additional Reading

Bruner, J.S., Jolly, A. and Sylva, K. (1976) *Play: Its role in development and evolution*. Hardmondsworth: Penguin.
One of the most significant books to appear on play in recent years. It contains a wealth of reference and research material, and spans all aspects of play in humans and animals.

Dunn, L.M., Horton, K.B. and Smith, J.O. (ed.) (1968) *The Peabody Language Development Kit*. Circle Pines, Minnesota: American Service Inc.
An approach to the learning of language and other skills through structured play experiences.

Garvey, C. (1977) *Play*. London: Fontana/Open Books.
A good general text.

Hohmann, M., Bernard, B. and Weikart, D.P. (1979) *Young Children in Action*. Ypsilanti, Michigan: High Scope Press.
A first-class examination of the way in which play can be used to produce learning experiences in young children.

Manning, K. and Sharp, A. (1977) *Structuring Play in the Early Years at School*. London: Ward Lock/Drake Educational.
Informative treatment of the place of structure in children's play drawing upon the Schools' Council Pre-School Education Project.

Opie, I. and Opie, P. (1959) *The Lore and Language of Schoolchildren*. Oxford: Oxford University Press.

The student interested in the verbal content of children's play and games will enjoy this classic.

Prosser, G. (1985) Play – a child's eye view. In A. Branthwaite, and D. Rogers (ed.) *Children Growing Up*. Milton Keynes: Open University Press.
A stimulating look at the function play has for children. (Also recommended for Chapter 3.)

Roberts, V. (1971) *Playing, Learning and Living*. Oxford: Basil Blackwell.
Looks closely at the way in which learning experiences can be provided through play.

Taylor, J.L. and Walford, R. (1972) *Simulation in the Classroom*. Harmondsworth: Penguin.
A good introduction to the use of simulation exercises. (Also recommended for Chapter 7.)

Wood, D., McMahon, C. and Cranstoun, Y. (1980) *Working with Under Fives*. London: Grant McIntyre.
This has a particularly good section on how teachers can 'tutor' young children's play. Part of a series arising out of the Oxford Pre-school Project, it contains much of practical value for teachers of young children.

Yardley, A. (1974) *Structure in Early Learning*. London: Evans.
A good examination of the use of structured play experiences with young children.

Yardley, A. (1984) Play. In D. Fontana (ed.) *The Education of the Young Child*: A Handbook for Nursery and Infant Teachers Oxford: Basil Blackwell.
A very good short introduction to play in the nursery and infant schools.

Part two

Cognitive Factors and Learning

The term *cognitive*, which derives from the Latin 'cognitio', to know, refers to all those psychological abilities associated with thinking and with knowing. These abilities attract particular attention within education since they help determine the facility with which children can learn, and therefore whether they come to be classed as forward in their work or as backward or perhaps even as educationally subnormal (ESN). Cognitive abilities include children's measured intelligence, their levels of thinking and even, to a certain extent, their creativity and the manner in which they conduct interpersonal relationships. Since language is the medium through which thinking usually takes place, and since much intelligent and creative activity is expressed through language, this too is usually regarded as a cognitive activity.

In Part II each of these aspects of cognitive functioning is studied, and the processes by which learning takes place are also examined, since learning and cognition are obviously closely related. The starting point is thinking, and the child's ability to develop and use concepts.

3

Concept Formation and Development

Thinking and education

The ability to think clearly and sensibly, which involves being able to follow a line of reasoning, to grasp concepts and to initiate lines of enquiry oneself, is obviously central to children's educational progress. No matter what subject is being studied, failure to understand what is required, or to identify and tackle the problems it involves, are obvious barriers to any real progress. Although they are fully aware of this, some teachers are unclear of the level of thinking they can reasonably expect of a child at a given age. Much educational failure, indeed, stems from the fact that forms of thinking are demanded of children that they are incapable of supplying.

The work of Piaget

The most sustained and ambitious attempt at studying children's thinking is that of the Swiss biologist-turned-psychologist, Jean Piaget. Piaget's findings led him to propose an essentially developmental theory of how children form the concepts involved in thinking. That is, a theory which proposes that children develop more sophisticated patterns of thinking as a consequence primarily of maturation, and according both to a set pattern and a more or less stable timetable. His theory is necessarily somewhat complex and elaborate in detail, but its basic ingredients can be understood readily enough.

Before we look at these ingredients, however, we must first define what we mean by a *concept*. A concept is the idea an individual has about a particular class of objects (including inanimate objects) or events, grouped together on the basis of the things they have in common. It is through concepts that we make sense of the world. Thus a small child will have a concept of 'big things', a concept of 'small things', a concept of 'wetness', and of 'dryness', a concept of 'things I like' and of 'things I don't like', and so on. When encountering novel objects or experiences, or faced with problems of any kind, a child attempts to make sense of them by fitting them into the range of concepts already held. If these concepts prove inadequate, he or she may have to modify them in some way, or perhaps try to develop a new concept altogether (as, for example, when encountering a dog or a snowstorm for the first time). Usually even new concepts can be related back in some way to concepts already held (e.g. the dog moves of its own accord like people do, the snow is wet like cold water), but if the relationships the child sees are not the right ones, and he or she thus cannot interpret anything important about the new experience correctly, then the child may be unable to develop a concept for dealing with it appropriately (e.g. the child may tear up a £10 note or Daddy's contract for his new book because he or she classifies them along with chocolate wrappers and newspapers which are known to be expendable).

Piaget's theory has attracted important criticisms, which are looked at later, but essentially the theory has it that the way in which we are able to form and handle concepts changes as we go through childhood into adolescense. Thus the child's thinking is not simply an immature version of the adult's, but differs from it in a number of radical and important ways. These ways can be classified in terms of several different stages which the child allegedly passes through on the way from the thought patterns of the infant to those of the fully developed adult. Piaget claims that the child goes through each of these stages in turn, at approximately the ages shown below, and that the speed of movement through each stage, though influenced by environment and by the richness or otherwise of the experiences it offers, is essentially governed by biologically determined maturational processes. Each of the stages is characterized by a particular cognitive *structure* (or structures): that is, by the particular strategy (or strategies) manifested by the child in his or her attempt to organize and make sense of experience. The stages are discussed in their chronological order below.

Stage 1. Sensori-motor: approximately birth to two years

In the early weeks of life, children's activity appears to be purely reflex in character. They suck, grasp objects, cry, throw out their arms and legs when startled and so on. Such actions are apparently entirely involuntary. The child is presented with a stimulus (e.g. something to suck, something to grasp) and the reflex response is evoked. There is no thinking on his or her part, just as there is no thinking on our part if we snatch our hands away from something hot or blink if something threatens our eyes.

At first these reflex activities are directed towards the child's own body, but somewhere between four and eight months of age they are increasingly directed towards external objects as well. This is an important development in that it indicates that an element of purpose is now being introduced into the child's behaviour, that is, the child is now apparently using sequences of movement directed towards the attainment of definite goals. Piaget calls such sequences *schemata*, and claims they are evidence of cognitive structures which allow the child to link actions together into stable and repeatable units. Between the ages of 12 and 18 months these schemata become increasingly elaborate as the child experiments with them to attain desired ends.

During the sensori-motor period, Piaget claims the schemata used by the child are principally circular reactions. These in turn are broken down into *primary* circular reactions which occur in the early period of reflex activity, *secondary* circular reactions which occur when the child starts more purposive activity, and *tertiary* circular reactions which happen when this activity becomes more elaborated. These labels are important if we wish to understand the development of thinking because they indicate that the child's reactions throughout the sensori-motor stage remain both overt and physical. That is to say, the child does not think about doing a particular action, but simply does it. As Piagetians express it, the child's relationship with the action is not a mental one, but is contained entirely within the action itself. It is only later on that he or she is able to internalize actions (i.e. to rehearse them mentally, to decide consciously to do A rather than B), and to think, rather than simply to do.

Stage 2. Pre-operational thought: approximately 2–7 years

This stage is divided by Piaget into two sub-stages, the *pre-conceptual sub-stage* (approximately age two to age four) and the *intuitive sub-stage* (approximately age four to age seven).

1. Pre-conceptual sub-stage: children's cognitive development during the years from two to four is increasingly dominated by the emergence of symbolic activity. Children become able to use symbols to stand for actions, and therefore are able to represent these actions to themselves without actually doing them (i.e. it becomes possible to internalize actions). We see this, for example, in the child's play, where dolls come to stand for babies, where a toy car stands for the real thing, and where the child can assume the role of 'mummy' or 'daddy'. With the development of language skills children also come to possess what Piaget calls *signs*: that is, sounds which, although they have no intrinsic relationship with objects and events (different languages use quite different sounds) nevertheless are used to represent them. Mathematical notations are another example of signs.

Note that Piaget holds the distinction between symbols and

signs to be an important one. The child is able to use symbols before signs, and therefore we must not equate the development of symbolic activity with the development of language, though the two tend to become increasingly linked as the child grows older. Nor, Piaget insists, does the emergence of symbolic activity indicate that the child is able to form concepts as adults and older children can (hence the title *preconceptual* for this sub-stage). For example, the child cannot form *generic* concepts, that is classes of objects, correctly (e.g. he or she may refer to all men as 'Daddy'), nor make *transitive* inferences (e.g. A is bigger than B, B is bigger than C, therefore A is bigger than C). The form of reasoning employed is known as *transductive* reasoning, since it goes from the particular to the particular (e.g. because A goes with B in this instance then A must always go with B; because we caught a bus to meet Daddy in town, then every bus goes to meet Daddy in town). Although such transductive reasoning is incorrect, it is clear evidence of the child's attempt to make sense of the world.

2. Intuitive sub-stage: of all stages and sub-stages, this is the one that has been most extensively studied by Piaget and his colleagues, and as it covers the early school years it is of particular interest to the teacher. The principal cognitive structures now employed by the child are labelled by Piaget *egocentrism*, *centration*, and *irreversibility* respectively.

- *Egocentrism* is characterized by an inability to see the world from anything other than a self-centred, subjective viewpoint. Therefore children at this time are unable to be critical, logical, or realistic in their thinking. This is not selfishness, it is simply that children are not yet aware that there can be points of view other than their own. This can be demonstrated experimentally if, for example, a child is asked to say what someone sitting on the other side of the classroom is likely to be able to see (typically the child will describe things from their own perspective only) or to name the brothers and sisters of a sibling in his or her own family (again the child will typically see things only from a personal standpoint and leave him or herself off the list).

- *Centration* involves focusing attention (centring) upon only one feature of a situation and ignoring others, however relevant. Investigation of centring has spawned a number of experiments. In one of the best known children are presented with two plasticine balls which they agree are the same size, and one is then rolled out into a sausage shape. When asked which is the larger now (or which has the more plasticine now), they will usually point to the sausage. In other words, they have focused upon only one aspect of the problem, namely the longer length of the sausage, and based their answer upon this. As a consequence of such centring, children are unable to practise what Piaget calls *conservation*: that is, they are unable to grasp in our example the fact that the amount of plasticine is conserved (remains the same) whatever happens to its shape. Another instance of the inability to practise conservation is allegedly produced if we lay out two rows of sweets, of equal number and length, then spread out one row to make it longer than the other. When questioned, the child shows *non-conservation* by saying we now have 'more' sweets in the elongated row than in the other. Similarly if we take two identical beakers each filled to the same point with liquid and pour the contents of one into a tall thin glass, children will now usually claim that we have 'more' liquid than we had before, and more liquid than we have in the remaining beaker, simply because the level has now risen higher. If we next pour the liquid into a square fat beaker so that the level falls they will now claim that we have 'less' liquid than before.

Irreversibility entails the inability to work backwards to one's starting point. Thus having gone, say, through a given sequence involving three steps, children find it hard to go back to step two and then to step one. Thus although they can add two and three in order to make five, they find it often impossible to reverse the procedure and subtract two from five in order to arrive back at three. It is not that they are incapable of carrying out the computation if it is presented to them as a separate sum; it is simply that they cannot grasp that because two and three make five then five minus two must make three. Similarly, they are also still unable to grasp the transitive inferences that eluded them in the pre-conceptual substage.

Stage 3. Concrete operations: approximately 7–11 years

This important stage, which essentially covers the junior school period, sees children achieve an organized and coherent symbolic system of thinking which enables them to anticipate and control their environment. This system still differs from that employed by the majority of adults, however, in that it is tied to concrete experiences (hence the term *concrete operations*). This means that although children can formulate hypotheses in the absence of any actual concrete evidence in front of them, and can go at least a step or two beyond the evidence by abstract reasoning, they nevertheless must have experienced such evidence in one form or another concretely in the past if they are to be able to do so. Essentially they are still limited in their thinking and tend to *describe* their environment rather than to *explain* it (one reason why they find it much easier to give examples of things than to provide definitions of them). They also find it hard to test a hypothesis against reality correctly, often changing a perfectly correct view of reality to make it fit rather than altering an hypothesis. Thus, for example, if they believe the football team they support is the best in the league they will continue to maintain this no matter how often it loses (a fault to which many adults are often by no means immune!)

Nevertheless children's thinking moves forward considerably during this stage. It becomes less egocentric, and they develop the ability to show both decentring (the opposite of egocentring) and reversal. With decentring comes conservation, and Piaget maintains that this conservation takes place in a definite order, with conservation of substance coming first at approximately age seven or eight, conservation of weight coming next somewhere between ages nine and ten, and conservation of volume being achieved by about the age of 12.

The main cognitive structure underlying these and the various other advances made during this stage is *grouping* (or categorization). Children are able to recognize the members of a true logical class, and thus organize objects and events into sets in terms of their common defining characteristics. Grouping increasingly enables them to make sense of experience, to solve problems, and to move towards a more realistic and accurate picture of the world. With the ability to group also comes what Piaget calls *seriation:* that is, the ability to arrange objects in rank order in terms, for example, of size or weight. This can be summed up by saying that grouping and seriation indicate that children are now able to see the correct relationship between things, and to use this knowledge to solve problems. Since this is remarkably like the definition of intelligence offered later in Chapter 5, it is appropriate to point out that for Piaget intelligence is indeed the result of the various genetically determined activities that we have been discussing under the various stages in this section, and that for Piaget intelligence is itself therefore closely bound up with the maturation of innate characteristics.

Stage 4. Formal operations: approximately 12 years and upwards

The onset of adolescence usually sees the emergence of what Piaget calls *formal operations*, which is the final stage in the developmental programme. Though children's thinking may still differ from the adult's in degree, it now begins to resemble it in kind. Children become able to follow the *form* of an argument or to set up an hypothesis without requiring actual experience of the concrete objects or situations upon which it depends. Of equal importance, having come to understand individual concepts or categories in isolation during the previous stages of development, they are now able to see that these may be interdependent in certain circumstances. For example, they may realize that speed, weight and time might all have to be considered in arriving at the answer to a particular problem, or that one might have to be varied while the others are held constant and so on.

The cognitive structure that underlies formal operations is called by Piaget *lattice-group structure*, to indicate that it is a form of thinking in which everything is capable of being related to everything else, thus allowing the individual to try out various combinations of hypothetical propositions when considering a problem or possible future event. The kind of reasoning thus generated is known as *hypothetico-deductive reasoning*, because the individual is able both to set up hypotheses and make deductions from results, thus furthering an understanding of the material which is being dealt with.

There is one further important aspect of Piaget's thinking that must be mentioned to have a good grasp of his theory, namely the processes that he calls *functional invariants*. It will be appreciated that all the forms of thinking described so far are dependent upon age and development. Children change their cognitive structures as they grow older (hence Piaget sometimes terms them functional variants). But they also have other cognitive processes that are inborn and remain constant throughout life (hence the term functional invariants). The most important of these are known as *accommodation, assimilation*, and *organization*. Borrowed from biology, the term *accommodation* implies that individuals have at times to adapt their functioning to the specific qualities of the things with which they are dealing. There are many things about the world that even at an early age children realize they cannot change (e.g. the force of gravity, the properties of water and fire), and therefore they have to accommodate their behaviour to these things rather than attempt to alter them to suit themselves. *Assimilation*, on the other hand (which is another term borrowed from biology), refers to the process by which objects or their attributes are incorporated into the individual's existing cognitive structures, often altering and developing these structures somewhat in the process. Assimilation and accommodation always go together, although at any one time one of them may be more important than the other. The reason why they go together is that individuals can only assimilate those elements of the environment to which they are able to accommodate themselves. If accommodation is impossible, then so is assimilation. For example, children accommodate themselves to a substance like water, assimilating in the process that water is wet, that you cannot breathe in it, that it makes a mess on the nice clean floor and so on.

The third of Piaget's functional invariants, *organization*, concerns the way in which cognitive acts are grouped and arranged to form sequences or schemata. In any intellectual act there is always a schema of some kind present, a kind of cognitive plan which individuals use to help tackle a given problem. If a certain schema proves inappropriate for a certain task, then individuals will try to reorganize it: that is, try to alter or add to or subtract from or rearrange the cognitive acts which it contains in order to try again more successfully. Obviously their ability to organize, just as their ability to accommodate and assimilate, develops as they grow older, but the three functions remain unchanged as processes from birth to maturity.

Criticisms of Piaget

Criticisms of Piaget focus primarily upon the fact that he seems to have underestimated the abilities of young children. Thus the failure of young children to tackle successfully the tests used by Piaget to assess their stage of cognitive development may be due less to immaturities in thought processes than to inadequacies in language or experience, or to an inability to separate relevant from irrelevant information, or to a range of other possibilities. For example in the egocentricity experiment mentioned on p. 46, which requires children to describe things from the perspective of someone else, the problem may not be an inability to *decentre* so much as an inability to decentre in situations which lie outside their immediate experience. Decentring depends upon the ability to take account of more than one viewpoint at a time, and there is now evidence that even children in Piaget's pre-operational stage can do this, provided that they are confronted with a test that reflects an activity in which they have engaged themselves. Thus Donaldson (1986) has demonstrated that when children even as young as three are asked to place a doll out of sight of another doll, they can correctly do so. From their bird's eye position above the table on which the dolls are situated, the children can see both dolls, but they know that if they put the first one behind an intervening barrier it will be 'hidden' from the second one. 'Hiding' is something young children know all about, since it is a game in which they often engage. In consequence, they have no difficulty in decentring and taking the viewpoint of the second doll, a viewpoint from which the first doll is now obscured by the barrier.

Rather than claiming young children are only capable of egocentric thinking, we should therefore say that *usually* their thought is egocentric.

Equally important, children's answers to the problems offered to them in Piagetian tests may be hampered by the fact that they tend to interpret words not in terms of general meaning but in terms of their own sense of the situation. Their failure to give correct answers to Piagetian tests may therefore often be due to the frequent use in such tests of terms like 'different from', 'same as', 'less', 'longer', 'shorter' and so on. Such words may be interpreted by children as referring to appearance rather than to actual size. Thus in the consevation experiment described earlier which asks children if we have 'more' liquid now that we have poured the contents of a standard beaker into a taller, thinner glass, children's wrong answers may stem from an association in their minds between 'more' and the changed, elongated appearance of the liquid, rather than from an inability to grasp the concept of conservation of quantity. In their own terms, the children's answers make perfect sense. Karmiloff-Smith (cited Turner, 1984) suggests that the child's apparent non-conservation is caused by his or her attempt to solve the problem. If children approach a task without an awareness that they are being specifically asked to provide an 'answer', then they will sometimes conserve quite naturally, just as they will sometimes decentre.

This is supported by several experimental examples cited in Sylva and Lunt (1985). For instance in the rows of sweets experiment (see p. 47) children will often say correctly that the number of sweets in the elongated row remains the same if their attention is partly distracted from the problem itself by a story line which includes a 'naughty Teddy' up to tricks of some kind. Even without a naughty Teddy element, I still remember the scorn with which both my children at the age of four assured me that the number of sweets remained the same ('Of *course* they're the same'), accompanied by the unspoken but obvious implication that it was a pity Daddy didn't have anything better to do with his time than ask such silly questions.

As with decentring and conservation, so with other aspects of children's thinking. Povey and Hill (1975) have shown that if pictorial material is used instead of verbal material with children at the pre-conceptual sub-stage, they appear to be capable of forming not only specific but also generic concepts. For instance, they appear to have a specific concept of 'dog', since they were able to identify a dog even when it was embedded pictorially in situations quite novel to them, and they appear to have a generic concept of 'food' since they could identify as food many different edible objects.

Similarly Bryant and Trabasso (1971) have shown that children in the pre-conceptual stage can grasp transitive reasoning provided that they are given appropriate previous training and steps are taken to prevent lapses of memory while they are carrying out the various comparisons. This means that in the 'A is bigger than B, B is bigger than C, therefore A is bigger than C' type of statement, children can understand the reasoning involved if they are first taught the initial two comparisons very thoroughly, and then are tested for memory of these comparisons at the same time that they are told about (or questioned on) the relationship between A and C.

Findings such as these have led some writers to conclude we should abandon Piaget to the occasional historical footnote. This is misguided. As Gellatly (1985) has it, Piaget's research has set the stage for all subsequent investigations. His towering contribution was to try and enter the world of the child, and understand it from the child's viewpoint. The vast output of literature that has been inspired by Piaget has concentrated on demonstrating improvements upon Piaget's theorizing or experimental approach, rather than on proposing an alternative methodology. No one has challenged Piaget's basic finding that children's understanding is determined by the expertise with which they can form concepts and build an internal model which approximates to external reality. From an educational standpoint, the implications of this are vast. Children's 'failure' to understand the questions and instructions and explanations offered to them by adults is due less to their own shortcomings than to the frequent inability of adults to present these communications to them in a form which is appropriate to the level at which conceptually they are able to function.

Other approaches to cognitive development

Although Piaget's work has attracted by far the greatest amount of attention within education, he is not the only psychologist who has made relevant contributions to our knowledge of the development of thinking in children. The American psychologist, Jerome Bruner, in a number of important publications, suggests children go through three main stages on their way to acquiring the mature thought processes of the adult. These are *enactive* (in which thinking is based upon doing), *iconic* (in which imagery comes increasingly to be used) and *symbolic* (in which complex symbolism including language is employed). These stages have obvious parallels with those of Piaget, but where Bruner differs markedly is in his insistence that although we acquire these three stages in chronological order, with symbolic coming last, we nevertheless retain and use all three throughout life. We do not 'grow out of' the earlier stages, as in Piaget's model, and although the major emphasis in adult thinking is upon the symbolic level, we can and do employ enactive and iconic thinking when the situation is appropriate.

Bruner's work is discussed in more detail in the chapter on learning (Chapter 7), which includes some of the implications of his ideas for the teacher's work. There remains one other worker in this field to whom we must draw attention, how-ever, and that is the Russian, Lev Vygotsky. Vygotsky differed from Piaget and Bruner in that his main concern was with the relationship between thought and language. His experimental apparatus consisted of a number of blocks of wood with nonsense syllables written on the hidden undersides. Each block was a variant of two heights (tall or squat) and of six shapes (circle, semicircle, square, trapezium, triangle, and a six-sided shape). The experimenter turned up one of the blocks and showed the child the nonsense syllable written underneath, and then asked him or her to pick out all the other blocks that they considered would carry the same syllable. Thus the child was being asked to isolate the parti-cular combination of shape and size that appeared to go with a particular syllable (or more technically to isolate the *spatial attributes* that appeared to accompany a particular verbal concept).

Broadly, Vygotsky's conclusions were similar to those of Piaget, though his terminology was different. He identified three main stages in the development of a child's thinking, namely the *vague syncretic stage* (in which the child depended primarily upon actions, and turned the blocks up on a ran-dom trial and error basis until he or she had found the right ones), the *complexes stage* (in which the child used strategies of varying complexity but still failed to identify the desired attributes), and the *potential concept stage* (in which the child was able to cope with the individual relevant attributes of the blocks but could not manipulate all of these at one and the same time). When the child could do so, the ability to form concepts was judged to have reached maturity.

Like Piaget, Vygotsky's ideas are complex, and there is considerable debate on the precise relationship of his three stages to those of Piaget. Nevertheless, from the practical standpoint of the teacher, it is easy to see the link between vague syncretic behaviour and Piaget's emphasis upon the child's need for physical activity before that activity can be internalized into thought. It is also easy to see the link between what Vygotsky saw as mature thinking and the lattice-group structures said by Piaget to be used when the child reached the stage of formal operations. In both there is an emphasis upon the child's ability to manipulate mentally several different ideas at the same time, and to see the rela-tionships between them. Vygotsky also agrees with Piaget and differs from Bruner in that he sees the child as moving through the earlier stages of thinking rather than as carrying them with him or her throughout life (though as with Piaget's stages there is always the possibility of regression to earlier, immature forms of thought in the face of extreme problems and stresses).

Cognitive
development
and the
classroom

For Piaget, intelligent cognitive activity is an extension of basic universal biological characteristics. The whole of intellectual functioning, in fact, is seen by him as a special form of biological activity. This factor, together with the four-stage developmental model that goes with it, might tempt some observers to suggest that in Piaget's view the role of the teacher is relatively unimportant. Children's ability to manage their environments and solve problems, it might seem, is dependent primarily upon maturation, with the teacher powerless to influence the speed with which a child progresses through each of the identified stages. This suggestion would be incorrect for two major reasons.

The first of these is that in his research Piaget concentrates upon how a child deals with information, not upon what kind of information we choose to give him or her. It is the teacher who decides upon the latter, and the teacher who therefore determines the content of the cognitive structures that a child uses in dealing with the world. The second is that the ages given for each of the stages and sub-stages identified by Piaget are *approximate only*. And as has been seen, there is firm evidence that Piaget has underestimated the abilities of children at each of these stages. Indeed the stages themselves may be more a convenient way of categorizing the development of a child's ability to reason appropriately and consistently across situations rather than invariable innate imperatives. Some commentators, in fact, prefer to refer to them as mental ages rather than chronological ages for this reason. Some children may move more quickly through some or all of the stages than the norm, others more slowly. Some children will never consistently attain formal operations, and even as adults may still function at the level of concrete operations. Granted this unevenness of progress, the question inevitably arises as to whether a child can be accelerated through the stages given the appropriate educational opportunities; if such acceleration does prove to be possible, the role of the teacher will then obviously be crucial to it.

The task of the teacher

What this unevenness of progress suggests is that the scope enjoyed by the teacher for accelerating children's progress through the various stages may be considerable, provided that material is presented to them in the appropriate way. And it is when making decisions about what is and what is not appropriate that the teacher finds Piaget's work to be of maximum help. This work suggests to us that many of the mistakes children make when tackling problems may be caused by the fact that, as presented, these problems are unsuited to their levels of thinking. Errors which may therefore at first sight seem to the teacher to be inexcusable may in fact simply be evidence of children's attempts to make sense of material in terms of their existing cognitive structures.

What this means to the teacher is summarized below:

- When working with children of any age the teacher should never make the assumption that a child's attempts to think through a problem are simply an immature version of his or her own. Often the answers children produce may make sense to themselves in terms of the way in which they are able to conceptualize the material in front of them. The task of the teacher should therefore be to assess the level at which the child is thinking. This does not, of course, mean going through a range of Piagetian experiments with each member of the class. The chronological age of each child is, as we have seen, some guide, and armed with this the teacher needs to remind him or herself of the level of thinking appropriate to this age, and then to ask whether children appear to be functioning at this level and whether learning material is being presented to them in a form appropriate to it.

- Although children should be given opportunities to conceptualize at levels higher than that associated with their chronological age, failure to take advantage of these opportunities should not be seen as a sign of inadequacy (or lack of interest) on their part. At no time should the individual child be left feeling confused or that he or she is to blame if the fault lies with an incongruity between the material presented and the child's own level of conceptualization.

- A child's level of conceptual development should be taken into account when devising teaching methods. At all stages below the onset of formal operations, for example, children's powers of conceptualization are linked closely to their physical activity, and they need therefore to experience problems (or previously to have experienced their defining characteristics) in a concrete form. Placed in an over-formal, exclusively teacher-orientated environment, children are therefore starved of the practical experience which serves as the raw material for their thinking. If we restrict their experience, we restrict their conceptualization.

- Having had the benefit of experience, children rely heavily upon symbolization in developing their concepts, and in particular upon that form of symbolization called signs which has already been referred to. Of paramount importance amongst the signs available to them are those which go to make up language. Language is discussed at length in the next chapter, and all that need be stressed for the present is that children should be given the benefit of a linguistically stimulating environment, and the teacher should endeavour to see to it that they understand the correct meaning of words used in the classroom. The same also applies to the signs (i.e. numbers themselves as well as plus signs, minus signs and the like) involved in mathematics.

- Piaget's developmental model of thinking emphasizes that children must master the schemata at the earlier levels if they are to go on to more advanced work. This is not just a question of children 'missing the groundwork' in a particular subject, but the much more fundamental issue of failing to master the patterns of thinking necessary for success in a wide range of educational endeavours.

- Closely allied to the last point, we derive from Piaget the notion that educational backwardness is bound up with the level at which the child is thinking. So-called backward children are functioning at a level below that of their chronological ages, and it is the task of the remedial teacher to establish what this level is and to ensure that material is presented to the children in a form consistent with it.

- The onset of formal operations makes the teacher's job easier in some ways in that he or she can now deal increasingly in abstract knowledge, but this brings potential problems of its own. It is suggested that part of the argumentativeness shown by some children at adolescence is occasioned by the fact that abstract concepts such as 'freedom', 'justice', 'truth', 'altruism', and so on now begin to take on a newer and deeper meaning for them, and often lead to their judging and rejecting the standards of their elders. Thus the idealism of the adolescent should be seen as a genuine attempt to understand the full implications of the nobler side of human nature, and should be welcomed and respected by adults who have perhaps had their own understanding blunted by problems and difficulties and the need to compromise over the years.

Finally, a word of caution; I have already said that the chronological ages attached to the various Piagetian stages are only approximations, but it must also be stressed that children's development may be uneven in that they may attain some of the thinking associated with a particular stage before attaining the remainder. Or, faced with a difficult problem in a stressful situation, they may revert temporarily to an earlier stage of reasoning. Children's errors should therefore be studied closely (as is stressed again in the chapter on learning) for the insights they give into the child's thinking. An error is not simply a matter of a cross rather than a tick on a child's work; it is essential feedback to the teacher not only on whether a child has understood a particular point or not but on the reasons why failure has occurred.

References

Bryant, P.E. and Trabasso, T. (1971) Transitive inferences and memory in young children. *Nature, 232*, 456–458.

Donaldson, M. (1986) *Children's Minds*, 2nd edn. London: Fontana.

Gellatly, A. (1985) Development of Thought. In A. Branthwaite and A. Rogers (ed.) *Children Growing Up*. Milton Keynes: Open University Press.

Povey, R. and Hill, E. (1975) Can pre-school children form concepts? *Educational Research, 17*, 180–192.

Sylva, K. and Lunt, I. (1985) *Child Development: A first course*. Oxford: Basil Blackwell.

Turner, J. (1984) *Cognitive Development and Education*. London: Methuen.

SOME QUESTIONS

1. What do we mean by the term 'concept'? Why are concepts so important in the development of thinking?

2. What is the process by which a child makes sense of novel objects or experiences?

3. List Piaget's stages of cognitive development and give the approximate ages associated with each.

4. What is the relationship between thought and action in the sensori-motor stage of development? How do we recognize when an element of purpose is being introduced into the child's behaviour?

5. Piaget claims that during the sensori-motor period the child's relationship with an action is not a mental one but is contained within the action itself. What do you think this really means?

6. Why is symbolic activity so important in the development of pre-operational (and later) forms of thinking?

7. Distinguish between 'symbols' and 'signs'.

8. Consider ways in which a child's play may give you insight into his or her level of symbolic activity.

9. Give an example of the kind of experiment used by Piaget to demonstrate centration. What aspects of the child's behaviour indicate that centration is taking place?

10. Write short definitions of egocentrism, irreversibility, and transductive reasoning.

11. Why do you think children tend to describe their environment rather than explain it during the stage of concrete operations?

12. Piaget considers both grouping and categorization are essential abilities in the development of complex thinking. Why do you think this is so?

13. What are the characteristics of lattice-group structure?

14. How important are Piaget's so-called 'functional invariants' to our understanding of the processes of thought?

15. List and define the three main stages which Bruner considers children go through on their way to the acquisition of mature processes.

16. What is the fundamental way in which Bruner's stages differ from those of Piaget?

17. What aspect of the child's activity indicated to Vygotsky that he or she had reached the ability to form mature concepts?

18. What is the link between Vygotsky's so-called 'vague syncretic behaviour' in children and Piaget's emphasis upon the child's need for physical activity before that activity can be internalized into thought?

Additional Reading

Boden, M.A. (1979) Piaget. London: Fontana Modern Masters.
A very readable brief survey of the whole range of Piaget's work and its relevance to philosophy and biology as well as to psychology and education.

Branthwaite, A. and Rogers, D. (ed.) (1985) *Children Growing Up.* Milton Keynes: Open University Press.
Reviews by expert authors of children's cognitive, social, personal and biological growth. Strongly recommended (also recommended for Chapter 2).

Brown, G. and Desforges, C. (1979) *Piaget's Theory: A psychological critique.* London: Routledge & Kegan Paul.
Good survey of Piaget's theory together with a detailed critique of some of his findings and the inferences drawn from them.

Bruner, J., Goodnow, J. and Austin, G. (1956) *A Study of Thinking.* New York: Wiley.
Bruner is easily tackled through his own writings, since he presents his ideas clearly and engagingly (and see Chapter 7 for other references to his work). This book deals particularly with cognitive development. (Also recommended for Chapter 8.)

Flavell, J.H. (1963) *The Developmental Psychology of Jean Piaget.* New York: Van Nostrand Reinhold.

Usually regarded as the most complete summary of Piaget's work.

Inhelder, B. and Piaget, J. (1958) *The Growth of Logical Thinking from Childhood to Adolescence.* London: Routledge & Kegan Paul.
Provides a comprehensive outline of Piaget's ideas on cognitive development for the non-specialist.

Kagan, J. (1984) *The Nature of the Child.* New York: Basic Books.
Excellent and sensitive examination of key aspects of the child's cognitive and social development. (Also recommended for Chapter 1.)

Modgil, C. and Modgil, S. (1984) The development of thinking and reasoning. In D. Fontana (ed.) *The Education of the Young Child*, 2nd edn. Oxford: Basil Blackwell.
Comprehensive resumé of the work of Piaget and of Bruner.

Modgil, S. and Modgil, C. (ed.) (1982) *Jean Piaget: Consensus and Controversy.* London: Holt Rinehart & Winston.

Modgil, S., Modgil, C. and Brown, G. (ed.) (1983) Jean Piaget: An interdisciplinary critique. London: Routledge & Kegan Paul.

Mussen, P.H., Conger, J.J. and Kagan, J. (1984) *Child Development and Personality*, 6th edn. New York: Harper & Row.
The chapters on cognitive development and allied topics, like the rest of the book, are first class. (Also recommended for Chapter 1.)

Phillips, J.L. (1975) *The Origins of Intellect: Piaget's theory*, 2nd edn. New York: Freeman.
A splendid book that makes even the more complex areas of Piaget's theories fully comprehensible.

Piaget, J. (1970) *Science of Education and the Psychology of the Child.* London: Longman.
A survey of Piaget's main concerns with education.

Tizard, B. and Hughes, M. (1984) *Young Children Learning.* London: Fontana.
A highly informative summary of the authors' own research which supports the view that Piaget underestimated the thinking capacities of young children.

Turner, J. (1975) *Cognitive Development.* London: Methuen.
A very useful, brief introduction to the general field of cognitive development.

Vygotsky, L. (1962) *Thought and Language.* Cambridge, Massachusetts, MIT Press.
Sets out his own ideas fully, but not an easy book for newcomers to the field.

4

Language

If I asked you to try and imagine a world without language, your first reponse would probably be that such a world would lack the means of proper communication. Without language, individuals would be unable to communicate anything other than the most rudimentary matters to each other. But if you thought further you would realize that a world without language would also be a world without thought. Or rather a world without complex thought. It is possible to think without language (using images, tactile sensations), but not at the kind of level we take for granted in even the simplest of daily activities. When humans developed language, their evolution took a quantum leap forward, not just in the ability of individuals to share their thinking with others, but in the quality and scope of that thinking.

The beginnings of language

Babbling. Language in young children is normally preceded by a pre-speech stage known as babbling which occurs spontaneously in the great majority of babies somewhere between the fourth and sixth months of life. In this stage, babies start producing a wide range of delightful little sounds, seemingly out of pure joy. These sounds have nothing to do with the sounds they hear around them, since whatever the country of their birth they babble in very much the same way, even reproducing in the process sounds that may occur only in languages other than their own. Nor is babbling a social phenomenon, for often babies will babble just as happily when they are alone as when they are with others.

Quite how a baby moves from babbling to actual speech is not clear. Since there are occasional babies who never babble but who nevertheless acquire perfectly normal speech, some authorities argue that there may be no links between the two; but with the great majority of children there does seem to be an orderly progression from the one to the other. This suggests that in most cases, a child's speech develops out of his or her early experiments with sound, partly perhaps as a result of social reinforcement and partly perhaps out of an innate tendency to acquire linguistic structures.

Dropping sounds from the repertoire. One thing is certain, we must not underestimate the staggering feats of learning and adaptation involved. Words are part of a highly complex process. They are sounds that we use to represent the objects and events in the world around us. For a baby to grasp the fact that these sounds stand for real experiences (and later on even for personal feelings, needs and intentions) is a marvellous feat of comprehension. At the purely descriptive level, what seems to happen is that babies become aware that some of the sounds they make during babbling correspond to the sounds other people are making. They then come to retain and repeat these sounds, dropping from their repertoire any sounds they do not hear around them. At the babbling stage, they could pick up any language and enunciate it perfectly, but once they have dropped sounds from their repertoire it becomes increasingly difficult for them to pick up these sounds again. Thus if later on we want a child to learn a foreign language containing a range of these discarded sounds, he or she is unlikely to re-acquire them perfectly. The result is that the child will have difficulty pronouncing the new language without traces of his or her native tongue.

Sadly, babies who are born deaf, although they usually go through the babbling stage, gradually fall silent as they hear no sounds around them. This is one reason why it is vital deafness is diagnosed as early as possible. If they have some slight hearing, and if we can amplify sounds sufficiently, deaf children's babbling stands a chance of developing into normal speech. Denied the chance to hear language during the babbling stage, any speech deaf children do acquire will have a characteristically laboured and unnatural quality to it.

Adding sounds to repertoire. During the babbling stage, babies usually add sounds to their repertoire in a fixed sequence (see e.g. Rogers, 1985). Details of this precise sequence lie outside the scope of the present chapter, but generally the 'baba' sound comes first followed by the 'meme' and then the 'dada' and the 'nana'. It is no coincidence that these sounds have been built into the most familiar English words in the baby's vocabulary (baby, ma, dad and nan). As the baby produces these sounds he or she is rewarded by the delight of parents, who think their offspring is consciously trying to refer to them by name, and this social reinforcement helps make these sounds an established part of early speech.

Ability to copy sounds. It is probable that this happens with a number of a baby's first words. Spontaneously the baby produces sounds which resemble words, is rewarded by parental approval, and through *operant conditioning* goes on to use the sounds increasingly and to associate them with specific people and objects. But there is more to language acquisition that this. Children appear to have an innate ability to imitate others (Bower, 1982). We see this in the manner in which small babies will copy the faces we pull at them, and the gestures we make. (Do not minimize this ability by the way; how does a baby know what groups of muscles to use in order to mimic the effects we are producing?) Nowhere is this copying ability more remarkable than with language. Infants innately know how to produce, often with complete accuracy at the first attempt, the sounds we make when we talk to them or when they hear us talking to each other.

The language acquisition device. But it does not end there. Having begun to copy our words, and to associate these words with the things they represent, young children then proceed to build these words into short sentences. And this is where they move beyond simple copying. For they *make grammatical errors which they do not hear other people make*, thus demonstrating that they are spontaneously experimenting with language usage. Again extended discussion of these childish grammatical structures lies beyond our scope, but so characteristic are these structures that Chomsky (1969) has suggested children are genetically programmed to acquire language in a particular way. Chomsky argues that children have an innate *language acquisition device* (LAD) which enables them to develop language in much the way they manifest other developmental skills. Certainly they would not learn to talk if they did not hear others use speech around them, but an innate structured predisposition for language is there in the first place. Without it, language would not happen.

Chomsky's ideas have been challenged by other experts, who argue that childish grammatical structures can result from the child's misapplication of grammatical rules he or she has already learnt from the speech of adults, and the debate rages on. But when experts disagree amongst themselves on such fundamental issues it is usually a fair sign that no one knows the complete answers. The more one studies the tremendous feat involved in a child's progress from pre-speech to a mature command of language, the more enigmatic the whole process looks.

Passive and active vocabularies. However, from an educational viewpoint, our interest lies less in the mechanics behind language development than in descriptions of the way this development takes place and of how it can best be encouraged. For this purpose we need to divide a child's vocabulary into *passive* and *active*, the former being the number of words understood and the latter the number of words that can

63

actually be used. Naturally the passive vocabulary is larger than the active, and much more difficult to assess in any detail. But careful recording by psychologists of the growth in children's active vocabularies allows us to draw up a list of average active vocabulary development.

15 months	–	First recognizable words.
18 months	–	Twenty words.
2 years	–	Fifty words. Two or three word sentences.
2 years	–	Two hundred words. Frequent use of short sentences.

Although these norms are useful to us, there are wide variations from them in individual cases. Some children still are not talking at two-and-a-half, while others are racing ahead. What is more, these variations do not tell us a great deal about a child's future progress. Provided they are not handicapped in any way, children who have not started to talk at two-and-a-half may have caught up and passed most of their contemporaries by the time they begin school, while children who are way beyond the norm at two-and-a-half may be only average at the age of five. For like most other aspects of development, language acquisition tends to go in fits and starts, with periods of rapid progress alternating with periods of consolidation. Nevertheless, at three the average child is talking so fluently that it is no longer possible to keep an accurate check of his or her active vocabulary, and by four most children have a command of everyday language which is virtually that of an adult.

Just as we can keep a check in the early years on the growth of children's active vocabularies, so we can look at the way they acquire a command of the various parts of speech. Nouns come first, followed by verbs, and somewhere between the ages of two and two-and-a-half by simple pronouns ('me', 'I' and 'you'). The use of pronouns shows a particularly significant advance. A child has to master the very complex idea that when I am talking about myself 'I' means 'me', but when you are talking about yourself 'I' means 'you'. Adjectives and adverbs are variable in their first appearance, but they usually appear sometime during the third year. Again their use shows a considerable feat of learning. A child has to grasp the idea that adjectives are *comparative* terms. That is, a 'big' object is only big as compared to other objects in the same category. Thus a 'big' spoonful is in fact much smaller than a 'small' doll. Similarly with adverbs. A person running 'quickly' is moving slower than a car going 'slowly'. All very complicated if we stop and think about it, and further evidence of how able small children are. Odd the readiness with which, when they get to school, we classify some of them as having learning problems.

Amongst the host of other landmarks in a child's language learning we can mention the appearance of 'what' and 'who' questions at around two-and-a-half, and the appearance of 'where' and 'why' questions at three or soon after. Plurals, the remaining pronouns, and even simple propositions (e.g. 'on', 'by', 'in') also appear around three, as does the ability to repeat short rhymes and songs by heart. Most children know their full name by two-and-a-half, and their address and birthday by four. By the age of four, most of their childish grammatical constructions have disappeared, and they can give accounts of events, name the primary colours, and show at least some appreciation of complex linguistic concepts like 'past' and 'future'. Once a child is at school, his or her language horizons widen even more rapidly.

Encouraging early language

Children's language, like most of their learning, responds to adult encouragement. We probably cannot speed up the age at which individual children first start using recognizable words, but once they begin employing language, the more verbally stimulating their environment the better. The more they hear others use words and the more others speak to them and respond to their own efforts, the more they will try and use language in their own turn. And once their vocabularies begin to grow, the process will be accelerated and enriched if they come from a home and attend a school in which language is fluently and flexibly used. Nor are the advantages of such an environment restricted just to vocabulary growth. With vocabulary growth comes increased opportunities for using words in the development of thinking, which in turn prompts further linguistic development. And if children are fortunate enough to have parents and teachers who encourage them to use language to express and communicate their feelings, then their emotional development will also be greatly enhanced.

In view of the importance of the link between a child's linguistic environment and the development of language, attempts have been made to study the way in which children's language use varies from one social context to another. At one time it was held that children from middle-class backgrounds could use both *elaborated* and *restricted* verbal codes (the former possessing a logically more complex linguistic structure than the latter), while working-class children used only restricted codes, thus placing limits on the complexity of their thinking. As indicated by Stubbs (1983) however, such sociolinguistic theories are now seen to be an over-simplification even by their principal author, Basil Bernstein (e.g. 1975), and are in any case supported by sparse research evidence and in many ways untestable. In addition, comparisons between different languages (e.g. English and Russian) show that grammatical structures which in one language look incorrect and unelaborated may be standard usage in another, with no apparent ill-effect upon the cognitive powers of native speakers of the latter tongue. Nevertheless, although the precise links between language and cognitive development are not yet clear, a highly restricted vocabulary or an ignorance of how to use language to express and convey meaning, does seem to be a major handicap to a child's powers of communication and therefore to the learning and thinking which arise from this communication.

One of the critical factors in the encouragement of language development is to provide children with the *objective necessity* for using words. If adults consistently 'guess' at children's meaning, instead of prompting them to put their meaning effectively into words, or if adults fail to reward children with attention when they are trying to communicate difficult concepts, then children have no incentive to develop beyond basic language usage. On the other hand, if adults use language which is way beyond the comprehension of children, the latter will find the whole exercise confusing and frustrating. Either way, the motivation to acquire language proficiency is likely to be hindered.

Language and the school

Much of the research into language function, as with research into other areas of linguistic competence, has focused upon early childhood and the pre-school years. This should not be seen as providing mere background knowledge for the teacher, however, because results provide us with invaluable pointers to how language is used in later childhood, since such usage is a development of, rather than a departure from, what happens in these early years. Children are active participants in the development of their linguistic skills: that is, language is not simply something that 'happens' to them as a result of the activities of others. They actively set out to acquire language, initially as an extension of their social interaction with those around them, and later as a deliberate attempt to find out more about, and increase their control over, their immediate environment. The response of their caretakers and teachers is, however, crucial to the level of success which greets their efforts. Failure to supply children with the linguistic information they request (e.g. the names of objects, the meaning of words), or to supply it in a form which they can assimilate, may result in children ceasing to make these requests, with obvious negative consequences for their speed of development. It must be said that some adults actively discourage children in their quest for language, for example by ignoring their questions, by laughing at them in their attempts to use new words, by censuring them too strongly for their errors, or just by making them feel guilty for 'chattering' or for using language at times which the adult finds inconvenient or irritating.

In all contexts, children are more likely to master language units if these units are relevant to daily life; if the units help them communicate the things they want to communicate, or understand the things they want to understand. Thus a child with a culturally stimulating environment will have more urge to acquire language than a child with an unstimulating one, since there are more things around the first child to be questioned and understood, and therefore a greater objective necessity to use words frequently and with a grasp of their correct meaning.

The role of the teacher

During the early stages of language development children frequently use what psychologists call *transitional* forms of syntax: they use parts of known (though, in the new context, incorrect) syntactical structures when attempting to master novel and more difficult ones. If frequently furnished with correct examples, children will soon abandon these transitional structures in favour of more advanced and suitable ones, but continual specific attempts to correct children may do more harm than good if they are unable to grasp and profit from them reasonably quickly. The disapproval implied by these corrections before they are able fully to profit from them may prompt children to abandon their transitional grammar structures and revert back to better-known, more primitive ones.

Research has identified four characteristics noted in mothers who have verbally advanced children, and these might be taken as the four 'golden rules' for any teacher concerned with a child's linguistic development. We can summarize these rules in a form appropriate for the teacher as follows:

1. Embed any new verbal structure to which a class is being intoduced in structures that are already familiar to the children.

2. Answer children's questions about language with relevant accurate replies that go beyond what is barely necessary. For instance, children might be furnished with examples of how the new word or the new syntactical structure might be used, or they might be invited to provide such examples themselves, or their attention might be drawn to words similar in meaning to the one about which they are enquiring, or they might be shown a helpful way of remembering the new linguistic skills they have just acquired.

3. Provide the children with helpful and appropriate feedback on whether they are expressing themselves correctly or not (though keep in mind the qualification already made and take care not to discourage them by showing undue disapproval of their errors).

4. Maintain linguistic themes where possible over several utterances, both when talking to individuals and to the whole class (i.e. keep the theme of a particular conversation going by prompting and responding to further contributions from the child or children, rather than simply giving short replies that close the discussion).

The rules of language

To these four rules a fifth can be added, namely that there is great value in teaching children the rules of language. From an early age (and certainly by the time they start school) most children are aware that there are rules underlying the construction of what they say, but their ignorance of these rules handicaps them in formulating new utterances to deal with novel situations. Over a period of time, by listening to others, they may gradually become more sensitive to these rules so that they use them without conscious deliberation (i.e. their use becomes an automatic skill), but this is a slow process. Often parents and even teachers are less help than they might be because they themselves are unable to formulate these rules and, importantly, to set up conditions in which the child can put them into practice. Thus the learning of language becomes an essentially haphazard process, based upon the amassing of instances of a particular rule rather than upon learning the rule itself and then gauging through direct experience the extent to which it enhances communicative skills.

The importance of language teaching

Clearly this indicates the importance of language teaching. By such teaching I am not implying the kind of formal grammar lesson in which theory may be taught divorced from practice, but the lesson in which theory and practice are closely linked, in which rules are related to children's ability to understand, and to the practical necessities of their particular stage of development. Once children have been introduced to these rules, then they can be used by adults in dealings with them to prompt them into developing new and ever more ambitious utterances. These utterances will help children communicate their ideas and feelings more clearly and comprehensively, and give them confidence in their ability to tackle new situations and new challenges verbally.

Maintaining the right balance between theory and practice in language teaching, and helping the child appreciate the immeasurable advantages of linguistic fluency, is not easy. Too often children see language work as 'boring' or 'irrelevant', rather than as a means towards the acquisition of a priceless tool which serves both practical and aesthetic ends. Precise guidance on how to go about language teaching belongs to a book on teaching methods and techniques, but the important psychological principle to bear in mind is that children should experience the tangible reward of an increasing command of language. They should be enabled to see that their developing linguistic skills help them to express more fully and precisely the things they want to say, rather than simply helping them tackle academic exercises in text books. Language should be a means towards the articulation of their problems and sentiments, the statement of their point of view, and towards a greater comprehension of the written word and of the exciting ideas it seeks to convey.

Teacher questions

Once children are at school, they come to rely more and more upon language as the principal means of communication. And increasingly their academic progress becomes tied to their ability to use the spoken and written word. Even those aspects of their intelligence assessed through tests of verbal reasoning will depend for expression upon this ability. In view of the crucial importance of the school as a linguistic environment, it is surprising that, as Stubbs (1983) puts it, we still know so little about what happens linguistically between teacher and pupil, and between pupil and pupil. The clear need exists for more research studies which employ interaction analysis (see p. 275) to study these linguistic exchanges, and to provide us with a reliable picture of how language is used in the classroom to convey and elicit ideas, to express attitudes and feelings, and to establish and develop personal relationships.

One area where progress of a kind has been made is in the study of teacher questions. Though the percentage varies dependent upon the children's age, the subject being taught, and the style of teaching, some 40 to 60 per cent of linguistic interactions between teacher and child appear to take the form of teacher questions (Hargie, 1978), with teachers on average asking questions every 70 seconds or so. Interestingly, a range of studies indicate that the great majority of these questions are of the factual, recall kind. Children are simply asked to give back to the teacher information in the precise form in which it was first offered to them. Few questions invite children to give evaluative answers, and fewer still are likely to be of the springboard type (see p. 148). Since so many questions are factual, perhaps not surprisingly research shows that a high proportion of teacher questions (up to 40 per cent in some studies) are answered by the teacher him or herself.

This high reliance on factual questions suggests that classroom language is only used in a minority of cases to prompt children to think and to develop their powers of linguistic expression. In fact teachers tend to assign these skills a relatively low priority when giving their views on the function of classroom questions (see Turney et al., 1974). Note that this not only may have an inhibiting effect upon children's acquisition of linguistic skills, it may restrict their whole concept of the purpose of education. If teachers demand from the class factual recall rather than evaluation or creative thinking, the child's likely conclusion is that education is not interested in the ability to go beyond the information given; its concern is first and foremost with memorizing.

Teacher language

The language used by the teacher to children should be familiar enough for them to be able to follow his or her meaning, while at the same time including enough new words and linguistic concepts to allow them to broaden their understanding. In a study some years ago Barnes (1971) showed that many teachers fail to meet the first and more basic of these requirements. In other words, they use a prescribed form of language which is not modified in response to children's inability to grasp what is being said. For example, when faced with the need to define an unfamiliar term to the class, many teachers do so by using equally (or even more) complex equivalents. They seem unable to present the original term to children in a form which relates to their experience and current level of comprehension. An allied example is provided by Brown (1973), who reports that 40 per cent of the questions asked by his sample of children received irrelevant teacher replies.

An equally frequent error by the teacher is to assume that because children appear to 'know' a particular word, it carries for them the same meaning it carries for him or her. This applies particularly to abstract terms (like 'fair', 'right', 'understand', 'interest') and also those terms whose meaning is always relative (such as 'high', 'near', 'fast'). It also applies to crucial terms like 'time' and 'space', and many a child's grasp of basic scientific and mathematical concepts is hindered by the teacher's assumption that these terms carry a common meaning. On the other hand, errors can arise if the teacher assumes that an inability to put things into words inevitably indicates an absence of understanding. Some children can demonstrate a complex grasp of logic when allowed to use mathematical symbols for example, or can show in mime what they mean by emotional responses such as compassion or joy or anger, while being quite unable to express these things linguistically. Even children whose writing obeys no observable rules for spelling or grammar (as in dyslexia) can nevertheless sometimes read it back correctly to the teacher, showing the soundness of their original concepts.

But one word of warning on language. In the West, we live in an intensely verbal environment, which tends both to place a high premium upon linguistic fluency and to undervalue forms of activity and communication which do not involve words. This has certain disadvantages. Language plays a vital part in our lives, and children must be given every encouragement to acquire and use it appropriately. But a skill with words can often obscure the *absence* of meaning. This is evident sometimes in the jargon used by scientists and social scientists, in the wilful obscurity of legal language, in the verbal evasions of politicians, and in the over-elaborations of civil servants and administrators the world over. Words, as Humpty Dumpty said to Alice, can mean whatever I want them to mean.

Coupled with this, there goes a common belief in the West that unless something can be put into words it has no validity, and conversely that if it can be put into words it has validity. This ignores the fact that many of the most important experiences in life, from happiness to falling in love, from spiritual intuitions to an appreciation of art, music and a beautiful sunset, often cannot be adequately represented in words at all. Such experiences carry a deep sense of meaning to individuals themselves, and can dramatically and permanently change the direction of their lives, yet they carry no precise verbal equivalents. To dismiss them as valueless because of their non-verbal quality is to ignore a vast area of human psychology and of the educational process.

Thinking critically about language. Thus along with teaching children how to use language, the teacher must also help children to think critically about it. Children need help in identifying the misuse of language by people in responsible positions. They need help in sorting out the meaning – or the absence of meaning – in the utterances of others. And they need help in distinguishing between those experiences which lend themselves to language and those experiences that do not. They need, in short, to appreciate that words are a *representation* of reality rather than reality itself, and that they are often only as reliable as the person who uses them. Because words are spoken by eminent people or because they appear in print does not automatically make them true, and because certain things cannot be put into words does not automatically make them false. Language is a tool available to us, of enormous power and potential beauty, but it is neither exclusive nor comprehensive. The job of education is to show children its strengths certainly, but not to neglect its weaknesses.

Dialects and accents

In the area of dialects and accents adults often fail to distinguish between aspects of a child's speech that indicate ignorance of language and those which simply mark social identity: that is, which are the marks of his or her home and subcultural group. The latter habits of speech may certainly be 'incorrect' in terms of standard English (i.e. the dialect of educated people throughout the United Kingdom), but children use them not because they know no better but because these habits help render a child more acceptable to family and friends. Where teachers treat these habits of speech with censure they run the risk of contributing towards the home–school conflict mentioned in Part I, a conflict in which the values of school and those of the home are seen to be in sharp contrast, and the child is forced to make some form of choice between the two. The school should certainly concentrate upon teaching standard English, but should recognize that children are readily able to learn both this and their own dialect, and use whichever is appropriate to the situation in which they find themselves. The school should be happy to see both exist side by side in the linguistic repertoire of individual children, since children may need both if they are to communicate fully and appropriately in the diverse circumstances that go to make up social life.

The same is true of the use of accents. People are often judged (quite inappropriately) on their accents, and again children may need to equip themselves with more than one method of pronouncing words if they are to find themselves fully acceptable to different groups of people. The important thing is that children should understand why there is this possible need to acquire more than one form of pronunciation, instead of being left to feel that one way of expressing their native language is inferior to another, or that one way marks them out as being 'affected' or 'ignorant' or 'ridiculous' as the case may be.

Enhancing language skills

Language is the basic teaching medium. Even in the science subjects and in mathematics and fine art, which each have their own grammar, the spoken word remains central to communication. It follows therefore that all teachers, no matter what their subject, are teachers of language, and of its associated skills reading and writing. No good teacher misses a teaching opportunity. One of their characteristics is they make use of each of the many daily incidents that lie outside the main content of their lessons but that nevertheless carry educational potential, and nowhere is this seen to better advantage than in the field of language. Much language teaching is best done within the context of lessons other than English, so that the child is able to see that language is an essential aspect of everyday life, and that the better our command of it, the better our potential for operating effectively within that life.

Thus the good teacher is always alert to opportunities for teaching language. Though constant correction of a child's speech is wearisome for him or her, and may even discourage use of words, sympathetic prompting and guidance whenever appropriate helps children see the linguistic possibilities open to them. And praise and encouragement for good language usage help them to see the dividends which accrue from a realization of these possibilities. Language is there to help one formulate one's thoughts, and to articulate these thoughts and the emotions and needs associated with them. Language is not there to provide children with yet another hurdle, yet another way of getting things wrong. It is there for their own benefit, and provided it is presented to them in a relevant and supportive way, they are quickly able to see its practical value.

The teacher as listener

The good teacher, whatever the subject, listens carefully to children when they are talking or reading, and identifies the occasions when they can be prompted towards improvement. The good teacher also listens carefully to his or her own speech and ensures it is appropriate to the class. Reference was made earlier in the chapter to the fact that teachers have to answer a large proportion of their own questions, and to the fact that teachers often use a prescribed form of language which is not modified in response to children's inability to grasp what is being said. Even definitions of unfamiliar terms are offered in language which is no easier to understand. Findings of this nature emphasize the gap between teacher language and child language. No teacher can function successfully unless able to communicate with children at their own level of comprehension. Tape recording lessons and then listening to their own language can be a great help to teachers in assessing whether they are using words appropriately. Identifying the key words used in a lesson, and then asking the class to provide written definitions of them, can be of equal value. Just as essential is a readiness to encourage children to ask questions and to indicate when they fail to understand the meaning of a word. Too often teachers inhibit children's questions by offering criticisms instead of answers ('If you'd been paying attention you wouldn't need to ask that question'; 'I don't see why you can't follow; it's simple enough'; 'I've already explained that. We haven't time to go over it again.'). Or by cutting the question short or by anticipating what the child is trying to say instead of allowing the latter to put it into his or her own words.

It is something of a reflection upon our teaching that in most lessons teacher questions far outnumber children questions. And the overwhelming majority of the language comes from the teacher rather than from the class. In any social encounter, most participants feel the need to have their say, to take part in the debate, to clarify points of difficulty, to voice their own views and from time to time their disagreements. The class lesson is a social encounter of a very particular kind, but it is a social encounter nevertheless, and many of the learning opportunities which it represents can only come through social interaction. Interaction analysis shows just how few of these interactions in many lessons are child initiated, and carried through to a proper resolution, with children receiving satisfactory answers to their questions or appropriate help in phrasing them and in asking necessary follow-up questions. The ability to manipulate the classroom into a successful linguistic environment is part of the art of teaching, and the ability depends primarily upon a simple readiness to listen both to one's own words and the words used by children, and to bring the two sets of variables into a proper harmony.

Language games

As mentioned earlier, one of the most vital ingredients in encouraging children to use and develop language skills is providing them with the *objective necessity* for language. Some children enjoy words from the start, and need little excuse to be verbal. But for many children, once they have mastered sufficient language to convey their immediate needs, further developments depends upon a clear awareness that their present skills are inadequate for coping with many of the tasks they are called upon to do. Work that began with children of West Indian background has shown that just such an awareness can be encouraged by the use of linguistic games (Wight, 1979). Certain of these games are now available commercially (for instance the *Concept 7–9* game from E.J. Arnold), and consist of such challenges as asking a child to describe a given shape to a partner, who then has to draw the shape entirely from the description.

The interest and amusement generated by such games prompt children to use every language strategy available to them, and to go on from there to invent and experiment with new strategies. Through playing the game, children are able to see not only the versatility of the linguistic tool they already possess, but also the inadequacies of that tool and the improvements they need to make to it. As an extension, they can record their own efforts at describing the shapes and the other target items presented in the game, both on tape and in writing, in order to look more closely at their language and see more clearly those areas in which it is deficient. Work of this kind is not designed to replace formal classroom verbal interactions, or creative writing projects, but used alongside them it accelerates and enriches linguistic development, and shows the child that above all language is both useful and fun.

Reading and writing

Coupled with language development are the language-related skills of reading and writing. Both of these skills are specialist areas in their own right, and space does not allow a comprehensive examination of them here. However, the teaching of reading in particular follows very similar principles to the teaching of language itself. First, the child is provided with the right reading environment. Thus children who are read to by parents and who have exciting ideas and events communicated to them through books, who see parents making use of reading in their own lives, and who have ready access to the printed word, come to see reading as a skill which broadens and enriches life. They come to understand the power and the pleasure which words can bring, and have the proper incentive to embark upon the joys of reading for themselves.

Second, children are presented with a specific reading method. The details of this method vary greatly across the various strategies advocated by reading experts, but they reduce for the most part to the simple principles of *Pause, Prompt, Praise*. The child halts at an unfamiliar word, the teacher *pauses* to give him or her a chance to say it, then *prompts* if they are unable to do so, and finally *praises* them as they repeat the word successfully. Research suggests that the pause should last for some five seconds, as this allows the child a space in which to concentrate upon the visual shape of the word, impressing it upon the memory before hearing the prompt from the teacher. This simple approach to the teaching of reading, coupled with patience and enthusiasm from the teacher and with a reading book at the right level of interest and difficulty for the child, cuts across much of the mystique that, intentionally or not, experts have allowed to accumulate around the subject.

The teaching of writing develops out of the teaching of reading. As children begin to realize that printed shapes carry linguistic meaning, so their natural bent for copying comes into play. The adult provides them with letters and simple words which they can trace or copy, and as their skill develops they become able to reproduce these letters and words from memory. Finally they begin to produce words on their own initiative, and the foundations of writing are laid. As with the teaching of reading, there are many variations on this basic approach, and I do not wish to oversimplify the teaching of these two vital skills. But it is equally misleading to over-complicate them. Many teachers (and parents), particularly those of older children, fail to provide slow learners with the help they need through a mistaken impression that reading and writing can only be effectively taught by teachers who have received lengthy specialist training in the techniques concerned. But as outlined here, the *psychological principles* behind these techniques are relatively straightforward. Allied to a cheerful and encouraging attitude on the part of the teacher and a stimulating learning environment, a grasp of these principles will allow most adults to make worthwhile contributions to a child's progress in these areas.

Language and intelligence   Further reference is made to language when intelligence is discussed in the next chapter. The concern here has been to discuss language as a function, as a method of communication between the child and the world. However, the role it plays in intelligent behaviour can in part be inferred from this discussion, with the linguistically fluent child possessing obvious advantages when it comes to conceptualizing and solving problems, and it is against this background knowledge that much of what is said in the next chapter must be viewed.

References

Barnes, D. (1971) Language in the Secondary Classroom. In D. Barnes, J. Britton and H. Rosen *Language, the Learner and the School*, revised edn. Harmondsworth:Penguin.

Bernstein, B. (ed.) (1975) *Class, Codes and Control*. Vols I–III. London: Routledge & Kegan Paul.

Bower, T.G.R. (1982) *Development in Infancy*, 2nd edn. San Francisco: W.H. Freeman.

Brown, R. (1973) *A First Language:The early stages*. London: Allen & Unwin.

Chomsky, N. (1969) *The Acquisition of Syntax in Children from Five to Ten*. Cambridge, Massachusetts: MIT Press.

Concept 7–9. Leeds: E.J. Arnold.

Hargie, O.D.W. (1978) The importance of teacher questions in the classroom. *Educational Research*, 20, 2, 99–102.

Rogers, D. (1985) Language Development. In A. Branthwaite and D. Rogers *Children Growing Up*. Milton Keynes: Open University Press.

Stubbs, M. (1983) *Language, Schools and Classrooms*. London: Methuen.

Turney, C., Cairns, L.G., Williams, G., Hatton, N. and Owens, L.C. (1974) *Sydney Micro Skills: Series 1*. Sydney: Sydney University Press.

Wight, J. (1979) *Dialect and Reading. Appendix to Supplementary Readings for Block 4, PE232*. Milton Keynes: Open University Press.

SOME
QUESTIONS

1. What kinds of thinking are possible without language?

2. What is the link in language development between babbling and speech?

3. Why is it vital to diagnose deafness in children as early as possible?

4. What role does imitation play in language development?

5. What is the evidence that children have an innate ability to experiment with language?

6. At what age do children have a command of everyday language comparable to that of adults?

7. List as many ways as possible of encouraging language development in children.

8. What are the simple principles behind most methods of teaching children to read?

9. What does the evidence tell us about the effectiveness of most teacher questions?

10. Think up examples of simple classroom games that will help children's language development.

11. Why is teacher language often unhelpful to children?

12. What are the dangers of an emphasis upon language to the exclusion of other forms of communication?

13. How might dialect and accent incorrectly influence teachers' perceptions of children's linguistic abilities?

Additional Reading

Aitchison, J. (1983) *The Articulate Mammal*, 2nd edn. London: Hutchinson.
In spite of the intimidating title, provides a comprehensive account of child language and of the main controversies and issues in the area.

Carter, R. (ed.) (1982) *Linguistics and the Teacher*. London: Routledge & Kegan Paul.
Most books on linguistics are heavy going, but this one links the subject clearly to the practical concerns of the teacher.

Gordon, J.C.B. (1981) *Verbal Deficit: A critique*. London: Croom Helm.
Examines comprehensively the various theories which explain language deficit in children.

Kennedy, A. (1984) *The Psychology of Reading*. London: Methuen.
A thoroughly practical and informative book. Written from no particular theoretical standpoint, it covers all approaches and is good on writing and speaking too.

Stubbs, M. (1983) *Language, Schools and Classrooms*, 2nd edn. London: Methuen.
Excellent short introduction to the relationship between language and educational progress, with a welcome practical orientation.

Stubbs, M. and Hillier, H. (ed.) (1983) *Readings on Language, Schools and Classrooms*. London: Methuen.
Excellent collection of papers covering nearly all areas of interest to the teacher.

Trudgill, P. (1975) *Accent, Dialect and the School*. London: Edward Arnold.
Argues the case for linguistic diversity and emphasizes the extent to which schools cause problems for children by their insensitivity towards this diversity.

De Villiers, J.G. and de Villiers, P.A. (1979) *Early Language*. London: Fontana/Open Books.
Straightforward and highly readable account of language acquisition. Those who wish to study the subject in more detail might like to go to the fuller account given by the same authors in their Language Acquisition, *Cambridge, Massachusetts: Harvard University Press (1978).*

Wells, G. (1985) *Language Development in the Pre-School Years*. Cambridge: Cambridge University Press.
An alternative to de Villiers and de Villiers, and equally good.

5

Intelligence

What is intelligence?

Of all aspects of psychology, none has achieved more attention within education than intelligence. The reason for this is not hard to seek. If we define intelligence as the ability to see relationships, and to use this ability to solve problems, then we can see that there are few aspects of a child's formal work in school that do not appear to be influenced by it in some way. Add to this the fact that high or low intelligence can carry important social and vocational significance, and it is not surprising that parents as well as teachers take a deep interest in the subject. It is probably in part because of this deep interest that many misconceptions have grown up about the nature of intelligence and its measurement, some of them actively detrimental to the child's educational progress.

The measurement of intelligence

Let us start with the problem of measurement because, unless we can understand this, we can have no clear idea of the limitations placed upon our attempt to study the origins of intelligence and the way in which its development can be best fostered and encouraged. Because intelligence is not something that can be directly observed, like a person's height or weight, we are only able to infer its presence by watching people's behaviour. If we bear this in mind we can see that any measurement of intelligence that we may be able to produce is less a measure of what people have than of what they do. If we take a crude analogy with running, we can say that one person runs fast and another runs slowly, but the running is essentially something they do, and not some identifiable physical quality that we can point to at any time whether they happen actually to be out on the running track or at home in their beds. True, the running may be the product of definite physiological characteristics, just as intelligent behaviour may be the product of neurophysiological characteristics in the brain, but it cannot be said to have any objective existence outside the activity itself.

This makes it very difficult for us to conceptualize what is meant by being a 'good' and a 'bad' runner in any absolute sense: that is, in the sense in which we can, for example, say that a tall man is tall by virtue of the fact that at all times and in all conditions his intact body is longer from head to toe than the bodies of the vast majority of his fellows. We may say that being a 'good' runner simply means running faster than the majority of one's fellows, but do we measure speed over 50 metres, 100 metres, or over 500 metres or a mile or a marathon of 26 miles and 385 yards? Do we measure it with the runner on the flat or going uphill or downhill; at altitude or at sea level; on a hot day or on a cold; after a big meal or before? It is quite clear that even with the same group of runners, measuring speed under all these different conditions would produce quite different results, with first one runner doing best and then another. Nor would it be sufficient simply to take the average results over all these conditions, since we could hardly say that one man is 'best' when he can easily be beaten by someone over 100 metres and by someone else over the mile. Nor could we even necessarily pick out the best sprinter, since although one runner might be fastest over 100 metres someone else might beat him or her if we shortened the race to 50 metres or lengthened it to 120.

I said at the start that the analogy between intelligence and running is a crude one, and it must not be supposed for one moment that I am suggesting that as abilities they come into similar categories. But our analogy serves to show that if we are measuring and placing judgements upon behaviour in this way, then the answer to the question 'who is best?', or 'how good is this person as compared to that?', depends very much upon the conditions under which we stipulate the behaviour must take place. And there cannot fail to be an arbitrary element about these conditions. To turn to running again for a moment, why should the shortest official sprint race run by adults out of doors take place over 100 metres? Why should it not be over 99 metres or 105 or over any other distance we like to suggest? So it is with intelligence. The designers of intelligence tests stipulate the conditions (i.e. they set the questions, determine the time limit by which these questions must be answered, and decide which answers are 'right' and which answers are 'wrong') under which intelligent behaviour is to be manifested; but we could if we wished propose quite different sets of conditions, and perhaps produce a quite different set of marks. Which set is the more appropriate would depend upon which gave us a better indication of how well the individuals performed when faced with problems solvable by intelligent behaviour in real life. But the range of these problems is so vast and their solution often dependent upon so many other factors in addition to intelligence (e.g. opportunity, the encouragement of others, motivation, degree of anxiety) that it is not always possible to allow such indication to emerge with any clarity.

All this is not an argument against the importance of intelligence or the attempt to measure it, just as it is not an argument against running races and using the results to predict how well someone might perform in real-life situations where running is required. But it is intended to highlight the problems associated with such measurement, and to indicate that the decisions we make on how measurement is to be undertaken inevitably influence the way in which we conceptualize the ability itself. It is for this reason that some psychologists define intelligence as simply the ability to do intelligence tests, a splendidly circular definition which is of little real help to us but which does serve to remind us of our difficulties.

Intelligence testing

ORIGINS. These points are further clarified, together with other important issues, if we now turn and look at the origins of practical intelligence tests for general use back in the early years of the present century; back, in fact, in 1905 when the French psychologist Alfred Binet and his collaborator Théodore Simon were asked by the Parisian education authorities to devise methods of identifying children who were too 'feeble-minded' for education in normal schools. Binet decided, sensibly enough, to compile a series of simple verbal and practical problems designed to test qualities of comprehension, reasoning, judgement and adaptation, all of which could be tackled by older children better than by younger, and by children classed as 'bright' by their teachers better than by children classed as 'dull'. A further sensible decision by Binet was that scores should be standardized so that each individual's mark could be compared to the norm for their age. This led eventually to the concept of *mental age* (or MA), a child's mental age being the chronological age at which most children obtained scores similar to his or her own (thus, for instance, a child of eight obtaining a score usually achieved only by ten year olds would have a mental age of ten).

Later, in 1916, the concept of mental age was developed by the American psychologist Lewis Terman of the University of Stanford into what came to be known as an *intelligence quotient* (or IQ). A child's IQ was arrived at by taking the ratio of mental age to chronological age and multiplying it by 100. Thus a child with, say, a mental age to ten and a chronological age of eight would have an IQ of:

$$^{10}/_8 \times ^{100}/_1 = 125$$

The great advantage of this method was that if individual children's mental ages matched their chronological ages (no matter what these respective ages happened to be) they would always have an IQ of exactly 100, and such an IQ would tell the psychologist or the teacher at a glance that the child's measured intelligence was 'average' for their chronological age. This method of computing the IQ was used for many years, but it had one major disadvantage. Experience showed that mental age does not appear to improve after about age 15 (i.e. in terms at least of intelligence test scores we seem to peak at around 15). Since chronological age goes on increasing, this would mean that, if one were to continue to use the equation, a person's IQ scores would automatically fall year by year once passed the age of 15. For instance, even the most able 30 year old would have an apparent IQ of only 50, well down in the feeble-minded category! Clearly therefore the equation was only suitable in the days when intelligence tests were used exclusively with very young children. In consequence we now use what is called a *deviation* IQ, which expresses an individual's score simply in terms of its deviation from the norm for their age, with the norm still being scaled to equal the convenient score of 100.

LATER DEVELOPMENTS. Although systematic intelligence testing may be said to have begun in a rather chancy, imprecise way, the same cannot be said for subsequent work in the field. The original Binet–Simon intelligence test has undergone a number of careful revisions at the University of Stanford and various other, now more widely used, tests have emerged since. Space does not allow me to go into great detail on how these tests are constructed but teachers need to know one of the basic principles behind them if they are to appreciate the true nature of this construction. This principle derives from the assumption that intelligence is normally distributed in the general population, just as are most physical attributes such as height and weight and size of feet. Normal distribution implies that if we, say, measured the height of every adult in the UK and plotted the results on a graph we would obtain a neat bell-shaped curve, with the hump in the middle representing the majority of people and the distribution on either side of the mean tailing off in a regular, symmetrical pattern as shown in Figure 5.1. Such symmetry would stem from the fact that the distribution of people with feet larger than average would be exactly matched by the distribution of people with feet smaller than average.

The assumption that intelligence is normally distributed means that intelligence tests have been so designed that if a large and representative sample of people is tested then scores will lie along this bell-shaped curve (usually called the *normal* curve). If they fail to do so (i.e. if many more people get high scores than get low scores or vice versa) then the difficulty

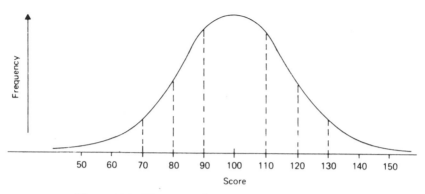

Figure 5.1. The normal curve.

levels of the tests are adjusted up or down until the required distribution is produced. There is only one snag, of course, and that is that intelligence may not be normally distributed amongst the population after all. There may indeed be more people with intelligence levels above the average than below (perfectly possible if the average is depressed by a relatively few very low-scoring individuals), or perhaps more with levels below the average than above, and it may be, therefore, that the principles upon which our tests are constructed serve to impose a pattern of IQ distribution upon the population that has no basis in fact. This could be important, for example, in selection exams or indeed in any exams where the assumption is that only people with scores above a certain standard will be able to profit from the opportunities offered, or master the skills necessary to make a success of a particular job.

Again, this is not an argument against the assumption that intelligence is normally distributed. Given the evidence from other human characteristics (such as the examples of height and weight referred to above), it is not easy to see in fact what other assumption could be made, but it is a strong caution against interpreting IQ test scores too rigidly, and assuming that small differences between one given group of children and another necessarily mean very much in practical terms. Test scores should ideally be viewed against a background of other measures, which may be tests of attainment in appropriate school subjects if we are making educational decisions, or perhaps tests of personality and motivation if we are concerned with some form of vocational guidance.

THE IMPORTANCE OF STANDARD DEVIATION. A further consequence of standardizing intelligence tests along the normal curve is that we have to take careful note of the *standard deviation* quoted by the test constructors. The standard deviation is a measure such that if we move one standard deviation above the mean and one standard deviation below we will have encompassed approximately 68 per cent of the sample, and if we move two standard deviations above and below we will have encompassed about 95 per cent. The standard deviation is thus a measure of dispersal, telling us how spread out the marks of a representative sample are likely to be. An example will make this clear, and also show why we need to know the standard deviation used by the authors of an intelligence test before we can interpret what a child's results on that test actually mean. Suppose one intelligence test (Test A) used a standard deviation of 10 and another (Test B) a standard deviation of 20. Using the normal curve we know that in the case of Test A sixty-eight per cent of children would be expected to have scores between 90 and 110, because these two scores represent respectively one standard deviation below the norm and one standard deviation above (the norm of course being 100). In the case of Test B, however, which has a standard deviation of 20, we know that 68 per cent will now have scores between 80 and 120, since on this test it is these scores which represent one standard deviation above and below the mean. If we now look at the scores of an individual child on both tests, and find that he or she has 110 on Test A and 120 on Test B we can see that these two scores, although apparently quite different, are in fact only telling us the same thing. They are telling us that the child is at the upper end of the 68 per cent of people who have scores (i.e. IQs) dispersed around the mean.

We can see the kind of confusion that can arise if we take the case of a child transferring schools. Let us assume that both schools keep records of children's IQs along with their attainment test results, and the first school attended by the child uses Test A while the school to which he or she transfers uses Test B. The headteacher of the first school forwards the child's records to the headteacher of the second school, and the latter sees that the child has a quoted IQ of 110. Now an IQ of 110 on Test B would indicate that the child is some way from the upper end of the 68 per cent of children with scores dispersed around the mean, and the headteacher may well assume that this is therefore the information that such an IQ score is seeking to convey. However, if the headteacher has details of Test A, and looks up the standard deviation, it will be found that this is not the case, and that on Test B the child's equivalent score would be 120.

GROUP AND INDIVIDUAL TESTS. Another feature of intelligence tests is that some are individual tests while others are of the group variety. The former are administered to the child individually by the tester, and sometimes involve structured apparatus such as bricks or cards, while the latter are essentially paper and pencil tests which can be given to more than one child at a time. Individual tests are more time-consuming for the tester, of course, and since the child has to respond orally, the *tester* can become an important variable in the exercise, since the child may find him or her intimidating or perhaps liable to give inadvertent clues through facial expressions, nods, etc. They do, however, have the advantage of not relying on the child's own ability to read the questions or to write down answers, and are particularly useful with younger children or with children who appear retarded in the basic subjects. One of the best known individual tests is the Wechsler Intelligence Scale for Children (WISC), which also exists in an adult form. The original Binet Scale which we discussed above is still in use in the revised Terman–Merrill versions of 1937 and 1960, while the British Ability Scales, standardized on British children and giving separate scores for a range of mental abilities, rather than an overall score, are also available.

More widely used and more readily available outside child guidance clinics are the various group intelligence tests. So popular are these that their use has proliferated outside education and into the world of job selection, vocational guidance, and management training (along with individual tests, they have also long been used in the armed forces). On one authoritative estimate (Vernon, 1979), over 200 million tests of intelligence or achievement are administered annually in the USA alone, though whether such colossal investment of time and money is altogether justified is another matter. Of the group tests currently available those devised by Alice Heim at the University of Cambridge (UK) are among the most useful, with versions available for use with children of school age and with students in higher education (the AH4 and the AH5 respectively). Psychological tests must be administered and interpreted by qualified users if they are to be of any value. Different tests require different user qualifications, and responsible test publishers and distributors will only sell standardized psychological tests to purchasers with the appropriate qualifications. Further details are available from The British Psychological Society.

Models of intelligence

Together with the advance in intelligence testing has gone an advance in attempts to build models of the intellect that help us understand how it may work. In the same year that Binet began his labours in Paris, Carl Spearman advanced what became known as the *Two-factor theory* of intelligence. We can see how this theory operates if we go back briefly to our analogy with running earlier in the chapter. It is possible to suggest that there is one general ability that underlies every performance of the running act and several more specific ability factors that come into play in particular kinds of running tasks (sprinting, middle distance, long distance, etc.). Similarly with intelligence, Spearman suggested the existence of a *general* intelligence factor (which he called 'g') and a range of *specific* ability factors (which he called 's' factors). Thus in any intelligent act, 'g' is involved, plus the 's' factor or factors appropriate to that particular act. Specific abilities are separate and distinct from each other and it is 'g', argued Spearman, that accounts for all correlations between cognitive abilities.

The measurement of general intelligence ('g')

A problem arises, of course, when it comes to trying to measure 'g'. For example, are verbal tests of intelligence a better measure of 'g' than spatial tests of intelligence or vice versa? We are told by Spearman that the level of correlation (i.e. the level of agreement) between the scores achieved by a child on the two sets of tests would be accounted for by the presence of 'g', but if we wanted to test for 'g', which would be the better test to use? We have no way of knowing. Moreover it would seem to be impossible to develop a test just to measure 'g' since as we have seen each intelligent act allegedly involves 'g' plus one or more 's' factors. Thus a verbal test of intelligence would involve 'g' plus the 's' factor of verbal ability; a spatial test of intelligence would involve 'g' plus the 's' factor of spatial ability, a mechanical test of intelligence would involve 'g' plus the 's' factor of mechanical ability; and so on. There seems to be no way of getting at 'g' on its own.

For this reason, alternative models of intelligence have been advanced that abandon the idea of 'g' altogether and propose instead a series of distinct clusters of intellectual abilities that may or may not be correlated with each other but which in measurement terms are better thought of as separate (e.g. verbal abilities, numerical abilities, spatial and mechanical abilities, or memory abilities). Generally, opinion these days, particularly in the USA, tends towards these alternative models, though for practical purposes tests yielding an overall composite IQ score, such as the ones we have been discussing (rather than separate tests for each of these clusters of ability), are still the more widely used. However, some of them do yield sub-scores which can be examined separately, such as *v:ed* scores (verbal and educational intelligence) and *k:m* scores (mathematical and spatial intelligence). But we must assume that if the alternative models become generally accepted then we may see the demise of the IQ test and the IQ score, and see instead a range of marks produced for each child, with each mark representing competence in a different area of intellectual skill (as with the British Ability Scales). The practical advantage of this would be that a child who might perhaps score poorly on certain of these areas (and therefore who might have ended up with a relatively low IQ score) could get a good result on one or more of the remainder, thus giving us clear evidence of giftedness in certain departments.

THE USE OF FACTOR ANALYSIS. The arguments in favour of these alternate models are based upon more than mere practical considerations, however. Recent research using *factor analysis* rather suggests that such models may approximate closer to reality than Spearman's 'g' and 's' model and the other so-called 'hierarchical' models based to a greater or lesser degree upon it. Briefly, factor analysis is a technique that examines a range of scores to establish whether groups of them correlate more strongly amongst themselves than they do with the rest. Thus, for example, in a range of scores that we can label A to Z, we might find that scores A, D and G form a group with this quality, while scores J, L and P form another and scores R, T and W a third. We would then say that each of these three groups has an underlying factor which accounts for the intercorrelation of the scores that it contains. Using tests of intelligence, we would expect that if there is such a factor as 'g', then instead of separate groups we would find that all the scores cluster together into a single group (i.e. that they all intercorrelate strongly due to the fact that all of them contain a high unifying measure of 'g'). In the event, such does not appear to be the case. When we correlate the results of various different measures of intelligence we find that not one but several separate factors emerge; hence the term *multi-factorial* that is given to the models of intelligence that reject the notion of 'g' and put in its place a range of separate abilities.

The usefulness of 'g'

Yet, in spite of this, the idea of 'g' lives on. Its supporters point to the finding that the separate factors to which we have just referred nevertheless show *some* correlation with each other, suggesting that there may be yet another factor (a second-order factor) in turn underlying all of them. At the educational level it is also pointed out that, like it or not, the IQ score is a pretty accurate prognosticator of academic success, suggesting that the notion of 'g' remains a useful one for certain purposes. It is also argued that some of the multi-factorial models, such as that of Guilford which postulates no fewer than 120 mental factors which singly or in combination are said to be involved in any given intelligent act, are highly complicated and often lack any very immediate appeal to busy class teachers. In any case, although teachers may make considerable use of the concept of 'g', they nevertheless are well aware that on its own it cannot account for all intellectual differences between children. Though a child who is good at, say, verbal reasoning is also likely to be good at tasks involving numerical ability, rote memory, inductive reasoning and so on, there will be fluctuations in his or her performance from one to another, suggesting that there is some degree of difference between the intellectual abilities involved. Thus although teachers may well describe a child as 'highly intelligent' or 'of average intelligence', they will make the reservation that this does not mean the child will perform uniformly at all tasks involving intelligent behaviour.

In practice, the use teachers make of the concept of 'g' will depend in no small measure upon the age of the children with whom they are concerned. Vernon (1979) considers the evidence and suggests that there is an increasing differentiation between abilities as the child grows older. The very young child's performance in different areas of intelligent behaviour tends to be relatively uniform, but in adolescents and adults there is often a marked discrepancy from one area to another. This may in part be the result of the increasing pressures towards specialization with which we meet after our primary school days, but there could also be other developmental factors involved. It could be that as our powers of thinking become more complex (see the discussion of Piaget's work on p. 43), so our ability to tackle certain kinds of intellectual problems develops more rapidly than our ability to tackle others, and our natural tendency to concentrate upon areas in which we are successful, at the expense of areas in which we are not, lends further impetus to the process.

Can IQ be enhanced?

We have seen that measured intelligence appears to be a consequence of both genetic and environmental factors, and since the teacher's concern is with the second of these the question that immediately arises is by how much, and in what ways, can measured IQ be improved by education? The answer to the first part of the question cannot be given with any precision, of course, but the consensus amongst both geneticists and psychologists seems to be that for children with similar genetic backgrounds a difference of up to 25 IQ points could be apparent at maturity given highly stimulating and very unstimulating backgrounds respectively. This could mean, for example, that a child averaging an IQ of 95 points at age four could reach the 100–105 range by school-leaving age if he or she received the right stimuli, or could slip back to the 80–85 range without it. This might well represent the difference between a well-paid skilled or lower managerial job, or an unskilled occupation offering neither fulfilment nor prospects.

Whether the school on its own can ensure that children each reach the upper end of their ability ranges is another matter. As with all social and academic factors, the school is limited in what it can do without the help of the home and, if need be, of other social services. Various ambitious intervention programmes based upon the school and designed to help under-privileged children have been tried (such as the Head Start programme in the USA) but have failed to eliminate all environmentally induced differences in IQ ratings. What they have sometimes succeeded in doing, however, is to maintain the IQ levels that these children show upon first being admitted to compulsory schooling (Lazar *et al.*, 1977). Since such levels tend to show the greatest deterioration in disadvantaged children in the years after leaving infant school (perhaps because in these years they are left increasingly to rely upon their own efforts) it seems essential that these programmes should therefore not be confined to the early school years, but should follow children right through to the time they leave.

It might be thought that the maintenance of IQ scores is only a kind of marking time, but this is not so. The items in an intelligence test presented to an 11-year-old child are much harder than those presented to a five year old. To maintain their IQ scores children must, therefore, be able to solve increasingly difficult problems and keep up with the intellectual development of their peers: no mean achievement for children from disadvantaged homes. Children will also come to possess more knowledge as a result of good educational programmes than they otherwise would. Education, after all, is not simply a matter of the skills required to do well in an IQ test, but of the accumulated factual and experiential knowledge necessary to understand an increasingly complex society. Even in more dispirited moments, teachers should never under-estimate the importance of their role in the child's life. Such under-estimation is likely to lead not only to career dissatisfaction but to a lowering of expectation, and there is no doubting the influence that teacher expectation can have upon children themselves.

Coaching for IQ tests

At one time, when the 11+ examination was widespread in the UK, teachers frequently used to ask whether children's IQ scores could be improved if they were given specific practice in answering intelligence test items. The answer is that some improvement in score (up to about ten per cent, in fact, with brighter children showing proportionally the greatest gains) can be achieved by systematic coaching of this kind, though whether such improvement also enhances the child's ability to deal with the real-life problems that intelligence test items are supposed to mimic is unclear. It is possible, in any case, that some at least of this improvement comes about simply as a result of greater confidence. We see in Chapter 7 on learning that anxiety can have a deleterious effect upon educational performance, and when a child is preparing for an examination such as the 11+ anything that helps to allay this anxiety to some degree is therefore likely to have consequences for the standard achieved. The problem faced by administrators of the 11+, however, was that children from schools which did not go in for coaching (and for the most part coaching was officially discouraged) tended to be at something of a disadvantage compared with those who came from schools which did. Now that the 11+ has become a relative rarity, coaching is only likely to be a problem if it is given to a child who subsequently is to be tested by the educational psychologist for possible placement in a special school. It could be that parents (or even a well-meaning teacher) might be tempted to offer such coaching in the belief that they are in some way helping the child. The opposite could be the case, of course, since the psychologist could be misled by an enhanced score and might be wrongly influenced in his or her recommendations as to placement.

IQ tests and the teacher

The teacher sometimes asks whether, for all the time and money that have been spent on IQ tests, they are really of very much value within the educational context. The answer is that for all their faults they remain one of the most (if not *the* most) accurate predictors of educational achievement, in that test scores correlate highly with both children's present and future levels of academic success. They thus serve as very useful diagnostic instruments. For example, children scoring high on an intelligence test but doing much less well at school than that score would predict are likely to be suffering from problems other than those caused by lack of cognitive ability. They might have problems at home or be unhappy with their teachers or classmates, or have missed vital groundwork through absence. An unusually high IQ score might indicate that they are in fact bored with school because it under-extends them. Or they might have undiagnosed physical problems such as poor hearing or poor eyesight, or might be from an ethnic minority with language problems (this would be indicated by much higher scores on non-verbal than on verbal test items), or they might be setting their sights too low so as to remain with friends or because of lack of confidence for some reason.

Thus the intelligence test could alert us to the real cause of a child's problems, allowing us to plan the right kind of remedial programme. Two qualifications need to be made about the diagnostic role of IQ tests, however. The first is that there is nothing to be gained (and much possibly to be lost) by trying to diagnose IQ levels in children who are already performing satisfactorily. There is sometimes a feeling on the part of headteachers and their staff that it would be of value to test children's intelligence routinely and keep records of the results. But I have already said that teacher expectations of individual children's performances can be influenced by a knowledge of IQ scores, and there is always a danger that a teacher will lower the standards demanded of a child who comes out with a score below the mean for classmates, even though to date he or she has been meeting these standards without difficulty. As was stressed earlier on, intelligence is not the only variable affecting school performance, and to know that one child scores five IQ points less than a neighbour is meaningless if the child is coping well with class work.

The second qualification is that the value of IQ tests for diagnostic purposes is only seen to best advantage where individual rather than group tests are used and where the administration and analysis is done by the educational psychologist or by a teacher trained in test usage. Many group tests, with their reliance upon reading and vocabulary skills, may fail to give a sufficiently accurate picture of the child's cognitive abilities. And, needless to say, even these individual test results must be treated themselves with great caution, and viewed ideally against a background of results from a variety of other diagnostic tests.

Improving intelligence

Of more relevance than specific coaching for IQ tests is the question of how we can improve the general problem-solving ability that these tests allegedly measure. The answer lies in part in doing the things that the good teacher will already be doing; that is, providing children with interesting and stimulating learning material, presenting them with problems that demand careful thinking strategies, encouraging their use of verbal skills and specifically of verbal reasoning, and motivating them generally to make best use of their cognitive abilities. But there may be more to it than this. Earlier in this chapter reference was made to multi-factorial models of intelligence and, in particular, to the model of Guilford. Guilford's model is, as was suggested, a complex one, but the basic elements are of considerable value to teachers who are trying to formalize their thinking on how best to encourage intellectual development in children.

Guilford's research (e.g. 1968) suggests that in any intelligent act there are three elements, namely *contents*, *operations*, and *products*. Individuals are first presented with the *contents* of a problem, which become the subject of their mental *operations*, and which in turn produce certain *products*.

Guilford recognizes four sub-categories under the contents category, five under the operations category, and six under that of products. These sub-categories are given below.

Contents	Operations	Products
figural	cognition	unit
semantic	memory	classes
symbolic	divergent thinking	relations
behavioural	convergent thinking	systems
	evaluation	translations
		implications

This means that the contents of the problem facing individuals can be of a figural or symbolic or semantic or behavioural kind (or a combination of these), that the operations they perform upon these contents involve cognition or memory etc. (or again a combination of these), and that individuals produce units, classes, relations, etc. in their attempts to understand and solve the problem. Since the four content categories, the five operational categories and the six product categories can all interact with each other we get $4 \times 5 \times 6 = 120$ possible mental factors.

For the teacher, the importance of this model lies in the fact that where a child fails to solve a particular item (and it could, of course, be an item from an intelligence test itself) the failure can be ascribed to one or other of the sub-categories or to the interaction between them. The child might, for example, be unable to cope with the symbols or the semantics involved in the contents (this would certainly happen if he or she could not understand the language in which the problem was couched), or with the memory task or the evaluation involved in the operations, or with the units or the systems in the products. Obviously, there is a limit to the amount of time a teacher can spend in diagnosing each individual failure of each individual child in the class, but a model of this kind has the virtue of directing the attention of the teacher towards the likely variables occasioning difficulty with an intellectual problem, and therefore of helping with decisions as to the kind of assistance that might best be offered.

Clearly, not all the sub-categories in Guilford's model make equal demands upon the child. Jensen (1969) believes that operations involving memory, for example, contain little in the way of reasoning and can be referred to as *Level I Skills*. Such skills are apparent in the recognition of symbols (arithmetical notation, vocabulary) and in the learning of physical movements, and are particularly evident in the early years of school life. *Level II Skills*, on the other hand, involve operations that require the child actually to do something with the information acquired (such as evaluating it or adding to it through the use of divergent thinking), and are likely to lead to products rather than to the simple regurgitation of information in the same form in which it was assimilated. These skills become increasingly important as the child moves up the school, and are sometimes referred to as 'higher order skills' or as 'learning how to learn'.

Intelligence and thinking

One psychologist who lays particular emphasis upon skills that require children to change or restructure the information they receive if they are to solve complex intellectual problems is Edward de Bono. De Bono maintains that, faced with one of these problems, children typically attempt to work through it using a sequential pattern (i.e. going from what seems to be one logical step to the next). Often they find, however, that each time they do this they reach a point where the sequence breaks down and they are unable to proceed further. What they require, de Bono argues, in some method of disrupting the sequence so that a new one is allowed to form. De Bono calls this method *lateral thinking* as opposed to the *vertical thinking* involved in sequential patterns.

De Bono's ideas are fully set out in his own books, to which the reader's attention is drawn at the end of the present chapter, and space does not allow us to look at them in great detail. Essentially, however, de Bono's argument is that both vertical and lateral thinking have their place and are involved in intelligent behaviour, but that too often we use the first where the second would be more appropriate. He also believes that in schools we teach vertical thinking but make little attempt to teach lateral. Children should be helped to see that at the point where a sequence of vertical thinking breaks down they need to move sideways, as it were (i.e. laterally), and pick up another vertical track going in a different direction. They may have to do this more than once in order to arrive at the desired solution, but each time they do so a better cognitive pattern emerges, involving not only movement towards the solution but also a better understanding of the critical issues involved in the problem, an understanding that will generalize to new problems in the future.

Lateral thinking therefore allows the juxtaposition of ideas which have no apparent logical or sequential connection. Such juxtaposition does not necessarily make sense in itself at first sight, but it triggers off something else that will do so. The reader will no doubt be able to think of examples of the value of this kind of thinking from personal experience, not only in academic life but in day-to-day living. A good example might be the gadget recently arrived through the post which we try to assemble following the manufacturer's meagre instructions. Each time, we reach a point where the thing stubbornly refuses to come together, and the experimental application of a little force produces only ominous noises. At this stage, in desperation, we try something that on the face of it looks ridiculous, like turning the object upside down or inside out, and to our relief it falls into place without further ado. In retrospect, the process of assembly looks so easy that we cannot understand why we did not think of it in the first place. The answer is that in following the inadequate instructions we were making certain false assumptions (e.g. that what looked like the top really was the top) that sent us off on the wrong vertical track each time. It was only when, in desperation, we introduced a lateral element like turning the item upside down that we were able to proceed along the correct vertical sequence.

Undoubtedly one of the best ways to come to grips with lateral thinking, and to see the implications it has for intelligent behaviour within one's own teaching subject, is to tackle some of the problems devised by de Bono to demonstrate its importance, as set out, for example, in his *Five Day Course in Thinking* (1969). These problems, of the brain-teasing variety, usually set the conventional thinker (or rather the person who is allowing him or herself to think conventionally) off on the wrong vertical track, and it is only by exploring lateral possibilities that one is eventually able to reach the goal. By working through a number of these problems de Bono maintains that the reader is able to give scope to lateral thinking abilities, and thus to be in a much better position to tackle any problems requiring intelligent behaviour. In a very real sense we can say, therefore, that de Bono's work supports the notion that by exposing children to carefully constructed problems (which could, of course, be problems framed within the context of any school subject) we can maximize their intellectual potential surely and divertingly.

Is intelligence inherited?

Early researchers were in little doubt that intelligence was an inherited ability. It might vary in its rate of development from individual to individual (as one child may grow physically more slowly than another or may perhaps put on less weight), but it was held to be essentially stable in its nature, susceptible to accurate assessment even in childhood, and a reliable indicator of future academic and vocational attainment. Such a viewpoint had important implications for education and for society in general since it supported strongly the notion that if the individual was not born clever then he or she could not be made so, and it tended to fit in with the hierarchical view that each person was born to a particular station in life.

It would be wrong to suppose that these early researchers deliberately set out to strengthen this socially divisive view of humans. On the contrary, one of their main arguments for the development of intelligence tests, and in particular for their use in such educational contexts as the 11+ examination, was that these tests would identify innately able children who had been born into economically straitened circumstances and allow society to give them a chance, through scholarships and so on, to make full use of their potential. But there is little doubt that their emphasis upon the prime importance of heredity did fit in neatly with the most influential social and political views of the time, and did help to perpetuate an educational system in which children with low or average IQs were given much poorer facilities and much less attention than children with IQs significantly above the mean.

In the 1930s, however, things began to change within psychology as a consequence of the so-called *behaviourist* movement, which argued that if psychologists were ever to turn their subject into an exact science then they must study the observable facts of human behaviour (i.e. what people actually do) rather than introspection and consciousness (i.e. what people tell you about their private mental world). With such a change in emphasis came a greater interest in learning, since the effects of learning can become immediately apparent in a person's behaviour. Once it was appreciated what a profound effect learning could have upon human behaviour, the door was opened to a new model of humans which argued that we become the people we are (intelligent behaviour and all) largely as a result of the particular learning experiences to which we are subjected from birth onwards. As a result, the view that intelligence was essentially an innate quality began to give ground to the notion that it was largely an acquired one. The stress upon *nature* was replaced by a stress upon *nurture*.

Obviously this change of emphasis is of great interest to teachers, concerned as they are with the child's ability to learn. The more a child can develop ability through learning, the greater the scope of the teacher. However, though the critical part played by learning in psychological development is not now open to dispute, it is still not clear whether the ability (or abilities) we call intelligence owes more to learning than it does to innate endowment; and in recent years the debate has been vigorously reopened, with some commentators now suggesting that the pendulum may have swung too far and that we may be in danger of neglecting the contribution made by inherited characteristics to the individual differences in behaviour between children. In a sense, of course, the existence of such a debate, with strong views on either side, may make us lose sight of the fact that it is not the separate contributions of either nature or nurture that are important so much as the *interaction* between the two. Whatever children's innate potential may be, if they are denied the environmental stimuli necessary for its development then it will be of little use to them. Similarly, whatever the environmental stimuli, if children lack the necessary degree of potential they may never be able to reach the same standards as other children more generously endowed. To return briefly to my first example of running, we can readily see that without the right training experiences no athlete would be able to break the world 1500 metres record. On the other hand, no matter what training we are offered, most of us would not be able to break the record because we do not have the (largely inherited) basic physiology for the job.

Nevertheless, the debate on the relative importance of the contributions of nature and nurture to individual differences in intelligence between children has achieved so much attention, and carries such profound implications for the political decisions that determine national educational policies, that the teacher must be familiar with some of the major issues raised by both sides. Let us start by looking at research that appears to favour the greater importance of nature, the so-called *twin studies*.

Twin studies

Genetically, all twins come in one or other of two categories, known popularly as identical and fraternal. Identical twins (known technically as *monozygotic* or MZ for short) are formed from the same ovum and sperm and therefore enjoy virtually identical genetic endowments, while fraternal twins (known technically as *dizygotic* or DZ) come from separate ova and sperms and are therefore genetically no more alike than any other brothers and sisters. Researchers have therefore postulated that if MZ twins are significantly more alike in terms of measured intelligence than DZ twins, then this is a strong argument in favour of the importance of inheritance, since twins in general receive very much the same kind of environment within their family and within their school. (It is often argued this is untrue, and that MZ twins are treated more alike by family and teachers than DZ twins, but this would probably only be sufficient to account for relatively minor differences in measured intelligence.) Another approach adopted by researchers is to study groups of MZ and DZ twins who have been separated at birth and reared apart in different homes. In this case both MZ and DZ twins will have received different environments, and if MZ twins are still significantly more like each other in terms of intelligence test scores, then this again will strengthen the argument in favour of inheritance.

A number of twin studies of both kinds have been carried out over the years, and some of the data have been collected and tabulated by Jarvik and Erlenmeyer-Kimling (1967). In

Table 5.1., which is adapted from their findings, the column headed 'genetic expectations' refers to the correlation (i.e. level of agreement) in intelligence tests scores between the respective twin pairs we would expect if inheritance were the only factor. Thus, on the basis of genetic theory, MZ twins would be expected to show a perfect correlation of 1.0, while DZ twins and siblings would be expected to correlate at 0.5 and unrelated children to show no correlation at all. Any deviance from these expected correlations would, on the purely genetic argument, be due to the unreliability of the tests used. On the other hand, if environment plays a major role then we would predict a major deviance from these correlations, with MZ twins in fact failing to correlate any more closely than DZ.

Table 5.1. Correlation in measured intelligence between various kinship relations. (Based on Jarvik and Erlenmeyer-Kimling, 1967).

Kinship relation	Number of studies	Median obtained correlation	Genetic expectations
MZ twins reared together	14	0.87	1.00
MZ twins reared apart	4	0.75	1.00
DZ twins of like sex reared together	11	0.56	0.50
DZ twins of opposite sex reared together	9	0.49	0.50
Siblings reared together	36	0.55	0.50
Siblings reared apart	3	0.47	0.50
Unrelated children reared together	5	0.24	0.00
Unrelated children reared apart	4	-0.01	0.00

The table indicates that, even when raised apart, MZ twins show a much higher correlation in their measured intelligence than do any of the other groups. Furthermore, it shows that

DZ twins reared together are no more alike than siblings (even though, being of the same age, they probably receive more similar environments), and that both DZ twins and siblings are more alike than unrelated children reared together. Results of this order appear pretty conclusive and have prompted some experts to suggest that, of the measured difference in intelligence between individual children, some 80 per cent is likely to be due to differences in inheritance and only some 20 per cent to be due to differences in environment.

However, the issue is not really as clear-cut as this after all. Data such as those summarized in Table 5.1. have been severely criticized on a number of important counts. Most notably Kamin (1974) points out the following:

- although raised separately, many of the identical twins included in twin studies were in fact placed in very similar homes: sometimes even raised by members of the same family. Thus it is incorrect to assume that they received very different environments;

- some of the data are themselves suspect, in particular those produced by the late Sir Cyril Burt. The evidence suggests that Burt may have, for various reasons, recorded inaccurate data for various groups of twins raised together and apart, data which have suggested the case in favour of inheritance is very much stronger than it is;

- even the data for siblings reared apart is inconclusive. In one study, for example (Freeman, Holzinger and Mitchell, 1928), we find that siblings raised apart but in similar homes show a correlation in measured intelligence of 0.30, while those raised in dissimilar homes show one of 0.19.

The problem is that it is very difficult to come by samples of twins and even of siblings raised apart and in quite different environments. And if twins raised together are studied and it is found that MZ twins are consistently more alike than DZ twins similarly raised, this is always open to the criticism that the environments of the former may be more similar than the latter. I have already suggested that this greater similarity may only account for relatively minor differences in measured intelligence, but nevertheless it remains what is called a *contaminating variable* in the research, and must leave all findings open to dispute.

Other studies

Is there some other way of solving the nature–nurture controversy, therefore, that is not subject to this kind of objection? Studies using animals are one possibility, though we must always be extremely cautious in the lessons for human behaviour that we derive from them. Quite apart from other major differences animals lack language and, as we saw in Chapter 4, language is of critical importance in the development of thinking and of intelligent behaviour in humans. Nevertheless, such studies are not without interest, and appear to indicate that selective breeding over a few generations can significantly improve certain animal skills (such as learning to find a way through a complex maze) which are possibly analogous to intelligence in humans, and this tends to support the importance of inheritance. Studies involving certain forms of mental subnormality in humans are another possibility, since it is known that some kinds of handicap (such as Down's Syndrome and Turner's Syndrome) are directly linked to genetic factors. The inference is that if genetic abnormalities appear to play a part in low measurable intelligence, then it is likely they also play a part in measurable intelligence across the whole spectrum of abilities.

One of the most interesting arguments in favour of the role played by inherited characteristics is that advanced by Vernon (1979), however. Vernon suggests that champions of the extreme environmentalist viewpoint have yet to explain the marked differences in intelligence often noted between children within the same family. These children in most cases received similar or very similar environments, yet their measured intelligence can differ by 10, 20 or even 30 IQ points on the same tests. Genetically we would expect this, as each child will have drawn a different combination of genes from his or her parents, but environmentally it is not what we would predict. Similarly, we sometimes find a very bright child born to relatively dull parents. This can be explained genetically as due to recessive genes (i.e. genes carried by parents which do not affect their behaviour but which can become dominant again in the child, just as two brown-eyed parents can have a blue-eyed child), but environmentally it is something of a puzzle, as the child will not have received a particularly stimulating upbringing. By the same token, we sometimes find highly intelligent parents who produce a relatively unintelligent child in spite of providing a great deal in the way of environmental stimuli.

Summarizing the evidence in all its different manifestations, Vernon concludes that it demonstrates a strong genetic component in the development of individual differences in intelligence. Although environment has a very important role to play, measurable IQ seems to 'depend more on genetic endowment than on favourable or unfavourable environmental opportunities and learning, at least within white culture'. But lest it be thought that this is an argument in favour of élitism in education, with genetically favoured children being given the best opportunities and the rest left to gravitate towards the social levels to which nature has called them, it must be stressed again that nature and nurture complement each other. In an educational sense, one is meaningless without the other. As Vernon goes on to say on the same page, 'both are essential, and neither can be neglected if we are to plan children's upbringing and education wisely'. To this we can add that the élitist argument can just as easily be turned the other way round. We can as readily argue that children with *lower* intellectual potential warrant *better* educational opportunities than children with higher, since it is important that they do not waste any of their more limited potential.

The approaches of Hebb and Cattell

Rather than spend more time discussing the precise percentage contributions of nature and nurture to human intelligence, we should turn now to a suggestion advanced by Hebb: namely, that instead of talking about intelligence in a general sense we should talk of Intelligence A, which is inborn potential and which we have no way of measuring, and Intelligence B, which is that part of Intelligence A actually developed by environmental influences. Thus one child, with a larger Intelligence A than another, might yet end up with a smaller Intelligence B due to environmental deprivation. This model has been augmented by Vernon, who suggests that since intelligence tests are imperfect instruments we should also talk of Intelligence C, which is that part of Intelligence B that we actually manage to measure.

A model along somewhat similar lines is proposed by Cattell (1963), who talks of *fluid* (gf) and *crystallized* (gc) intelligence, the former representing the influence of biological factors on intellectual development and the latter the outcome of environmental experiences. Where Cattel differs from the Hebb–Vernon model is that he claims both gf and gc can be measured, in that they emerge from factorial analysis of the results of a range of ability tests. Further, he considers that such measurement indicates a deterioration of gf with age, which is an important point since, as we have already said, measured intelligence does not appear to increase much in most people after the age of 15, and in fact may show something of a decline from early adult life onwards. Cattell's findings would seem to show that the biological mechanisms involved in intelligence reach full maturity by this age, and then are subject to the ageing process, whereas crystallized intelligence (gc) can go on developing with experience throughout life. Within the context of the nature–nurture debate this would suggest that, given appropriate experiences, people are capable of increasing their capacity for certain kinds of intelligent behaviour long after leaving school, and this perhaps helps to explain the great success of many mature students who performed with only limited success during their earlier formal education.

Before leaving this section I must stress that, although we have been talking about the nature–nurture controversy and its possible implications for educational policy, intelligence is only one of the many psychological variables that influence a child's progress at school. Motivation, creativity, vocational aspirations, child–teacher relationships, personality, self-esteem, peer-group pressures and many others all have their part to play, and these are, of course, dealt with at the appropriate points throughout this book.

Intelligence and ethnic groups

It will be noted in the quotation from Vernon (on p. 99) that the words 'at least within white culture' were used, and this unfortunately raises the whole vexed question of whether or not genetically determined differences in intelligence exist between the different ethnic groups of the world. With so many factors creating distrust and dislike between ethnic groups we could well have been spared this one, but a lively controversy has sprung up in recent years, with some bitterness on both sides, and as with the nature–nurture controversy it is important that the teacher should know the issues involved.

Our starting point must once again be with the difficulties in defining and measuring intelligence. If intelligence is the ability to solve problems, which in summary is what I have suggested, then the Australian aborigine or Kalahari bushman, for example, would regard the average westerner as highly unintelligent in view of his or her lack of ability to survive unaided for long in their harsh environments. And so indeed might the Eskimo. These examples might seem extreme, but they illustrate the point that, historically, different ethnic groups have been faced with different kinds of problems, and it is therefore inappropriate (and unfair) for one group to claim that its intelligence tests are the correct way of measuring intellectual ability (i.e. problem-solving ability) in every part of the world. Aborigine children might well smile at a psychologist who expects them to answer one of the standard items on a western intelligence test (e.g. 'complete the sequence of numbers 8, 20, 50, 125, ?') yet who could not find the nearest source of water in order to save him of herself from an agonizing death. Similarly, a Buddhist monk might doubt the intelligence of the whole of western society, with its emphasis upon material possessions and upon weapons of fearful mass destruction, and its inability to solve the problems of living at peace with oneself and one's fellow men.

What I am saying, therefore, is that our concepts of intelligence and our methods for measuring it are *culture bound*, and may not have validity outside western White society. In the light of this, it should come as no surprise to find that in one piece of research a sample of White American children emerged with an average of 14 IQ points higher than a sample of American Indians on verbal reasoning tests, but that the position was more than reversed when non-verbal intelligence tests such as the Goodenough or the Harris were used (Gaddes, McKenzie and Barnsley, 1968). The latter tests, it would seem, with their emphasis upon visual detail, are more suited to the culture of the American Indian than are the verbal tests with their extreme emphasis upon linguistic skills.

The most extensive investigations into racial differences in intelligence have been carried out, however, not with American Whites and American Indians but with American Whites and American Blacks. Literally hundreds of studies using these two populations have been undertaken over the last half century, and Vernon (1979) considers the consensus which emerges from them is that Black IQs are, on average, 15 points below those of Whites (85 as opposed to 100). In a study that aroused great controversy, Jensen (1973) attacked the argument that differences of this magnitude can be caused by environment alone, and pointed out that even when steps have been taken to improve the environments of Black communities these differences have not fully disappeared.

Does this mean, therefore, that the supposed intellectual inferiority of American Blacks as compared to American Whites must be taken as a proven fact, and that the genes which cause differences in skin pigmentation and the other superficial differences which mark one race off from another are also connected in some way with the development of intelligence? No, it emphatically does not. The picture is much more complex than this, and the closer one studies it the more anomalies one finds. For example, Vernon (1969) shows that IQ gains of 15 points and more are by no means uncommon amongst West Indian children who have attended London schools for six or seven years. In addition, the observed gap between White and Black children in America is nowhere near as marked in the pre-school years as it is later on. Although it is not easy to test intelligence very reliably in children as young as two years, the available evidence we have using the Gesell test in fact shows no difference at all between the two groups. Summarizing world-wide evidence, Werner (1972) even suggests that on psychomotor tests (i.e. tests involving the solution of physical problems) both African and American Black races show the highest mean scores of any group tested while western Whites show the lowest. It is only at school age, when intelligence tests come to involve more verbal problems, that the gap begins to open up in the other direction.

The implications of these and the various other issues involved are far too numerous to pursue in detail here, but it is fair to conclude that there are no conclusive grounds for supposing genetic differences in intelligence exist between races. Such measurable differences as do exist would seem to be far too strongly contaminated by environmental variables to allow us to explain their origins with any confidence. Western White culture is highly verbal in its current orientation, and success in many walks of life seems to go to those who are able to use language at a fluent and complex level. Groups who themselves place a lower emphasis upon the importance of language (and after all language is not the only form of communication), or who have less opportunity to acquire and use it to a high standard, will therefore inevitably appear to be less able on tests demanding verbal reasoning and other verbal skills. Until such time as we develop genuinely culture-fair tests, or until such time as we decide money spent on exploring racial differences in intelligence is better spent in other areas of human need, there is little that one can usefully add.

Intelligence and socio-economic factors

From the educational standpoint, probably the most important differences in measured intelligence between groups are those associated with socio-economic status. Socio-economic status (SES for short) is usually determined by reference to paternal occupation. In the UK the Registrar General classifies such occupations into five groups, starting with Group I which includes such luminaries as doctors, politicians and university teachers and proceeding down through managerial, skilled, and semi-skilled to the unskilled workers who make up Group V. Research has consistently shown that the higher one moves upwards through these groups the higher the mean IQ becomes, both for parents and children (the mean for children of parents in Group I for example is reported to be about 115, while for those in Group V it is around 92).

The reasons for these differences are again by no means clear. Children from low SES homes are, of course, less likely to have the material possessions that stimulate intellectual activity, such as books and constructional toys. They are also less likely to be read to, to have a room where quiet study is possible, to hear complex verbal structures in the speech of their parents and siblings, and to be motivated to do well at school by parents who have high ambitions for them. But it has also been suggested that there may be genetic factors at work, with people of lower intelligence tending to gravitate to SES Group V and to pass on lower intellectual potential to their children, while people of higher intelligence tend to move up towards SES Group I and to pass on a higher potential. Lest it be thought that this will result in a steady widening of the gap between the two groups, geneticists suggest we should take account of an interesting phenomenon known as *filial regression to the mean*. Put simply, this represents the tendency of children, over a wide range of geneti-cally determined factors, to score nearer to the mean for the whole population than do their parents in instances where the latter obtain unusually high or unusually low ratings. With height, for example, the average stature of sons of very tall fathers is 50 per cent nearer the mean than is that of their fathers, while the sons of very short fathers again show an average height nearer the mean by the same percentage than do their fathers. This is nature's way, if you like, of ensuring that the race remains relatively uniform, and does not consist of giants and dwarfs. If filial regression to the mean operates in the field of intelligence (and the evidence that it does has been hotly disputed) this would mean that parents in Group I would on average have higher IQs than their children, while in Group V the reverse would be the case.

Urban and rural differences in intelligence

Turning away from socio-economic status, we find that differ-ences in measured intelligence also exist between urban and rural children. One study (McNemar, 1942) found that at school entry the difference is some 5.7 IQ points in favour of urban children, and rises to 10.4 by top junior age and to 12.2 in school leavers. Again, this could be a compound of genetic and environmental factors. The trend since the eighteenth century has been for people to seek their fortunes in the cities and the large towns, and it could be that historically it has been the intellectually more able who have tended to up and leave the quiet rural life. Thus the genetic pool could have been gradually depleted of its high intelligence genes in coun-try districts, while the pool in towns and cities was constantly being augmented. On the other hand, it could simply be that there is more environmental stimulation in the cities (at least of the kind that leads to success in intelligence tests!), better school facilities, and higher motivation. Or it could simply be that in the urban–rural dichotomy we see in miniature the kind of things we suggested may exist between races: that is, country people place less emphasis on the verbal and other skills measured in intelligence tests, and prefer to develop a more measured and perhaps profounder way of life which is more in keeping with the kind of problems that present themselves for solution in their environment.

Gender differences in intelligence

A third between-group difference in measured intelligence that has attracted research interest is that between the sexes. The extensive literature that this research has spawned is extensively reviewed by Maccoby and Jacklin (1974), but if one summarizes their findings and those of more recent workers one can say that no conclusive general difference in IQ scores appears to exist between boys and girls, though in certain specific intellectual skills such differences do seem to be apparent. Of most direct interest to the teacher are those differences in reading and mathematics. In the former, twice as many boys as girls are diagnosed as backward in the USA, while the picture is probably not substantially different in the UK. Girls also tend to be more verbal and articulate than boys at first, through these differences disappear by around the age of 16 or so. However, cross-cultural studies show that this picture is not duplicated in all societies, and it may therefore be primarily a culturally induced one. In western societies girls spend more time within the home than do boys, and are more concerned for parental approval. They are thus more likely to be exposed to a verbally stimulating environment and to good parental reading habits. With less in the way of physical activities open to them, they may also turn to reading as a way of employing their time.

In support of this culture-orientated argument there is some evidence that when boys are presented with reading books that have a high interest content (i.e. are orientated towards a 'typical' boy's pursuits), differences in reading ability between boys and girls tend to disappear (Stanchfield, 1973). There is also some evidence, though it has not gone undisputed, that when boys are taught by men in the early schoolyears, and therefore come to identify school with masculinity rather than with femininity, they perform up to the same standards as girls in reading and other verbal skills.

In mathematics, we find the position reversed, with boys showing significant superiority over girls, this time right up to school leaving age. But here again, this may primarily be a culturally-induced phenomenon. Mathematical and spatial skills traditionally (and unfairly) are associated with the male world and with male vocational choice. Even in the early school years, the more interesting and exciting mathematical problems can tend to be presented in terms of masculine occupations and preoccupations rather than in terms of feminine (the latter being restricted to problems to do mainly with shopping and household budgets). As with boys and reading, there is evidence to show that where these and other opportunity and emotional variables are held constant there is no evidence that one sex is markedly superior to the other, and findings of this kind should make educationists reflect very carefully on the degree to which girls and boys can be handicapped by the very agencies that are supposed to be helping them develop their potential and widen their occupational choice.

In particular, we should stop believing that girls are naturally more literate than boys and boys naturally more numerate than girls, as it seems that teacher attitudes and expectations can materially influence child performance. If we expect one child for some reason to be better at something than another child then we will, consciously or unconsciously, tend to convey this expectation to the children themselves, who will allow it to influence their own views as to their ability. We will also tend to expect higher standards from the first child than from the second, and perhaps work that little bit harder ourselves as teachers to get him or her to achieve them. Very few teachers are ever consciously sexist in their approach at any level, but misconceptions about the relative abilities (and interests, inclinations and emotions) of boys and girls lead without doubt to a great deal of unconscious bias within the school, as indeed they do within society in general.

References

Cattell, R.B. (1963) Theory of fluid and crystallized intelligence: a critical experiment. *Journal of Educational Psychology, 54,* 1–22.

Freeman, F.N., Holzinger, K.J. and Mitchell, B.C. (1928) The influence of environment on the intelligence, school achievement and conduct of foster children. In *Twenty-Seventh Yearbook of the National Society for the Study of Education, Part 1.* Bloomington, Illinois: Public School Publishing.

Gaddes, W.H., McKenzie, A. and Barnsley, R. (1968) Psychometric intelligence and spatial imagery in two northwest Indian and two white groups of children. *Journal of Social Psychology, 75,* 35–42.

Guilford, J.P. (1968) The structure of intelligence. In D.K. Whitla (ed.) *Handbook of Measurement and Assessment in the Behavioral Sciences.* Reading, Massachusetts: Addison-Wesley.

Jarvik, L.F. and Erlenmeyer-Kimling, L. (1967) Survey of familiar correlations in measured intellectual functions. In J. Zubin and G.A. Jervis (ed.), *Psychopathology of Mental Development.* New York: Grune & Stratton.

Jensen, A. (1969) How much can we boost IQ and scholastic achievement? *Harvard Educational Review, 39,* 1–123.

Jenson, A.R. (1973) *Educability and Group Differences.* New York: Harper & Row.

Kamin, L.J. (1974) *The Science and Politics of IQ.* Harmondsworth: Penguin.

Lazar, L. *et al.* (1977) *The Persistence of Pre-school Effects: A long-term follow-up of fourteen infant and pre-school experiments: final report.* Denver, Colorado: Education Commission of the States.

Maccoby, E. and Jacklin, C. (1974) *The Psychology of Sex Differences.* Stanford: Stanford University Press.

McNemar, Q. (1942) *The Revision of the Stanford–Binet Scale.* Boston: Houghton Mifflin.

Stanchfield, J. (1973) *Sex Differences in Learning to Read.* Bloomington, Indiana: Phi Delta Kappa Educational Foundation.

Vernon, P.E. (1969) *Intelligence and Cultural Environment.* London: Methuen.

Vernon, P.E. (1979) *Intelligence: Heredity and environment.* San Francisco: W.H. Freeman.

Werner, E.E. (1972) Infants around the world: cross-cultural studies of psychomotor development from birth to two years. *Journal of Cross-cultural Psychology, 3,* 111–134.

SOME QUESTIONS

1. Can you account for the great interest that educators and parents have taken in intelligence over the years?

2. What particular problems does the measurement of intelligence present?

3. In the chapter 'running' was used as an analogy in our discussion of the measurement of intelligence. Can you think of any other analogies that could usefully have been employed instead?

4. Why do some psychologists simply define intelligence as 'the ability to do intelligence tests'? Why is this definition of little real help to us?

5. What are the origins of formal intelligence tests? Why is it of value for us to know about these origins when discussing the concept of intelligence within education?

6. What is meant by mental age? How was this originally used in the computation of IQ?

7. What was the disadvantage of this method of computation and what is the method that has superseded it?

8. How has the notion that intelligence is normally distributed affected the design and construction of intelligence tests?

9. Why is it important to know the standard deviation of an intelligence test before we try interpreting the results produced by it?

10. What is meant by 'g' and what part does this concept play in models of intelligence?

11. Why is the term 'multi-factorial' given to certain models of intelligence?

12. How does age apparently affect the usefulness of the concept of 'g'?

13. Why is the nature–nurture controversy over the origins of intelligence of interest to teachers?

14. Give examples of some of the methods psychologists have used to try and resolve the nature–nurture controversy.

15. Give some of the objections raised to the data on nature–nurture yielded by twin studies.

16. How do the models proposed by Hebb and Vernon on the one hand and by Cattell on the other deal with the relative influences of nature and nurture?

17. What do we mean when we say that our methods for measuring intelligence are 'culture bound'?

18. Give some reasons why children from LSES backgrounds may show lower measured intelligence than children from USES.

19. What is meant by 'filial regression to the mean'?

20. Discuss the apparent differences in intelligence and ability between girls and boys noted by some researchers. Can you account for these differences?

Additional Reading

Block, N. and Dworkin, G. (1977) *The IQ Controversy*. London: Quartet Books.
Contains much of the relevant evidence thrown up by both sides.

De Bono, E. (1969) *The Five Day Course in Thinking*. Harmondsworth: Penguin.
Readers interested in sharpening their own wits might like to work through this.

De Bono, E. (1970) *Children Solve Problems*. Harmondsworth: Penguin.
An interesting, amusingly illustrated record of how children tackle some of the problems presented to them using de Bono's methods.

De Bono, E. (1978) *Teaching Thinking*. Harmondsworth: Penguin.
All his books are fun to read. This is one of the best for the teacher, and gives a variety of strategies that the teacher can adopt with a class.

De Bono, E. (1979) *Word Power*. Harmondsworth: Penguin.
An illustrated and highly diverting dictionary of the key words used in the world of business and management today. Of obvious relevance to education.

De Bono, E. (1980) *Future Positive*. Harmondsworth: Penguin.
Discusses the ways in which positive and lateral thinking can be put to good use in planning for the future and solving our environmental and social problems.

Eysenck, H.J. and Kamin, L. (1981) *Intelligence: The battle for the mind*. Harmondsworth: Penguin.
An excellent debate between two of the major proponents of nature and nurture theories of intelligence respectively.

Kail, R. and Pellegrino, J.W. (1985) *Human Intelligence: Perspectives and prospects*. San Francisco: W.H. Freeman.
A good survey of the present position, and with interesting pointers for the future. Highly recommended.

Kamin, L.G. (1974) *The Science and Politics of IQ*. Harmondsworth: Penguin.
The book that sparked off the current debate over the relative contributions of nature and nurture to measured intelligence.

Richardson, K., Spears, D. and Richards, M. (1972) *Race, Culture, and Intelligence*. Harmondsworth: Penguin.
Deals with cross-cultural issues in intelligence and intelligence testing.

Sternberg, R.J. (ed.) (1985) *Human Abilities: An information processing approach*. New York: Freeman.
A useful overview of human cognitive abilities. More comprehensive but not so practical as de Bono's books. (Also of relevance to Chapter 7.)

Vernon, P.E. (1979) *Intelligence: Heredity and environment*. San Francisco: Freeman.
The student keen to find a good general text on all aspects of intelligence need look no further. In spite of its title, this book covers virtually all areas of the subject of interest to the teacher and does not concentrate solely on the heredity versus environment debate. It is scholarly, fair-minded, and eminently readable.

Watson, P. (ed.) (1973) *Psychology and Race*. Harmondsworth: Penguin.
Closely concerned with racial issues, though it deals with other psychological matters in addition to intelligence.

6

Creativity

What is
creativity?

Creativity is a familiar yet oddly elusive concept. We all think
we can recognize creativity in others (and even in ourselves at
times), since this is regarded as one of the abilities of the good
teacher, but we would probably be hard pressed to advance a
definition acceptable to all our colleagues. And we might find
some disagreement over whether one can be creative in the
sciences as well as in the arts, in the home as well as in the
potter's studio, in bringing up children as well as in writing
books. Further disagreement would probaby arise if we began
to discuss ways of teaching creativity to children, or even
whether such teaching is possible; whether in fact creativity
can be learnt at all or whether it is a precious gift with which
we are born (or not as the case may be).

Lateral/divergent thinking

One approach to the problem is to see creativity as a special
kind of thinking, a kind of thinking that involves originality
and fluency, that breaks away from existing patterns and
introduces something new. Obviously, on this count de Bono's *lateral* thinking (see p. 93) would involve creativity,
whereas his so-called *vertical* thinking would not. Indeed,
creativity would also be involved in the *divergent* thinking
included in Guilford's model of the intellect which was also
discussed in the last chapter. In fact, it is this divergent
thinking, together with other aspects of Guilford's work, that
has tended to attract maximum attention in the debate over
the nature of creativity that psychologists have been conduct-
ing during the last four decades.

Guilford claims that divergent thinking is the ability to
generate a range of possible solutions to a given problem, in
particular to a problem to which there is no single right
answer (like 'think of all the meanings you can for the word
"bolt"'). It will be readily seen that such an ability is likely to
play a part in the creative act, since the artist will often need
to explore a range of possible ways of painting a picture, or
finishing off a novel, or writing a poem before finally deciding

on the one that looks best. Obviously we also expect a creative act to bear the stamp of originality (at least in the sense that the individual concerned has not thought of the idea before), but here again divergent thinking will play a part, in that the wider the range of possibilities we are able to generate the more likely it will be that one of them will carry originality.

Creativity and intelligence

It will be noted that in his model Guilford also refers to what he calls *convergent* thinking. In convergent thinking individuals are said to converge upon the single acceptable answer to a problem rather than to diverge and throw up as many solutions as they can. It is sometimes said that conventional intelligence tests concentrate only upon convergent thinking in that there is only one single acceptable correct answer to each item, and that divergent thinking can only really be demonstrated in tests of the so-called open-ended type. This is probably true, and it is always an interesting exercise to ask children to look at certain intelligence test items (particularly those of the 'underline the odd man out' type) and see whether they can find reasons for more than one acceptable solution to each. In doing so we are asking them to think divergently rather than convergently, and the results might come as something of a surprise to intelligence test designers.

Nevertheless, I am not suggesting that divergent thinking is in any way superior to convergent, or that we have made mistakes in the past by emphasizing convergent thinking in schools. Often the latter is more appropriate to a particular problem, and we should therefore at the outset regard divergent thinking as complementary to convergent rather than as some kind of competitor. The point that Guilford and others have tried to make is that, in our emphasis upon convergent thinking, we have tended to neglect divergent altogether, and in consequence we have done little to teach (or develop) creativity in schools.

The problem is, however, that we have no conclusive findings as to the degree of correlation between the ability to perform well on divergent thinking tests (more will be said about these tests shortly) and the ability to achieve success in obviously creative subjects such as fine art, writing, and musical composition. Nor is it as yet clear whether convergent and divergent thinking are separate operations as suggested by Guilford, or whether they are part and parcel of the same group of mental abilities. In an early work, Getzels and Jackson (1962) studied groups of children having on the one hand high divergent thinking scores and relatively low IQ scores (the 'high creative' group), and on the other high IQ scores and relatively low divergent thinking scores (the 'high

IQ' group). Both groups were found to have similar school achievement records, but the former emerged as less conformist than the latter, less popular with teachers, more prone to over-achieve (i.e. to exceed expectations), and more likely to have a lively sense of humour. Importantly from our point of view, there appeared to be no significant correlation in the sample between divergent thinking and IQ scores.

One drawback to this study, however, was that the children were all in the high ability range (the mean IQ for the whole sample was 132). Using a broader ability band, other psychologists have failed to replicate these findings, and have concluded that convergent and divergent thinking abilities do appear to be linked, though it is not yet clear how strongly. Supporters of Getzels and Jackson have countered by saying that this link is a consequence of test procedure rather than of psychological fact. Divergent thinking tests, they argue, should be administered untimed, and in a deliberately light-hearted and playful atmosphere, since the serious exam-orientated climate in which IQ tests are undertaken is inhibiting to creative thinking. If we insist on producing such a climate, we penalize the diverger and end up with inaccurate results. In support of this argument they point to an extensive study by Wallach and Kogan (1965) which showed that younger children, in particular, seem to produce their best divergent thinking results when there is an absence of stress in the air.

In the light of present knowledge, the fairest conclusion seems to be that the link between convergent and divergent thinking abilities appears to be strongest for children with moderate or low IQs, where a straightforward linear relationship may apply. Above an IQ threshold somewhere in the 110–120 range, however, the relationship becomes a much more complex and even random one. That is, we become much less able to predict whether a given highly intelligent individual is likely to score at a comparable level on divergent tests. Up to this threshold level, therefore, increased intelligence seems usually to go with increased divergent abilities, but above this level gains in the former do not necessarily appear to go with gains in the latter. Assuming that divergent thinking abilities do go with recognized creative ability in the arts, this means that, for example, a painter with an IQ of 150 would not, simply by virtue of that fact, emerge as a greater artist than a painter with an IQ of some 30 points less.

We must not lose sight of the fact, though, that certain activities may demand both IQ and high divergent ability. This could well be true of certain areas of science. In this chapter's opening paragraph it was suggested that there might be disagreement on whether creativity is apparent in science as well as in arts, but the examination of the creative act in due course below (together with common sense) would indicate strongly that it is so apparent, particularly in areas of scientific research and invention. One of the differences between high level performance in science, as opposed to high level performance in the arts, is that more convergent ability may be needed to understand the grammar of science, to identify and clarify research problems within it, and to see the relationship between these problems and other relevant issues.

Having read this far, the reader may consider that I have ducked rather neatly out of the attempt to provide a precise definition of creativity. Certainly there is a tendency to avoid the issue, since any definition is likely to be some way short of perfect. Some definitions advanced in the past, with their emphasis upon the ability to see relationships, look in fact very similar to those associated with intelligence, while others are so vague that they cover almost every informal thought and action. A definition that has some merit, however, is that creativity is *the ability to generate fluent and novel ways of tackling problems and of organizing material*. Such a definition shows quite clearly that one can have creativity in the home as well as in the art room, in dressing a shop window as well as in writing a symphony, in educating children as well as in advancing scientific theory and practice. What it cannot do without becoming unwieldy, however, is to stress that by 'novel' we mean novel for the individual concerned. Thus a child who spends happy hours inventing something only to be told someone else thought of it years ago is nevertheless being creative. He or she has gone through the creative process just as did the original inventor, and probably derived as much value (though regrettably perhaps not in financial terms!) as did that worthy individual.

Divergent thinking tests

I have already indicated that divergent thinking can only be assessed by tests of the *open-ended* variety: that is, by tests that have no set right and wrong answers. They can, of course, be of the verbal kind, but can also be spatial or even musical. In each case the emphasis is the same. Children are asked to think of as many appropriate ways as they can for solving some particular problem. For example, we can have what is called the 'Uses of Objects' test, in which children are invited to write down as many uses as they can for everyday objects such as a housebrick, a paper clip, a barrel, a blanket, a book and so on. Another example is the 'Meanings of Words' test in which they are invited to record all the meanings they can for appropriate words like 'iron', or 'carpet', or 'bolt', and yet another is the 'Consequences' test in which they are asked to think of as many results as they can for a particular change in the usual order of things (e.g. the caretaker losing the school keys, or everyone living to be 100 years old).

Turning to non-verbal tests, we have such things as the Guilford 'Circles' test, in which subjects are confronted by a sheet of small uniformly-sized blank circles and are asked to use pencils to turn as many of them as they can into recognizable objects. Tests using a random pattern of lines instead of a circle are also popular, while a simple musical test would be to ask subjects to think of as many endings as they can for a given musical phrase. Commercial tests (such as the 'Torrance Tests of Creative Thinking') are available, but it will be readily appreciated that teachers can devise their own without much difficulty. Scoring is simple in that marks are usually given for *fluency* (the number of appropriate responses the subject makes), *originality* (the novelty of these responses) and *flexibility* (their variety). The usual method for arriving at the originality score is to compare each child's responses with those of the rest of the class, and award, say, 5 marks for every response that is offered by one child only, 4 marks if it is offered by two children and so on down to zero. Flexibility is scored by grouping responses into categories (e.g. 'domestic', 'sporting', 'animal'), and counting how many of these categories a subject has offered.

Since divergent thinking tests lay emphasis upon individuality of response, far less work has been done on standardization than is the case for intelligence tests, and in consequence most commentators regard them as rather crude devices. They are also criticized as being somewhat dull, which may inhibit the full creative response from subjects. To date, results on these tests do not always correlate very well with proven success in creative work or with peer group ratings of creativity, and it is probably as a consequence of this that research in the field has tended to taper off after the hectic activity of some years ago. It would seem at the moment to be badly in need of fresh impetus and of a new sense of direction.

The creative act

Turning now from the definition and the measurement of creativity to the creative act itself, we find that studies of creative men and women suggest that a creative act typically involves four stages (see Perkins, 1981).

- **Preparation**, which is primarily concerned with the recognition that a particular problem is worthy of study, or a particular theme is suitable for a book or a picture or a piece of music.

- **Incubation**, during which the problem or the theme is mulled over, often at an unconscious level.

- **Inspiration**, when the possible solution to the problem or a flood of ideas for the book, etc., come abruptly into the conscious mind.

- **Verification,** when the solution is put to the test or the ideas are tried out on paper or on canvas.

Each of these stages carries its own importance. The ability of the highly creative person to recognize the significance of a problem or of a theme which has lain disregarded under the noses of other men and women often for very many years is legendary: Pavlov spotting the anomaly that dogs salivated on hearing the footsteps of the attendant bringing their food rather than solely on seeing or smelling the food itself; Freud recognizing the existence of infantile sexuality; Cervantes spotting the absurdities in the medieval system of chivalry; Dvořák realizing the symphonic potential of simple folk songs; in fact, practically any artist's or research scientist's work that leaves us wondering, 'Now why on earth didn't *I* think of that?'

During the *preparation* stage the creative person explores various possibilities associated with the problem or theme in question, and then often comes to a full stop. The solution, or the precise methods of procedure, fail to come to mind, and there then follows the period of *incubation* during which the creative person often puts the whole subject aside, sometimes only for days, at other times perhaps for years. We can only guess at what happens during this incubation period, but if the model of the unconscious suggested by Freud and other depth psychologists is correct, then the processes of thought continue at the unconscious level, though without employing the kind of logic which characterizes conscious thought. This apparent illogicality perhaps assists the lateral thinking discussed in connection with de Bono's work in the last chapter. Freed from logical, sequential thought, the mind is able to rove freely over its accumulated store of knowledge, trying new permutations and new juxtapositions until one eventually makes recognizable sense and in a surge of creative excitement comes up into the conscious mind in the form of *illumination* (Nierenberg, 1982).

This flash of illumination (or inspiration, though perhaps this term should apply to the whole of the creative act) has been well illustrated by, for example, the poet Houseman, who maintained that most of his verses came to him 'ready made', or the mathematician Poincaré who solved the problems associated with Fuchsian functions in a series of inspirational flashes which occurred at odd moments when he was engaged in quite different activities, or the scientist Kekulé whose revolutionary discovery of the chemical structure of benzene came to him in a dream. Illumination is then followed by *verification*, which is the perspiration stage of the creative act. The scientific theory must now be put to the test in the laboratory, often over careful months or years, or the novel or the symphony has to be worked out in detail and revised and re-revised.

This four-stage model of the creative act sometimes comes as something of a surprise to the person who supposes that the scientist, in particular, works carefully through the data and only arrives at a new theory by a process of deduction when he or she comes to the end. In reality science, just as much as the arts, seems to rely for its major advances upon the creative leap of the brilliant mind. Obviously such a leap is only normally possible (I say 'normally' because there are exceptions) where the scientists concerned are already steeped in their subject, and have the accumulated knowledge necessary not only for the permutations and the juxtapositions that I have suggested take place at the unconscious level, but also for recognizing the potential value of their illumination and for undertaking the verification procedure. But the importance of the incubation period and of the moment of illumination do not seem open to much doubt. If readers want to test this personally they have only to remember the occasions when, stuck over a particular form of words or a particular idea in an essay, they put it to one side and banish it from the conscious mind, and then find on returning to the fray a little later that the problem now resolves itself without difficulty.

Does this mean, therefore, that it is impossible to have a creative act without incubation followed by illumination? Since, as we have seen, creativity appears to cover such a wide area of human endeavour, and to be practised to a greater or lesser extent by each individual member of the human race, it would be unwise to generalize to this extent. The process of incubation may, in any case, often be very brief, particularly when we are working with very familiar material or where the problem to be solved is a relatively simple one. Journalists regularly meeting the editor's deadline with their copy can hardly afford the luxury of long periods of incubation, and neither can the teacher attempting to deal creatively with a wide range of classroom problems. Again, some creative people work very much more quickly than others, and the time from the conception of a creative idea to its final delivery in book (or whatever) form may be relatively short. But as a model for formalizing one's thinking about the creative process and developing strategies for helping children work creatively, the four-stage model of preparation, incubation, illumination and verification seems to approach most closely to what creative people themselves feel to be happening when they engage in creative activity. It also leaves us wondering whether formal examinations, where the candidate has both to read the questions and produce the answers all within the space of three short hours or so, really allows much scope for creative thinking. Along with the nervous stress of the examination situation itself, the absence of sufficient time for incubation may well be one of the reasons why all the best answers seem to come to us after leaving the examination room!

Creativity and the school

Just as all teachers are teachers of language, whatever their actual subject, so all teachers are teachers of creativity. This applies to science teachers as much as to those in the arts field. Earlier findings by Hudson (1966) that at sixth-form level high divergers tend to be on the arts side and high convergers on the science side are now thought primarily to be due to encouragement and opportunity rather than to anything inherent in either the academic disciplines concerned or in the pupils themselves. It seems arts students, in certain schools at least, are simply allowed to operate divergently more often than science students because the disciplines they are studying are held to be more subjective (more 'inspirational' perhaps) than those followed by the latter. Where science students are given examples of what is meant by divergent thinking, their scores on divergent thinking tests show immediate improvement. Assuming that such tests are a good measure of creativity, this would indicate that science students have no lack of creative ability, but simply need the impetus to bring it out.

Encouraging divergent thinking

The first point for teachers to bear in mind, therefore, is that whatever their subject they must be alive to opportunities for the encouragement of divergent thinking in students. It is argued by both Bruner (to whom reference was made in Chapter 3 and to whose work we return in more detail in the next chapter) and de Bono that within education we tend to reward only the 'right' answers and penalize the 'wrong'. This makes children reluctant to attempt novel or original solutions to problems, since the chances of error are inevitably greater when they do. In other words, they play for safety. Yet the imaginative leap, the production of an answer different from the conformist one, the readiness to take what one might call cognitive risks, are inseparable from creative endeavour. The teacher should be prepared to operate in an atmosphere where this endeavour is encouraged and rewarded, rather than in one where only cautious, convergent solutions are countenanced.

This does not mean, of course, that we have no regard for accuracy or precision. Remember that in the creative act the final stage is one of *verification*. The solution must be put to the test to see if it will work. If it fails it must be discarded, though the child can still be praised for an imaginative attempt. And even this failure may spark off fresh ideas which in turn can be tested and which may lead to the desired solution. In de Bono's terminology, the creative act is often a lateral endeavour that moves our thinking out of its narrow path and on to a new tack, while Bruner has it that creative thinking is *holistic* (i.e. productive of responses greater than the sum of their parts) while rational convergent thinking is *algorithmic* (i.e. productive of responses that are unambiguously themselves). Both kinds of thinking have their vital roles to play, but they should be used to complement and support each other, and not be regarded as in some sense mutually exclusive.

Before we protest too strongly that we already understand the value of both forms of thinking in the classroom, and would never penalize the child for holistic endeavour, we should remember that one of Getzels and Jackson's findings was that high divergers were less popular with teachers than high convergers. Schools have their rules and regulations, their patterns of procedure and conduct, and often the conformist child is more comfortable to live with than the nonconformist, highly imaginative one. In addition, divergent ideas may often be original and valuable, but they can also be bizarre and silly, leading the teacher to suspect the child may just be playing up. Unfortunately (or fortunately), creativity is an unpredictable thing, and we cannot expect it always to emerge in a form appropriate to the circumstances of the moment. By studying children's responses, and in particular by watching where ideas that initially appear silly actually lead, the teacher can soon recognize when children are trying to use their imagination and when they are simply trying to be difficult. By neglecting such study, the teacher runs the risk of stifling the good ideas along with the not-so-good, and giving the class the impression that originality quite simply is not welcome when he or she is around.

Classroom organization and creativity

If the first point in encouraging creativity is therefore to be open to its operation in the classroom, the second point must be concerned with the nature of classroom organization itself. Does creativity flourish better in an informal classroom, where children are responsible for much of their own work and for initiating a great deal of what goes on, or is it at its best in a more formal, structured context? Before we automatically plump for the former it is as well to remember that many artists have talked of the need for discipline in their subject, of the need for set work routines and for hard work and sustained application. The great teachers of the arts, whether they be dancers, musicians, or painters, have all insisted on their pupils learning the grammar of their subject, and on putting their creative gifts to constructive use rather than dissipating them without discipline or dedication. It is one thing to encourage creative expression, quite another to take that expression and mould it into a form that does it full justice.

With this in mind, it is perhaps not surprising to find that the evidence does not unequivocally support the informal classroom as the best way of nurturing creativity. Haddon and Lytton (1977) did indeed find that children from informal primary schools out-performed those from formal on divergent thinking, and that the differences persisted even after transfer to secondary schools, but in a more extensive study Bennett (1976) found that when he used actual creative endeavours (such as creative writing) instead of divergent thinking tests as his variable, results did not differ significantly between formal and informal primary schools. It could be that these apparently conflicting findings are fully explained by the different experimental variables used, divergent thinking tests as opposed to creative writing and so on, but it could be that the teachers themselves were far more important than the simple matter of classroom organization. Wallach (1970) showed that creative adults appear in general to have been exposed in childhood to a rich variety of experiences, and to an environment in which they were encouraged to ask questions, to test out their ideas by active experimentation, and to pursue their interests through hobbies and through the development of special talents and skills. Since this can be done as readily in the good formal as in the good informal classroom this seems to suggest that we should look first at teachers' general approach to their task.

Creative teaching techniques

We have already seen that teachers should encourage the generation of ideas in their work with children, but the above suggestion indicates that we should also ask what kind of personal interests and enthusiasms do individual teachers bring into the classroom? Teachers who themselves have wide interests, and who enjoy sharing them with children both in and out of timetabled school hours, who themselves have lively enquiring minds and enjoy playing with ideas, and above all who like posing and listening to questions, would seem much more likely to prompt creative development in their children than teachers who are stereotyped and rigid. Torrance (1962) suggests specifically that teachers should help children to indulge in speculation along the 'What would happen if . . . ?' (or 'What would have happened if . . . ?') line, and to teach them that everyone has creative potential and not just a few outstanding individuals.

Parnes (1967) proposes a method called *brainstorming* which has achieved wide popularity in industry and which has obvious educational implications. Participants in a brain-storming session work as a group and are encouraged to generate ideas in response to a particular problem. Nothing is regarded as too wild or inappropriate, and no criticisms of any kind are offered. The session can be tape-recorded, and at the end the tape played back and allowed to stimulate further inspiration or work of the verification kind. Often seemingly intractable problems are solved in this way, with each parti-cipant sparking off creative ideas from the rest of the group. The non-judgemental atmosphere allows each person to let his or her thoughts on the problem come without check or censure, and at school level it is this process, as much as the solution of the problem itself, that has educational value.

The importance of this open-ended approach is emphasized further by Davis (1976) who presented three student groups with a problem (how to change or improve a doorknob) and then tried different methods with each to stimulate their creative thinking. The first group was presented with a list of specific examples of how the problem might be solved, the second was given a number of possible general strategies (e.g. try thinking about changing the materials from which the knob is made), while the third was given a matrix with which to work. This matrix allowed one set of variables to be placed along the first axis (e.g. the various materials from which a doorknob can be made) and another set along the second (e.g. the various possible shapes a doorknob can take), thus mak-ing it possible to combine the variables into new arrange-ments.

Not surprisingly, in view of the points made so far, indivi-duals within the third group produced the most ideas and individuals within the first the least. These last individuals in fact spent all their time working through the long list of specific possible solutions which they had been given instead of trying to think up something new. The implication of this for the classroom is that if we constantly present students with our ideas, even if these are simply offered as examples, the situation becomes less open-ended in that they will con-centrate upon these to the exclusion of any new ideas of their own. Present them with stimuli by all means, but in a form which allows for rearrangement and juxtaposition. Even if we are concerned simply with a classroom discussion or debate, teachers must beware of 'closing' the situation by constantly attempting to sum up or to offer their own solutions. Carrying as they do the authority of the teacher, these solutions will inevitably be regarded by many children as the 'right' an-swers, and will put an end to further creative individual thinking. Even at the end of the debate teachers should avoid the temptation of always providing their own judgements on the virtues of the ideas that have been put forward. Far better often to leave things deliberately rather open, and send children away thinking further, than to give the class the impression that the last word has now been uttered and nothing further remains to be said.

Finally, it is essential that children should be helped to see the distinction between different kinds of thinking, and to come to decisions as to which is appropriate in a given context. A number of studies show that, faced with the same problem, children produce different kinds of solutions if they are asked on the one hand to be creative and original about it, and on the other to be practical. Practicality is usually interpreted as meaning, 'stick to the known methods', while invitations to be original prompt children to use their imagination in the search for something new. In creativity, as in so many other classroom activites, the things we get out of children depend not only on their own abilities but on our cleverness in phrasing the questions we put to them.

References

Bennett, N. (1976) *Teaching Styles and Pupil Progress*. London: Open Books.

Davis, G. (1976) Research and development in training creative thinking. In J. Levin and V. Allen (ed.) *Cognitive Learning in Children: Theories and strategies*. New York: Academic Press.

Getzels, J. and Jackson, P. (1962) *Creativity and Intelligence: Explorations with gifted children*. New York: Wiley.

Haddon, F.H. and Lytton, H. (1971) Primary education and divergent thinking abilities – four years on. *British Journal of Educational Psychology*, 41, 136–147.

Hudson, L. (1966) *Contrary Imaginations*. Harmondsworth: Penguin.

Nierenberg, G.I. (1982) *The Art of Creative Thinking*. New York: Simon & Schuster.

Parnes, S. (1967) *Creative Behaviour Guidebook*. New York: Scribner's.

Perkins, N.D. (1981) *The Mind's Best Work*. Cambridge, Massachusetts: Harvard University Press.

Torrance, E. (1962) *Guiding Creative Talent*. Englewood Cliffs, New Jersey: Prentice-Hall.

Torrance, E. (1974) *Torrance Tests of Creative Thinking*. Windsor: NFER.

Wallach, M. (1970) Creativity. In P. Mussen (ed.) *Carmichael's Manual of Child Psychology*, 3rd edn. Volume 1. New York: Wiley.

Wallach, M. and Kogan, N. (1965) *Modes of Thinking in Young Children*. New York: Holt, Rinehart & Winston.

SOME
QUESTIONS

1. How would you define creativity?

2. What are the differences between so-called 'convergent' and 'divergent' thinking?

3. How would you convert a question which calls upon convergent thinking into one which calls upon divergent? Give examples.

4. Do convergent and divergent abilities appear to be correlated?

5. Is creativity as important in advanced work in science as it is in advanced work in the arts?

6. What is an 'open-ended' test?

7. What are the usual variables used in marking divergent thinking tests?

8. Give the four stages that appear to be associated with the creative act.

9. What appears to happen during the 'incubation' stage of the creative act?

10. Give further examples of the ability of the creative person to recognize the importance of a problem that has lain disregarded under the noses of other men and women for years.

11. Is the notion that creative scientists work systematically through their experiments and only arrive at a new theory when they come to the end generally an accurate one?

12. Is it appropriate to talk of creativity in the bringing up of children and in the work of the teacher, for example, or is creativity confined to the work of the artist?

Additional Reading

Anderson, B.F. (1980) *The Complete Thinker.* Englewood Cliffs, New Jersey: Prentice-Hall.
Tackles the whole field of thinking, with a good chapter on creativity.

Bransford, J.D. and Stein, B.S. (1984) *The Ideal Problem Solver: A guide for improving thinking, learning and creativity.* New York: W.H. Freeman.
Full of relevant information and practical examples and exercises. Excellent in every way.

Foster, J. (1971). *Creativity and the Teacher.* London: Macmillan.
Remains a useful guide to creativity at school level.

Ghiselin, B. (1952) *The Creative Process.* New York: New American Library.
A classic in its field. The creative process as experienced and reported first-hand by creative individuals in the sciences and arts.

Hudson, L. (1966). *Contrary Imaginations*. London: Methuen and Harmonds-worth: Penguin.
Overstresses the arts/science dichotomy, but another classic which did much to focus attention upon creativity and work in schools.

Pickard, E. (1979). *Development of Creative Ability*. Slough, Bucks: NFER.
Full of ideas for encouraging creativity in the classroom.

Torrance, E.P. and Myers, R.E. (1970) *Creative Learning and Teaching*. New York: Dodd Mead.
An alternative to the above. Rather older but still highly relevant.

7

Learning

In spite of its critical importance within education, the problem of explaining how learning takes place, and analysing the factors that influence it, remains a confused area. Teachers, and educators generally, often blame psychologists for this, and claim that they either present them with several conflicting explanations of learning, each one based upon a different psychological theory, or a single coherent explanation with which it is admitted other psychologists would probably not agree. Yet perhaps this blame, though understandable, is a little unfair. The problem is that learning is such a highly complex activity. We each of us receive a constant and varied stream of experiences throughout our waking moments, each one of which potentially can give rise to learning, yet most of which apparently vanish without trace from our mental lives. What is it that makes some things memorable and others not? Why is it that a particular event can prompt learning in one person yet have no measurable effect upon someone else? Why does an individual learn readily from one teacher but not from another? How is it that we are able to make sense of our experience, and put that knowledge to good effect when it comes to tackling new situations and problems? Questions such as these and many others make the psychologist's task of understanding and explaining learning, and above all of advising on how learning can be made more efficient and more permanent for all types and conditions of learner, an almost herculean one. Perhaps the wonder is not that psychologists have so far failed to come up with all the answers during the 50 years or so in which a systematic study of learning has been made, but that they have come up with as many as they have.

What constitutes learning?

Since it is always helpful to start with a definition, let us say that most psychologists would agree that learning is a relatively persistent change in an individual's potential behaviour due to experience. This definition draws attention to three things: first, that learning must change the individual in some

125

way; second, that this change comes about as a result of experience; and third, that it is a change in his or her potential behaviour. The first of these points of emphasis is obvious enough. Unless we are changed in some way, learning cannot be said to have taken place. This change can, of course, be at a relatively simple level (as, for example, when we learn a skill like tying a shoelace) or at a more complex one (as, for example, when we encounter a great work of art for the first time), but the principle remains the same. The individual is in some definable way a different person with this learning from the person he or she was without it. The second point of emphasis stresses that the change must come about as a result of experience. This therefore excludes the kind of changes that accrue from maturation and physical development. The third point stresses that although a change has taken place, it is a change in potential rather than in actual performance. We may learn something, but give no hint of this learning in our actual performance until months or years later (as, for example, when a child sees some facts about a foreign country on television and surprises everyone by trotting them out when the class starts to study that country at a later date).

Armed with this definition, we can now look at the psychologist's attempt to develop a convincing theory of how learning comes about. At this point we must acknowledge the existence of the sharpest divergence between psychologists, a divergence which in effect sometimes puts them into two opposed camps, neither of them prepared to accept the potential usefulness of the other's point of view. Without wishing to become drawn too deeply into the issues that divide these two camps, we can say that one adopts an essentially *behaviourist* (or connectionist) approach and the other a *cognitive* (or cognitive-field) one.

The *behaviourist* approach maintains that if psychology is to be an exact science it must focus upon the study of observable behaviour: that is, upon the responses made by the individual and upon the conditions under which they occur. Such an approach sees learning in terms of connections between stimulus and response or between response and reinforcement, and places great stress upon the role played by the environment. Structure the environment correctly, and learning will usually follow, irrespective of the particular volition of the learner.

The *cognitive* approach, on the other hand, holds that if we are to understand learning we cannot confine ourselves to observable behaviour, but must also concern ourselves with the learner's ability mentally to reorganize his or her psychological field (i.e. the inner world of concepts, memories, etc.) in response to experience. This latter approach, therefore, lays stress not only upon the environment, but upon the way in which the individual interprets and tries to make sense of the environment. It sees the individual not as the somewhat mechanical product of the environment, but as an active agent in the learning process, deliberately trying to process and categorize the stream of information received from the outside world.

These two sets of theories are not mutually contradictory. Teachers, concerned as they are with the practicalities of learning, can draw usefully upon them both, and see each of them as having greater or lesser relevance dependent upon the level at which learning is intended to occur. To clarify this we must look in turn at one example from each of these sets of theories, examples which have direct practical relevance for education and which will provide us with a theoretical underpinning for much of what has to be said in this chapter.

Theories of learning

Although usually referred to as theories, the two views of learning that are about to be discussed are really descriptions. That is, they confine themselves to describing what actually happens when learning takes place, instead of entering into theoretical speculation on why and how it happens. This will come as something of a relief to the teacher, since it is a common complaint that theories of learning, for all their undoubted complexity, are not really that much help when it comes to the practicalities of helping students learn. Descriptions of learning, on the other hand, are of much more immediate benefit because they describe the kinds of activity carried out by both pupil and teacher that appear to lead to enhanced levels of learning on the part of the former. They thus assist teachers to plan classroom strategies, to monitor pupils' learning, and to isolate the possible reasons for the success and failure of this learning.

The first of these descriptions of learning is drawn from the behaviouristic school of thought and is known as *operant conditioning*.

Operant conditioning

The principle of operant conditioning is most clearly expounded by the American psychologist B.F. Skinner, who has spent over 50 years in the experimental investigation of learning. Skinner (1969) holds that the learning act involves three identifiable stages: first, the *stimulus* or *situation* (S) with which the learner is confronted; second, the *behaviour* (B) which it elicits from the learner; and third, the reinforcement (R) which follows this behaviour. Such reinforcement can best be thought of by the teacher as the results that follow on from B. Obviously these results can either be favourable to the learner (in which case they are known as positive reinforcement or R+), or they can be unfavourable (in which case

127

they are known as R−). R+ increases the likelihood of the learner producing the same piece of behaviour again in the future, while R− decreases this likelihood. To take a straightforward example: a boy is asked by the teacher to give the present participle of the French verb *avoir* (S), he answers 'ayant' (B), and the teacher says 'correct' (R+). When confronted by the same question in the future, the likelihood of his answering 'ayant' is accordingly increased. Had he responded with 'avant', however, the teacher would have said 'incorrect' (R−), and he would have been less likely to offer this answer again.

Obviously R+ and R− need not always come from the teacher. The learner can find out in all sorts of ways whether his or her answer to a particular task or problem is right or wrong. But the principle that R+ increases and R− decreases the likelihood of behaviour recurring remains the same. The reader may regard this as self-evident, but Skinner and his associates consider that the relative inefficiency of much school-based learning stems from a basic failure to grasp both the S–B–R (or operant conditioning) model itself and its many implications. I look at some of these implications in due course, but first an example of the second view of learning, namely the cognitive-field approach, must be examined.

Instrumental conceptualism

This somewhat intimidating title is used by Bruner to define one of the most coherent and consistent cognitive descriptions of learning (Bruner, 1966). Bruner's approach is very much in the cognitive tradition since it sees learning not merely as a passive unit of behaviour elicited by a stimulus and strengthened or weakened by reinforcement, but as an active process in which the learner infers principles and rules and tests them out. Learning, in other words, is not simply something that happens to individuals, as in the operant conditioning model, but something which they themselves make happen by the manner in which they handle incoming information and put it to use. For the teacher, the main difference between Bruner's model and that of Skinner is that, while not denying the potential importance of the stimulus and the reinforcement in the S–B–R paradigm, Bruner considers that Skinner pays insufficient atention to the element that comes in between S and R, namely the learner's own behaviour (B). This behaviour is not simply something 'elicited' by a stimulus and strengthened or otherwise by the nature of the reinforcement that follows, it is in fact a highly complex activity which involves three major processes, namely:

- *acquisition* of information
- *transformation* or *manipulation* of this information into

a form suitable for dealing with the task in hand
* *testing* and checking the adequacy of this transformation (Bruner, 1973; Bruner and Anglin, 1973).

The learner achieves transformation by codifying and classifying incoming information: that is, by fitting it into (and sometimes thereby modifying) the categories he or she already has for understanding the world. This codifying and categorizing therefore consists of an internal mediating process upon which the overt behaviour itself depends. As this process becomes more developed through age and experience, the learner increasingly transforms the stimulus and gains freedom from stimulus control. What this means – and we must understand it if we are to grasp fully the differences between Skinner and Bruner – is that whereas Skinner sees the stimulus as a relatively discrete unit, an objective event distinct from the learner and evoking a fundamentally mechanistic response, Bruner sees it as something identified and recognized by the learner in his or her own individual and subjective way. Thus the stimulus, in a sense, becomes a personal thing, which individuals interpret (or misinterpret) and transform in their own fashion dependent upon their previous experiences, thoughts, and aspirations. Far from a response being purely mechanical, therefore, a stimulus can be ignored altogether if it is regarded as inappropriate, or it can be used to help construct internal hypotheses and models ('anticipatory categories' as Bruner calls them) which allow the prediction of future events and which in turn influence the way in which fresh stimuli are perceived and transformed. Similarly, the learner can also become increasingly independent of immediate reinforcement (R), and work towards long-term goals since such goals are essentially the anticipatory categories which he or she predicts will give the greatest satisfaction.

Before leaving this theoretical discusssion and moving on to more practical matters, we must say something about the manner in which the learner transforms incoming information. Bruner believes this transformation is linked to three methods of representation (i.e. systems for representing past experiences in the memory and utilizing them to deal with the present). The mature person is capable of using all three systems, and acquires them one by one in childhood at ages determined both by environmental opportunities and by maturation. These systems, in the order in which they are usually acquired, are labelled by Bruner, Goodnow and Austin (1965) the *enactive*, the *iconic* and the *symbolic* respectively (see also Chapter 3).

The *enactive* is a highly manipulative mode, using neither imagery nor words. It operates through action, and is apparent in, for example, motor skills, which we learn by doing and would find difficult to represent internally in terms of language or pictures.

The *iconic* mode is more developed in that it does use imagery, though still does not employ language. This imagery, which depends upon visual or other sensory organization, represents a concept without fully defining it. A child of five, for example, has mental and aural images of a wide range of things which allow him or her to recognize and use them, though the child would be unable to define or describe them in terms of words. Similarly an adult may, for example, have a clear picture of the workings of a piece of machinery, yet be hard put to it to give a verbal description of it.

Finally, the *symbolic* mode goes beyond action and imagery and employs representation through language. Such representation leads to thought and learning of a much more abstract and flexible kind, allowing the individual to engage in reflective thinking, to consider propositions as well as concrete examples, and to arrange concepts in a hierarchical structure. Symbolic representation can, of course, employ symbolic systems other than language, such as the symbolism used in mathematical and scientific logic.

Let us look at a simple example of how an adult might use each of the three modes. Suppose you are asked by a stranger the way from A to B. You might respond that you cannot explain the route to him, but you *can* accompany him and show him (enactive mode). Or you might say you cannot explain but you can draw him a map (iconic mode). Or you might say you can explain, and proceed to provide him with a verbal description (symbolic mode). Each of these three levels of explanation shows an increase in complexity, but each is valuable in its own way. Thus, depending on their degree of knowledge of a subject, and upon their command of the three modes, adults will use one or other of them as appropriate to process learning experiences and communicate the results to others. Small children, by contrast, will be restricted to the enactive mode, and will acquire the iconic and later the symbolic modes only as their powers of thinking develop.

Bruner (1966) considers that Skinner's operant conditioning model may be an adequate account of the way learning takes place when the learner is operating in the enactive mode, but that it tells us little about the iconic and symbolic modes. Whether this is correct or not, the teacher may well find that Bruner's description of learning is of more practical help than Skinner's when it comes to dealing with the problems of facilitating pupils' abstract learning, though as we see both have their place in helping the teacher plan learning experiences at different levels.

Finally, Bruner and Anglin (1973) consider that when we undertake such planning, or indeed when we think about any learning activity, we must consider three important variables, namely *the nature of the learner, the nature of the knowledge* to be learned, and *the nature of the learning process.* Although we are not concentrating simply upon Bruner in the remainder of this chapter, this threefold division forms a convenient and productive way of ordering our thinking on the practical aspects of learning, and accordingly we examine each of these variables in turn.

The nature of the learner

There are a number of factors within learners themselves that influence their ability to learn. Perhaps best known of these are cognitive factors such as intelligence and creativity, but there are many others of equal relevance to teachers with which they are often much less familiar. These include affective (i.e. emotional) factors, motivation, maturational factors, the learner's age, sex and social background, study habits and, above all, memory.

Affective factors

Anxiety. Strictly speaking, the term 'affective' refers only to the emotions, but psychologists tend to use it more broadly to cover all the things related to personality. Of particular importance amongst these from our point of view is the learner's level of anxiety. From general classroom experience the teacher soon discovers that a mild degree of anxiety can be a useful aid to learning, but that too much can have an inhibiting effect and interfere with it. Precisely what degree of anxiety motivates and what degree inhibits varies from child to child and from task to task (the more difficult the task, the more likely a high degree of anxiety is to interfere with it). One of the most potent sources of anxiety in children is the fear of failure. We see this particularly in exams where a great deal is often at stake, or in unhappy classrooms where teacher anger or ridicule from classmates is the usual consequence of failure. But some sources of anxiety are less obvious than this. Trown and Leith (1975) and Bennett (1976) produce evidence that suggests habitually anxious children may find the informal classroom, where they are often unsure of what is expected of them, more anxiety-provoking than a more formal, less ambiguous environment. Even in higher education, where habitual anxiety seems to be more of an advantage than it does at school (for the possible reason that it motivates students to make better use of their time outside lectures!), research (Franson, 1977) indicates individuals do better at specific learning tasks in the presence of low rather than high anxiety.

Self-esteem. Closely linked to anxiety is the question of self-esteem (i.e. the regard in which we hold ourselves). In a number of studies, Coopersmith (e.g. 1968) has demonstrated that children with high self-esteem consistently perform better than children of similar ability with low self-esteem (see pp. 236–238). They also set themselves higher goals, show less need for adult approval, are less deterred by failure, and have a more realistic view of their own abilities. High self-esteem seems to be due in large measure to parental attention, encouragement, physical affection, consistency, and democratic behaviour (i.e. to the things that make a child feel a valued, significant and responsible member of the family), but the teacher can help to give children confidence in their own abilities by giving them opportunities for success, by encouraging rather than censuring them when they are confronted by failure, and by demonstrating personal belief in their competence.

Extraversion–introversion. High and low self-esteem can be referred to as a dimension of personality. Another such dimension that has implications for learning is that of extraversion–introversion (see p. 175). Typically the extravert is an individual who enjoys change and variety and is orientated towards the external world of people and experiences, while the introvert is more concerned with stability and with the inner world of thoughts and feelings. All of us find our place at some point on this dimension between extreme extraversion and introversion, and research with children (Entwistle, 1972) suggests that success in primary school (where the emphasis is often upon group work and social activity) may be linked to some extent to extraversion, but that the balance swings towards introversion (more rapidly for girls than for boys) in the secondary school and even more markedly in higher education (where the emphasis is more upon solitary study habits). Further evidence that extraverts prefer unstructured and introverts structured learning environments comes from Rowell and Renner (1975), while Lewis and Ko (1973) demonstrate that introversion may be of most value in terms of school learning and achievement when it is combined with high levels of intelligence.

Note that the relative progress of introverts and extraverts at school level appears determined, partly at least, not so much by some quality in themselves as by the way in which we organize the learning environment for them. The inference for teachers is that just as they adopt different approaches for children of differing cognitive ability, so should they for children of differing personality, making sure that the introvert enjoys ample opportunities for quiet, structured work and the extravert for more active, socially orientated activities. In particular, they should avoid ordering the classroom (and personal value systems) so that only children with personalities similar to their own find it a suitable environment for learning.

Motivation

Satisfactory school learning is unlikely to take place in the absence of sufficient motivation to learn. I have already mentioned one possible source of motivation, namely anxiety, but there are many others. For convenience we can divide these into *intrinsic* forms of motivation, which come from the individual, and *extrinsic*, which are imposed upon him or her by the environment.

Intrinsic motivation. Taking intrinsic first, research studies suggest (e.g. Harlow and Harlow, 1962; Charlesworth, 1966) that there may be a natural curiosity drive in animals and man, a drive that does not appear to be directed towards an apparent material end, but is engaged in for itself and which prompts exploration and discovery from an early age. As children mature, so the response of others to this drive will help determine its development. If their attempts at exploration are met with adult disapproval and consequent frustration, then through operant conditioning such attempts are likely to become less frequent, and to be replaced by apathy or posssibly by random purposeless activity. If, on the other hand, they are frequently rewarded and reinforced by discovery, excitement, and adult approval they are likely to continue, and to become more directed and productive.

Closely linked to children's curiosity as a motivator is the degree of interest derived from a learning experience. If we had to say why some things capture a person's interest and others do not we would probably argue that the former have direct relevance to daily life. Either they amuse or take the mind off unpleasant thoughts, or they enable one to cope more effectively with the tasks and people one meets. As the individual grows older they may also help him or her towards self-understanding and the development of some coherent and consistent philosophy of life. But the problem with much school learning is that it appears to lack this relevance. It takes place in an environment distinct from the outside world, and much of what it teaches is a preparation for tasks way ahead in the future rather than in the present (or for tasks which the child meets only in school and nowhere else). By knowing both one's subject and one's children, the lively imaginative teacher can do much to make school work appeal directly to children's interests. Essentially, this means starting from what children already know, their curiosities, their ambitions, their problems, and showing how these relate to what is studied in school, and how such study can provide answers that will help them lead more satisfying lives.

Extrinsic motivation. Nevertheless, however stimulating the

133

teacher, there will always be occasions when the children's intrinsic motivation is insufficient and recourse has to be made to motivation of an extrinsic kind. Such motivation usually consists of marks, grades, school reports, tests, examinations and, of course, teacher approval. Success at such things helps build up children's prestige in their own eyes and in the eyes of teachers, peers, and parents, and thus assists the development of what is called *achievement motivation* (sometimes called need for achievement, or nAch for short). Children find success to be rewarding, and build up expectations which they have to work ever more purposefully to fulfil. But extrinsic motivation raises a number of important considerations at school level (quite apart from the danger that it may increase anxiety to an inhibiting level), the most important of which are summarized below.

- Instead of success, some children experience only failure (Fontana, 1984). This tends to produce either low self-esteem or a rejection of school as 'boring' and 'stupid' (i.e. a defensive attempt to convince everyone that 'I could do the work if it was worth doing'). In combatting the harmful effects of constant failure, the golden rule for the class teacher is to provide opportunities for success at however low a level. Through this experience of success the child gradually builds up a new self-image, and can be encouraged to set sights progressively higher.

- Sometimes motivation suffers because children have to wait too long for the results of their work. The operant conditioning model demonstrates that the longer the gap between performance and results the less efficient the learning, and the greater the likelihood that children will lose interest in the task and in how well they have done it.

- Competition between children is a useful motivator, though if it becomes too intense it can lead to bad feeling and the harmful effects of failure. A situation where children compete against themselves, steadily improving their performance, is often more helpful, as is a spirit of co-operation where children adopt group norms and work together to achieve them.

- Wherever the pressures of extrinsic motivation are too strong, children may resort to strategies like cheating, absenteeism, or feigned illness to avoid the consequences of failure.

Age, gender and social factors

Age variables in learning bring us to the concept of readiness. Such a concept has it that children are unable to undertake certain kinds of learning (whether it be simple skills like colour discrimination or more complex ones like classification and seriation) until their cognitive processes have matured to the appropriate levels. Piaget's well-known developmental stages of sensori-motor operations, concrete operations, and formal operations (with their various subdivisions) provide a context within which to study this concept (see pp. 43–50), as do the enactive, iconic, and symbolic systems of Bruner referred to above. Both Piaget and Bruner stress that learning is related closely to thinking. As children become more capable of complex thinking, so the nature of the learning they are able to undertake changes in a range of important and subtle ways. For the teacher the most important difference between the developmental psychologies of Piaget and Bruner is that although Bruner believes we acquire the stages proposed by his system in a set order and we continue to use each of them throughout life, Piaget argues that generally we progress beyond each stage as we acquire the next one above it. The teacher should study both the systems of Piaget and Bruner and ensure that learning experiences are presented to children in a form suited to their particular level of thinking. Thus, for example, a child in the early stages of concrete operations (Piaget) and capable only of iconic thinking (Bruner), should not be taught by methods that employ elaborate linguistic definitions, and highly abstract concepts. Bruner, in particular, stresses that a child is ready to tackle virtually any subject *provided* it can be presented in a form appropriate to his or her level of thinking.

Just as the ability to learn is influenced by age variables, so is it influenced by gender (see pp. 104–106). As we've seen, girls are generally more verbal than boys at school age, and have fewer reading, speech, and general backwardness problems (Davie *et al.*, 1972), while boys are more advanced in number skills. These verbal and speech differences tend to disappear by the age of 16, and boys between five and ten years old also appear twice as likely to show an increase in measured intelligence as girls. Throughout school life, however, girls tend to be better all-rounders, while boys are better at the subjects they enjoy and spurn those they do not. These gender-related differences could be in part genetic and in part related to the home (where girls are taught to be more dependent, and more concerned for parental approval), but research in the USA summarized by Mussen, Conger and Kagan (1984), suggests they could also be due to the fact that most early school teaching is done by women, and boys therefore associate school with feminine values. Where such teaching is done by men, the higher rate of backwardness and school rejection shown by boys apparently declines. Sadly, at all ages, girls tend to show lower self-esteem than boys, and may even artificially depress their levels of performance in conformity with an outmoded and unfortunate social conception of the inferiority of the female role.

A number of studies (e.g. Davie *et al.*, 1972) show that children from deprived social backgrounds lag behind children from more favoured environments in every aspect of school learning. Extended discussion of the reasons for this belong elsewhere, but obviously poorer economic circumstances, fewer facilities, less parental interest and encouragement, and a higher level of emotional upheaval will all play their part. It may be also that since schools, for better or worse, uphold the so-called middle-class values of thrift, respect for authority, professional ambition, politeness, and deferral of satisfaction (i.e. the willingness to put off short-term gain in the interest of long-term), then children who share these values are more likely to fit in successfully than those who do not.

Memory

Clearly, learning and memory are interdependent. At the practical level, some psychologists recognize the functional existence of two kinds of memory, short-term and long-term respectively (a further subdivision into immediate or sensory memory is of little practical importance to the teacher). All information received by the senses and to which we pay attention seems to enter short-term memory, but it can only be held there briefly and is either then forgotten (as when we look up a telephone number and forget it the moment we have dialled it) or transferred to long-term memory where it can be held more permanently (though it is still, of course, subject to forgetting). Obviously this transfer from short- to long-term memory is vital for learning. Available evidence suggests it involves some form of consolidation, typically a short pause during which the information is held consciously in the mind. Even after an interesting lesson children often remember little, probably because each piece of information is so quickly followed by the next that there is no time for consolidation. However, a number of strategies exist both for helping consolidation and for increasing the efficiency of long-term memory generally.

- *Pausing, repeating, and questioning*: each of these prompts children to dwell sufficiently upon material for transfer from short- to long-term to take place.

- *Relevance and interest*: children best remember those things that appeal directly to their own experience and feelings.

- *Attention span*: the process of concentrating on a task for any length of time is difficult for some children. Their attention wanders, and material is neither listened to nor remembered. A rough rule is that the teacher can expect to hold attention with a normal class at any one point, even with interesting material, for no more than a minute to a minute-and-a-half for each year of the children's age (e.g. 10–15 minutes for a class of ten year olds).

- *Practical use*: material that is put to practical use tends to be remembered better than material which is not.

- *Meaning*: material which is understood by the child is more memorable than material which is not.

- *Overlearning*: skills or knowledge that children go on practising and revising even after they have apparently got them off to perfection (i.e. material that is over-learned) persist better in the memory than material that they do not. This is especially true of material required to be remembered in a stressful situation (e.g. in the examination room, or on the concert platform).

- *Association*: unfamiliar material is remembered more effectively if it is associated with something familiar. Realization of the truth of this lies behind the old (and good) primary school adage that learning should always go from the known to the unknown; that is, that new material should be keyed in by reference to the association between it and something already known. Visual association is also particularly helpful: hence the importance of visual aids. Such aids need not necessarily be closely linked in terms of meaning to the material to be learned (witness the highly successful advertisements on television!), but they must be presented concurrently with this material so that a strong association is built up.

- *Recognition and recall*: there appears to be a functional difference between recognition (where we spot as familiar some stimulus physically presented to us) and recall (where we have to retrieve some word or fact from memory itself). Recognition appears to come more readily than recall (e.g. it is easier to recognize a face than to recall a name, to recognize a word in a foreign language than to recall it from memory), and in consequence, where practical, the teacher should aid children's recall by providing appropriate recognition cues.

So much for the factors that aid long-term memory. Now for those that appear to interfere with it. One of these, anxiety, has already been touched upon. Material that can readily be recalled in a relaxed state may prove elusive when in a stressed state. Two others of importance are known as *retro-active* and *proactive interference* respectively. Retroactive interference occurs when recently learned material appears to inhibit the recall of that learned earlier. The phenomenon appears to take place at all levels of learning and is apparent in students, for example, who cram for an examination and find the facts they learned the night before keep coming back when they try to recall those studied earlier in the week. Proactive interference, on the other hand, occurs when earlier learning seems to block the recall of later, as when, for example, children start learning a second foreign language and find themselves unable to remember the word they want because the equivalent in the first foreign language keeps coming to mind. We shall discuss ways of minimizing the risk of retroactive interference we deal with study habits below, but little can be done, within the confines of the classroom, to lessen proactive interference in the early stages of a new learning task. Such interference is more likely where the two subjects being studied share certain similarities, but it is generally less of a problem than retroactive interference and tends to disappear as the new material becomes more familiar and overlearning takes place.

Memory training. Finally, we come to the subject of memory training. Some teachers still assume they are 'training' children's memories when they require them to learn long pieces of poetry, as if the act of memorizing in itself effects improvement. There is no consistent evidence that it does. True, actors and others who spend their professional lives memorizing material seem to become extra good at it, but this comes from acquiring skills on how to memorize rather than from memorizing *per se*. Some of these skills have already been mentioned, and others are discussed in the next section, but some reference should be made here to *mnemonic* devices, which are devices created specifically to aid recall. They range from simple tricks like tying a knot in a handkerchief and short jingles like 'thirty days hath September . . .' to the elaborate devices used by stage 'memory men'. One such device is the so-called peg-word system, where the digits 1–10 (or more) are each associated with a rhyming word (e.g. 1 is a bun, 2 is a shoe, 3 is a tree, etc.). These associations are learned, and then facts to be memorized are associated with them in turn, preferably using visual imagery. Thus, for example, if we wished to learn (for some reason) the agricultural produce exported by New Zealand we could visualize first butter spread on a bun, second a lamb wearing shoes, and so on. Such devices are remarkably effective in the learning of lists of facts, but their use beyond this is limited.

Study habits

As children grow older and come to take more responsibility for their own learning, so good study habits become increasingly important. Some of these habits, like working in an environment free from distraction, are obvious while others, like overlearning, have already been covered. The remainder can be summarized as follows.

- *Realistic work targets*: realistic work targets, which the student plans in detail, are far more effective than impossibly ambitious or vague commitments. Ideally these targets should be expressed publicly, so that the student will stick to them to protect his or her prestige.

- *Rewards*: the student can build small rewards, as reinforces, into a work schedule, like a cup of coffee and a five-minute break after every hour of solid work. He or she should be strong enough to withhold the reward if it fails to be earnt.

- *Punctuality*: work should be started promptly at the appointed hour. This forestalls the elaborate (and plausible) strategies we each develop to put off actually sitting down at our desks and getting on with it.

- *Whole and part learning*: a new learning task should be read through first in its entirety, to get the general drift of it, before being broken down into small units and learned methodically.

- *Organizing material*: often textbooks (and lecturers) do not present material in a way which accords best with the learner's own experience and understanding. Time spent making notes and reorganizing the material into a more palatable form is never wasted. Similarly, time spent in ensuring that notebooks are attractive and neat is also time well spent. Scruffy notes, with pages out of order, are a powerful disincentive to learning. Revision notes should also contain all important references and information likely to be needed later. Many things that seem unforgettable at the time soon fade from memory, as does the meaning of the cryptic, home-made shorthand that many students employ in lectures!

- *Oral as well as visual memory*: revision material which a student tape-records and plays back is often more effectively remembered than material which is simply read.

- *Revision*: a programme of phased revision throughout the duration of a course is of far more value than an attempt to cram everything in during the final few weeks before an exam. Retroactive interference is the almost inevitable consequence of such cramming. Phased revision, however, leads to a growing mastery of the whole course as students work their way through it, with each new piece of knowledge being placed in its proper context. When it comes to final examination preparation students are therefore looking back over material that has already been overlearned. Revision is best done before material has actually been forgotten. This is known as maintenance revision.

The nature of the material to be learned

From time to time one still hears the view expressed that the experienced teacher can teach any subject, no matter how unfamiliar, simply by keeping one page ahead of the class in the textbook. The fallacy of this view is most clearly emphasized by Bruner (1966), who insists that the ultimate aim of teaching a subject is to help children understand its *structure*: that is, the basic principles that help define it, give it identity, and allow other things to be related to it meaningfully. Without a thorough specialist knowledge of the subject, the teacher can neither understand its structure nor help others achieve such an understanding. By knowing the structure of a subject the teacher is able to abstract from it material that is suited to the level of comprehension of the class, and that represents coherent, logical, and meaningful elements of the whole. This material can then be expressed in terms of clear learning objectives which state the purpose behind each particular lesson.

Emphasis upon the essential nature of such objectives, if learning is to be rendered efficient, also comes from operant conditioning theorists who argue that such objectives must be couched in behavioural language so that we can judge by the changes in student behaviour whether or not the desired learning has taken place. In other words, objectives must state clearly what a student should be able to do at the end of a successful lesson (see e.g. Pearson and Tweddle, 1984). The most detailed attempt to provide guidance on the preparation of learning objectives comes from the work of committees under the direction of Bloom (1956) and Krathwohl (1964) working respectively in the *cognitive* domain (the area of learning concerned with intellectual outcomes) and the *affective* domain (the area concerned with feelings and emotions). Bloom and Krathwohl and their colleagues have produced a set of general and specific categories that encompass all the learning outcomes that might be expected in the class or lecture room. These categories are arranged in hierarchical order, from the simplest to the most complex. Each of the higher categories includes the outcomes at the levels inferior to it (e.g. outcomes at level 2 will include those at level 1 also), and these are now summarized in ascending order, taking the cognitive domain first).

The cognitive domain

Categories in the cognitive domain (after Bloom et al., 1956)

1. **Knowledge:** simple knowledge of facts, of terms, of theories, etc.

2. **Comprehension:** an understanding of the meaning of this knowledge.

3. **Application:** the ability to apply this knowledge and comprehension in new and concrete situations.

4. **Analysis:** the ability to break material down into its constituent parts and to see the relationships between them.

5. **Synthesis:** the ability to reassemble these parts into a new and meaningful relationship, thus forming a new whole.

6. **Evaluation:** the ability to judge the value of material using explicit and coherent criteria, either of one's own devising or derived from the work of others.

Armed with this taxonomy teachers are able to examine whether or not they are keeping a balance between their expectations. For example, are they placing too great an emphasis upon expectations connected with level 1 of the taxonomy (e.g. by concentrating the attention of the class upon the memorization of facts and figures) at the expense of the more complex outcomes? More important still, are they able to separate educational *outcomes* (i.e. the behaviour expected of children at the end of the learning task) from educational *processes* (i.e. the behaviour expected of children – and of the teacher – during the task itself)? Educational processes are, of course, a major concern, and these are dealt with in the next section, but the tendency to confuse these processes with outcomes is a prime cause of the vague and well-nigh valueless objectives with which many teachers and student teachers preface their lesson notes. For example, a teacher may state that the objective is to demonstrate to a class a particular skill (whether it be in science, craft, sport or whatever). But this is not really a learning objective at all. It is simply a statement of what the teacher plans to do, and therefore belongs more properly under the category of process (or methodology). It fails to say why the skill is to be demonstrated, and how children's behaviour is going to be changed as a consequence. Instead of a mistated objective of this kind, therefore, the teacher should have said that the objective was one or more of the following (dependent upon the level of Bloom's taxonomy at which the work is planned). At the end of the lesson the class should be able to:

1. **recognize and identify** the various elements involved in the particular skill (these elements would then be specified: this is an objective at the *knowledge* level);

2. **define** these elements and to know the part they play in the particular skill (an objective at the *comprehension* level);

3. **practise** the skill itself (an objective at the *application* level);

4. **describe** what is happening – and why – during this practice (an objective at the *analysis* level);

5. **utilize** elements of this skill in solving a particular novel problem (an objective at the *synthesis* level);

6. **assess** the degree of success achieved in this solution and to propose improvements (an objective at the *evaluation* level).

Note that if we were using objectives at more than one level we would not necessarily always deal with them in their hierarchical order. To do so would lead to formal and stereotyped lessons. We might prefer, at times, instead of first presenting the class with knowledge and then going on to the practical activities, to start by confronting the class with the problem and then feed in the knowledge (and the comprehension) as the objective necessity for it arose during the course of problem solving. Note also that the verbs in the extended example above of how to write objectives are of an essentially unequivocal behavioural kind. Bloom and other workers in the field lay great stress upon the need for this. It is all very well for teachers to write that they want the class 'to appreciate' a particular thing, or 'to become proficient' at something else, but what do these terms actually mean when translated into directly observable changes in children's behaviour? Instead of such imprecision, Bloom proposes examples of the kind of concrete verbs that should be used, with appropriate variations dependent upon the level at which we are working. Thus if we were working at level 1 (knowledge) we would express objectives in terms of class members being able to state, or list, or identify, or reproduce; at level 2 (comprehension), we would talk of their being able to explain, or distinguish, or infer, or give examples; at level 3 (application), we would expect them to be able to demonstrate, or operate, or show, or solve, or use; at level 4 (analysis), to describe, or break down, or discriminate, or select; at level 5 (synthesis), to combine or compile, or design, or create, while at level 6 (evaluation), we would expect behaviour that would show them able to appraise, to contrast, to criticize and to justify.

The affective domain

The categories in the affective domain are rather different from those in the cognitive, and can be taken to refer not just to classroom learning but to all those values and attitudes that students derive from the institution of which they are members. Thus the affective domain must not be seen as something quite separate from the cognitive. The affective categories advanced by Krathwohl and his colleagues are summarized below, and this time we include in each of the categories the kind of concrete verbs in which objectives might be expressed.

Categories in the affective domain (after Krathwohl et al., 1964)

1. *Receiving* (willingness to attend): the student listens, or asks, or sits erect, or looks at.

2. *Responding* (willingness to participate actively): the student answers or complies, or helps, or obeys, or reads, or writes.

3. *Valuing* (the ability to assign value to things; this differs from evaluation in the cognitive domain in that it involves attitudes and moral and social judgements rather than the application of the specific principles of a given subject or discipline); the student joins, or justifies, or prefers, or commits him or herself or shares.

4. *Organization* (the ability to bring separate values together and compare and relate them): the student modifies, or relates, or organizes, or accepts responsibility.

5. *Characterization* by a value or value complex (the ability to take the organizational level a step further and build up a coherent value system or philosophy of life which informs all of one's behaviour): the student serves, or acts, or influences, or shows self-awareness.

The psychomotor domain

The committees that met under Bloom and Krathwohl originally intended to produce a taxonomy of educational objectives in the third major domain, the *psychomotor*, in addition to those produced in the cognitive and affective domains. This work was never finished, but various attempts have been made to remedy this omission, the best known probably being that by Simpson (1972). The psychomotor domain is concerned with motor skills, such as those used in sport, in operating machinery and equipment, and in manipulative exercises such as handwriting. Simpson's taxonomy, in ascending order, consists of: *perception* (the acquisition by the senses of cues to guide motor activity); *set* (the readiness to take a particular kind of action); *guided response* (the ability to copy an instructor or to be guided by knowledge of results); *mechanism* (the ability to carry out simple movement patterns with confidence and proficiency); *complex overt responses* (the ability to carry out more complex patterns with smooth and accurate control); *adaptation* (the ability to modify established movement patterns to meet special situations and problems); and finally *origination* (the ability to create new movement patterns).

It would be wrong to suggest that all psychologists and curriculum theorists interested in school-based learning agree that with the help of the above (or any other) taxonomies it is necessarily possible to write specific objectives for all learning situations. Stenhouse (1970) argues, for example, that the teacher cannot plan in advance the precise impact that great literature is likely to have upon young minds and behaviour, and this argument is perfectly valid. Indeed, it would not be a good thing if the teacher could. Great literature is an intensely personal experience and it is not the teacher's job to circumscribe this experience by imposing too many of his or her own reactions upon the class. Nevertheless, even with great literature the teacher should have a good idea of the *kinds of responses* from children that can be regarded as appropriate and those that cannot. He or she will expect, to give an instance, that even those who reject the literature will be able to show some knowledge and comprehension of it, that they will be able to analyse the plot, the characterization and perhaps the techniques that it contains, and that they will be able to offer some considered evaluations and take part in informed debate.

Assessment

The preparation of specific learning objectives plays an important part in helping the teacher to structure the learning experience and evaluate its success. Such evaluation, however, involves more than teachers sitting back and observing whether or not the children evidence the kind of behaviour hoped for. Often they will want to offer children specially devised opportunities for such behaviour, and this brings us to a consideration of assessment in its various forms.

The first point to stress is that the teacher's choice of assessment techniques will be strongly influenced by the level (in terms of the taxonomies discussed above) at which learning is intended to take place. All too frequently, particularly in arts and social science subjects, assessment simply takes the form of a written essay, which may be ideal for gauging progress at the more complex cognitive and affective levels (such as synthesis and evaluation, or valuing and organization), but which is a very limited measure of such things as knowledge and comprehension. It may also be that students

144

have little idea of the kind of essay likely to appeal to a particular teacher, or the precise meaning of a given title, or of the criteria which will be employed in marking it. Thus their essays may be a poor reflection of the actual learning that has taken place, and of the use to which they can put this learning in environments other than the classroom. The value of essays in assessment can be increased considerably if teachers pay attention to these points, making their expectations clear to their students and explaining the details of their marking schedules.

The main alternative to the essay, in the cognitive domain at least, is the so-called objective test, each of whose items carries only a single right answer. The principles behind the construction of such a test can be simply stated.

(a) From the objectives of the various lessons that the teacher wishes to assess, a list is made of the student behaviour that represented the desired outcomes of these lessons. This behaviour yields the general area to be tested.

(b) From the contents of these lessons a list is made of the knowledge and comprehension (or whatever) that were expected to figure in this behaviour. For example, the lesson objective may have stated that the student should be able to quote the terms or the parts of speech or the procedures associated with a particular skill, while the lesson content will have stated what these various things actually were. This knowledge and comprehension yield the precise subject matter to be tested.

(c) From these two points, a schedule is drawn up of the relative importance of each of the various items of subject matter to be tested. This provides guidance on the number of test questions that will be constructed for each item.

(d) Finally, the test questions are prepared. In an objective test these are usually of the multiple-choice variety, with the student being asked which of a range of possible answers is the correct one: for example, 'The Theory of Association was first advanced by: Herbart/William James/Francis Galton/none of these.' However, some operant conditioning theorists claim that in getting a multiple-choice question wrong, a student may unwittingly form a mental association between the question and the incorrect response. To avoid this, it is sometimes suggested that the question should be left to stand on its own, without the addition of a range of possible answers. The reader will note at once that in this form such a question would be testing recall, whereas when presented in its multiple choice guise it is testing recognition.

It is often objected that tests of this kind take much longer to construct than does a test of the essay type. There is no gainsaying this, but on the other hand they are much quicker to mark, and teachers are left with the satisfaction of knowing that they have adequately tested the knowledge, comprehension and application that they set out to test. Further, students are motivated to acquire this knowledge since they know it is to be comprehensively tested, rather than fractionally sampled as in an essay. They are also left with the reassurance that good marks really do mean that they know the field and are equipped with the basic grammar of their subject.

The nature of the learning process

The learning act. Consideration of the practical aspects of the learning process brings us to the question of teaching methods and techniques. Many of these are specific to the particular subject or subjects being taught, and therefore lie outside the scope of a text in psychology. However, there are a number of general points to which we can draw attention. Gagné (1974), who draws upon both Skinner's operant conditioning model and (though to a lesser extent) the kind of conceptual model associated with Bruner, suggests that the learning act typically consists of a chain of eight events, some internal to the learner and others external. These are, in their usual order of occurrence:

1. **motivation** (or expectancy)
2. **apprehending** (the subject perceives the material and distinguishes it from the other stimuli competing for his or her attention)
3. **acquisition** (the subject codes the knowledge)
4. **retention** (the subject stores the knowledge in short- or long-term memory)
5. **recall** (the subject retrieves the material from memory)
6. **generalization** (the material is transferred to new situations, thus allowing the subject to develop strategies for dealing with them)
7. **performance** (these strategies are put into practice)
8. **feedback** (the subject obtains knowledge of results).

Where there is a failure in the learning process, Gagné argues, it will take place at one of these eight levels, and it is the task of the teacher to ascertain which. Motivation has already been discussed at some length, but Gagné considers that the teacher can help avoid failure at the other levels by bearing in mind that a learning sequence should consist of five steps:

- Step 1: learners are informed of the performance to be

146

expected of them at the end of the learning experience. This is best done by presenting them with a list of the teacher's objectives. Neglect of this basic step, suggests Gagné, is a frequent cause of learning failure. Learners are unsure of teacher expectations and thus unable to monitor their own progress adequately.

- Step 2: learners are questioned in a way that requires a restatement of earlier concepts upon which the current learning depends.

- Step 3: the teacher provides cues that help learners put together the current learning as a chain of concepts in the correct order.

- Step 4: learners are questioned in a way that allows them to demonstrate concrete applications of their learning.

- Step 5: learners are questioned in a way that allows them to make statements of the rule or rules that they have learned.

Note that the 'questions' referred to in Steps 2, 4 and 5 can take the form of project work and discovery learning as well as simple verbal presentations on the part of the teacher. Such project and discovery work is also likely to incorporate Step 3, and here we can turn from Gagné to Bruner (1966) for further helpful comment. Bruner believes that far too often when providing learners with the cues mentioned in Step 3 we deal only in the 'middle language' of our subject: that is in the facts, formulae, techniques, ideas and so on developed by other people. Learners are not allowed to discover these facts for themselves. True, if we do allow them to discover these facts for themselves they are not 'new' discoveries in any absolute sense, but this, suggests Bruner, is not the point. The point is that the facts are new for *them*, and by going through the discovery process they are much better able to grasp the concepts and the structure that underlie them.

Discovery learning. By allowing the learner to use the discovery method, Bruner argues, we are also closing the gap between elementary and advanced knowledge. After all, the university professor and the higher degree student employ the discovery method, and if we deny it to learners functioning at a less exalted level we are preventing them from really experiencing the subject they are attempting to study. An academic subject is defined not just by the knowledge that it has amassed over the years, but also by the methods used to amass it. If we teach merely the middle language of the subject we are teaching the one without the other, and hindering genuine understanding on the part of the learner.

Bruner is aware that too often discovery learning is used as an excuse for vague and haphazard goings on, with neither teacher nor class very certain of what is supposed to be happening. This is one of the reasons for his emphasis upon objectives. The teacher should hold the *ends* of learning constant, while providing a scaffolding within which the *means* can be varied to suit the level of thinking and of conceptualization of the class. For example, when teaching the working of an electrical circuit the teacher will be quite clear on the principles that have to be learned, yet instead of simply listing these principles to the class he or she will present them with the necessary wires, bulbs, and batteries and set them a problem which can only be solved when they are connected up correctly. Having done these connections, the class will then be expected to state the rules that can be derived from the experience (Step 5 of Gagné's learning sequence above). It is sometimes objected that this approach is less suited to arts and social science subjects than to mathematical, technical and scientific subjects, but here Bruner stresses the value of *simulation exercises*. Such exercises present the learner with imaginary problems designed to mimic those faced, for example, by historical figures, economists and social workers, and ask him or her to produce solutions. These solutions are then compared with genuine case histories, and comparisons and contrasts are drawn which promote debate, understanding and the efficient workings of memory.

Reflective thinking. Naturally it is not possible to carry out all classroom learning by means of the activities advocated by Bruner. However, whatever the nature of the lesson, teachers can ensure that the questions directed at the class (whether verbal or in the form of written exercises) contain a fair proportion designed to prompt the kind of reflective thinking that leads to discovery. Too often questions invite only middle language answers, such as 'What is the population of Great Britain?'; 'What is the formula for water?'; 'In what metre is this poem written?' Such questions are useful at their own level, but they demand nothing from students other than a single answer delivered in the form in which they first heard or read it. On the other hand, *reflective* questions (or *springboard* questions, as they are often called) usually contain an element of controversy or contradiction. They introduce material which may not fit in with the student's knowledge or beliefs, and which therefore stimulates him or her to produce an answer which is more personal and original. Good springboard questions often contain the word 'why'. For example, 'The north and south poles are equidistant from the equator yet it is colder at the south. Why?' 'Christianity teaches you to love your enemies, yet many of the most terrible massacres have been carried out in its name. Why is this?' 'The higher an aeroplane flies, the nearer it gets to the sun, yet the colder the air becomes. Why?' Springboard questions can also take the form of statements, such as 'You have to be unscrupulous to succeed in business', 'Milton was a greater poet than Shakespeare', or 'There is no such thing as a scientific law'.

Creating springboard questions is, of course, best done by a teacher who is an expert in the subject being taught, and who knows its structure and its challenges. Their essential feature is that, by making students reflect upon some critical aspect of the subject being studied, they help them understand the subtle ways in which the subject works, the relationship between cause and effect, and the methods of procedure and enquiry. Thus they are helped actively to advance their understanding of the subject and of the structure that underlies it. As a consequence, not only do they acquire knowledge, they acquire a grasp of the way in which that knowledge is generated, and of how it may be generalized to solve new problems.

By contrast, *programmed learning* concentrates upon providing learners with a simple unit of knowledge and then testing retention of it. It owes much to the operant conditioning techniques of Skinner, with their emphasis upon learning by small steps and immediate knowledge of results. An example of an item from a programme on electrical wiring illustrates the principles behind this form of instruction.

Stage 1 (information): in wiring a 13 amp plug the brown wire is connected to the live terminal.

Stage 2 (question): what colour wire is connected to the live terminal of a 13 amp plug?

Stage 3 (response):
   A. the blue
   B. the brown
   C. the green and yellow

Stage 4 (answer): the brown

Students look at each of these stages in turn, and if they get the answer wrong turn back and re-read Stage 1. Programmed learning is a vast subject in its own right, and we have no space to deal with it fully here. However, since the principles behind it are so simple teachers can easily select programmes suitable for the class or, indeed, construct their own programmes which children can work through individually.

Programmed learning theorists criticize discovery learning because it allows children to make frequent mistakes, thus setting up incorrect associations which may persist in the child's mind. Advocates of discovery learning, on the other

149

hand, claim that mistakes are an essential part of learning, because they prompt learners to ask questions of their own in an attempt to discover why and how they went wrong. Too often the teacher instils in children a fear of making mistakes and of showing their failure to understand, and this leads to conservative and stereotyped patterns of learning which inhibit reflective thinking and a genuine grasp of the principles upon which knowledge is based. Doubtless readers will want to make up their own minds on these matters, but a crucial consideration could be the level at which learning is intended to take place, with programmed learning proving particularly effective where the objective is to impart straightforward knowledge, and the reflective springboard approach where the aim is to stimulate thinking and further enquiry.

Managing the learning process

Precision teaching

In addition to an understanding of how children learn, good teachers also understand the need for good management techniques if this learning is to be maximized. One approach to good management goes under the general heading of *precision teaching* (Raybould, 1984). Precision teaching stresses the need for the continual measurement and evaluation of learning, thus providing teachers with the necessary feedback to modify and develop classroom procedures as appropriate. Teachers are thus acting somewhat like managers of a successful commercial enterprise, continually monitoring the quality of their work and subjecting it to constant development and improvement. We must not push the commercial analogy too far (children and teachers are human beings not merchandise and machinery), but there is no doubt that by managing learning, teachers can make it both more efficient and more pleasant.

Precision teaching suggests there are five key questions the teacher must ask if good management is to take place:

- It is the pupil on the right task in terms of interests and abilities?
- What level of performance should be expected?
- Is the pupil learning?
- Is the pupil learning quickly enough? (This is particularly important if there is lost ground to be made up.)
- What should be done if the pupil is not learning or is not learning quickly enough?

In order to answer these questions, the teacher must be able to carry out four particular strategies.

1. *Specify* in advance the nature of the learning task to be offered to children (i.e. specify necessary learning objectives) and the level of performance that will indicate their mastery of it.

2. *Record pupil performance* regularly and systematically. This requires the use of frequent assessment probes (the term 'probe' is used instead of 'test' to emphasize that children are not being judged; the teacher's intention is simply to identify what has been learnt and what remains to be done). The probes should always be presented to the class in an informal and unstressful way.

3. *Record teaching arrangements* in relation to performance. This makes it possible for teachers to evaluate their own performance. It enables them to see what methods worked and what methods did not.

4. *Analyse the data* regularly to see what changes are needed. This is part of the quality control and product improvement aspect of the teacher's role. By retaining and further developing successful methods, and eliminating or improving less successful ones, teachers make their work increasingly appropriate to the children they teach and the subject matter they propose to teach.

Teachers who are not methodical in their keeping of records and in their assessment of children's progress and of their own methodology quickly make life difficult both for themselves and for their class. Lack of organization, together with the omissions and inadvertent repetitions to which this lack of organization gives rise, produce an inefficient and ineffective learning environment, and one in which the teacher has little knowledge or understanding of children's individual learning difficulties. Not surprisingly, teachers who operate in such an inefficient environment run an increased risk of class control problems, and an increased risk of forfeiting the respect and co-operation of their children.

The 'slow learner'

Most psychologists and many teachers are increasingly unhappy about labelling children with such terms as 'slow learner' and strenuously resist any such attempts, preferring rather to understand all children in terms of their special needs (and strengths). Children are individuals, and each of them works at his or her own pace. Thus each child at some point or other is likely to be 'slow' when compared with classmates, and the label 'slow learner' therefore does not of itself tell us very much. It may mean simply that a child is falling behind the other members of what is a very able group, or that a child is slow at grasping new work (but tends to catch up later). For practical purposes, however, 'slow learner' is usually taken to mean any child who is consistently unable to cope with the work of his or her age group to the satisfaction of teachers. Far from being pejorative, the earlier a child who is having difficulties of this sort is diagnosed and offered appropriate help the better. As was stressed very firmly earlier, consistent failure in itself has a handicapping effect upon children because it lowers their esteem in their own eyes and in those of their classmates and teachers, and usually leads to reduced self-confidence, reduced aspirations, and often reduced effort as children resign themselves to the belief that they just 'can't do' the required work.

Having identified a child as a 'slow learner', the next task of the school is to have this identification confirmed by the use of attainment tests, and to establish why the child is having difficulty. Often an intelligence test is useful at this point, administered together with other diagnostic instruments by the educational psychologist. Viewed against the child's attainment age scores, the results of this administration help place the child in one or other of the two main categories of slow learning, namely children with *low or very low IQs* (sometimes described as 'mentally dull') and those who are *retarded in achievement*. The child with a low IQ is by definition one with limited intellectual endowment, and is unlikely ever to develop into a 'bright' child whatever educational provision is offered. Children who are retarded in achievement, on the other hand, are those whose intellectual endowment appears to be within or above the normal range, but whose speed of work is held up by some factor or factors in their background. Such children, with appropriate help, are well capable of making up lost ground and rejoining their classmates. These two categories need now to be looked at separately and in more detail.

Children with low IQ scores

Many teachers and psychologists are put off by the label 'low IQ' (or 'mentally dull'), and for the best motives strenuously resist having it placed upon a child. (I am talking here about teachers of young children, since it is usually early in a child's career that such a diagnosis is made.) However, as already indicated, the sooner a child who comes in this category is recognized as such, the better the chances of avoiding the psychological damage that constant failure can bring.

Some children with low IQs are eventually categorized as *educationally subnormal* (ESN), and transferred to special units where the ratio of pupils to teachers is lower and where the latter are specially trained for their remedial role. In terms of measured IQ, ESN children usually fall within the 50–80 range. Below 50, the child is usually categorized as *severely subnormal* (ESN(S), more commonly referred to now as SSN), and it is unlikely that the teacher will encounter any children in this category in the normal school. Usually the handicaps shown by SSN children (which often include physical handicaps) are so severe that they are diagnosed before the child

152

reaches school age, and he or she is placed in a special school designed to cope with these particular problems. An intermediate category ESN(M), with the 'M' standing for 'moderately severe handicap' is now also recognized and usually covers children in the IQ range of 50–70. Only some 3.7 children per thousand fall into the SSN category, whereas some ten per thousand fall within the broad 'mentally dull' category.

Children with low IQs, then, have special needs and require special help. Recently, however, it has been argued with increasing conviction that for children simply classed as ESN (i.e. not as ESN(M) or SSN), this help is better provided within the normal school than in special schools. One of the problems of special schools, no matter how good, is that children become labelled, in their own eyes as well as in those of adults and other children, as being 'different' from their fellows in an undesirable way. This kind of stigma places additional burdens upon children and their parents, and it is ironic that it should arise from the way in which we organize the child's formal education, since the purpose of such education after all is to enhance children and not to handicap them further.

Remedial classes within the normal school, the argument has it, go some way towards lessening the stigma of being of 'low IQ', particularly if such children work with the rest of the school wherever possible, and only join the remedial group for certain subjects. More recently, the trend has gone even further towards integrating 'low IQ children' into normal classes for all subjects. True, they may still be labelled to some extent by their fellows, but it is up to the school and its general system of values and behaviour to see that this labelling is kept to a minimum. Perhaps the most important variable here is to let everyone see that such children are prized by the school. This means they should be given positions of trust and responsibility, that their expertise and qualities as individuals should be praised at every opportunity, and that they should be taught by teachers who are respected and admired by all school members and who take a full part in running the school and helping with general school activities. However, where remedial groups do exist they should at no time be treated as units 'set apart' from the rest; for example, by putting them in a separate part of the school buildings, by giving them different break or lunch periods, by timetabling them separately for games or sports activities, by denying them access to school facilities such as laboratories and workshops, or by refusing them subject options which are given freely to the rest of the school. Obviously, in many of these situations children with low IQs may need special help and supervision, but they must be seen by all (themselves included) as equal members of the school.

Teaching children with low IQ scores

A detailed discussion of the teaching skills necessary for use with children with low IQ scores lies outside the scope of this book, but in every context it is vital for the teacher to keep in mind that these children, as emphasized earlier in this chapter, must be allowed to experience success at however low a level. The experience of success itself is the important thing, rather than the absolute standard achieved. Through such experience children gain in confidence, escape from the 'can't do it' syndrome, and are encouraged gradually to raise their sights until they are performing up to their maximum potential. The teacher must also remember that in Piagetian terms (see pp. 43–50) children with low IQ scores are usually operating at conceptual levels below their chronological ages. They may never, for example, reach the stage of formal operations, and this means it is valueless to expect them to grapple with abstract concepts, or to grasp the principles behind sets and categories simply because these are crystal clear to the teacher. Often it is difficult for the teachers, if they have no special training for remedial work, to avoid becoming irritated if a child seems particularly obtuse in the face of an apparently simple idea. But such irritation only makes matters worse, with all concerned ending up frustrated and with a sense of defeat. Teachers should instead remind themselves that children usually learn *if they can*. It can be little fun to sit in a classroom and fail, especially if one's peers find no difficulty in forging ahead. Where the child experiences particular problems, therefore, teachers need first to look at the way in which material is being presented, and to ask whether this is appropriate to his or her level of thought.

With their lower developmental stage of conceptualization and their problems with abstract ideas, children with low IQ scores profit particularly from practical activities. They like to be doing things, not only art and craft and domestic skills but also music, where a low IQ does not appear to be a necessary barrier to high levels of performance. They may also enjoy working outdoors with animals and with plants, and taking part in sport and physical activities. In fact, the curriculum can be made so interesting and exciting that children will come to take a particular pleasure in school, and see themselves as performing there relevant and socially useful skills. The absence of examination pressures, and the more favourable teacher–pupil ratios within remedial groups, can also mean that these children come to have a much closer and less formal relationship with teachers than do children engaged in more academic work, and the realization that they are liked and respected by teachers can further enhance the growth of their self-esteem and self-confidence.

This close relationship also means that children's opportunities for linguistic communication with verbally fluent and articulate adults are greatly increased. I have already stressed in earlier chapters the critical importance of language to cognitive development, and I need only remind the reader here that far too often children of low IQ, by virtue of the fact that they may come from verbally unstimulating homes, mix mostly with other verbally retarded children, and experience reading and comprehension difficulties, usually have few chances outside the classroom for improving their linguistic skills. Thus the teacher carries a particular responsibility for providing such children with good examples of appropriate verbal communication, and for encouraging them to respond in kind. Good linguistic development will not only help the children's cognitive growth, it will help them avoid the frustration of being unable to communicate feelings and ideas in a form comprehensible to those around them. It is this frustration that lies behind a good many of the behaviour problems that children with low IQ scores often develop.

Children retarded in achievement

I have specified that the child who is categorized as retarded in achievement is one whose failings do not appear to be due to low intelligence. Generally such children have IQs from about 80 upwards, and may even fall into the very superior category. The teacher's first task, therefore, once it has been established that such children do not belong to the 'low IQ' category, is to isolate the factor or factors responsible for their retardation. The school psychological service, who will assess the children and provide statements of their abilities and problems, together with social workers and school welfare officers, will be of help here, but it is the teacher who usually remains the person who knows individual children best, and his or her role in this diagnostic procedure is therefore a crucial one. The major factors likely to lead to retardation in achievement are covered below.

1. **Physical problems**. The child may suffer from some ailment which has led to long absences from school, or which renders it difficult for him or her to perform certain of the motor skills associated with learning. Ailments in the second category (e.g. poor sight, poor hearing, bronchial problems, or mild brain damage affecting motor co-ordination) may have gone unrecognized for some years, even by the child him or herself. Alternatively, in the case of stammering or stuttering for example, they may be all too painfully obvious, and may hold the unfortunate child up to ridicule from other children or (unforgivably) from teachers themselves.

2. **Personal problems**. These could include such relatively

simple factors as frequent changes of school or of class, or more complex ones such as limited attention span and high distractability. Frequent changes of schooling lead to problems of adjusting to new teachers, new syllabuses and new teaching methods, and to new peer groups and surroundings. Such changes, in addition to the cognitive strains they impose, leave children feeling emotionally insecure and vulnerable. They have to re-establish their status in their new environment, prove their competence to strange teachers, learn new rules and standards (both formal and informal), and make new friends. Small wonder that they are often left struggling, and it is the teacher's job to ensure that they are integrated into the life of the school as soon as possible. This means ensuring that they get relevant textbooks and exercise books at once, that trouble is taken to find out what they already know about current work and to give them guidance on where some catching up is necessary, that immediate interest is shown in them as people, and that they are warmly welcomed in front of the class and sympathetic children asked (formally or informally as appropriate) to show them around and see to it that they are not left on their own at break and lunch times.

Limited attention span and high distractability are not dealt with so easily. Children faced with these difficulties find it extra hard to settle to work, to concentrate for any length of time, and therefore to undertake learning tasks successfully. In some cases, where the distractability is of a particularly marked kind and accompanied by almost constant physical activity, children are called *hyperactive*, and it is recognized that they present particular problems. At one time it was thought that such hyperactivity was a symptom of brain damage, but it is by no means clear that this is necessarily the case. Children obviously vary innately in their activity levels, and problems are sometimes caused by the fact that a particularly active child is made to keep unnaturally quiet at home or school, leading to frustration and explosions of random and undirected activity. The remedy with such children is simple. Too much should not be expected of them in the way of passive behaviour. Given free range for their activities and their energies, and provided with as much interesting and stimulating material as possible, their attention span gradually increases as they grow older, and they show themselves well able to cope with school and its demands.

With some children, however, the picture is not as straightforward, and there seems to be a genuine psychological problem that may need specialist help. Typically such children (and they are the only ones who genuinely merit the term hyperactive) are retarded from an early age in important skill areas such as language and reading, and show an inability to concentrate (or even to stay in one place) for any but the very

156

briefest interval, placing great strains upon parents and upon nursery and infant teachers. Usually these strains become so severe that in the end, after specialist diagnosis, the child may be recommended for transfer to a special school. In such a school the child is given more scope for restless behaviour without the fear that he or she may be disrupting the rest of the class, and often special schooling is therefore the best solution for all concerned.

Typically, however, if children are not made to feel excess frustration or guilt as a result of their behaviour, hyperactivity tends to lessen as they grow older, and may disappear as a major problem by about the age of eight or so. Retardation in speech and reading may also disappear, often even before this age is reached, allowing the child eventually to be transferred back to normal schooling. It is as if hyperactivity is due to some neurological immaturity that eventually corrects itself, and if children are not allowed to develop psychological problems or to fall too far behind their peers in those areas where they need to develop competence, then their long-term educational prospects may be good.

3. **Environmental problems**. These include a poor or depressed background in which the child has no encouragement to read or to use language, in which there are no facilities for homework or private study, and in which the values of the school are rejected and perhaps even held up to ridicule. There may also be cases of actual physical deprivation (such as shortage of food or extreme shortage of sleep), of physical or sexual abuse, or of outright physical rejection, perhaps brought about by a broken home or by alcoholism in one or both parents. These issues have been discussed in Chapter 1, and the task of the teacher in relation to them outlined.

4. **Emotional problems**. The cause and treatment of emotional problems will be dealt with more fully in Chapter 12 and again when we come to look at discipline and class control in Chapter 13. Mild emotional problems can, however, be caused by any or all of the three categories of problems discussed above. They can also arise from the fact that children may feel disliked or rejected by their classmates or teachers, or even because they happen to take a rooted dislike to one teacher in particular and find it hard to remain in his or her class (such apparently irrational over-reaction is not uncommon, particularly at adolescence). This dislike can stem from a real or imagined injustice, or from some mannerism of speech or dress on the teacher's part. Alternatively children may develop an exaggerated fondness for a teacher, and become too eager to please, or too hurt by the slightest suggestion of criticism. More rarely, children may feel acute physical fear of a teacher, and go in dread of his or her lessons

and teaching subject, and find that even the general school atmosphere becomes a source of disturbance and anxiety to them.

Whatever their cause, emotional problems can become a major hindrance to learning, and if allowed to go untreated can lead to a syndrome in which children and their teachers become increasingly alienated from each other. Such children's parents, disappointed by lack of progress in school, may unwittingly make matters worse by bringing pressure upon them to work harder, thus leaving the children with the feeling that no one understands their difficulties nor takes an interest in helping solve them. Thus what perhaps started out as only a minor problem, which could readily have been handled given the appropriate action on the part of those concerned, becomes a major crisis which perhaps permanently affects children's chances of making a success of their school careers.

Helping children retarded in achievement

Having diagnosed the reasons for a child's retardation in achievement, the teacher is part way towards providing the solutions. Usually allowance can readily be made for physical problems, with the child being referred to the relevant medical authorities, moved nearer to the front of the class, given extra time to complete work or extra help to catch up with what has been missed and so on. Frequent changes of school and/or of class teachers can also be made good with appropriate remedial assistance and encouragement. Where the problem is environmental teachers cannot, as we saw in Chapter 1, put things right single-handed. What they can do, however, is to convince the child that the school is there to help. Even if children appear to reject this help, it is nevertheless important to their self-esteem to know that the school considers them worth bothering about and is anxious not to make their lives any more difficult. Children who feel at odds with both home and school are likely to develop rapidly into the maladjusted category, and present extreme behaviour disorders in addition to retardation in achievement.

Where teachers suspect that their own behaviour may in part be the cause of slow learning in one or more members of the class (and there is no need to feel shame on this score; we cannot expect to be perfect all the time any more than we can expect this of the child) it is a useful exercise to tape-record all or part of a lesson or, better still, videotape it if this is possible. By studying the tape teachers may be surprised to hear how complex (or unstimulating or confused) some of their questions to the class are, or how little praise or encouragement they give to certain members of it, or how many irritating little mannerisms they have developed or are developing. Chapter 11 looks at these matters in more detail, but the point to be stressed here is that the more teachers know about what is actually going on between themselves and the individual members of the class (as opposed to what merely seems to be going on), the better they will be able to assess their own role in slow learning, and take steps to remedy it where these are seen to be necessary.

Finally, at no point should slow learning of any kind be seen exclusively as the child's own problem. It is the school's problem, and all associated with the child are equally involved. If the child fails to respond to help, then questions must be asked as to whether this is after all the most appropriate kind of help, whether causal factors have been correctly identified, whether the child perceives the help in the same light as do teachers (the child may, for example, see any extra work he or she has been given as a punishment rather than as a learning aid, perhaps because the motives behind it were not correctly explained or because it was handed out in an unsympathetic way), and perhaps even whether other children are playing the constructive role that they should. Slow learning is, as I have said, the school's problem, and that means classmates as well as teachers. Have these classmates been helped to understand the slow learner's problems? Have they been shown how they can offer assistance? Have they been taught, through the value systems operating throughout the school and through the example set by the staff, that it is the job of everyone to offer sympathy and help to those less well off than oneself? The school is there to enable slow learners to become quick learners, and this means a constant reappraisal by staff of the methods they use and the values they uphold.

References

Bennett, N. (1976) *Teaching Styles and Pupil Progress*. London: Open Books.

Bloom, B.S. *et al.* (1956) *Taxonomy of Educational Objectives. Handbook 1: The cognitive domain*. London: Longmans Green.

Bruner, J.S. (1966) *Towards a Theory of Instruction*. Massachusetts: Harvard University Press.

Bruner, J.S. (1973) *The Relevance of Education*. New York: Norton.

Bruner, J.S. and Anglin, J.M. (1973) *Beyond the Information Given: Studies in the psychology of knowing*. New York: Norton.

Bruner, J.S., Goodnow, J.J. and Austin, G.A. (1965) *A Study of Thinking*. New York: Wiley.

Charlesworth, W.R. (1966) Persistence of orienting and attending behavior in infants as a function of stimulus locomotion uncertainty. *Child Development, 37*, 473–491.

Coopersmith, S. (1968) Studies in self-esteem. *Scientific American, February.*

Davie, R., Butler, N. and Goldsmith, H. (1972) *From Birth to Seven.* London: Longmans.

Entwistle, N.J. (1972) Personality and academic attainment. *British Journal of Educational Psychology, 42,* 137–151.

Fontana, D. (1984) Failures of academic achievement. In A. Gale and A.J. Chapman (ed.) *Psychology and Social Problems: An introduction to applied psychology.* Chichester: Wiley.

Franson, A. (1977) On qualitative differences in learning: IV – Effects of intrinsic motivation and extrinsic test anxiety on process and outcome. *British Journal of Educational Psychology, 47,* 244–257.

Gagné, R.M. (1974) *Essentials of Learning for Instruction.* Hinsdale, Illinois: Dryden Press.

Harlow, H.F. and Harlow, M.H. (1962) Social development in monkeys. *Scientific American, November.*

Krathwohl, D.R. *et al.* (1964) *Taxonomy of Educational Objectives. Handbook II: The affective domain.* New York: David McKay.

Lewis, D.G. and Ko, P. (1973) Personality and performance in elementary mathematics with special reference to item type. *British Journal of Educational Psychology, 43,* 24–34.

Mussen, P.H., Conger, J.J. and Kagan, J. (1984) *Child Development and Personality,* 6th edn. New York: Harper & Row.

Pearson, L. and Tweddle, D. (1984) The Formulation and use of behavioural objectives. In D. Fontana (ed.) *Behaviourism and Learning Theory in Education.* Edinburgh: Scottish Academic Press.

Raybould, E.C. (1984) Precision teaching. In D. Fontana (ed.) *Behaviourism and Learning Theory in Education.* Edinburgh: Scottish Academic Press.

Rowell, J.A. and Renner, V.J. (1975) Personality, mode of assessment and student performance. *British Journal of Educational Psychology, 45,* 232–236.

Simpson, E.J. (1972) The Classification of Educational Objectives in the psychomotor domain. *The Psychomotor Domain, Volume 3.* Washington: Gryphon House.

Skinner, B.F. (1969) *Contingencies of Reinforcement: A theoretical analysis.* New York: Appleton-Century-Crofts.

Stenhouse, L. (1970) Some limitations of the use of objectives in curriculum research and planning. *Paedogogica Europaea, 6,* 73–83.

Trown, E.A. and Leith, G. (1975) Decision rules for teaching strategies in the primary school: personality-treatment interactions. *British Journal of Educational Psychology, 45,* 130–140.

SOME
QUESTIONS

1. Identify your own attitude towards the behaviourist and the cognitive approach to learning respectively. Which seems to accord more closely with your own experience?

2. What is meant, in Bruner's language, by freedom from stimulus control? Skinner considers such freedom is illusory. Why?

3. Give examples of Bruner's three modes of representation as you might witness them in normal classroom work.

4. Make a list of the extrinsic motivators in common use in schools. Can you decide what effect they are each likely to have upon different types of children?

5. Why is it that the experience of consistent failure is so damaging to a child's readiness to learn?

6. If you found a child cheating in your class what action would you take? What would this cheating tell you about the child?

7. Bruner maintains that children are ready to tackle virtually any learning task provided it is presented in a form appropriate to their level of thinking. Is that realistic? Can you think of exceptions?

8. Define short- and long-term memory respectively. What are the strategies the teacher can use to aid children in effecting transfer from one to the other?

9. Define the difference between recognition and recall. How can the teacher convert a recognition task into a recall task (and vice versa)?

10. When and in what circumstances must the teacher be alert to possible interference with the process of remembering?

11. List the six suggested ways in which study habits can be improved. Can you think of any further ways of your own?

12. Write a set of learning objectives for teaching students to do one or more of the following: (i) make an omelette; (ii) become more aware of nature by reading a particular poem; (iii) solve simultaneous equations; (iv) mend a bicycle puncture; (v) construct a simple histogram.

13. Why do correctly written educational objectives lay stress upon learning outcomes rather than upon learning processes?

14. Take each of the major subjects in the school curriculum in turn and discuss in which of the three domains it predominantly lies.

15. Discuss some of the problems a teacher of children with a handicap (e.g. deaf, blind or ESN) would have in using a taxonomy in one or more of the three domains.

16. Select a particular aspect of your teaching subject and indicate

how it can be taught either (i) in a direct practical way using Bruner's discovery method, or (ii) through the medium of a simulation exercise.

17. Construct a list of knowledge questions and a list of reflective (or springboard) questions on some aspects of your own teaching subject. Indicate the purpose behind each question.

18. What are the major causes of slow learning in children?

Additional Reading

Ainscow, M. and Tweddle, D. (1984) *Early Learning Skills Analysis*. Chichester: Wiley.
Thorough and practical examination of the foundations of learning experience.

Baddeley, A. (1983) Your Memory: A user's guide. Harmondsworth: Penguin.
Excellent popular approach. Highly recommended.

Bellezza, F.S. (1982) *Improve Your Memory Skills*. Englewood Cliffs, New Jersey: Prentice-Hall.
Full of practical and intriguing exercises which can be used in the classroom.

Bigge, L. (1982) *Learning Theories for Teachers*, 4th edn. New York: Harper & Row.
One of the best and most comprehensive surveys of learning theories and their application to teaching.

Bruner, J.S. (1961) *The Process of Education*. Cambridge, Massachusetts: Harvard University Press.

Bruner, J.S. (1966) *Towards a Theory of Instruction*. Cambridge, Massachusetts: Harvard University Press.

Bruner, J.S. (1973) *The Relevance of Education*. New York: Norton.
Bruner's ideas are expounded in a number of highly readable texts, of which the above three are good examples.

Carl, J. (1980) *Helping Your Handicapped Child*. Harmondsworth: Penguin.
Aimed at parents, but of great value for all those working with children with handicap.

Claxton, G. (1984) *Live and Learn: An introduction to the psychology of growth and change*. London: Harper & Row.
A stimulating, highly personal approach to cognitive issues.

Fontana, D. (ed.) (1984) *Behaviourism and Learning Theory in Education*. Edinburgh: Scottish Academic Press. (*Also recommended for Chapter 12.*)
Surveys the whole field and outlines practical implications for the teacher.

Fontana, D. (1986) *Teaching and Personality*. Oxford: Basil Blackwell.
Gives a general discussion, with an examination of the implications for the teacher. (Also recommended for Chapters 8 and 14.)

Gagné, R.M. (1975) *Essentials of Learning for Instruction*. Hinsdale, Illinois: Dryden Press.

Gagné, R.M. (1977) *The Conditions of Learning*, 3rd edn. London: Holt, Rinehart & Winston.
Gagné's work is best tackled through his own writings, particularly these two books.

Gronlund, N.E.R. (1978) *Stating Objectives for Classroom Instruction*, 2nd edn. London: Collier Macmillan.
There are also ·many books available now on the writing of educational objectives and on the taxonomies produced by Bloom, Krathwohl and Simpson respectively. This is one of the best – and shortest – of them. It also has something useful to say on the construction of objective tests.

Hintzman, L. (1978) *The Psychology of Learning and Memory*. San Francisco: Freeman.
A good choice for those who want to take their study of learning theories rather further, and examine their relationship to memory.

Howe, M.J. (1984) *A Teacher's Guide to the Psychology of Learning*. Oxford: Basil Blackwell.
Immensely readable and practical book on cognitive aspects of learning.

Jones, R.M. (1972) *Fantasy and Feeling in Education*. Harmondsworth: Penguin.
Contains a good discussion of Bruner's ideas within the practical classroom context.

Laing, A.F. and Chazan, M. (1984) Educational handicap. In D. Fontana (ed.) *The Education of the Young Child*. Oxford: Basil Blackwell.
Deals more specifically with the young child, but is immensely thorough and helpful.

Lindsey, G. (1984) *Screening for Children with Special Needs*. London: Croom Helm.
Excellent on the definition and diagnosis of children with physical and mental handicaps. A multi-disciplinary approach.

Marjoribanks, K. (1979) *Families and Their Learning Environments*. London: Routledge & Kegan Paul.
Provides a thorough and scholarly survey of the research into the relationship between intelligence, personality, family variables and learning.

Neisser, U. (1976) *Cognition and Reality*. San Francisco: Freeman.
Contains some of the major tenets of the cognitive position.

Rowntree, D. (1974) *Educational Technology in Curriculum Development*. London: Harper & Row.
Provides a good introduction to programmed learning and the whole field of educational technology.

Rowntree, D. (1976) *Learn How to Study*. Harmondsworth: Pelican.
A good example of the many useful texts available on study habits.

Skinner, B.F. (1969) *Contingencies of Reinforcement: A theoretical analysis.* New York: Appleton-Century-Crofts.
Sets out Skinner's own theoretical position fully.

Skinner, B.F. (1972) *Beyond Freedom and Dignity.* London: Jonathan Cape.
Covers the application of his ideas to learning within society generally.

Taylor, J.L. and Walford, R. (1972) *Simulation in the Classroom.* Harmondsworth: Penguin.
Gives a comprehensive explanation of simulation exercises, with examples. (Also recommended for Chapter 2.)

Wheeler, H. (ed.) (1973) *Beyond the Punitive Society.* London: Wildwood House.
Provides a full debate on Skinner's ideas.

White, D.R. and Haring, N.G. (1980) *Exceptional Children.* Columbus, Ohio: Merrill.
A valuable survey of the nature of special needs.

Part three

Affective Factors

Introduction The term 'affective', strictly speaking, applies to the emotional factors associated with human behaviour, but is generally taken to refer more broadly to all those elements which go to make up personality. Personality can be defined as the relatively stable and persisting characteristics of a person's non-cognitive psychological life. As such, it covers attitudes and value systems, emotions and feelings, ambitions and aspirations, personal complexes and self-regard. It takes in both conscious and unconscious elements, and incorporates many of the things that help define people as individuals.

At this point the reader may argue that the distinction between cognitive and affective factors is surely an artificial one, since thinking (cognition) must enter into many of the things just listed. There is some force in this argument, since obviously we cannot disregard the individual's patterns of thinking – or allied factors such as intelligence and powers of creativity – when we are considering personality. But we all know highly intelligent people who are nevertheless petulant and childish for much of the time, or given to uncalled-for displays of temper, or prey to all kinds of anxieties that rationally they know are quite unjustified. Conversely, we all know people of apparently modest measurable intelligence who are serene and well-balanced, helpful to friends and to strangers alike, philosophical and realistic in the face of problems. Similarly, if we turn to value systems, we all know intelligent folk who are devious and vindictive, who use their

165

cognitive abilities to deceive and beguile others, and who delight in scoring off those they consider inferior to themselves. By the same token we know people of much lesser intelligence who are honest and courageous, and who speak ill of no one.

I could develop these examples further by pointing to highly creative individuals whose gifts are expressed in a form indicative of internal turmoil and anguish, and to others whose works of art bring tranquility and delight to the onlooker, but the point being made should already be clear. Affective factors interact with, and are modified by, cognitive factors, but the two nevertheless have a functional independence. We cannot take the measure of a man or a woman by simply looking at their results on cognitive tests, however good these tests are for their own purposes.

Within formal education the main emphasis has been upon cognitive factors though, as was indicated in the last chapter, children's emotional states (together with other personality variables) may have a profound effect upon their school performance. Within the last few years psychologists have been urging that this fact be recognized, and that teaching strategies be adapted to children's personalities as well as to their cognitive abilities. In the chapter that follows the measurement of personality is discussed, since an understanding of the techniques of measurement is essential if the teacher is to be in a position to assess the practical value of personality research in the classroom. Also discussed are descriptions of personality and theories of personality: that is, the models advanced by psychologists to explain how personality develops and influences the individual's behaviour.

8

Personality

Psychologists have developed a number of different approaches – some conflicting, some complementary – to the study of personality. But before examining these we need to ask whether personality owes anything to heredity or is entirely dependent upon the environment. The answer may give an indication of the influence which teachers have upon the personality development of their children. If personality is in part a consequence of heredity, then the teacher's influence has clear limits. But if personality is acquired, then those limits may be much broader. To provide an answer, we have to look briefly at the early years of life, and see if research can tell us how and when personality makes its first appearance, and what happens subsequently.

The origins of personality

Many parents remark on the fact that their children show identifiable differences in behaviour as early as the first weeks or even days of life. One baby may be happy and contented while another, though enjoying the same parental care and in equally good physical health, may be demanding and awkward. A third may be particularly active and involved in all that goes on. Clearly, since these characteristics are evident so early in life, they are far more likely to be due to inheritance than to learning, but the question is whether they form the basis of the individual's mature personality in later life, or whether they are simply superficial variations in behaviour that quickly become superseded by more enduring qualities as he or she begins to react to the world and commence the process of learning.

The most ambitious attempt to answer this question was inaugurated some years ago by the American paediatricians Thomas, Chess and Birch. They took an initial sample of 141 children at the age of 12 weeks, and with the co-operation of parents studied them closely in their own homes and rated them on a number of different behavioural characteristics. These included such things as activity levels, regularity of bodily functions (feeding, sleeping, excreting) and general disposition (cheerful, cranky). Results (Thomas, Chess and Birch, 1970; Thomas and Chess, 1977) showed that 65 per cent of the sample could be assigned at this early age to one or other of the following three groups.

- *The easy group* (40 per cent of sample), characterized by regularity of bodily functions, by a high level of adaptability, by a generally friendly and positive disposition, and by a normal reaction to stimuli.

- *The difficult group* (10 per cent of sample), characterized by irregularity of bodily functions, by low adaptability, by negative responses to new people and situations, by a general crankiness of disposition, and by an over-reaction to stimuli (i.e. they tended to fuss if everything was not quite right).

- *The slow-to-warm-up group* (15 per cent of sample), characterized by low activity and adaptability levels, by an inclination to withdraw in the face of novelty of any kind, by a slight general negativity of mood, and by mild reaction to stimuli.

The children were then followed through into later childhood and adolescence, and it was found that membership of the three groups remained remarkably constant. 'Easy' children at 12 weeks tended still to be easy children at 12 years, while 'difficult' children remained difficult and those 'slow to warm up' remained slow to warm up. Obviously the precise aspects of behaviour studied by the researchers changed as the children grew older, but they still focused upon the same general areas. Perhaps not surprisingly, it was found that 70 per cent of the 'difficult' group had developed distinct behaviour problems by adolescence, as opposed to only 18 per cent of the 'easy' group.

Of particular relevance to the teacher, it was found that when the children first started school the 'easy' group quickly adapted to the new routine, participated cheerfully and readily in all activities, and showed the general friendliness and sociability that had been apparent in their early weeks of life. The 'difficult' and 'slow-to-warm-up' groups, on the other hand, presented more problems, often showing considerable reluctance to settle in, to make friends, and to join in the various activities.

Examining the environments in which the children were reared, the researchers found there were no significant differences between the three groups. All the parents were good parents, in the sense that they provided and cared for the children well (a factor, indeed, which had been taken into account when the sample was selected), and the groups each contained similar proportions of authoritarian and permissive parents. The inescapable conclusion, therefore, was that the observed differences between the children were due to heredity. The children, it seemed, had been given the raw material of their personalities, usually referred to by psychologists as *temperament*, at birth.

The role of parents

However, lest it be thought that environment was relatively unimportant, it was found that parents exerted a major influence on the extent to which children adapted to their temperaments. In particular, children from the 'difficult' and 'slow-to-warm-up' groups were much more successful at coping with their potentially troublesome natures if they were blessed with parents who were extra-patient, consistent and objective in their manner. The 'difficult' children, especially, tended to become even more negative and awkward when confronted by parents who were rigid and punitive, and who met childish tantrums with outbursts of their own. 'Difficult' children, it seemed, could be taken to water but could not readily be made to drink, and the more their parents insisted the more stubborn they tended to become. It appeared they responded best to parents who were gentle but firm, who were prepared to reason and explain, and who had clear standards but preferred to enlist the child's co-operation rather than to rely on force and punishment.

The 'slow-to-warm-up' children also benefited from this kind of sympathetic handling. If they were pushed too precipitately into new experiences they tended to withdraw into themselves. If, on the other hand, they were left to their own devices they still showed little inclination to take part. Their best responses were forthcoming if they had parents who provided a wide range of stimuli and interests, and who relied upon encouragement and support rather than upon ultimatums. They needed, it seemed, time to adjust and have their interest aroused if they were to become involved.

The enduring nature of temperament

Thomas, Chess and Birch do not claim that their three categories are the only possible ways of classifying temperamental factors, but their general finding that these factors exist from an early age and remain reasonably constant over the years has been supported by a number of other studies. Maccoby and Jacklin (1974), in a similar approach, have also shown that there seem to be temperamental differences between the sexes at this age, with boys tending to be more active, initiatory and aggressive than girls, and girls more watchful, attentive and vocal. As shown in Chapter 1, such differences are likely to be quickly overlaid by learnt characteristics, since even in the first months of life parents tend to show subtle differences in their behaviour towards the two sexes. But at least the greater incidence of aggression in young males seems to be partly genetic in origin, since it is observable in other primates besides humans.

By the time a child starts school, of course, its early temperament will have been considerably modified by learning. The 'difficult' child (using the terminology of Thomas, Chess and Birch) who has received sympathetic handling may well show determination rather than stubbornness, while the 'slow-to-warm-up' child may show interest rather than apathy. In addition, of course, we must remember that 35 per cent of the sample studied by Thomas, Chess and Birch could not be assigned to any of the categories with any consistency, which may indicate that their temperaments were more malleable (or that a wider range of variables should have been studied in the children). But such work on temperament indicates, particularly to the teacher of very young children, that account must be taken not only of the child's home background when considering individual differences in personality, but also of the child's own disposition. Children can hardly be held to blame if they find new experiences, or joining in things, or meeting new people, or distractions in their immediate environment more disturbing and upsetting than do many of their peers, or if they find it harder to take an active and lively interest in some of the things that are on offer. The role of the teacher is to help children adapt and adjust to the social and academic demands of the school and, like the successful parents in the Thomas, Chess and Birch sample, this may mean showing particular patience and sympathy towards certain children. The so-called 'easy' child may find life rather less of a problem than do children from the other two categories, and may appear much more receptive to what the teacher is trying to do, but it is often the children in these latter categories who have most need of the understanding, supportive adult, and who in the long run may derive most benefit from this relationship.

Approaches to personality

But temperament is only the start of the story. As the child grows, temperament interacts with environment, with cognitive factors, and with other maturational variables such as physique and physical appearance, and all these play their part in determining personalities and giving them their rich complexity. In measuring this complexity and in developing theories to describe and explain it, psychologists immediately face the problem of whether personality is something relatively stable or relatively unstable. Things do not have to be stable to be accurately measured, but their degree of stability or instability influences the way in which we undertake measurement and the interpretations we put upon that measurement when it is obtained. A useful analogy here is between a ruler and a thermometer. A ruler is used to measure fixed objects, and the results of this measurement usually remain constant, at least in the medium term. A thermometer, on the other hand, is used to measure a quality which is constantly fluctuating, and the results obtained a few hours (or even minutes) ago may tell us nothing of what is happening now. Both rulers and thermometers are valuable in their place, but it is important not to confuse the two. To treat ruler measurements as if they were constantly fluctuating, and to treat thermometer measurements as if they were fixed and invariable, would lead to no end of problems.

Ruler or thermometer?

With personality we need to ask whether what we are measuring calls for the ruler or the thermometer, and from the practical viewpoint of the teacher the best answer is that certain aspects of it require the former and certain aspects the latter. For convenience, these aspects can be labelled personality *traits* and personality *states* respectively. Personality traits are relatively fixed and enduring, and may be linked to temperamental factors, while personality states are fluctuating and have to do with moods and the moment-by-moment way in which individuals experience themselves and others. Traits may influence states, but knowing someone's traits does not tell us what state they are experiencing at any particular moment. For example, knowing that someone has a high score on the personality trait of introversion does not tell us whether they are in a happy state when tackling the solitary task of changing the car wheel. Conversely, knowing that someone is in a worried state when reading their electricity bill does not tell us whether they score highly on the personality trait of anxiety. Each of the states and traits in these examples is measurable, but each requires measurement of a different order and provides different kinds of information about the individual.

Personality traits

If I asked you to describe your personality, you would say perhaps that you are an outgoing, sociable person, who likes meeting people and seeks new challenges and experiences. Or you might say you are a worrier, who takes a rather pessimistic view of things. If I probed further you might say you are bored with your own company or that you often feel depressed without good reason. Notice that some of these things are really quite closely linked. Thus a person who is outgoing and sociable may also usually be rather bored with their own company, while a person who is a worrier may often also feel depressed without obvious cause. Far from being a range of different qualities, many of the terms which we use to describe ourselves may simply be expressions of certain common, underlying personality characteristics. It is these underlying characteristics that psychologists term *personality traits*. Some years ago Allport (1961) identified over 4,500 terms in the English language which can probably be used to describe personality, but research has since shown that the great majority of them can be related back to a surprisingly small number of these underlying traits.

This has been demonstrated by assembling batteries of questions which people can answer about their own person-alities, and then factor analysing their responses. *Factor analysis* identifies all those response variables which show an inter-relationship, thus allowing identification of groups of questions which individuals tend to answer in the same way. For example, people whose answers reveal them as gregarious may also reveal themselves as inclined towards sensation-seeking and as fond of challenge. Such an inter-relationship suggests that each of the responses concerned stems from the same underlying personality trait. Having established the existence of this trait the researcher can then decide what to call it and can construct from the questions that measure it a personality test which, after standardization, can be used to identify other people's scores on this trait.

The work of H.J. Eysenck

One of the best-known psychologists working in this area is H.J. Eysenck whose three tests of personality, namely the Maudsley Personality Inventory (1959), the Eysenck Person-ality Inventory (EPI) (1964) and the Eysenck Personality Questionnaire (1975), have been used in a wide range of educa-tional and psychological settings. (A number of variants of these tests exist, of which the most relevant to teachers is the Junior Eysenck Personality Inventory (JEPI) for children between the ages of 7 and 15.) The research that went into the develop-ment of these tests indicated the existence of three major personality traits (or *dimensions*, to use Eysenck's preferred term), which Eysenck labels *extraversion, neuroticism* and *psychoticism* respectively. The first two are measured by the Maudsley Personality Inventory and the Eysenck Personality Inventory, while the Eysenck Personality Questionnaire mea-sures all three.

High scores on extraversion indicate that the individual is orientated primarily towards the external world of people and experiences, while low scores show him or her to be more withdrawn and more concerned with inner states of mind (a condition which Eysenck terms *introversion*). High scores on neuroticism indicate that the individual is prone to anxiety and to the reactions and fears associated with it, while low scores show good psychological balance (termed by Eysenck *stability*). High psychoticism scores indicate an individual who is relatively independent, tough-minded, aggressive and cold, while low scores go with dependency and tender-mindedness.

Most research to date, particularly in the educational context, has been carried out using the extraversion and the neuroticism scales (the 'E' and 'N' scales). Since these scales are not correlated with each other (i.e. scores on the E scale give no indication of how an individual will score on the N scale), they can be used to yield four distinct personality 'types', namely people with high scores on both scales (the *unstable extravert*), people with low N scores and high E scores (the *stable extravert*), people with high N scores and low E scores (the *unstable introvert*), and people with low scores on both (the *stable introvert*). People with mid-point scores on both scales are sometimes termed *ambiverts*. The interesting thing about these personality types is that they fit remarkably well with the four types identified by the ancient Greeks and Romans, namely the choleric, sanguine, melancholic and phlegmatic. They also give clues as to how the two personality dimensions interact with each other. Thus a stable extravert manifests stability through a breezy, exuberant approach, while a stable introvert will do so through calmness and tranquility. Similarly, an unstable extravert will manifest instability through mood swings and volatile over-reactions while an unstable introvert will do so through brooding and depression.

The work of R.B. Cattell

The other major champion of the trait-based approach is R.B. Cattell (e.g. 1980). Cattell argues that his research, though conducted along similar lines to that of Eysenck, reveals many more than three underlying personality traits. On the basis of his findings he has constructed a number of personality tests for specific age groups which measure up to 16 relatively distinct factors such as excitability, strong super-ego (i.e. moral sense), conscientiousness, shyness, individuality and guilt-proneness. The personality tests consist of the 16 Personality Questionnaire for adults, the High School Personality Questionnaire for children from 12 to 18, the Child's Personality Quiz (8 to 12), the Early School Personality Quiz (6 to 8) and the Pre-School Personality Quiz (4 to 6). However, as Eysenck points out, Cattell's factors are only *relatively* distinct, and do in fact show clusters of intercorrelations. He argues that they should therefore be seen as surface traits which originate in a few broad underlying categories (*source traits*), the most important of which look very much like Eysenck's own E and N dimensions. Thus there would seem to be no major disagreement between Eysenck and Cattell's respective approaches.

Pros and cons of the trait-based approach

The value of the trait-based approach lies in the fact that it yields specific, carefully identified areas of personality which can be explored in relation to other variables. For example, we can look at whether success in such things as school work or certain vocations goes with extraversion or introversion. Or we can look at whether criminality or sexual deviance or creativity or any other relevant behaviour goes with high E or N or P scores. Or we can look at personal relationships and see which personality types seem most compatible with each other. Or we can study social groups or popularity or leadership and see the role played in them by personality. Or we can look at changes in personality over age, asking whether people become more introverted as they grow older, or more stable or less psychotic. Or we can see whether certain kinds of physique go with certain kinds of personality. The possibilities are extensive and inviting, and many have been explored by researchers. There is no doubt that the trait-based approach has considerable appeal for psychologists, particularly for those psychologists who practise psychological measurement (psychometry) on a large scale.

The disadvantages of the trait approach, however, lie partly in this very versatility. It is all too easy for researchers to include personality inventories in their test batteries with no theoretical justification beyond the vague hope that some correlation or other may emerge. Such a ubiquitous practice means that on chance grounds alone some researchers will from time to time throw up apparently significant results, only to discover that further research by others fails to support their findings. It thus becomes difficult to establish any consistent pattern of correlation between personality traits and many of the other variables against which they have been studied. A further disadvantage, this time perhaps inherent in the trait-based approach itself, is that even where such patterns do emerge, the actual correlations are often low. This suggests that, in spite of their inter-relationship, the various aspects of personality subsumed by the traits are so many and varied that the traits themselves are too general always to be of much help when investigating detailed hypotheses.

Finally, an emphasis upon personality traits may hide from us the fact that personality is perhaps much less fixed than we believe. Consistent with the ruler as opposed to the thermometer approach, personality inventories are expected to show test-retest reliability. This means that in their construction any questions which individuals tend not to answer consistently in the medium term are discarded. Test construc-

tors retain only those questions which support their precon-
ception that personality characteristics are relatively enduring, changing only slowly (if at all). But the questions that are
discarded may be an important part of the story, presenting us
with valid evidence that personality is to a significant extent a
dynamic, ever-changing quality, unsuitable for measurement
solely by test-retest reliability and the ruler approach.

Personality traits and learning

The idea that personality has an influence upon the child's
learning is not new to teachers. Classroom experience shows
that it is not cognitive variables alone which determine children's progress. These variables interact with children's individual attitudes and interests, their motivation, and a wide
range of emotional responses such as excitement, sympathy
and empathy and, perhaps above all, anxiety. The specific
relationship between learning and anxiety was discussed in
Chapter 7 (see p. 131), and it was pointed out how anxiety
can affect not only the assimilation of knowledge in the first
place but also its recall at a later date, particularly if this recall
is demanded under test and examination conditions or in a
generally unsympathetic environment. But as indicated by
trait-based theories, some children have habitually higher
levels of anxiety than others, so much so that these can be
regarded as constituting an enduring personality dimension.
Thus we say that one child is timid and nervous, that another
is full of confidence, that a third is a real worrier, and that a
fourth takes things as they come, and so on. These labels
mean that, whatever the situation in which the respective
children find themselves, we would expect them to show the
behaviour patterns in question in response to any kind of
stress.

Trait theories figure prominently in explorations into the
links between personality and learning, and both Eysenck's
neuroticism–stability dimension and his extraversion–introversion dimension have yielded interesting information at classroom level.

The extraversion–introversion dimension

From the educational point of view, the main interest lies in
whether or not any discernible relationship exists between
either of these categories and classroom achievement. Using
the JEPI, and reviewing the evidence up to 1972, Elliott (1972)
in fact detects an interesting relationship between educational
achievement and personality that changes with time. By the
age of eight there is a statistically positive relationship in
children between extraversion and academic attainment. Ten
years later the relationship is reversed so that achievement is
positively related to introversion. Although statistically

significant, the magnitude of the effect is small. Since Elliott is pooling the results of a number of separate investigations rather than carrying out an investigation of his own using stratified samples (i.e. samples matched for all relevant variables except age), this pattern must be treated with some caution, but it seems to suggest either that extraverts are better workers than introverts in the primary school, with the position reversed by the time higher education is reached, or that some factor or factors in the primary school environment favour extraverts and some factor or factors in higher education favour introverts.

Of these two suggestions, the second would seem the more plausible, since one can readily make out a case that the sociable, outgoing, active teaching environment of the normal primary school suits the study habits of the extravert, while the more individual, even lonely, academic environment within which the student has to work in higher education suits those of the introvert. In the secondary school, where the teaching environment may vary from subject to subject, it could be argued that it is sometimes the extravert who is favoured and sometimes the introvert, so that no clear pattern emerges (though there is some evidence that introversion in girls proves beneficial quite early on in secondary school life).

However, there is a third, more subtle, suggestion that is sometimes advanced to explain why introversion gradually becomes more advantageous than extraversion as the child moves through secondary school and into higher education. This suggestion cites the known evidence that in most people extraversion increases up to about the age of 14, and then shows a steady decline towards introversion throughout the rest of life (in other words, people become more introverted as they grow older). It could be, therefore, that children who are intellectually precocious are also precocious in terms of personality, and show an extraversion peak in the primary school (i.e. some years ahead of the average), where such a peak is at its most useful. Thereafter they become increasingly introverted, and are scoring more strongly on this quality than their peers in the upper secondary school and in higher education, where introversion is at a premium.

The neuroticism–stability dimension

In the light of current knowledge it is not possible to say whether this last suggestion is more important than the more widely advocated one that the primary school environment tends to favour extraverts and that of higher education introverts. Possibly both contain some truth. But before considering the matter further, it is as well to turn to Eysenck's other dimension, *anxiety* (or the *neuroticism–stability dimension*, as Eysenck prefers to call it), and examine its relationship to

176

educational achievement. And here we find that the position is rather more complex. One way of explaining this complexity is to refer to the Yerkes–Dodson law, that states that moderate levels of anxiety act as motivators and improve performance, whereas high levels lead to inhibition and a deterioration in performance. This suggests that children who score highly on Eysenck's dimension (i.e. have high neuroticism scores) will do their best work in relatively unstressful environments, while children with lower scores will receive optimum motivation in environments where the pressures are rather more severe.

There is some evidence, however, that students with high neuroticism scores tend to do *better* than those with low scores in higher education, where the stresses (at least around examination times) are quite intense. Since this applies particularly to students following arts courses, it has been suggested that there may be a subject discipline variable at work here. Arts subjects, particularly those which have a literary basis, may demand a kind of sensitivity in students which goes with a certain degree of anxiety. Put rather fancifully, it may be impossible to appreciate the emotional sufferings that writers and poets pour into their work unless one has experienced at least a degree of similar suffering oneself. It may also be that anxiety is less inhibiting in an arts examination, where one is not quite so concerned with the recall of factual information, than it is in science and technology. Thus anxious arts students are able to give a rather better account of themselves than are anxious students in other disciplines.

The evidence, extensive as it is, gives no final very clear answers. Indeed, the most important conclusion that one can reach is that personality variables cannot be viewed in isolation when it comes to assessing their impact upon learning, but must be viewed within the context of a range of other variables that interact with them at every point. This is amply demonstrated by the work of Bennett (1976), who looked at children's personalities in relation to teaching styles within the primary school. I have already said that most studies show a link between extraversion and classroom success in the primary school, but Bennett seems to show that this may be an over-simplification. He found, for example, that well-motivated extraverts actually did *better* in formal than in informal primary schools, which calls into question the idea that it is simply the free atmosphere of the primary classroom that favours extraversion. Able extraverted children may certainly shine in a very informal primary school environment, but it seems that where they are well motivated they will do even better (at least in terms of results in reading and the other basic subjects that Bennett used as his criterion variables) in a more formal environment, where they find themselves better able to concentrate upon the work in hand.

Bennett also found that children with high neuroticism scores did better in formal than in informal primary schools, and in fact spent only half as much time on work activities in the latter as did children with low neuroticism scores. This may again seem odd in view of my suggestion that anxious children do better in less stressful environments, but the probable answer here is that, in the formal classroom, anxious children felt less worried because they were given a more structured atmosphere in which to work and therefore knew more of what was expected of them. In the informal classroom they actually avoided work, probably because they were less sure of what they were supposed to be doing, and this uncertainty made the work itself rather anxiety-provoking.

Note that I am being somewhat speculative here in the absence of any firm evidence, but the point to be emphasized is that we must keep a range of variables in mind before we try to reach any conclusions on the part played by personality in school success. Another important variable is that of gender. Lynn (1971) demonstrates that females tend to have higher neuroticism scores than males throughout the years of formal education. This may be one of the reasons why they tend to shy away from science subjects, and to concentrate upon the arts where, as we have seen, higher neuroticism may be less of a handicap. (Other reasons might be the greater human interest of the arts, the cultural myths that suggest women are less good at science than men, and the fact that hitherto women's education has been regarded as less important from a career point of view.) A further important variable is the teacher's own personality, to which I return in Chapter 14.

The trait-based approach and individual differences

Before leaving personality traits, I should point out that, although we have looked mainly at work done in schools and in higher education using the JEPI and the EPI, in America in particular wide use has been made of Cattell's Sixteen Personality Factor Questionnaire (16 PF), and of the three versions of this questionnaire developed for use with school children. Recently increasing attention has been focused as well upon the third of Eysenck's dimensions (psychoticism), and evidence is accumulating of a possible link between high scores on this dimension and creativity (Eysenck, 1983).

I should add, however, that in most of the studies within education using the Eysenck or Cattell measures, the levels of correlation between these measures and academic success are not very high. This means that although the findings are statistically significant when we are testing children in large groups, they do not necessarily tell us a great deal about the position of individuals within the groups. We can often say no more than that if children are extraverted there is some chance that they will do better in primary school than if they are introverted, with the position reversed in higher education. This indicates clearly the need for caution when making statements applicable at class level.

Modifying personality traits

So far, apart from a reference to possible age-related changes, I have suggested that the trait-based approach sees personality as a relatively enduring, fixed quality. But does this mean that trait-based theories see the teacher as powerless to influence this aspect of children's development? Perhaps the first point to make is that with all personality dimensions, it is not necessarily more desirable to be at one extreme than at the other. Extraverted people may seem to have more fun on the face of it than introverted people because of their greater sociability and their generally more outgoing behaviour, but there is not much evidence that they are very much happier or experience a great deal more self-satisfaction. And though introverted people may seem on balance to do better in higher education this does not necessarily mean that they are more scholarly, but simply that the way in which we organize teaching and examinations in universities and colleges may be more suited to their personalities than to the personalities of extraverts. Even if we look at the neuroticism–stability dimension it would be inappropriate to say that stable people are better people than those who are on the neurotic side. Neurotic people may experience more difficulties in life as a result of their tendency to worry unduly, but they may, in learning to cope with these difficulties, find an eventual maturity and serenity that escapes the person to whom life has come more easily. They may also be more sensitive to mental distress in others. It is not part of the teacher's role to look constantly for ways of passing value judgements on children's personalities, but rather to understand the manner in which these personalities affect the ways in which children behave and learn.

This brings me back to my point: namely, is it possible for the teacher to change children's personality traits as measured by scores on the dimensions included in such tests as the JEPI? The answer is that although there is no hard research evidence (research projects deliberately designed to 'change children's personalities' would rightly be given short shrift by most parents and teachers), it is debateable whether we could effect more than limited changes. We could, for example, urge introverted children to be more sociable, in the hope that they would quickly come to enjoy social events and therefore change into extraverts, but it is probable that they would not like these events and would blame us for pushing them into something they did not want to do. In any case, many introverts are just as fond of other people as are extraverts, but prefer to mix with small gatherings of friends rather than be constantly meeting new people and going to new places.

More realistically, we might try to help children stop worrying so much, in the hope that this would render them less neurotic and thus lower their neuroticism scores. In theory this should certainly be possible, but in practice many worriers already know all the reasons why they should not be worrying, but confess that this does not stop them from doing so. There may indeed be physiological reasons for this, in that the neurotic person may have a more readily aroused *autonomic nervous system* than does the more stable individual. The autonomic nervous system is that part of our neurophysiology that controls our involuntary processes (sweating, heart rate, rise and fall in blood pressure, digestion, shivering, and the like), and it can easily be appreciated that if this system is quickly aroused then we may find ourselves with butterflies in the stomach and nervous shivers when confronting a situation that leaves someone else quite unmoved. The point is that there may be nothing in our experience to make such situations more frightening to us than they are to the next person, it is just that our bodies respond at once and send us all sorts of alarm signals, whereas someone else can remain physiologically unaroused and can view the whole thing with calm detachment.

It is possible that with *biofeedback* techniques (which relay information to the individual on the performance of his or her autonomic nervous system) and some forms of relaxation, both of which lie outside the scope of this book and of the teacher's normal role, neurotic people can learn to control the rate of arousal of their autonomic systems, but they are unlikely to be able to do so simply by being told to stop worrying and to take things more as they come. When working with highly anxious children the job of teachers is therefore primarily to understand and sympathize with their problems, and to give practical proof of this sympathy by not exposing them unnecessarily to stressful situations. Teachers should also, of course, try to equip such children with the skills necessary for dealing competently with most of the problems they are likely to meet, and should help to build their confidence by giving them the experience of success, which, as I have stressed repeatedly, is essential if children are to make satisfactory progress. Thus what teachers are trying to do is not so much radically to alter children's personalities as to help them cope more effectively with the kind of people they are.

Personality and academic success

Turning again to the relationship between personality and academic success, it is as well to repeat that even if we could produce consistent evidence which proved that the extravert does better in a formal than in an informal classroom, it would be purely statistical. As we have seen, it would tell us only that this proof holds good when we compare large groups of children in one of the categories mentioned with large groups of children in one of the others. Depending upon the strength of the correlations they would indicate what the chances are that individual children will conform to the pattern, but no more than that. The value of the research that has been done to date in the field lies primarily in the fact that it alerts teachers to the existence of important links between personality and learning, not that it tells them unequivocally what these links actually happen to be. As explained earlier, personality seems to be in a complex relationship with a number of other variables such as the material being taught, the teaching methods being used, the study habits open to the individual child or student, and the personality of teachers themselves. Teachers must therefore operate as their own researchers, sensitive to the individual personalities of each child in the class, and alert to the reaction between these personalities and the other variables involved.

Cognitive style

Very similar to the trait-based approach, in that it also employs the notion of dimensions, is an area of personality study known as *cognitive style*. As the name implies, cognitive style is to do with thinking, and it could be argued that it thus more properly belongs in Part II, along with concept formation, language development, intelligence and so on. This is a valid point, but it is usually dealt with under personality because it links closely with affective factors as well. Eysenck argues that intelligence is really only another dimension of personality, and Cattell does in fact include it as one of his personality factors in the 16 PF.

Whether one accepts Eysenck's argument or not, the link between intelligence and various personality traits is well attested by research. Children who evidence significant increases in measured intelligence between the ages of six and 10 years have been shown to be more independent, competitive, and verbally aggressive than children who evidence a decline. They are also more likely, it seems, to work hard, to show a stronger desire to master intellectual problems, and to show less readiness to withdraw in the face of challenge. In their classic long-term study of high IQ children, Terman and Oden (1947) found that those most likely to make good use of their gifts were high on self-confidence, on perseverance, and on work interest, and had well-integrated life goals that were realistic and single-minded. The more successful children also showed themselves to be better adjusted and more socially balanced than the less successful, and to be more likely in later life to make successful marriages and to achieve satisfaction in their personal and professional lives. Comparing high and low IQ children, McCandless (1969) considered that research shows the former to be taller, better looking, less anxious, more popular, and physically stronger than the latter and, not surprisingly, to be better judges of other people.

Whether it is the high intelligence that prompts the desirable personality traits or whether it is the other way round is open to debate. Probably the two interact with each other at every point, making it impossible to establish the precise nature of causal links. What we can say, however, is that certain kinds of personality traits seem to be desirable if children are to make the best use of their intelligence, while high intelligence allows children to be more independent, self-confident, competitive and so on.

It seems that creativity interacts with personality traits in similar ways. Creative people appear to be more autonomous, self-sufficient and resourceful than the average, and also to be more introverted and aware of their impulses, and more ready to confess to the irrational in themselves. They also appear to be more prone to engage in abstract thought, and to have a higher tolerance of ambiguity. This close link between creativity and personality has led some people to suggest that creativity (or rather the divergent thinking that apparently goes with creativity) should be regarded as a cognitive style, and, like intelligence, should be seen primarily as a dimension of personality. However, research into cognitive styles has tended to focus on areas other than divergent and convergent thinking (convergent thinking, as explained on p. 112, being the form of thinking associated with intelligence), and it is to these areas that we now turn.

Theories of cognitive style

Cognitive style theorists start from the fact that we are bombarded with stimuli from the environment every moment of our waking lives, and attend to only a small part of it, which we make sense of by *coding*; that is, by assigning it to a range of categories, each of which carries its own rating of importance. In any situation, things belonging to categories relatively high in importance gain our attention, while those belonging to categories relatively low do not. For example, children sitting in a classroom will not be attending to the physical sensation of their chairs pressing against their bodies, or the feeling of the ground under their feet, or the air entering their lungs, or the backs of the heads around them, but they will (one hopes) be attending to what the teacher is saying, since this will fall into categories such as 'interesting' and 'important' and be further coded into categories associated with meaning as it becomes assimilated. However, if somebody has put drawing pins on their chairs, or if the air entering their lungs becomes charged with the smell of cooking from the kitchen, or if one of the heads in front turns round and pulls a face, then their attention may be diverted from the teacher to these other stimuli, because such stimuli have suddenly moved up into categories of greater importance.

The way in which we assign things to categories will be determined to a great extent by previous experience. Children have learnt that when the teacher is talking this experience must be placed in a category of high importance and attended to, either because it gives them relevant and useful information or because the teacher has a habit of directing questions at people who are not listening. As they assimilate what the teacher is saying, they match it with what they already know and categorize it accordingly (into sets if the lesson happens to be mathematics perhaps, into time-charts if it happens to be history). But such assignment may also be influenced by innate factors, including how we actually perceive things. Some people, it seems, are innately more sensitive to certain stimuli (loud noises, bright colours, subtle differences in shape) than others, with the result that such stimuli may impinge on their awareness, whereas to somebody else they would go unnoticed. When faced with any kind of problem, therefore, children will attend to what they consider important within it, will categorize the information concerned, and will hunt through their internal reference system until they find data coded into a similar category which will help them form hypotheses as a means towards a solution.

Cognitive style theorists consider that there is an identifiable consistency about the way in which each of us carries out this coding process, and that we do not change our methods drastically from problem to problem. They further consider that such consistency applies not only to how we tackle academic problems but to social problems as well, and indeed all the problems with which we are confronted in daily life. It is for this reason that they see cognitive style as an integral part of personality. This is readily apparent when we say, for example, that certain people let their hearts rule their heads (i.e. that they tend to code information into categories associated with emotional responses rather than into those associated with rational thinking), that others tend to rush into things headlong (i.e. to categorize without due thought), while others are too slow in making up their minds (i.e. they deliberate too long over which categories to use), and that yet others are disorganized or precise or methodical and so on. Useful as these general categories are, cognitive style theorists have tried to go beyond them and identify certain very definite dimensions along which we can all be placed. Research continues and no one is as yet sure how many common dimensions there may be, but there are three that have obvious relevance to education, and we will look briefly at each of these in turn.

Focusing–scanning. The first dimension of cognitive style was identified by Bruner (Bruner *et al.*, 1956), whose work was discussed in Chapters 3 and 7. Bruner labels this dimension focusing–scanning and argues that extreme focusers, when faced with a problem, characteristically delay hypothesis-making until they have amassed sufficient evidence, while extreme scanners form a hypothesis quickly and usually have to go back and start all over again if this hypothesis eventually turns out to be untenable. This is well illustrated by the test originally designed by Bruner to place people on this dimension. The test involves presenting individual subjects with a number of pairs of cards, each card consisting of varying arrangements of squares, circles, lines and colours, and then telling them that one card in each pair is 'correct' and the other 'incorrect'. As each successive pair is revealed individuals are asked to determine what particular features of the squares, circles, etc. denote 'correctness' and 'incorrectness' respectively. Clearly, if we carry this over into the classroom, we can see that focusers sometimes might delay hypothesis-making longer than necessary, and therefore appear over-deliberate in their work, while scanners might make up their minds too quickly and be at a disadvantage in problems presented to them orally, where they cannot go back and look at earlier information if their hypotheses prove to be wrong.

Field dependence–field independence. Another well-researched dimension of cognitive style is that called field dependence–field independence, but also sometimes referred to as *global–articulated*. The discoverer of this dimension, Herman Witkin, noted that certain people (those who are said to have *global* cognitive styles) appear less able than others (said to have *articulated* styles) to separate out the relevant from the irrelevant stimuli in a given situation. That is, they appear less able to decide which information belongs to important categories in that situation, and should be attended to, and which information belongs to unimportant ones and can be ignored. For example, Witkin showed in early experiments that people with global styles are unable to tell very precisely whether a chair in which they are sitting is tilted or upright when they are placed in a tilted visual field. They are, it seems, unable to separate the relevant stimuli (i.e. the bodily sensation of whether they are upright or not) from the irrelevant (the visual stimuli at which they are looking). Witkin has since shown that global individuals seem less able to remember details when given recall tests, seem less perceptive, and appear to be more easily influenced by their fellows.

There seems to be some link between the global–articulated dimension and intelligence, in that global individuals appear to do less well on analytical items in IQ tests than do articulated people, though there is no difference on verbal items. Witkin suggests (1965) that this imbalance between analytical and verbal skills in global children may work to their disadvantage, in that high verbal skills may disguise inadequate analytical ones, leaving the teacher unaware of the real reasons that may lie behind the difficulties such children experience with certain learning tasks. He suggests in consequence that cognitive style tests may be of more use to the teacher than IQ tests, and should indeed be used in place of them since the former are more comprehensive and 'recognise the rooting of intellectual functioning in personality'.

Reflectivity–impulsivity. A third dimension of cognitive style of relevance to the teacher is that proposed by Jerome Kagan (1966), namely that of reflectivity–impulsivity. Reflective children tend to make fewer errors than impulsive ones, particularly on challenging and difficult tasks, since they show a strong desire to be right first time, and seem able to tolerate the ambiguity, say, of a long silence in front of the class while they think out the right answer before responding. Impulsive children, on the other hand, adopt a 'shotgun' approach, firing off answers in the hope that one will be right and that in any case errors will provide appropriate feedback from the teacher to help them to get nearer the solution next time.

On each of the above dimensions it might be supposed at first sight that one end is very much better than the other (i.e. the reflective, analytical and focusing ends of the dimensions respectively). This is not so. All cognitive style theorists stress that ideally we should be able to operate at either end of a dimension, depending on the circumstances. To take the reflectivity–impulsivity dimension as an example, it is easy to see that over-reflective children, unwilling to commit themselves until they are sure they are right, may be showing an undue fear of ever being wrong. They may also be denying themselves the valuable learning opportunities that come from making mistakes. Similarly, the analytical approach of the person with an extreme articulated style may be inappropriate in social situations where humanity demands that we respond to individuals themselves as well as to the information they are trying to convey. Again, as we have already seen, the extreme focuser may be at a disadvantage in a situation where early hypothesis making is essential and where decisions based on only limited evidence have to be made.

Note that there may be some overlap between these dimensions. In particular, the focuser would appear to have much in common with the person with a reflective style, but the two are not necessarily the same thing. In focusing we are talking about a situation where information is fed to the subject in a number of stages, whereas reflectivity is a response to any situation, whether the information is present at one go or whether some of it is more delayed. Note also that although my examples have been of people at the extreme ends of each of the dimensions, most people will tend to cluster towards the centre: that is, they will tend to make up their minds in an interval of time that does not categorize them as extremely impulsive or extremely reflective.

Cognitive style and learning

Since cognitive style may in a variety of important ways influence the manner in which we tackle learning tasks, teachers often ask whether it is possible for them to help children alter their position on a particular dimension. Here the answer is rather less clear than it is with the personality traits discussed earlier. Certainly some important aspects of cognitive style would appear to be learnt, though others might be due to temperamental and emotional factors, and it seems probable that the teacher might be able to modify and develop the former. It is illuminating to consider how much of our educational effort is directed towards the transmission of knowledge and skills, and how little of it is concerned with helping children understand and shape their own patterns of thinking and categorization. As was pointed out in Chapter 7, failures in learning are not caused only by failures in memory, in attention, in attitude and motivation and so on, but by the way in which sense is made (or not made) of the material to be assimilated. Yet, as Chapters 5 and 6 showed, little thought is given within education to the best methods of helping children to extend the ways in which they explore and recognize the meaning of the material in front of them, and develop the thinking strategies most appropriate to it. It is not that educationalists are unaware of the importance of children's thinking, or are unaware that one of their tasks is to encourage and help shape this thinking: it is simply that to date they are by no means sure how this can best be done. Research into cognitive style will provide valuable pointers in this area, and will show besides that the child's thinking must be considered within the context of personality as well as within the context of cognitive abilities.

Personality states

We turn now from personality traits and dimensions, (which I have termed the 'ruler' approach), to personality states (the alternative 'thermometer' approach). As indicated earlier, personality states are fluctuating and have to do with the mood of the moment, the social context in which one finds oneself, the task in hand, and so on. Some psychologists are divided on the question of which is more important, states or traits, or whether the two are equal, and the debate is unlikely to be quickly resolved.

One example of a state-based approach is the work of George Kelly, which is discussed in Chapter 10. It might be helpful to read pp. 233–236 in order to follow the argument. Kelly's *repertory grid technique* allows one to explore the shifting nature of the individual's psychological space. Though the repertory grid does not measure emotions and feelings in any direct sense, it gives us a clear picture of how the individual's cognitive and effective experiences relate to each other and together construct his or her view of reality. For example, we can use the repertory grid to assess how individuals feel about themselves and their relationships with family, friends, teachers and the like, thus allowing us to deduce how they feel about their lives. We can then use the grid to observe how the way they feel can change over time, particularly in response to variations in life circumstances such as a switch from failure to success at school, or to new insights into the concepts others have about them. Evidence of the speed at which such a change can take place comes from exercises such as measuring individual students' self-concepts in the nervous days before an important examination and measuring them after the exam when they learn they passed with flying colours.

Arguments against permanence in personality

Work with repertory grids has prompted some state theorists to see the notion of fixed traits as actively harmful, since it leads us to relate to people *as if* their personalities are permanent structures and therefore resistant to change. Thomas and Harri-Augustein (1985) maintain that the notion of permanence in any area of human psychology is a handicap to our understanding and to our attempts to educate ourselves and others. This handicap is particularly damaging when it comes to assessing and working with children. We mistake a child's present state for something permanent, and by reacting to him or her accordingly we actually help make it so. Learning failure, low intelligence, personality problems may therefore be in part the creation of psychologists and teachers who purport to 'measure' these states, and convince other adults and the children themselves that they are measuring something solid and real.

State theorists argue that we should concentrate upon determining what affective (and cognitive) *entry behaviours* children need if they are to tackle a particular task effectively. That is, we should ask ourselves what mood they need to be in (and what they need to know) if they are to be in the state needed for success (Bloom, 1983). Once we have determined this, we encourage that mood (and that knowledge) and proceed to the learning task itself. One state theorist from whom we can draw guidance on these issues is Apter (1982). Apter suggests that personality can be conceptualized in terms of a number of dimensions, like the trait theorists, but he differs from them in maintaining that instead of fixed positions on these dimensions we can reverse from one end to the other in response to circumstances. In terms of Eysenck's dimension of extraversion–introversion this would mean that we can be extraverted in certain situations and introverted in others, indeed that psychological balance is best served if we *are* able to reverse in this way. Similarly, we can be anxious in certain situations and unruffled in others.

Telic–paratelic behaviour

Apter does not, however, take Eysenck's dimensions as his example. Instead, he puts forward a number of different dimensions of his own. The most fully researched and the most relevant of these from the teacher's viewpoint is labelled by Apter the telic–paratelic. In the *telic* state we are in a purposeful mode, using the present activity primarily as a means towards the attainment of a definite goal. In the *paratelic* state on the other hand we are in a playful mode, with the present activity all-important and the actual objective (if there is one) simply an excuse for engaging in the activity. For example, I can swim to save my life (telic), or I can swim for the pleasure of swimming (paratelic). I can walk to the newsagent because I want my newspaper (telic), or I can walk to the newsagent simply as an excuse for stretching my legs (paratelic). Although the behaviour in both cases is the same, my reason for engaging in it is fundamentally different. As indeed would be my response to other people. If I am swimming to save my life I would welcome the intervention of a lifeguard. If I am swimming for pleasure I would regard this intervention as something of a nuisance. If I am walking to the newsagent because I want my newspaper I would welcome the newsagent's offer to deliver it to me in future. If I am walking to the newsagent as an excuse for stretching my legs I would reject this offer and stick to my walk.

Apter argues that although individuals usually prefer one end of the telic–paratelic dimension to the other (they may *prefer* to be purposeful or *prefer* to be playful), they are normally able to reverse between the two ends as necessary. Failure to reverse suggests psychological problems, as in the person who can never relax at a party (i.e. become paratelic) or the person who cannot be serious (i.e. become telic) at a funeral. But often individuals fail to reverse simply because they do not properly understand the situation in which they find themselves. This is particularly important at school level. Certain school subjects or certain activities within school subjects require a telic state (preparation for examinations, detailed scientific experiments, the use of potentially dangerous equipment for example), while certain others require a paratelic state (sport and games, creative expression, musical appreciation). The teacher and the child who are unable to discriminate between the two, and reverse along the telic–paratelic dimension accordingly, are seriously handicapped. As is the teacher who tries too abruptly to change children from one state to another (e.g. when a maths lesson follows a games lesson, or a creative writing lesson follows a foreign language lesson). Serious misunderstandings may also arise between teachers who prefer the telic state and a class which prefers the paratelic ('why do teachers always want us to work?') and between teachers who prefer the paratelic state and a class which prefers the telic ('why don't teachers get on with it?').

The state-based approach and counselling

Dimensions such as the telic–paratelic are also of value when it comes to counselling children with behaviour and personality problems. For example, children may truant in the telic state *or* in the paratelic. In the telic state they truant with the definite intention of avoiding a teacher or a group of children they dislike, or of staying at home to stop the violent behaviour of parents towards each other. In the paratelic state they truant simply for the pleasure of being off school. Similarly they may steal in the telic state (as a way of getting something they want) or in the paratelic state (as a way of experiencing excitement). Unless teachers are aware of the child's state, their efforts at counselling are unlikely to get very far. On the broader front, a child who has been made anxious by the constant telic insistence of parents or teachers upon getting 'good marks' may produce a much more relaxed and successful performance if the teacher is able to present class activities more in the form of paratelic 'games', while a paratelic child who seems unable to take anything seriously can be helped to become telic if the teacher offers rewards which the child sees are worth working towards and adopting as goals.

The whole emphasis of the state-based approach is therefore upon opening up the possibilities for desirable change, rather than assuming that the personalities of the children we teach are basically fixed and enduring. Admittedly, carried to extremes, the state-based approach could suggest there is nothing consistent in personality, and that the idea we are the same people today as we were last week or even yesterday is an illusion. This is manifestly unworkable, both in our inner lives and in our relationships with others. But properly interpreted, the state-based approach tells us that it is a feature of living systems that they are subject to constant change. Since the individual aspects of that change do not all happen at the same speed, enough is carried over from one day to the next to make us recognizable as ourselves. But these changes are nevertheless taking place, many of them very rapidly, and if we accept this then we can guide these changes in desirable directions, instead of assigning to the personality set labels and categories which can serve as hindrances to our understanding of it.

The psycho-dynamic approach

A very different approach to personality from that of the trait- and state-based theories referred to so far in this chapter is that of *psychodynamics*. Whereas both trait and state approaches are concerned primarily with the individual's personality as it is now, psychodynamic psychologists argue that we can only understand the present if we look back at the formative influences at work upon personality in earlier years. They go further and suggest that the personality is shaped by the interaction of these influences with innate psychological dynamics, that is with strong inborn psychological drives such as the sex drive and the drive towards self-preservation.

The best-known psychodynamic psychologist is Sigmund Freud (who founded the *psychoanalytical* school). His proposed system is so complex and far-ranging that detailed discussion lies outside the scope of this book. Psychodynamic psychology has little immediate classroom relevance for the teacher, though it has so influenced the way in which we think about childhood and about personality problems that some acquaintance with it is called for. Also called for is some acquaintance with the deep divide between trait theorists and psychodynamic theorists. The former argue that the models of personality advanced by the latter are hopelessly unscientific, cannot be put to proper experimental test, and are so vague they can be used to 'explain' almost any aspect of human behaviour. On the other hand psychodynamic theorists argue that trait theories ignore the fact that each individual is unique, and that attempts to study personality by the use of questionnaires and large sample work are doomed to failure. Thus psychodynamic theorists do not emphasize measurement at all, either with ruler or thermometer, and propose instead a model of personality development against which each person can be studied individually.

Sigmund Freud

In Freud's view, the crucial years in the forgeing of the personality are from birth to six or seven. During this period children have their inborn drives socialized by those around

190

them. If this is done with understanding and a due regard for the strength of these inborn drives, then all goes well. But if children meet with frustration and harsh punishments, then they grow up full of guilt and inner conflicts, and with all manner of neurotic problems. Neurosis, in Freud's view, is essentially the result of preventing people from doing what they are strongly motivated to do, without allowing them to understand the reasons for this prohibition and without providing them with alternatives into which they can channel their frustrated psychological energy.

THE ID. In Freudian psychology, the personality is seen as composed of three separate levels. The first level is the *id*, the instinctive energies with which the child is born. These energies have a survival value, and obey the *pleasure principle*. Their aim is to provide the individual with gratification for basic animalistic needs. Shorn of the elaborate explanations used by Freud to explain these needs, they consist primarily of personal survival needs (food, comfort, warmth, shelter and so on) and species' survival needs (sex). The id is entirely selfish and unconscious, and has no knowledge of the needs of others or of the consequences of its actions.

THE EGO. Around the end of the first year of life the second level of personality, called by Freud the *ego*, begins to develop. The ego operates at the conscious level, and obeys the *reality principle*. That is, it contains the child's growing knowledge of the world and of the behaviour and reactions of others. With the development of the ego, the child's social learning begins, and with it comes an initial awareness of the limits which the world places upon the demands of the id. The ego realizes that these demands cannot always be met, that sometimes they may lead to physical dangers and punishments, and that often they are best served by obedience and politeness and other learnt strategies rather than by simply grabbing and insisting. Note however that in Freud's view the ego itself has no psychological energy. All such energy comes from the instinctive drives of the id. As long as the ego is successful in obtaining satisfaction for the needs of the id, then the id is prepared to channel its energy into the ego. If, however, the ego is unsuccessful, then the id demands direct expression and we get outbreaks of uncontrolled anger or aggression or lust (or whatever other emotional form the id's energy happens to take). For satisfactory personality development, it is essential for the id and the ego to strike a proper balance, with the latter obtaining gratification of the needs of the former, which in turn transfers energy to the latter.

THE SUPER-EGO. Round about the age of six, the third level of the personality, the *super-ego*, develops. Part conscious and part unconscious, the super-ego is the internalization of the moral beliefs and strictures passed on to children by their parents, and obeys the *morality principle*. It contains both the 'conscience' (which produces guilt when children know they have done wrong) and the 'ego-ideal' (which produces ambition when children get a picture of the people they would like to be). Like the ego, the super-ego has no psychological energy of its own, and like the ego can be overwhelmed by the animalistic id if the needs of the latter are constantly frustrated.

One useful example of the respective workings of id, ego and super-ego is the child who sees some mouth-watering cakes on a tray in the kitchen. The id says 'go get one' (the pleasure principle) but the ego says 'no, mummy or daddy would find out and I'd be punished' (the reality principle). Assuming the id's need to avoid punishment is greater than its need for a cake, then the reality principle prevails and the child does not take a cake. However, if the ego is satisfied that mummy or daddy has no way of knowing that a cake has been taken, and that there is no risk of punishment, then the reality principle of the ego will agree 'go ahead' and the child gets the mouth-watering delicacy. But – and it is a big but – if the super-ego has developed, it chimes in with 'even though mummy or daddy won't find out, it's *wrong* to take the cake' (the morality principle). If the id's need to avoid the emotional punishment brought on by feelings of guilt is greater than its need for the cake, then again the child will not take a cake.

This example shows how id, ego and super-ego are all involved in the child's behaviour from the age of six or so onwards. In the case of the cake, they are all operating in response to the child's personal survival instinct (hunger). But important as the personal survival instinct is, Freud held that the species' survival instinct is sometimes more important (or at least causes more problems!) From birth onwards, Freud saw the child as an intensely sexual creature, with a number of erogenous zones in the body which crave sexual gratification (principally the mouth, the anus and the genitals). There is no relevance for the teacher in going over the intricate theories which Freud developed in relation to these erogenous zones. Suffice it to say that Freud argued that if children are made to feel excessively guilty or 'dirty' at the thought of touching or playing with these zones, and are constantly frustrated in their efforts to do so, then there will be serious long-term effects upon the personality. Sexual energy must be recognized and given opportunities to channel itself into other creative outlets (the arts, good human relationships, imagination, initiative and so on) if orderly development of the personality is to take place. Freud never advocated unlicensed sex. Quite the contrary. But he did insist that such a powerful drive must be accepted and understood if it is to develop into psychological health. Thwarted, punished, frustrated it turns into violence, perversions, aggression and other harmful impulses on the one hand, or leads to a rigidly over-controlled and obsessional personality on the other. Either way, we have the foundations for neuroses, and for the kind of personality problems that lead not only to destructive behaviour within individual lives but within whole communities. For nations to live at peace with each other, individuals must first be able to live at peace with themselves.

For Freud, the healthy personality is one where there is an orderly transfer of energy between id, ego and super-ego. A personality where the ego knows, understands and accepts the needs and the emotional pressures of the id (from anger to sexuality), and is able to control them and channel them into socially acceptable behaviour at a conscious level instead of rigidly repressing them or remaining at their mercy. And a personality where the ego knows and appreciates the moral principles that underlie the super-ego, and can do what is right because it is known to be right and not because to do otherwise would lead to torments of guilt.

EGO DEFENCE MECHANISMS. If the personality is not able to produce the appropriate balance between the id, ego and super-ego, then in Freud's view a number of *ego defence mechanisms* are created. These are strategies developed by the ego to defend itself from the demands of the id. The most comprehensive of these is *repression*. The ego pushes emotions, feelings, unpleasant memories and thoughts down into the id, thus putting them beyond the reach of conscious awareness. In this way hostility towards others, for example, or sexual desire, or forbidden longings, go unacknowledged and remain down in the id where they cannot be subjected to rational, objective debate. But repressed material does not just go away. The emotional energy behind this material may become so powerful that it emerges back into consciousness in a disguised form; that is, in a form which the individual can more readily accept (e.g. repressed and unacknowledged anger towards parents may emerge as hostility towards superiors at work). Or it may become the source of inner conflicts in which individuals go in dread of some dark force inside themselves which they sense but cannot explain.

Another important ego defence mechanism is *reaction-formation*, in which individuals maintain repressions by emphasizing the very opposite behaviours. For example, a strong sex drive is repressed by exaggeratedly moral behaviour. Another is *denial*, in which individuals over-emphatically deny possessing those very motives or emotions which trouble them most. Another is *projection*, where they insist on accusing others of having the characteristics they fear in themselves. Another is *regression*, where they go back to earlier forms of childish behaviour which used to be successful in protecting the ego from fears and frustration. And there are many others.

THREE KINDS OF ANXIETY. One final aspect of Freudian theory of potential relevance to the teacher is Freud's three-way categorization of anxiety. If anxiety is caused primarily by the repressed emotional energy in the id, then individuals suffer from *neurotic anxiety*. This is free-floating anxiety in which individuals are always afraid of something, though they often do not know what. The fear really comes, argues Freud, from a fear of oneself; a fear of those strong forces which lie just below the conscious level of one's psychological life and which force one to maintain a rigid control over all one's actions and emotions. If anxiety is caused primarily by actual events going on around one and operates at the level of the ego, then the individual suffers from *realist anxiety*, while if the anxiety comes from the punitive and guilt-arousing super-ego, then the individual suffers from *moralistic anxiety*.

The ego has, therefore, potentially to fight on three fronts. Against the neurotic anxiety caused by the id, against the realistic anxiety caused by contemporary life events, and against the moralistic anxiety caused by the super-ego. In individuals who already have a great deal of their energies tied up in fighting neurotic and moral anxiety, a relatively small dose of realistic anxiety may cause a breakdown. In individuals with low neurotic and moralistic anxieties on the other hand, even high levels of realistic anxiety can be coped with successfully.

Arguments rage as to whether these three different forms of anxiety, and indeed the whole construction of id, ego and super-ego, can readily be put to experimental test (see e.g. Fisher and Greenberg, 1985). But they do provide useful ways of conceptualizing the personality, and yield implications for the teacher when it comes to helping children handle their emotions. With Freudian theory, the best approach is often to see if it provides useful insights into your own mental and emotional life. If it does, then it is worth exploring the theory further. Most teachers adopt an eclectic approach to psychology, borrowing from it those aspects which help them in their task of understanding children, rather than identifying exclusively with any one theory or set of theories. Working at this level, you may find that Freud does have something to teach us, though this does not mean taking over all or even most aspects of his thinking. The conclusion reached by Brown

(1964) on Freud remains one of the best, namely that without knowing all the answers, Freud did know the kind of *questions* psychology ought to be asking.

Personality
and
motivation

One important area of personality linked to both the trait and the state-based approaches is motivation. We can talk reasonably of a general trait of motivation within people (one person may be strongly motivated to succeed in a career, another strongly motivated to get on with others and so on), while at the same time we can talk of fluctuating motivational states ('I'm strongly motivated to get on with my work this week, but didn't feel so enthusiastic last week'; 'I'm motivated at task A but not at task B'). Many of the general principles behind motivating children were discussed in Chapter 7 (pp. 133–134), so I will look now at motivation in its more personal sense as an aspect of personality, an aspect which touches a child's chances of success and failure in education at a number of points.

Most theories of motivation begin with the basic survival motives with which we are born. Often referred to as *drives*, these include the desire to seek for food when hungry, for warmth when cold, for physical safety when threatened, for drink when thirsty, and for sexual activity when sexually aroused. The suggestion is that hunger, thirst, etc. set up tensions within us which we seek to relieve by appropriate action. If we did not experience tension as uncomfortable, of course, we would simply stay where we were and die. In young babies whose activity, and therefore whose independence, is limited by physical immaturity, crying is used to attract the attention of others who then initiate tension-reducing activity for them.

However, in our highly complex, artificial environment these survival drives (with the exception of sex) are rarely strong determinants of behaviour once early infancy is past, since the needs associated with them are met with routine ease. Even aggression, which also seems to be a natural survival drive, rarely needs to be given physical expression in a civilized society, and indeed is often discouraged in most of its manifestations by social mores and taboos. Thus we are faced with the conclusion that for all their obvious importance, survival drives have little direct influence upon the motivational structures that help define the personalities of older children and adults. There is also a range of important motives that sometimes appear to work *against* survival drives, and others that have no obvious relationship to them. Examples of motives in the first category would be concern for others and for society in general, self-denial and self-sacrifice and even, in many instances, conscientiousness, honesty and sympathy. In the second category we might instance love of music and of the arts, many hobbies, and a delight in beauty and in nature generally.

Motivation and reinforcement

From the discussion of learning theories in Chapter 7 (pp. 127–131) it can be seen that one possible explanation of these motivational systems is that they develop in response to strong reinforcement. Thus the individual's love for a hobby, for example, might have come about because the activities connected with it received generous praise and encouragement from parents in childhood. Parental praise (and even parental attention) is, as we have seen, a potent form of reinforcement, and the child may well have found that turning to these activities was an excellent way of attracting such praise. In consequence, the activities became an established part of his or her behavioural repertoire, and soon produced further reinforcers unconnected with the home (e.g. teacher praise, success in competitions, the establishment of new friendships, prestige, release from boredom). Similarly, helpful actions and concern for others could also have attracted adult approval initially, and then gone on to attract wider reinforcers that serve to sustain them into adult life (e.g. the grateful thanks of recipients, the feeling that one is a significant and necessary member of the community, or the warm feeling of self-approval).

Obviously the reinforcement model can account for many motives of this kind, but it cannot account for them all. It cannot account, for example, for hobbies and enthusiasms that arise suddenly and with no apparent preconditions in later life. Nor can it account for acts of self-sacrifice where the tangible rewards would seem to be much less than those to be gained by acting selfishly. We can, of course, say that nevertheless there must be schedules of reinforcement to account for these behaviours if we were only able to study the individuals concerned and their life histories closely enough to discover what they are. But this is simply a statement of belief, since there is no direct evidence to show that this is the case. Hence motivation remains one of those problem areas in psychology where there is no general agreement that any one model or set of models is adequate.

Maslow's theory of motivation

An alternative and less ambitious way of approaching the subject is to attempt simply to *describe* motivation rather than to account for it. The best-known descriptive model of this kind is suggested by Maslow, and takes the form of a hierarchy going from personal needs at the bottom to intellectual ones at the top as shown in Figure 8.1. (e.g. Maslow 1943).

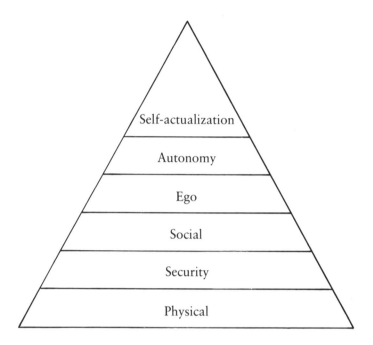

Figure 8.1. Maslow's hierarchy of needs.

The implications are that the lower, personal levels of the hierarchy, which consist of physiological needs (food, drink, shelter, etc.) and needs associated with survival and security, are largely innate, while the social and intellectual levels consist of innate factors combining more and more with learnt responses. In the light of our present knowledge it is not clear how this process of combination happens, but Maslow does not rule out the possibility that innate factors may still play the more important part even at the intellectual level: that is, that the thirst for ego strength and autonomy may be something inherent in humans, and something which they will pursue even when these qualities are not necessary for their physical or even social needs.

Maslow thinks that we can only attend to the three highest levels of the hierarchy, however, if the lower levels of physiological and social needs have been satisfied. Thus a society living perpetually in near starvation conditions or at war with its neighbours would have little time or energy left to allow individuals to develop the creativity and wisdom associated with autonomy and self-actualization. The great upsurge in artistic endeavour noted in Europe during the Renaissance, for example, only became possible because at this point in history certain nations had advanced to the stage where primary needs were reasonably easily met, and certain sections

tions of the community had the time to divert their attention to loftier matters. Note that this does not mean that the satisfaction of primary motives will of itself lead us on to higher things, but simply that unless this satisfaction is forthcoming all of our motivational energy goes into the simple business of keeping ourselves alive, with none left over for more exalted considerations.

Maslow's hierarchy therefore suggests that if individuals have their physiological needs satisfied, together with their need for safety from aggressors, they then become chiefly concerned with being accepted by their families and the social group (social needs). Once accepted, they will next concern themselves with ego needs such as being esteemed by others, so that they may come to think well of themselves. Having satisfied these ego needs, they then move on to autonomy, that is to a sense of independence and personal freedom, and finally to self-actualization, which is a more difficult concept but one upon which Maslow lays great stress. Self-actualization means in effect that individuals develop those characteristics peculiar to mature and well-adjusted people. They become, for example, realistic, independent, creative, problem-centered rather than self-centred, and with a ready appreciation both of other people and of the world about them.

Locus of control

Of course, although we are each faced with this same hierarchy, some of us will climb higher up it during our lifetime than will others. We will also tend to tackle the problems associated with it in different ways. Rotter (1954) suggests that one important way in which these differences are expressed is evidenced by what he calls *locus of control*. This refers primarily to the way in which individuals expess their successes and failures. Those with external locus of control tend to ascribe these things to factors outside themselves (e.g. 'I did well because I had the lucky breaks'; 'I failed because my teacher was no good'), while those whose locus of control is internal feel the responsibility usually lies with themselves ('I got through because of my own hard work'; 'I failed because I didn't take it seriously enough'). Not surprisingly, research shows that people in the former category prefer usually to work in conditions where chance plays an important part, while people in the latter prefer circumstances where skill is the deciding factor. This does not imply that success is always more likely where the locus of control is internal. Many prestigious and lucrative occupations depend upon a high-risk factor (not only sporting occupations but such things as stockbroking, starting new businesses and commercial undertakings, and being prime minister). In addition, the tendency of internalizers to lay all their problems at their own door can lead to feelings of inadequacy and personal failure which may deter them from attempting new tasks even though such tasks may be well within their talents. However, within the school and the educational world in general, an internal locus of control seems the more desirable.

Weiner (most recently 1979), working along similar lines to Rotter, has developed what is known as *attribution theory*, which explores in more detail the way in which we attribute the reasons for success and failure in our personal and professional lives, and even the way in which we attribute meaning to the terms 'success' and 'failure' themselves, and has shown that the most highly motivated students are those who:

- prefer situations in which the consequences of their actions can be ascribed to themselves;
- have learnt to attribute outcome to effort;
- are sensitive and reactive to cues that indicate the importance of effort expenditure in any particular area.

In the light of present knowledge we cannot say for sure whether locus of control and the various factors associated with attribution theory are innate or acquired; probably both, but it would seem that of the two learning plays the more important part. Some children are taught by parents and teachers from an early age that it is no good putting the blame on somebody else, or complaining about bad luck when poor results are achieved. Instead, they are told, they must rely upon their own efforts, and if they meet with failure they must try extra hard to develop the skills that are lacking. Of course, blaming things on others can be a form of self-defence. If it is always somebody else's fault then we never have to face up to our own inadequacies. Children who are allowed to get away with this attitude find it a comforting one therefore, which in itself acts as a strong reinforcer and helps to make the attitude habitual. (It is worth while pointing out that teachers who always lay the blame for classroom failure upon pupils may also be exhibiting the same attitude.)

The teacher's reaction to success and failure in children

One of the most important aspects of the teacher's role is his or her reaction to success and failure in children. Most teachers have few problems in recognizing and rewarding success (though they sometimes neglect the fact that success should be interpreted in terms of what the individual child can do and not merely in terms of the subject itself and the usual standards achieved in it by other children of the same age), but more problems arise with failure. The point has already been emphasized very strongly indeed that making mistakes is not evidence of failure but is an integral and essential part of the learning process. By puzzling over where and how they went wrong children learn from these mistakes, and develop strategies for dealing with them in future. Slow learning, as has been indicated, is not failure but evidence that the child needs special kinds of help. So failure at school level, therefore, is more an attitude of mind than an objective reality. Children who develop this attitude, perhaps encouraged by teachers who give them consistently low marks and show them up in front of the class, will tend to give up and show low levels of motivation even when the work is theoretically within their grasp. If their locus of control is external they may blame their failure upon others or upon the subject itself; if it is internal they may feel it is their own fault, but the end result will be the same, with individual children coming to make failure a habit. Faced with low motivation, the first questions the teacher must ask are 'What has been the child's experience of failure to date?' and 'How has this experience affected his or her general motivation to learn?'

Mood

Turning from motivation to mood, which we can define as a state of feeling of varying duration, we find that again there are links with both personality traits and personality states. The anxious person, for example, will have a tendency to manifest a different pattern of moods from the cheerful, optimistic person, thus suggesting the pattern depends in part upon the underlying trait of anxiety. On the other hand, even given this pattern, the anxious person may well vary in mood from one situation to another, suggesting that we can sometimes best understand him or her if we adopt the state-based approach and see the mood simply as a transient phenomenon.

But whether looked at in terms of traits or states, mood seems to be the creation in part of heredity and in part of environment. It will be recalled from earlier in the chapter that the children labelled 'difficult' by Thomas, Chess and Birch had a general crankiness of mood, suggesting the influence of innate temperament. The influence of environment is, however, equally clear in that individuals who experience secure, happy childhoods are more likely to see the world as an optimistic place than are people from more difficult backgrounds. People who experience constant failure are more likely to show dejection and apathy (or anger) than people who predominantly experience success. Children who are encouraged to discuss their problems and feelings fully and openly with their parents, without fear of rejection, are less likely to indulge in sullen brooding than children who have always had to bottle up their feelings and keep their mouths closed. Children who are taught a humane and balanced moral code are less likely to be tortured by guilt at imagined misdemeanors than children who are brought up in an unrealistic punitive creed. At each point the child's mood is in part a response to the behaviour of people around him or her, and can only be understood if it is viewed within the context of this behaviour.

Moods are often thought to be at their most *labile* (i.e. subject to the most rapid fluctuation) at adolescence. Body chemistry again may play some part here, with the child undergoing the rapid adolescent growth spurt, and maturing in the space of some two or three short years from physical childhood to physical adulthood, with all that the latter implies in terms of bodily size and strength, sexual energy, and brain maturation. But environment is also important in that adolescents often feel the restrictions that society still lays upon them are particularly irksome, and keep them in the subservient, dependent role of the child when physically they clearly belong to the grown-up world. In addition adolescents are, of course, trying out various new patterns of behaviour, experimenting in a sense with their personalities to see how other people react to them, and to see what kind of people they really are and what kind of people they would like to become. Met with sympathy and understanding (and consistent firmness where necessary) adolescents gradually come to terms with their moods, and learn where self-control is preferable to self-expression. This whole phase, linked as it is to the vital question of personal identity and the development of the self, is so important that I return to it at greater length in the next chapter.

Teachers have moods too

Before leaving the question of moods, however, it is appropriate to point out that teachers are themselves also subject to these varying states. How individual teachers feel at any given moment will depend upon a number of factors, such as their own temperament, their relationship with the children concerned and with colleagues, the way they feel about the subject to be taught, the state of their private lives outside school, and so on. But sheer physical fatigue can also play an important part. Particularly towards the end of term some teachers experience what is often called *fatigue debt*: that is, they find the tiredness of the preceding day is not fully dissipated by an evening's rest and a night's sleep, and in consequence they have to draw upon their energy reserves to keep going. At such times minor irritations which normally would pass almost unnoticed may take on major significance, and the teacher will perhaps start snapping at children in consequence. Far from improving matters this may only serve to irritate the children in turn, leading to further problems for the teacher and a rapidly escalating state of tension for all concerned.

The best advice that can be offered here is that teachers should be aware of their own changing moods, and aware of the effect that these moods can have upon the class. As I have stressed already in the book, children thrive best upon consistent treatment from the important adults in their lives. Such treatment allows them increasingly to predict what is likely to happen next in their relationship with these adults, and to see their social world as an essentially lawful and understandable place. As they grow older, of course, they come to realize that a degree of fluctuation in the behaviour of those around them appears unavoidable, but there should still be sufficient consistency for them to feel secure and to learn appropriate workable strategies for managing relationships with parents and teachers and other adults in positions of authority over them. Where adults fail to show consistency of this kind children are left feeling confused and uncertain, and perhaps even resentful and hostile at what they see as the adult's inexplicable and unfair behaviour towards them.

Thus, however difficult it may seem, the teacher cannot really afford the luxury of moods that significantly alter behaviour towards individual children or towards the class as a whole. Children come to respect the teacher with whom they 'know where they stand' (one reason why even the stern, remote teacher usually commands respect), and in the long run have scant regard for anyone who fluctuates wildly from good humour to bad, from friendliness to aloofness, from sympathy to indifference, and from leniency to strictness. Provided it does not happen frequently, and therefore come to be seen by the children as a tiresome excuse, it is better for unwell or over-fatigued teachers on a particular day to tell the class of their moods at the outset of the lesson, so that children can understand why their behaviour may be a little different from usual. Some teachers strongly condemn such a practice, and see it as a sign of weakness, but it is better that children should know and sympathize than that they should be left puzzled and hostile. Where the relationship with the class is a good one, teachers will also be heartened at the thoughtfulness and kindness that many of the children show. Needless to say, this will be particularly noticeable where teachers themselves are noted by the children as being sensitive to their problems in turn.

Interest

In addition to motivation and moods, the study of personality is also linked to such important variables as interest and attitudes. It is relatively easy to test the nature and strength of both of these even in children of junior school age and below, but it is more difficult to trace their origin and to make decisions on how the teacher can best encourage the development of those deemed by society to be of most value.

If we take interest first, I have already suggested (p. 133) that children tend to become interested in those things that help them deal with problems and difficulties in their lives because they see these as having 'relevance'. In the discussion of play (p. 29), I also proposed that there seems to be a natural inclination towards hedonistic activities. In addition, an interest in hobbies (and of course in school subjects) can come about in response to parental reinforcement, and even as a consequence of association between these hobbies and parents themselves. To this we can add the possibility that innate factors also play some part, particularly in those interests demanding skills which may to a certain extent be genetic in origin. Thus the child with a good ear for music even before receiving musical training, and with good manual dexterity, might show more interest in learning a musical instrument than a child less favourably endowed, while a child with a good visual imagination might be more ready to show an interest in developing drawing skills than a child with one less good.

The development of interest would seem, therefore, to be dependent upon a number of interrelated factors. In helping the child to develop an aptitude or interest in things considered to be of value, however, the role of the teacher is essentially:

- to provide the relevant opportunities
- to demonstrate the relevance of the interest concerned to children themselves
- to refrain from passing judgements on children's competence at the skills associated with the interest until they have been given the opportunities they require to develop these skills
- to show personal enthusiasm and involvement in the interest.

To these four basic points can be added a fifth, namely that the teacher should not react angrily if children, after due opportunity, do not feel the same way towards the interest in question as does the teacher. A negative reaction of this kind by the teacher is usually counter-productive, in that it turns children further against the interest (either through hostility towards the teacher, or through anxiety, or through feelings of personal inadequacy at not experiencing the enthusiasm which the teacher claims they 'ought' to be experiencing). Sometimes, although nothing may be apparent at the time, if children are left to themselves the interest will flourish at a later date. At other times, it is as well simply to remember that each of us is an individual, with our own particular set of psychological endowments and life experiences, and it would be impossible for us all to enjoy precisely the same things.

It must be stressed that we are not talking at this point about a child's feelings towards basic school subjects, (which are dealt with in the discussion of learning and motivation in Chapter 7), but about the more general enriching experiences that are a part of the school's educational life. The teacher is quite right to think that children would benefit from these experiences if they came to appreciate them to the full, but such appreciation is not something the teacher can compel. By its very nature it even lies to a great extent outside the conscious control of children themselves. They can learn to write, for example, an elegant criticism of a poem or of a painting or of a piece of music, but few teachers would regard this as the same experience as being deeply moved by the work of art concerned: that is, stirred by it emotionally because it strikes a chord with important aspects of their own life history or with the dreams and hopes they have about the future. There may come a time when we will have learnt so much about the techniques of teaching that we will be able to produce this kind of reaction from children for any great work of art or for any of the interests that we feel are important; but I doubt it. I also think it likely that if such a day does come, many teachers will feel that the things that make their job worth doing (and the things that make the arts and most other interests worth studying) will have disappeared.

Attitudes

Turning now to attitudes, we find ourselves on rather more precise ground. Psychologists define attitudes as the relatively enduring orientations that individuals develop towards the various objects and issues they encounter during their lives, and which they express verbally as opinions. Attitudes therefore clearly contain elements of value and belief, as well as varying degrees of factual knowledge (or what the holder takes to be factual knowledge). Less obviously, they may be partly *conscious* and partly *unconscious*, with the two sometimes even in conflict with each other. Freudian theorists lay great stress upon this conflict, and regard it as playing an important role in the development of the personality. We can see this exemplified by the ego defence mechanism of reaction-formation which was explained earlier in the chapter. In terms of this mechanism, an individual might harbour hostile attitudes towards people of other races, yet refuse to admit to these consciously because they arouse in him or her strong feelings of guilt. The attitudes are therefore kept repressed in the unconscious, and in an attempt to make sure they stay there the individual adopts an exaggeratedly solicitous and pious attitude towards every foreigner they meet. The presence of the unconscious attitudes are, however, revealed by surreptitious acts of nastiness (such as blocking the promotion of a coloured colleague or voting against a local councillor because of the liberal stand he or she takes on ethnic groups), which the individual nevertheless attempts to explain away as being in the 'best interests' of the person concerned or as being 'for the sake of peace' or because 'the majority would never stand for it'.

Attitudes and ego defence

The main problem here, however, is that we have no accurate way of measuring unconscious attitudes or of assessing how important the conflict between them and consciously held views is in normal life. Some psychologists hold that Freud greatly over-stressed the case, and that in the light of current knowledge we should concentrate upon *conscious* attitudes and keep an open mind on any other kind. However, teachers will want to examine their own attitudes on important moral and social issues closely to see whether there are any grounds for supposing that these attitudes are influenced or affected in any way by deeper beliefs which so far they have refused to face.

Closely linked to reaction-formation is another of the Freudian mechanisms of ego defence, namely *rationalization*. Rationalization applies where individuals express a socially acceptable reason for behaviour that in fact stems from much more dubious attitudes or motives whose existence they are reluctant to admit even to themselves. Thus the military man might claim he is in the Services because this is the best way of deterring the aggressor, whereas in fact he is drawn to the life by a liking for violence. Similarly, the anti-pornography campaigner might claim that she watches a salacious film only because this enables her (or him) to press for legislation to prevent other people from seeing it, whereas actually she enjoys the titillation provided by the experience.

This is not to suggest, of course, that teachers have much in common with either of these examples, but simply to urge that people entrusted with the task of helping form the attitudes of the young should strive first for self-knowledge, and should examine their own attitudes and beliefs for signs of the things against which I have been warning. Of equal, if not greater, importance is that they should look closely at the origin of their conscious attitudes (particularly where these concern education or children) and at the evidence that supports them. Sometimes they may find that these attitudes have been taken over, on trust so to speak, from authority figures and have not been subjected to proper critical scrutiny. At other times they may find them stemming from emotional reactions rather than from any reasoned argument. On other occasions they may find that attitudes lead them to prejudge important issues (e.g. their disapproving attitude towards a certain child may lead them to presume the latter's guilt whenever trouble has been caused instead of pausing to look at the evidence), and to take action which may in the event be inappropriate and even unjustified.

Attitudes and behaviour

Before leaving this general discussion and turning to the more specific matter of attitude change in children I should add an additional word of caution, namely that behaviour does not always match up even to consciously held attitudes. This is often because such attitudes set individuals standards that appear to be beyond their reach. One example is New Year resolutions, in which we consciously vow to match our behaviour to our attitudes, but which rarely survive beyond the end of January (or beyond the first day of January in some cases). A man may know he should work harder, or be kinder to his family, or watch less television, or take more exercise, or give up certain bad habits, but although his attitudes towards these things are right, his determination to carry these attitudes through lags some way behind. So the teacher may indeed have a fine turn of phrase, and send children away after morning assembly resolved to mend their ways and live henceforth lives of blameless purity, but the resultant changes in behaviour may not survive the first classroom skirmishes.

This means that paper and pencil tests of attitude, in which children (or adults for that matter) claim to prize desirable things like honesty, kindness towards others, thrift, and hard work, may tell us disappointingly little about how the children concerned will actually behave when faced with opportunities to live up to the attitudes in question. Certainly they may feel twinges of conscience at each failure, but these may be insufficient to make them behave differently next time. Similarly, some people may endorse the desirable things in an attitude test yet make mental reservations that under certain circumstances these attitudes may legitimately be abandoned. The businessperson may endorse the virtues of fair play, for example, yet consider that these do not apply when it comes to winning business from a competitor. The child may endorse the value of honesty, yet feel this does not apply when it comes to copying homework from a friend a few minutes before it is due to be handed in.

Cognitive dissonance

Closely linked to such anomalies we have what Festinger (1962) calls cognitive dissonance. Cognitive dissonance is said to arise where individuals hold a particular attitude, yet find that their behaviour (or another attitude) is at variance with it. Such variance can set up tension (dissonance) which individuals find uncomfortable, and which they try to reduce by modifying one of the variables concerned. They may do this by distorting it, even if this means tampering with what they believe to be the truth. For example, if a person has a confident attitude towards their own abilities, yet fails an examination that hitherto they considered to be an accurate measure of such abilities, they may suddenly find all sorts of reasons why the examination after all is no good. Once having made a dissonance-reducing change of this kind they will often go to great lengths to maintain it by misinterpreting new evidence. In the above example they might interpret a change in the examination syllabus the following year as 'proof' that it was unfair in the past. Or when they hear that someone who passed the examination has nevertheless failed to get a coveted job they may regard this as demonstrating that employers have little regard for the qualification it carries, and therefore must also be convinced of its worthlessness.

Dissonance-reducing changes are also apparent sometimes after individuals tell a lie. If an individual has a positive attitude towards the truth, they are now faced with dissonance between this attitude and their own behaviour. To reduce this dissonance they may decide that what they said was not really a lie at all because of the careful form of words used (e.g. 'it was all right to say I did not go for a swim because in fact we only splashed about in the shallows'). Individuals, it seems, will often show great ingenuity in convincing themselves that a lie was not really a lie, or in changing their recollection of events so that it appears to fit with the account of such events that they actually gave. This is particularly true, Festinger tells us, if the lie was over something small. It is as if our view of ourselves as truthful people can survive the knowledge that we have told a lie over something important more readily than the knowledge that we have told it over something trivial. To give way to great temptation, it appears, is seen by the individual as being human. To give way to minor temptation looks suspiciously like weakness. All this is not to say that people do in general give in to great temptation more readily than to minor, or necessarily feel less badly about it if they do, but simply that the individual's view of him or herself as basically honest seems less subject to dissonance where the falsehood is over something important.

Attitude change

In effect, a great deal has already been said about attitude change, both in this chapter and in Chapter 7. To interest children in something and to motivate them to succeed at it usually involves changing their attitude towards it. To reward them for changes in behaviour is also often likely to lead to changes in attitude (e.g. the child finds that hard work begins to pay off in class because the teacher deliberately sees to it that every example of it is reinforced, and the child then comes round to the view that lessons are not so bad after all). We can, however, add one or two further points that the teacher needs to keep in mind when thinking about shaping children's attitudes.

- Children's attitudes towards a particular activity benefit from seeing that activity performed (or *modelled*) for them by a prestigious figure. This does not mean, of course, that watching somebody else is a substitute for the children actually taking part in the activity themselves. But to attend, say, a top level games match, or to visit a factory to see certain skills and crafts in operation, or to watch inspired acting in the theatre, can be invaluable experience (provided, of course, that the children are not then expected immediately to match up to the observed standards themselves!)

- Linked to this notion of modelling, children's attitudes also benefit from the *example* set by teachers, particularly in matters of social conduct. Teachers who are themselves considerate and fair-minded towards the class are far more likely to see children taking over this behaviour than teachers who simply talk about these things but do not follow their own precepts.

- Arising from the discussion of learning in Chapter 7, it will be appreciated that where we have tried to change attitudes by modelling and by discussing important issues with children, we should take every opportunity to watch for and immediately *reinforce* the changes in behaviour that arise from these new attitudes. Otherwise, like New Year resolutions, these changes may be temporary in the extreme. Often, of course, the teacher will want to engineer specific opportunities for the children to put this new behaviour into effect, and the sooner this happens after changes in attitude have been noted the better.

- Finally children, like adults, respond readily to *enthusiasm* in others. Provided this enthusiasm is not forced on them (teachers have already been cautioned against expecting children necessarily to share their interests), they are likely to be fired by it and want to participate in the activities associated with it. The same is true of success. Where children witness success they quickly want to be associated with it through participation: as witness the upsurge in interest in a particular sport after a national competitor has won a gold medal in it for his or her country. One quality of successful teachers about which there is little dispute is their ability to inspire enthusiasms in others for their teaching subjects, and to carry others along with them until a point is reached where enthusiasm becomes self-reinforcing and their pupils are able to continue on their own. Another quality of successful teachers is that they set an example that children want to emulate: they have, in other words, skills and techniques that children would like to possess for themselves.

References

Allport, G.W. (1961) *Pattern and Growth in Personality*. London: Holt, Rinehart & Winston.

Apter, M.J. (1982) *The Experience of Motivation*. London: Academic Press.

Bennett, N. (1976) *Teacher Styles and Pupil Progress*. London: Open Books.
Bloom, B.S. (1983) *Human Characteristics and School Learning*. New York: McGraw Hill.

Brown, J.A.C. (1964) *Freud and the Post-Freudians*. Harmondsworth: Penguin.

Cattell, R.B. (1980) *Personality and Learning*. New York: Springer.

Elliott, C.D. (1972) Personality factors and scholastic attainment. *British Journal of Educational Psychology*, 42, 23–32.

Eysenck, H.J. (1983) Human learning and individual differences. *Educational Psychology 3*, 169–188.

Festinger, L. (1962) Cognitive dissonance. *Scientific American, October*.

Fisher, S. and Greenberg, R.P. (1985) *The Scientific Credibility of Freud's Theories and Therapy*. New York: Columbia University Press.

Kagan, J. (1966) Developmental studies in reflection and analysis. In A. Kidd and J. Rivoire (ed.) *Perceptual Development in Children*. London: University of London Press.

Lynn, R. (1971) *An Introduction to the Study of Personality*. London: Macmillan.

McCandless, B. (1969) *Children: behaviour and development*, London: Holt, Rinehart & Winston.

Maccoby, E. and Jacklin, C. (1974) *The Psychology of Sex Differences*. Stanford: Stanford University Press.

Maslow, A.H. (1943) A theory of human motivation. *Psychological Review, 50*, 370–396.

Rotter, J. (1954) *Social Learning and Clinical Psychology*. Englewood Cliffs, New Jersey: Prentice Hall.

Terman, L. and Oden, N. (1947) *Genetic Studies of Genius, Vol. IV*, Stanford: California University Press.

Thomas, A. and Chess, S. (1977) *Temperament and Development*. New York: Brumner-Mazel.

Thomas, L. and Harri-Augstein, S. (1985) *Self-organised Learning*. London: Routledge & Kegan Paul.

Thomas, A., Chess, S. and Birch, H. (1970) The origin of personality. *Scientific American, August*.

Weiner, B. (1979) A theory of motivation for some classroom experience. *Journal of Educational Psychology, 71*, 3–25.

Witkin, H.A. (1965) Psychological differentiation and forms of pathology. *Journal of Abnormal Psychology, 70*, 317–336.

SOME
QUESTIONS

1. Discuss the relative merits of the 'ruler' and the 'thermometer' approaches to personality assessment.

2. What is a personality dimension?

3. How would you define social introversion and social extraversion?

4. What are the disadvantages of trait-based personality tests?

5. What is meant by cognitive style?

6. Give some examples of the links that apparently exist between personality and intelligence.

7. What are the factors that influence the way in which a child codes incoming information?

8. Define personality states.

9. Why is the notion of 'permanence' a potential hindrance to our understanding of human psychology?

10. Which notion do you find of more help in understanding your own personality, personality traits or personality states?

11. Give examples of items of behaviour which can be carried out in either a telic or a paratelic mode.

12. Why is it important to know whether a particular learning task requires a telic *or* a paratelic mode?

13. What are the major formative influences at work upon personality according to the psychodynamic approach?

14. Give an example to show the relative workings of id, ego and super-ego.

15. Discuss the implications of ego defence mechanisms.

Additional Reading

Bruner, J., Goodnow, J. and Austin, G. (1956) *A Study of Thinking*. New York: Wiley.
A classic text which fully outlines Bruner's approach to cognitive style.(Also recommended for Chapter 3.)

Cattell, R.B. and Kline, P. (1977) *The Scientific Analysis of personality and Motivation*. London: Academic Press.
Explains in detail the factor analytical approach to personality which lies behind trait theories.

Eysenck, H.J. (1985) *Rise and Fall of the Freudian Empire*. Harmondsworth: Penguin.
A sustained critique by a confessed opponent of Freudian theory.

Fisher, S. and Greenberg, R.P. (1985) *The Scientific Credibility of Freud's Theories and Therapy*. New York: Columbia University Press.
The most fair-minded and comprehensive survey of the scientific status of Freudian theories.

Fontana, D. (1983) Individual differences in personality: State-based versus trait-based approaches. *Educational Psychology 3*, 189–200.

Fontana, D. (1986) *Teaching and Personality*. Oxford: Basil Blackwell.
A general introduction to personality and its significance at classroom level. (Also recommended for Chapters 7 and 14.)

Freud, A. (ed.) (1986) *The Essentials of Psychoanalysis*. Harmondsworth: Penguin.
Freud's classic work is The Interpretation of Dreams, *also available in Penguin. But this version edited by his daughter of many of his major papers provides the reader with the best introduction to his work.*

Hall, G.D. and Lindzey, G. (1973) *Theories of Personality*. New York: Wiley.
For the reader with a particular interest in personality who wants an overview of the best-known theories.

Kagan, J. and Kogan, N. (1970) Individual variation in cognitive processes. In P. Mussen (ed.) *Carmichael's Manual of Child Psychology, Vol. I*, 3rd edn. New York: Wiley.

Kline, P. (1983) *Personality: Measurement and theory*. London: Hutchinson.
Especially good on the subject of personality assessment.

Maslow, A.H. (1976) *The Farther Reaches of Human Nature*. Harmondsworth: Penguin.
Maslow was a prolific and highly readable author. This is a particularly comprehensive summary of his main ideas.

Naylor, F.D. (1972) *Personality and Educational Achievement*. Sydney: Wiley.
Still a useful introduction to the various ways of exploring links between personality and learning.

Warr, P.B. (1970) *Thought and Personality*. Harmondsworth: Penguin.

2

Still one of the best introductions to cognitive style and its practical implications.

Warren, N. and Jahoda, M. (1973) *Attitudes*, 2nd edn. Harmondsworth: Penguin.
A good general survey of the field.

Witkin, H., Moore C., Goodenough D. and Cox, P. (1977) Field-dependent cognitive styles and their educational implications. *Review of Educational Research*, 47, 1–64.
A very comprehensive summary by Witkin of his own work and its relevance to education.

Wolheim, R. (1971) *Freud*. London: Fontana.
One of the leading introductions to Freud's life and work.

9

Values and Moral Development

What are morals and values? The discussion of attitudes in the last chapter leads on to the broader issue of morals and values. Morals and values are elusive concepts, and there is no single definition of them that satisfies everyone. Many psychologists find it helpful to divide morality into two related aspects proposed by the philosopher Fichte, one subjective (the individual's inward observation of a personal code of of behaviour) and one objective (the attitudes and behaviour generally prized by the cultural group to which the individual belongs). The latter aspect is the one more thoroughly researched by psychologists, particularly in the context of a child's development of objective behaviour in general. The moral behaviour prized by one's cultural group may or may not be defined by rules, and these rules may or may not carry the force of law, but this behaviour is nevertheless seen by responsible members of society as representing imperatives in matters of conduct and of interpersonal relationships. These imperatives may be derived from religious, philosophical, or political teachings, and usually they have had an important influence upon the historical development of the cultural group concerned, providing guidelines for the emergence of civilized practices and even (ostensibly) for dealings with other countries. Sometimes within a culture, subgroups become apparent which differ from each other in the morals and values held (e.g. religious groups, socio-economic status groups), and this can lead to friction and to attempts to put down opposing value systems by force.

The origins of value systems The generally held view amongst psychologists is that morals and values are largely learnt structures, with young children acquiring them initially from parents and later from teachers, peer groups, the media, and society generally. One psychologist who made a particular study of the way in which this seems to happen was Freud (see pp. 190–195). Freud considered that the development of moral attitudes and behaviour in the child is due to the *super-ego*, which is largely the internalization by the child of the moral codes and strictures taught by

213

parents, but which are taken over so completely by the child that he or she often loses sight of their point of origin. The super-ego becomes, therefore, not just a collection of parental 'dos and don'ts' but an autonomous part of the mental life of individuals which they may come to regard as the voice of conscience or as their own carefully formulated moral code, operating at both the subjective and the objective levels.

Freud considered that an over-developed super-ego could lead to psychological problems such as excessive guilt and feelings of personal inadequacy and worthlessness and even, in extreme cases, to severe neuroses. Nevertheless, he saw the formation of the super-ego as on balance a good thing, since without it the child would only behave correctly when parents or other adults were there to reinforce good behaviour. In their absence, and when detection was unlikely, the child would feel quite free to follow selfish interests, no matter what the consequences for others might be. As suggested in Chapter 8, Freud's ideas attract much criticism nowadays in some quarters, and space does not allow me to go into them in any great detail, but it is interesting to recall that he saw the super-ego as developing two distinct elements. These were the *conscience*, which provides children with feelings of guilt when they do wrong and is equivalent to the punitive function of the parent, and the *ego-ideal* which provides feelings of satisfaction when they do right and is equivalent to the parental rewarding function. It is through the ego-ideal also that the child builds a picture of 'the person I would like to be', which may be important not only in determining day-to-day contact but in setting long-term life goals and ambitions.

Freud's model of the super-ego is a useful way of conceptualizing what may happen in the mental life of children as they build up a moral sense. An alternative view, based upon a study of the child's thinking, is proposed by Piaget (1932), however. Piaget, whose work was examined in detail in Chapter 3, observed the changes in the level of moral reasoning shown by children as they move through the various Piagetian stages of cognitive development. His findings suggest that children go from egocentric thinking, where everything is seen from the point of view of the self, to a form of thinking which allows them to put themselves in the place of others. Only when they are able to engage in the latter form of thinking are they capable of true moral judgement. We need not examine this model in detail, however, because a more comprehensive one, again related to the child's levels of thinking, is proposed by Kohlberg (1969). Kohlberg has it that the child passes developmentally through six major stages (grouped under three more general headings related to Piaget's stages) in moral development. The terminology used to describe these stages is varied by Kohlberg in his different publications, but a general summary appears below.

214

Kohlberg's six stages of moral development

Preconventional morality (Piaget's pre-operational stage of thinking). Age approximately 2–7 years.

1. *Obedience.* Children have no real moral sense, but their behaviour can be shaped by simple reinforcement.
2. *Naïve egoism.* A 'right' action is one that works for the child personally. The child may appear able to meet the needs of others, but this is only because the result is directly favourable to him or herself.

Conventional morality (Piaget's concrete operational stage of thinking). Age approximately 2–11 years.

3. *Good boy/girl orientation.* Children try to please their elders, initially only in specific situations, but later more generally as they come to acquire a concept of the 'good' child.
4. *Authority maintaining orientation.* Moral ideas generalize even further, and children try to live up to them not simply for personal gain, but because they now develop a sense of duty towards authority and the maintenance of the existing social order.

Postconventional morality (Piaget's formal operational stage of thinking). Age approximately 12 years onwards.

5. *Contractual legalism.* The sense of duty is still strong, but a sense of fairness and legality become even more important than the simple maintenance of the status quo. Rules are increasingly seen as arbitrary things subject to possible and often desirable change.
6. *General principles of conscience.* Moral ideas become integrated into a consistent and coherent philosophy. Moral decisions are able to take into account all the relevant variables, and the individual can now look beyond surface fairness and legality.

As with Piaget's stages themselves, the rate of progress through these six levels can vary from child to child, and some individuals may never reach the higher levels just as they may never achieve formal operations. In fact, it seems that reaching the appropriate level of thinking is an essential prerequisite for arriving at the corresponding level of moral development, though simply because children have achieved the former does not necessarily mean that they will also have achieved the latter. Learning and opportunity play a major part, and simply because children are capable of a certain level of moral thinking does not mean that they will automatically have arrived at it.

Measuring moral development

One way of measuring the stage of moral development of individual children is to confront them with a teasing moral problem and see how they solve it and why. Ideally, this should be in the form of a story, with children as the central characters. The plot should present these children with a dilemma of some kind, and the child taking the test should then be asked what he or she thinks they should do next. An example of one of these problems is given below.

> Jane's mother promises her she can go to the dance on Saturday if she washes the dishes all week. Jane does the dishes, but on Saturday her mother tells her she has changed her mind and will not let her go after all. Jane steals secretly out of the house and goes to the dance, and confides in her sister Mary. Should Mary tell their mother?

Clearly there is no easy right answer to this problem. Most children tend to agree that Mary should tell on her sister, but their reasons for taking this line vary and help us to decide their level of moral development. Children at Stage 1 typically say that Mary should tell because if she does not do so and her mother finds out that she kept the information back she will be punished. By Stage 3, however the emphasis has usually shifted and is now placed upon the relationship between Mary and her mother rather than upon the fear of punishment, and children typically say that it is wrong for children to keep secrets from their parents. By Stage 5, the reasoning is much more subtle and children tend to say that if Mary does not tell her mother then she is conspiring in her sister's lie, and lies are always morally wrong even though Mary's mother was also wrong to break her promise to Jane. By Stage 6, children show less agreement in their responses, and now tend to invoke their own moral codes. Some will argue that two wrongs do not make a right, while others will consider that Mary should not break a confidence of whatever kind, and yet others that Mary's mother has acted unreasonably towards Jane, and Mary's silence should be regarded as the lesser of two evils.

It is not, of course, possible to distinguish clearly between each of Kohlberg's stages even with tests of this kind, and the stages are therefore better regarded as guidelines in our approach to children's moral thinking than as rigid categories. We should not, for example, expect Stage 5 reasoning from a child who clearly is in Stage 2, but we should not be surprised if a child who solves one problem at a certain level reverts to a lower level when confronted with a dilemma of a different kind. A further difficulty, to which attention has already been drawn in the discussion of attitudes in Chapter 8, is that a child who expresses a moral attitude in response to a

Kohlberg-style problem willl not necessarily behave in accordance with this attitude when faced with a similar problem in real life. For example, the real-life Mary might decide not to tell on her sister simply for fear of what Jane would do to her if she did, or simply out of loyalty to Jane, or simply because at that particular moment in time she also had been treated unfairly by her mother and carried a brief grudge against her. It is also true, paradoxically, that children sometimes feel less guilt if they do what they claim is the 'wrong' thing (e.g. refuse to tell on Jane) than if they do what they claim is 'right' (tell on her after all).

It is also true (again, this can be implied from the discussion of attitudes in Chapter 8), that children may change their values dependent upon circumstances; that is, that they may show failure to generalize their moral codes. They may, for instance, find it acceptable to lie to the teacher but not to a best friend, to steal from a shop but not from their parents, to cheat in a class test but not in a public examination. Their moral codes may also be overriden by what appear to them to be more important considerations. Thus they may behave badly because this makes them more acceptable to a peer group, or cheat in an examination because this will get them into a higher set which in turn will please their parents, or steal from a shop because this is the only way they can get presents to give to family and friends. In our modern society, children are faced with increasingly difficult problems when it comes to moral decisions, due to constant bombardment by the media with materialistic and acquisitive concepts, and to the decline in the moral imperatives that go with religious beliefs (to say nothing of the general decline in the authority of parents and of the school). Perhaps in view of all this it is a wonder not that the moral standards of the young have slipped, as we are sometimes told, but that they have held up so well.

Criticisms of Kohlberg

Evidence for the importance of cultural factors in moral development comes from a number of cross-cultural investigations into Kohlberg's stages. Indeed, such studies suggest we must have reservations as to the universality of these stages. Kohlberg himself has found no evidence for Stage 6 amongst Turkish subjects, and has suggested in consequence that Stage 6 may simply be an advanced form of Stage 5 (Kohlberg, 1978). Bergling (1981) goes further, and casts some doubts on Stage 5 itself. Even Stages 1–4 are less apparent in some cultures than in others, and there is some suggestion that stage jumping may take place in certain instances.

However, what is at issue is not whether the stages can

always be identified or whether they form a useful basis for the development of curricula materials in moral education. Rather one must ask whether the stages are tied to precise levels of cognitive development such as those claimed by Piaget. There is little doubt in fact amongst most commentators that Kohlberg's theory is an appropriate starting point for those designing moral education programmes for use with children. At the same time, the consensus seems to be moving towards the idea that while Stages 1–3 or 4 are linked to the cognitive-developmental process, Stages 5 and 6 are very culture dependent, and are not normally reached in cultures which do not practice or teach a post-conventional morality (see Modgil and Modgil, 1985 for extended discussion).

The role of the teacher

The task of teachers in assisting children's moral development is never less than a delicate one. I have already discussed (pp. 207–209) the way in which they can help children develop desirable attitudes (in moral matters as well as in all other areas), and there is no need to go back over this ground except to stress two things: first, the enormous importance of the teacher's own example. It is of little value to emphasize to children the necessity for tolerance and sympathy if teachers, in their own dealings with the class, show themselves to be intolerant and unsympathetic. Similarly, it is of little value to teach honesty if teachers show themselves to be not above a bit of sharp practice when it suits them, or to teach even-handedness if teachers then treat children with manifest inequality. Not only will children fail to learn the desired moral codes under these conditions, they may even end up regarding them with the same disrespect with which they regard teachers who behave in this way.

The second thing to be re-emphasized is that teachers should take every opportunity to reinforce the right moral behaviour when they see it taking place. It is no good teaching children the importance of consideration for others, for example, and then sweeping past the child who rushes to open the door for us without a word of thanks; or teaching the value of honesty and then imposing a harsh penalty, without even a word of approval, upon a child who owns up to a certain misdeed. It is all very well to argue that virtue should be its own reward, but this is asking a great deal of children. As they grow into adulthood so their moral behaviour should become self-sustaining once they come to appreciate its importance to a civilized community *and* to their own personal (and spiritual) development. But during their less mature years, and in particular while they are still in Kohlberg's first three stages, feedback from the environment is vital in assuring them that they really are learning and applying moral codes successfully.

Some specific moral problems

There are also a number of specific aspects of their moral role that sometimes trouble teachers. In particular they often ask what kind of action should be taken against children who contravene moral codes in important ways, such as by stealing or cheating in examinations. The answer is that, as in all aspects of child behaviour, we must look first for the underlying causal factors. If we take stealing first, I have already implied that children may steal to compensate for material inadequacies in their own lives. Children from an impoverished economic background, faced with the constant blandishments of press and television advertising and by the temptation of goods prominently on display in shops will, not surprisingly, think from time to time of helping themselves. If they have been given little in the way of moral guidance by parents, they may well put such thoughts into action. Such children must obviously be viewed in a different light from children with a more affluent background who may be stealing simply for excitement (though they too could have real problems, such as worry over their parents' marriages, or feelings of neglect which drive them to steal in order to draw attention to themselves).

Teachers should, therefore, try to understand something of the motives of children caught stealing, and should use this understanding to decide what help needs to be given. But whatever these motives may be, children must be shown that their actions were wrong, and inevitably carry certain consequences. I discuss what these may be, and the relationship of the school to the police, etc., when dealing with counselling in Chapter 12, but the basic principle to be kept in mind at all times is that children should be shown that, whatever they may have done, as people they still have the sympathy and support of the school. We can hardly expect to teach them the value of moral behaviour, of compassion and concern, if we abandon them to their fate at the time they need us most. It is sometimes argued that, where stealing and other misdeeds put children on the wrong side of the law, they become the responsibility of the social or probation services rather than of the school. These services are, of course, of great importance, but involve children, who may already be insecure, in forming relationships with strangers. Their teachers, however, are already familiar to them, and may be better placed to help them come to terms with their mistakes and learn desirable lessons for the future. The practical involvement of the school at times like this will also demonstrate to all concerned that schools are not simply there to impart academic knowledge but to serve the children with whose care they are entrusted.

Turning to cheating, the treatment of which also causes teachers some problems, again the first question to ask is why should children cheat? Obviously, they are likely to do so for one overriding reason, namely fear of the consequences if they

219

do badly in the work concerned. This fear could simply be fear of the teacher's anger (or of the punishment that might be meted out), in which case the teacher needs to query his or her own behaviour. I have already stressed on a number of occasions that making mistakes is an aid to learning, both because the rectification of such mistakes helps the child directly, and because these mistakes give the teacher clues as to where the child most needs help. If, therefore, a child prefers to cheat rather than to acknowledge mistakes, it looks as if the teacher has in the past been misunderstanding the importance of mistakes, and has been adopting the wrong attitudes towards their occcurrence. Or the teacher may (perhaps unwittingly) have been humiliating children who receive low marks by reading these marks to the class or getting the children to read them out themselves (the reader will probably remember from his or her own schooldays the delighted horror with which the rest of the class greeted the unfortunate child forced to confess to zero marks out of ten).

On the other hand, children may simply be afraid of their own anxieties. Better to have cheated than to go home with the knowledge that you got nought out of ten, since the former is perhaps more readily forgotten than the latter. Poor marks deliver a blow to children's self-esteem if they happen to be people who care about their work, and if they happen to have parents who make a habit of asking how well they got on. Or they may be afraid that poor marks will put them in a low set next year away from friends, or in a set with an unpopular teacher instead of in one with a teacher they happen particularly to like. None of this should be taken to mean that we can condone cheating, of course; simply that we should not take a lofty moral stance in the matter and regard it always as exclusively children's own fault. We may rest assured that if they do not care in the least about their work (or about their teachers) then they will not be bothered to go to the trouble of falsifying marks. Far better then, when the teacher finds evidence of cheating, to take the child on one side in private and try to find out the cause, than automatically to harangue him or her in front of the class and hand out a stiff penalty which may do nothing to help the child get work right next time by his or her own unaided efforts.

A third example of a common contravention of the school's moral code is telling tales on other children. This is almost exclusively a problem of the primary school, since by the stage of secondary education the child is too concerned about peer group approval to attempt such an exercise. Often the teacher's response to the problem is to refuse to listen to the saucer-eyed innocents who are attempting to pour out details of some heinous crime, at that very moment being perpetrated elsewhere in the playground or school building, unless the crime involves damage to another child or to school property.

220

Sometimes the tale bearers are warned briskly not to come running on such an errand again. Not surprisingly they go away feeling a little confused, as if they themselves are in the wrong. Having tried to absorb the school's moral code, and seeing one of their number apparently breaking this code, they went to the teacher to put things right but met only with stern dismissal. Now it is perfectly reasonable that teachers should dislike tale-telling (particularly if they suspect it is done simply for the smug delight of getting another child into trouble), but this should be explained to children as part and parcel of their normal moral education, not thrust at them out of the blue when they feel they are doing the right thing. Teachers should at the same time explain to children why they dislike this activity.

Teaching
moral
behaviour

In conclusion, something must be said about the actual teaching of moral behaviour as a formal lesson. At one time such teaching tended to come almost exclusively under the heading of religious education, but it is now recognized that many other subjects (e.g. literature, current affairs, general studies, history and geography) can also raise moral issues, and that these should not simply be left to a single period a week and to one teacher on the timetable. Where the teacher deliberately wishes to raise questions of morals and values, this can be done by inviting the class to debate the kind of question used in the measurement of moral development and exemplified above in the discussion of the work of Kohlberg. Through such debate children are helped to see the various issues relevant to particular moral dilemmas, and to express their own views (and misgivings). The teacher might also like to consider composing springboard questions (see p. 148) related to moral problems, and to allow children to think creatively about the answers. The emphasis at each point should be upon helping children to get at the underlying variables and to ponder the full implications of their own ideas rather than upon producing cut and dried solutions.

Since moral development, as seen from the stages proposed by Kohlberg, depends to a great extent upon appreciating the other person's point of view, much of the class work should be devoted to this end. Here two processes can be recognized, namely *sympathy* and *empathy*. To sympathize with someone is to feel sorry for their plight, while to empathize with them means actually to experience the kind of emotions that they may be feeling. Empathy requires a more finely developed sensitivity than does sympathy, and obviously cannot be 'taught' in any complete sense. It comes more readily to some children than to others, but role-playing in drama lessons, together with simple imaginative descriptions of the kind of emotions we think others may be going through, both help.

Unless prompted by such activities, some children even at the stage of formal operations seem never to have considered what it must be like to be the butt of class teasing, or to be old and unwanted, or to grow up against a background of family violence. To speculate on the emotions of others, and then to apply these to oneself, is an essential first step for many children in developing the sensitivity towards others that is an integral part of moral development.

No matter how good the moral education within a given school, however, some of the impact is lost unless the staff show common standards in their day-to-day dealings with children. This is easier in a small than in a large school, of course, but children need to feel they are part of an institution that has some readily definable set of values. After all, if these values are important enough to be demanded of them, then the children are bound to reason that they should be important enough for the staff to demand them of each other. To be treated one way by one teacher and quite another by someone else leaves the child feeling that the school only pays lip service to values when it suits itself, and really does not care enough about them to ensure that they apply to adults as well as to children. Reaching a workable general consensus amongst staff on even the most important standards of behaviour is not easy, particularly where members of staff come from different backgrounds and different religious and political creeds, but this is as much a task of any school staff as agreeing on general policy matters relating to syllabuses and to teaching techniques.

References

Bergling, K. (1981) *Moral Development: The validity of Kohlberg's theory.* Stockholm, Sweden: Almqvist & Wiksell International.

Kohlberg, L. (1969) Stage and sequence: the cognitive-developmental approach to socialisation. In D. Goslin (ed.) *Handbook of Socialisation Theory and Research.* Chicago: Rand McNally.

Kohlberg, L. (1978) Revisions in the theory and practice of moral development. *Moral Development, 2,* 83–88.

Modgil, S. and Modgil, C. (ed.) (1986) *Lawrence Kohlberg: Consensus and controversy.* London: Falmer Press.

Piaget, J. (1932) *The Moral Judgement of the Child.* New York: Harcourt, Brace, & World.

SOME QUESTIONS

1. From where does western society derive its morals and values?

2. Discuss the origins and the nature of the super-ego in Freudian theory.

3. From your own personal experience and from your knowledge of children, how appropriate do you consider Kohlberg's model of moral development to be?

4. To take an example from Kohlberg's model, why do you think that the stages of 'good boy/girl orientation' and 'authority maintaining orientation' are related to Piaget's stage of concrete operations?

5. What are the characteristics of 'contractual legalism' as defined by Kohlberg?

6. Describe one method we can use to test which stage of moral development a particular child has reached.

7. Why does achievement of formal operations appear to have an important influence upon moral thinking? (Look back to the comments on formal operations in Chapter 3 (p. 48) for further help here.)

8. Are young children likely to be consistent in their moral behaviour? Give reasons for your answer.

9. Give some of the reasons why children may perform acts that they know to be morally wrong. Do these reasons always show them up in a bad light?

10. Is a child born with moral sense?

11. Why do children sometimes feel less guilt if they do what they claim is wrong than if they do what they claim is right?

12. Why are children these days faced with increasingly difficult decisions when it comes to moral problems?

13. Suggest some reasons why children may unwittingly contravene the school's moral code.

14. Discuss some of the factors relevant to the successful teaching of moral behaviour.

Additional Reading

Kohlberg, L. (1964) Development of moral character and ideology. *Review of Child Development Research, Volume 1*. New York: Russell Sage Foundation.

Kohlberg, L. (1969) Stage and sequence: the cognitive-development approach to socialisation. In D. Goslin (ed.) *Handbook of socialisation Theory and Research*. Chicago: Rand McNally.
Kohlberg's ideas on moral development can be approached through his own work, especially the above two publications.

Lockwood, A. (1978) The effects of values clarification and moral development curricula on school-age subjects: a critical review of recent research. *Review of Educational Research, 48, 325–364.*
A good survey of school programmes designed to enhance moral development.

May, P.R. (1971) *Moral Education in Schools.* London: Methuen.
Provides a good introduction to the practicalities of moral education in schools, as do the books by Sugarman (1973) and Wilson (1972) which appear below. All three are highly recommended.

Modgil, S. and Modgil, C. (ed.) (1986) *Lawrence Kohlberg: Consensus and controversy.* London: Falmer Press.
The latest and perhaps the last word on all aspects of Kohlberg's work.

Piaget, J. (1932) *The Moral Judgement of the Child.* London: Routledge & Kegan Paul.
Presents Piaget's work on moral development.

Purpel, D. and Ryan, K. (ed.) (1976) *Moral Education . . . It comes With The Territory.* Berkeley: McCutchan.
Also of value in a practical context.

Sugarman, B. (1973) *The School and Moral Development.* London: Croom Helm.

Wilson, J. (1972) *Practical Methods of Moral Education.* London: Heinemann.

Wright, D.S. (1971) *The Psychology of Moral Behaviour.* Harmondsworth: Penguin.
A very good general text on moral development.

10

The Self

One of the most interesting exercises we can attempt with anyone is to ask them to write an essay entitled 'Myself'. Interesting not only from our point of view, since it is a good way of learning about people, but interesting from the other person's point of view as well. Faced with the task of writing about 'myself', most individuals find themselves rather daunted. It is not just that they feel shy at the thought of writing about who they are, it is that they genuinely do not know what to say. We each of us experience ourselves at every moment of our waking lives, yet when it comes to putting ourselves into words, we uncover all kinds of problems.

Defining the self

Basically these problems stem from the fact that we do not really know that much about ourselves. People say rather vaguely 'well I suppose I'm *me*', and then they get stuck. Who is this 'me'? Is it my body? Is it my thoughts? Is it my emotions? Or is it perhaps a combination of all these things? The trouble is that body, thoughts and emotions keep changing. We know that the cells in our bodies are constantly wearing out and being replaced, so much so in fact that we do not have a single cell now that was there eight years ago. Over an eight-year cycle, the body is completely renewed. And thoughts change even more rapidly. Observe your thinking for a moment, and you will see that it is an ever-changing stream of consciousness. One thought pops into your mind, suggests another, which in turn suggests another, and off you go on a roller-coaster of associations, often ending up with no recollection of the particular thought that started it all off. Emotions change equally rapidly. Open a letter one morning that tells you that you have won a fortune and your spirits soar. Open the next letter that tells you it was all a mistake and your spirits drops into your boots. Watch a small boy running happily towards you and your heart fills with joy. See him trip and fall flat on his face and your joy turns to compassion and concern.

225

All this makes it rather hard to see body, thoughts and emotions as 'me'. So usually what happens is that people say 'okay, if I'm not any of these things, I must be my memories: it's the fact that I remember what I did yesterday and last week and last year that gives me the feeling that I'm me'. Fine. But what would happen if you lost your memory? Would you cease to be 'me'? And in any case, memory is a very fragmentary process, notorious for playing us tricks. We have the *feeling* that our memory stretches way back into childhood, an unbroken record of the person we are. But try and remember in detail even what happened yesterday. Or harder still what happened in detail on any particular day last week. Try and remember what you were doing on 1 July last year. Try and remember your fifteenth birthday, or your tenth, or your fifth. You made the journey to and from school literally thousands of times. How many of those journeys can you remember?

Once we start delving into the past in this way, we find that if our sense of self depends upon memory, then we must be like a jigsaw with most of the pieces missing. A little bit of detail here. A little bit there. And all the rest just large blank spaces. So where do we go from here? At this point, people normally start defining themselves in terms of labels. They give their name, or their occupation, or their status within the family or within the community. But these labels are general terms. They apply to lots of people. There are many folk around with the same names as yourself, or with the same family status (father, mother, daughter, son) or with the same occupation. None of these labels are exclusively *you*. What is more, they are simply labels that other people have decided to stick on you. Even your name, which seems a very personal expression of who you are, is simply the label that your parents decided to give you at birth.

Faced with the realization that labels of this kind are simply general terms, people usually dig rather deeper, and start to tell you things about their behaviour. 'I'm the kind of person who likes peace and quiet.' 'I'm a sociable sort of chap.' 'I worry a lot.' 'I like to be in control.' Some of these descriptions even include judgemental terms. 'I'm good at sport.' 'Though I say it myself, I'm a woman who gets things done.' 'I'm not very good at putting my thoughts into words.' 'I seem to get on well wth everyone.' 'I speak my mind and I don't care who knows it.' 'I'm at my best when I'm looking after people.' Again, none of these labels is really '*me*', since they are descriptions of 'me' rather than an expression of that elusive awareness of experience which underpins 'my' life, but which it is seemingly impossible to put into words. But nevertheless these judgemental labels are enormously important in any study of the self, because they tell us how people feel about their own existence. Whether they think well of themselves or not. Whether they accept themselves, or are constantly finding fault. Whether they experience themselves harmoniously or as constant conflict. And it is this picture of oneself, this set of self-concepts, that particularly interests the psychologist, since it has such a profound effect upon the individual's behaviour and psychological health.

What determines the self?

Where does an individual's picture of himself or herself come from? We can be sure of one thing. Individuals are not born with these pictures ready-made. In fact, they are not born with a picture at all. We cannot get inside the minds of small babies, but it would seem that their mental life consists simply of a stream of perceptions. They are very aware of the world around them and aware of the sensations from inside their own bodies (and insistent that people come and attend to them if they are uncomfortable ones!), but they are not aware of themselves as separate, unified 'people' experiencing all these things. This sense of a separate, integrated 'I' does not appear to develop until the third year of life, which is one reason why many children go through a particularly negative phase at this time. They are in the process of discovering themselves as autonomous people in their own right, and they have a strong and perfectly natural urge to start asserting this autonomy. 'I'm me and I *won't* do as you tell me!'

The importance of learning in self concepts

But it is one thing to be aware of yourself as a separate human being, and quite another to know what kind of human being you are. This is where learning comes in. Small children know that they exist, but they do not know much about that existence. Left to themselves, they would begin to find out about it, to get to know themselves, to familiarize themselves with their emotions and likes and dislikes. But they live in a social world, and the adults around them usually are not content to leave them to get on with their self-exploration. Instead, these adults begin early to tell the child things about him or herself, to assign labels. He's 'good' or he's 'bad'. She's 'truthful' or 'untruthful' and so on. Since small children have no way of knowing the accuracy or otherwise of these labels, and since they are so dependent for their every need in life upon the adults who assign these labels, they come to accept them without question.

Thus essentially a child's self-picture is a learnt one, dependent upon the descriptions provided by others. The picture may or not be a fair one. The point is that it is taken over largely ready-made from others, internalized, and used to provide self-definition. If children are told often enough they are naughty, they come to see themselves as naughty. If they are told often enough they are good, they come to see themselves as good. Thus the same child, brought up in two very different households, would end up with two very different self-pictures.

Notice that telling children they are naughty does not necessarily make them good, any more than telling them they are good makes them naughty. Small children are in the grip of very strong emotions, and have as yet very little control over their own behaviour. They also lack the language and the powers of thinking to be able to deliberate fully over their behaviour and make decisions on what is expected of them. And crucially they live very much in the present moment without any real thought of the future and the likely consequences of a particular course of action. So constantly telling children they are in the wrong will certainly make them feel inadequate and guilty as they internalize the labels people are tying on them, but it will not necessarily make 'good' children of them. Moreover behaviour produced by the fear of disapproval, lacking in any real concept of responsibility and thought for others, can hardly be called good anyway.

Once children start school, they have further important adults ready to assign labels to them. Like parents and any other adults close to them, their teachers begin to pass judgements on them, showing variations dependent upon their attitude towards children and towards their role as guides and educators of children. Sometimes the labels teachers give children reinforce those they have been given at home. Children who are told they are 'good' at home are told they are 'good' at school, while children who are told they are 'bad' at home may be told they are 'bad' at school. On other occasions there may be a conflict. Both reinforcement and conflict carry potential dangers. Children who are victims of unsatisfactory self-images in the home suffer even more if these self-images are confirmed by the school. On the other hand, children who are given one picture of themselves in the home and quite another in school have difficulty in deciding who they really are. Both sets of children are being denied the necessary opportunities for developing the positive and coherent notion of self that, as seen later, is essential for psychological health.

Can we know our real self?

But if the picture we have of ourselves is essentially learnt from the reactions of other people to us early in life, does this mean that we can never properly know our real selves, and have very limited powers to change things about ourselves that we dislike or that make us unhappy? In a way, this brings me back to the questions raised at the beginning of the chapter, questions as to what is the real self. The German philosopher Kant once said that self-knowledge is the beginning of all wisdom, and no doubt he was right. If we can fully know who we are, this gives us a firm foundation upon which to build our lives, (since it means we can recognize our likes and dislikes, our strengths and weaknesses, etc.), and allows us to identify what needs to be changed and how to go about this change. But Kant did not tell us the psychological meaning of self-knowledge, or the psychological strategies for acquiring it.

Another philosopher, G.H. Mead (1925), is more help when he suggests we should think of the self as separated into *subject* and *object*. 'I' (subject) know about 'me' (object). The 'I' is pure awareness, and the 'me' is the things about myself of which I am aware. This model allows us to talk about important issues like self-image and and self-concepts, issues which profoundly affect the way in which I feel about my life and the way in which I try and live it. The picture 'I' have of 'me' includes what I know about my personality, the personal memories that give me a sense of continuity as a person, my body-image, my physical sensations, and all the other things I carry around with me and which give me the sense of being who I am.

Carl Rogers's theory of the self

Since psychology is essentially a practical discipline, psychologists focus their attention primarily upon the self-as-object, the 'me' aspect of self. This is the aspect we can know about, explore, and attempt to change in desirable directions. This is the aspect produced largely by the early learning experiences already discussed, and this is the aspect that is of most immediate interest to educators. Of the psychologists who have contributed to our knowledge of self-as-object, perhaps the best known is Carl Rogers. Rogers's theory is an extensive one, (e.g. 1961), but for present purposes the most relevant part of it has to do with his concepts of the *organism*, the *self*, and *congruence*.

The *organism* is the total person, including all our basic inborn needs such as our survival needs (food, shelter, sex etc.), our emotions and feelings, our sensations, and our social needs, the most important of which in Rogers's view is what he calls the need for *positive regard*. Children are born with a basic need for the positive regard (the acceptance and approval) of others, and it is this need, says Rogers, which is the main socializing force behind their behaviour. It is this need ultimately that makes them obedient to parents and teachers, since without other people's positive regard they cannot develop positive regard for themselves. If the various needs of the organism are satisfactorily met, then the individual develops a *self* which is *in congruence* with it. Where these needs are not met, then there is a degree of incongruence, and it is this incongruence which in Rogers's view prompts the development of psychological ill health.

Let us clarify this a little, taking our example from the need for positive regard. Children are born with this need, and therefore one can say it is a basic characteristic of the organism. If children are given positive regard, then the self develops a picture of itself as someone worthy of self-regard, and the organism and the self are allowed to be in congruence (in harmony if you prefer) with each other. If by contrast children are starved of positive regard, then the organism and the self are out of congruence. On the one hand the organism has a strong desire for positive regard, while on the other the self is convinced it is unworthy of this regard. Not surprisingly, incongruence between the organism and the self leads to inner conflict, and feelings of self-rejection and alienation, many of which become directed outwards into hostility towards the rest of the world.

Rogers adds to this model a further concept, that of the *ideal self*. The ideal self is the picture we carry within us of the kind of person we would like to be. Once again, if there is congruence (in this case between the self and the ideal self, between the person we think we are and the person we would like to be) then we have a balanced and integrated person. Similarly if there is incongruence, with a big gap or with actual conflict between the self and the ideal self, we have imbalance and disintegration. Since it is not possible always to have congruence between organism, self and ideal self, Rogers accepts that we all of us carry some degree of incongruence around with us, and that helping children deal with incongruence is one of the main tasks of education.

Conflict between the *organism* and other people

For example, children have to learn that the wishes of their organism may conflict directly with the wishes of other people's organisms. Children want their own way in order to satisfy the needs of their organism for creature comforts, or for possessions, or for adult attention, but other children also want their own way because they have the same kind of organismic needs. So there has to be a compromise. Children have to learn to wait their turn, to share, to ask instead of grabbing, to curb their desire to hit out at people who thwart them. If they have the help of wise adults who allow them to see that there is nothing basically *wrong* about wanting to satisfy organismic wishes, and that in a social world we have to learn to respect the similar needs of others as well, then the learning will take place without undue incongruence. Children will be allowed to accept and understand their organisms, and to channel its needs into socially approved forms. They will be able to develop pictures of themselves as valued and successful individuals, with good self-insight and self-control. And there will be congruence between the self and the ideal self too, in that the people they are will approximate to the people they would like to be.

If by contrast children are exposed to adults who are constantly putting them at odds with themselves, making them feel guilty even for having organismic needs and wanting to assert them, then the result is incongruence between organism and self. Similarly, if children are always allowed to indulge their organismic needs, they are going to have to learn sooner or later that such behaviour will not win the positive regard of anyone but the most doting of parents, and again the result is incongruence, this time between self (the way they are) and ideal self (the popular people they would like to be).

Measuring the self

The use of Q-sorting. Rogers has shown that a technique called Q-sorting is a very useful way of exploring children's pictures of themselves. In Q-sorting a number of cards are prepared, each one of which carries a self-descriptive statement (e.g.'I work hard', 'I'm popular', 'I'm nice-looking'), and the child is asked to arrange the cards into five separate piles, going from 'most like me' at one end down to 'least like me' at the other. To combat any tendency to place most of the cards in only one or two piles, a limit can be placed upon the number of cards each pile contains (often one asks for most cards to be put in the middle piles and fewest cards in the two outer ones, so as to achieve a normal distribution). The number of cards is not critical, but for the secondary school child 25 is about right, with appropriate reductions for primary school children. By observing what cards are put by individual children into which pile, one gets an outline of the way they see themselves.

The semantic differential is even more versatile than Q-sorting. As illustrated in Figure 10.1 'The Person I Am' is written at the top of the page, and then a number of pairs of adjectives are arranged down the page, each separated from the other by five (or seven) spaces. Individual children are asked to put a tick in the space which best represents their self-images relative to the adjectives in each pair.

By looking at the pattern of ticks, we can get a pretty fair idea of the way in which children see themselves. And if we want to compare their self-concepts with the way other people see them, we ask their teachers and any others who know them well to fill in a similar sheet for them. Any major discrepancy between the children's views of themselves and the view of them held by everyone else would need investigating, as it could mean that the children have unrealistic self-images.

The person I am

Nice		✓				Nasty
Weak	✓					Strong
Clever				✓		Slow
Popular		✓				Unpopular
Plain				✓		Pretty

Figure 10.1. The semantic differential.

George Kelly and the self

The other modern psychologist who has made most contribution to our study of the self is George Kelly. Kelly's starting point (Kelly, 1955) is that humans are innately curious. They wish to make sense of the world and of their own existence, and operate in their daily lives very much as does the scientist, exploring, experimenting, constructing hypotheses about reality, predicting the future, working out strategies and procedures. The term Kelly uses to cover the units of meaning we develop in order to make sense of the world in this way is *personal constructs*. We have personal constructs about every aspect of our lives, including ourselves. These constructs are essentially the means by which we define and understand existence, and once formed they influence the way in which we interpret future events.

No two people ever share an identical construct. For example, if I mention the word 'mother', this immediately summons up your unique personal construct 'mother', a construct which will have been formed over the years in response to your experiences of what mothers are like. If you have a good relationship with your mother, your construct will be very different from that of someone who has had bad child–mother experiences. If you are a Roman Catholic, your feelings for the Virgin Mary as a universal symbol of motherhood will enter into it. If you are married and pregnant your feelings about your own readiness for motherhood will play a part. If you value the concept of 'Mother Nature' that will also be mixed in. And so on. Your construct of 'mother' is exclusively your own, and inevitably it colours your response every time you hear the term used.

Since we have these constructs about every aspect of life, and since it is in and through them that we interpret and respond to reality, individual children's constructs about school and about everything to do with school will profoundly influence their educational progress. They will have constructs about all the subjects in the curriculum, about teachers, about their abilities, about their educational aims, about their class, about other children. Take for example mathematics. Each child will have a construct 'mathematics' which will contain elements of all their previous experiences with the subject. If they have not liked their mathematics teachers, if they have not seen the point of mathematics, and if they have constantly experienced failure in relation to mathematics, the very mention of the word will arouse a whole host of negative feelings and resistances, all of which they will carry with them even when they go into a new class and begin to work with a new teacher. Thus unless the teacher can find a way of changing this negative construct, he or she is unlikely to be able to make much of a job of teaching them how to do their sums.

Kelly recognizes the existence of a range of different kinds of personal constructs. There are for example:

broad constructs, which can be widely applied (e.g.'all politicians are dishonest')

tight constructs, which have a specific application and collapse altogether if proved faulty (e.g. scientific laws)

loose constructs, which can be varied dependent upon circumstances (e.g.'a book can be interesting or boring')

impermeable constructs, which are strongly resistant to change (e.g.'I was good at sport when I was in school')

constricted constructs, which have a narrow application (e.g.'the only thing I like about school is English')

core constructs, which refer to the self and are vitally important in maintaining our identity (e.g.'I'm the kind of person who gets on well with others').

Obviously the more a child is able to develop positive constructs about school (particulary where these are impermeable constructs or broad constructs) the more likely he or she is to work well and enjoy the experience. But all too often children are given negative constructs, simply because the school does not realize that encouraging the development of more favourable ones is as important a part of the educational process as the actual transmission and assessment of subject-based knowledge.

The use of the repertory grid. Kelly's work is important to us however not simply because it suggests a model of how we represent and make sense of experience, but because it also provides us with a highly sensitive methodology for exploring these personal constructs, a methodology even more sensitive than Q-sorting and the semantic differential. The method is known as the *repertory grid* (see e.g. Bannister and Fransella, 1980), and consists essentially of establishing the similarities and dissimilarities which the individual sees between the people and things in his or her life. Let us take an example by looking at an aspect of the core construct 'self'. If we were exploring this construct in a boy (or girl) we would begin by asking him who are the important people in his life. As he names them, we write each one in turn on a separate card, and then add a card labelled 'myself' to the pile. The number of important people named by individual children varies, but we would normally expect a dozen or more, consisting of such folk as 'mother', 'father', 'grandma', 'grandad', 'uncle', 'teacher', 'brother', 'sister', 'best friend John' and so on. Our next step is to shuffle the cards, and then draw any three at random. The boy is asked to look at the three names on the cards, and tell us one way in which one of the three people concerned differs from the other two. Suppose the three cards are 'grandma', 'teacher' and 'sister'. The boy may say that teacher is clever, and that grandma and sister are not. We accept what he tells us without question, and then go through the rest of the names with him, applying the distinction 'clever – not clever' to each one. 'Is mother clever?'; 'Is father clever?'; 'Is myself clever?' and so on.

Having done this, we return the first three cards to the pack, shuffle and again draw three. This time we may have 'uncle', 'myself', and 'sister' again. Once more we ask him to tell us any way in which one of these people is different from the other two. This time he says that 'uncle is fun but myself and sister are not'. As before, we then apply the distinction 'fun – not fun' to all the other names, before returning the three cards to the pack, shuffling, drawing another three, and repeating the procedure.

Many of the cards will be drawn from the pack a number of times, and we may get the same combination of three names cropping up more than once. No matter; we go on putting the same question to the boy until he has exhausted all the ways in which people important to him are similar and different, and begins simply to repeat himself. We now have all the similarities and differences, and therefore all the ways in which he conceptualizes the important people in his life and the ways in which he conceptualizes himself.

Our results are set out in the form of a grid (hence the term *repertory grid*) and by looking at it we can see at a glance the way in which individual children construct themselves and the significant others in their lives. The boy's possible response pattern is illustrated in Figure 10.2., with an X representing a 'yes' response and an 0 a 'no' response.

Usually a child will produce many more items (called *events*)

	Clever	Fun	Cross	Young	Truthful	Nice-looking	Strict	Unfair
Mother	X	0	0	0	X	X	0	0
Father	0	0	X	0	0	0	X	X
Grandma	0	0	0	0	0	0	0	X
Grandad	0	X	X	0	0	0	X	X
Uncle	0	X	0	0	0	0	X	X
Teacher	X	0	0	0	0	0	X	X
Brother	0	X	X	X	0	0	X	X
Sister	0	0	0	X	0	0	X	X
John	0	X	X	X	0	X	0	X
Nigel	0	0	X	X	0	X	0	X
Paul	0	0	X	X	0	0	X	X
Cousin	X	0	X	X	0	0	X	X
Myself	0	0	X	X	0	0	X	X

Figure 10.2. Repertory grid showing 'myself and significant others'.

for entry across the top in a grid on 'myself and significant others' than are shown in the example. But one can see even from the above brief list that the boy in question sees himself in unfavourable terms, and lives in a world where the adults are a rather elderly and untruthful bunch, given to strictness and unfairness. Using exactly the same procedure, we can elicit his constructs about school (listing on the left for example all the teachers and subjects he comes into contact with), about his leisure interests, and about any other aspects of himself or his life space that we want to explore. Thomas and Harri-Augstein (1985) give a comprehensive range of different areas in which they have used repertory grids, and the possibilities are virtually endless. They also give details of computer programmes now available which allow individuals to explore their life space for themselves, and to experiment with what would happen within the grid if they were to change some of their constructs. Other programmes allow two people (e.g. parent and child, teacher and pupil) to hold a dialogue through the computer, mutually eliciting constructs on how they view each other and the consequences for their relationship of any changes they may choose to make in these constructs.

Constructs can be changed

Repertory grids are widely used by educational psychologists and can be employed equally readily by teachers interested in exploring the way in which children see themselves and the world. What Kelly is saying is that we each experience reality in our own way (indeed that we each have our own reality), and that this way is essentially a consequence of learning. The more we understand about our own constructs, the more effective we can be in identifying desirable change and the more effective we can be in bringing it about. And the more we understand about the constructs of others, the more we can help them change too. The self is simply a learnt construct like any other, and subject to the same possibilities for alteration and development in positive directions. We see ourselves in the way in which we have learnt to see ourselves, and we have the power to unlearn this way and put a more positive one in its place.

Self-esteem   The development of self-esteem

The work of Rogers and of Kelly helps indicate how we build up knowledge of ourselves, and how dependent this knowledge is upon what other people tell us about ourselves, both directly and, through the way in which they treat us, indirectly. This is illustrated by research into aspects of the growth of self-concepts, some of which have great practical relevance to the teacher. The best example is probably Stanley Coopersmith's investigation into the development of self-esteem (e.g.1968), and it is appropriate to look into this in some detail.

Self-esteem (or positive self-regard as Rogers calls it) is concerned with the value we place upon ourselves, and of all areas of self-concepts it is one of the most important. It is sometimes claimed that one of the major factors (if not *the* major factor) in the development of psychological ill health is the inability of some individuals to value themselves at their true worth. I mean by this that the people concerned seem unable to regard themselves as significant acceptable members of the community, but labour instead under feelings of inadequacy and even hopelessness, and consistently underestimate both their abilities and the regard in which they are held by other people. As we shall see from Coopersmith's work, these feelings of inadequacy are apparent by the time children

236

reach junior school (and probably long before), and do not seem necessarily to be related realistically to the child's academic potential or to any other factors closely associated with it.

Coopersmith began his investigation with a sample of ten-year-old boys, and followed them through into early adult life. Using a battery of psychological tests and self-ratings, Coopersmith found his sample could be divided consistently into three groups which he labelled 'high', 'medium' and 'low' self-esteem respectively. High self-esteem boys appeared to enjoy what Rogers calls congruence. They showed themselves to have a positive, realistic view of themselves and their own abilities. They were confident, not unduly worried by criticism, and enjoyed participating in things. They were active and expressive in all they did, and were generally successful academically and socially. Medium self-esteem boys showed many of these qualities, but were more conformist, less sure of their worth, and more anxious for social acceptance. Low self-esteem boys, however, were described by Coopersmith as a sad little group, isolated, fearful, reluctant to join in, self-conscious and over-sensitive to criticism. They consistently under-rated themselves, tended to underachieve in class, and were preoccupied for much of their time with their own problems.

It might be thought that the high self-esteem boys were more intelligent than the rest, and had proved their ability to themselves, or that perhaps they were physically more attractive or came from wealthier homes or had some other quality that made them more popular and better liked. Careful research showed this not to be the case. Boys in all three groups came from middle-class homes (in fact, they were deliberately chosen from the same socio-economic background), and there were no significant measurable differences between them on any of the other variables just mentioned. Where they did differ sharply, though, was in the relationship which they had with their parents. The high self-esteem boys came from homes in which they were regarded as significant and interesting people, and in which respect was shown for their opinions and points of view. Homes, in other words, where they experienced the positive regard so emphasized by Rogers. Their parents had higher and more consistent standards than did those in the other groups, and their methods of discipline were less erratic. Though not necessarily permissive, this discipline eschewed corporal punishment and relied instead upon rewards for good behaviour and upon withdrawal of approval for bad. Parents knew a great deal about their children (such as their interests and the names of their friends), showed physical affection towards them, and clearly signalled to them in all sorts of ways that they mattered very much as people. Interestingly, the boys regarded their parents as being fair towards them ('fairness', remember, is a quality highly prized by ten-year-old children!)

By contrast, the low self-esteem boys often regarded their parents as unfair. Within the home, discipline veered from over-strictness to over-permissiveness, and the boys were obviously not sure where they stood. There was less clear guidance than in the homes of the high self-esteem boys, standards were less apparent, and parents knew significantly less about their children. Here the signals seemed to suggest to the boys that they were not as significant and important within the home, and did not count for as much as people.

Causal factors in self-esteem

Since, as has been said, there was no apparent difference between the boys on cognitive, physical or socio-economic variables, we can conclude that their high and low levels of self-esteem were linked significantly to parental behaviour. The boys, in large measure, took over and internalized the picture that their parents appeared to have of them. The consequences of this for their performance in school were considerable. The high self-esteem boys set themselves more elevated (and realistic) goals. Because they were not unduly frightened by the possibility of failure they were much readier to meet challenge, to participate, and to express their feelings. When they met occasional failure or criticism they were undaunted by it because they had a firm conviction of their own worth. The low self-esteem boys, on the other hand, saw failure as yet another blow to their small store of self-confidence, and tended to play safe and set themselves artificially low goals. (Note that sometimes, however, low self-esteem individuals set themselves unrealistically high goals, perhaps because no one could then blame them when they failed or because of some obscure desire for self-punishment.) They were unduly wounded by criticism, and generally anxious for approval because they set great store by what others thought of them.

Value to the teacher

These findings have relevance for teachers for two reasons: first, because they reveal a great deal about the development of the child's self-concepts within the home, and second, because they give some practical guidance on how teachers can best influence this development for good in the classroom. If, in exploring the development of self-esteem above, the word 'teacher' had been substituted for the word 'parents', we would still have been providing ourselves with a valid model. Certainly the parent has more influence normally over the child than the teacher, but children tend to take over and internalize the teacher's picture of them just as they take over and internalize their parents' picture. Many teachers signal to their children, consciously and unconsciously, that they value them as people, that they consider them capable of developing the necessary skills to cope with their work, and that they consider them important enough to spend time listening to their views (and advice) on most of the things that go on in the classroom. They set their pupils consistent and realistic standards, encourage them to be undaunted by failure, and urge them to have the confidence to act independently and responsibly when the occasion arises. Other teachers, disappointed perhaps that progress with particular individuals and groups of children is not as fast as they would like, send signals of the opposite kind, and leave children with negative feelings about themselves and their abilities. Such teachers forget that they should be concerned first and foremost not with making comparisons between children and finding some wanting, but with indicating clearly to each member of the class that he or she matters as much as does everyone else, and has qualities and abilities which can be developed and which can help towards enjoyment of the positive things in life and towards coping with its problems and difficulties.

Other influences on self-esteem

Coopersmith has now followed this sample through into the adult world and shown that his high self-esteem boys have consistently outperformed those of low self-esteem and have proved more successful vocationally as well as within their education. One limitation of his study, however, is that he did not examine the influence of socio-economic status or of sex upon self-esteem (his sample, remember, consisted only of middle-class boys). Nevertheless, there is evidence, as was mentioned when discussing the influence of socio-economic status in Part I, that children from working-class homes generally suffer from lower self-esteem than children from homes higher up the socio-economic scale, and it was suggested that this is hardly surprising as the former children tend to have contant reminders of their own supposed 'inferiority' in the form of dilapidated environments, limited facilities, older school buildings and so on. Much can be done, of course, by parents and teachers to combat this unwarranted sense of being less good than the children from more affluent environments, but the task is not an easy one. As also indicated in Part I, delinquent groups tend to suffer from low self-esteem, and often their 'toughness' and antisocial behaviour would appear to be an attempt to protect this self-esteem by demonstrating their power to destroy things that society deems to be important, and thus prove to all and sundry that they do really matter after all. It is interesting to note that the low self-esteem middle-class boys in Coopersmith's sample, with their greater respect for authority, appeared to accept docilely the negative view that others had of them, whereas working-class boys showed a greater tendency to fight back and blame their failures at least in part upon authority itself.

Turning now to the position of girls, we find that they generally (again as suggested in Part I) have lower levels of self-esteem than boys. As with most of the sex differences discussed in the book so far, this would appear to be largely the result of cultural factors, and the general status of women in society (though the stronger musculature and the greater average physical height of the male sex at maturity may also play some part). We find evidence for lower self-esteem in girls, for example, in the fact that when paired with boys in a problem-solving task they sometimes artificially depress their performance levels so as not to outshine their partners (a phenomenon that does not work in reverse). Some girls, it seems, feel uncomfortable in the superior role, as if they are performing in a manner inconsistent with their true position in life. Girls tend to rate themselves less highly than do boys on written tests of self-esteem, to set themselves lower goals in life, and to be more inclined to underestimate their abilities than do boys (even in primary school where in reading and language skills they often tend to outshine the latter). Depressingly often, even in our supposedly more enlightened times, they seem prepared to accept second-best for themselves, even though they are prepared to be just as hard-working and conscientious.

Encouraging self-esteem

With both children from working-class backgrounds and with girls, teachers can do a great deal to help the development of self-esteem if they pursue the methods outlined above, and indicate firmly the regard and respect with which they view their children. It is also important, with all children, to encourage them to articulate their picture of themselves. Low self-esteem children can do little to subject their negative self-concepts to critical scrunity until these concepts are defined and recognized for what they are, which in turn is not possible until children have found some way of expressing them. Once each child has learnt to communicate the nature of self-doubts to others, he or she can be helped to face up to them and to recognize their lack of substance. I am not suggesting by this that teachers should spend all their time in a counselling role, or be continually taking children on one side to get them to talk about themselves, but simply that they should be at all times alert for opportunities to ascertain how children themselves perceive their own successes and failures. Often children become quite skilled at hiding their feelings,

even from themselves, and teachers may be misled into thinking that low marks, or criticisms directed towards them in
class, have no real effect upon their self-esteem, or their
confidence in their own abilities. Teachers may even feel
rather angry about this, and redouble these criticisms in the
hope that they will finally 'sink in'. The result is often to
wound children further, or to make them defend their self-
esteem by ignoring the teacher and pretending that neither the
teacher's opinions nor the subject being taught are of any
value.

This does not mean that the teacher should not criticize
children, or challenge them to greater efforts, or correct work:
far from it. The teacher must always be concerned to help
each child reach his or her potential. What it does mean,
however, is that the teacher should do things in such a way
that the child's self-esteem is protected. Children will differ in
the extent of their needs, and the robust, high self-esteem
child will, as we have seen, be less sensitive than the low; but
in all cases it means giving children work that is appropriate
to their competence, drawing attention to successes rather
than harping upon failures, giving work back personally to
children wherever possible (particularly if the marks are
rather low) with a quiet word of encouragement rather than
simply handing it back in class. It also means helping children
to understand and profit from their errors, choosing any
words of criticism with care, and making sure that they are
applied to the work rather than to the child him or herself,
and emphasizing at all times by actions as well as by words
that, whatever happens, each child retains the teacher's concern and respect.

Self-esteem is not the same as conceit

In any discussion of self-esteem, the objection is sometimes
raised that we must not give children inflated pictures of
themselves which will only be rudely destroyed one day. This
is a fair point, but I am not suggesting that teachers be
dishonest towards their pupils. Self-esteem should not be
equated with conceit. It stems not from an exaggerated view
of oneself but from the realization that one matters to the
people one loves, or those in authority over one, or those with
whom one works. It stems from the knowledge that one is
doing the best one can with one's abilities, and that the rest of
the world is not critically watching one's every move ready to
pounce as soon as there is any hint of error. And, finally, it
stems from the knowledge that one should extend to oneself
the understanding and sympathy that one extends to others.
Some low self-esteem people are full of excuses because they
cannot bear the thought that something or other was their
fault and is therefore further proof of their inadequacy, but

many of them are quick to excuse others but never themselves. Such people (and this is easier in childhood than in later life) need to be helped towards self-acceptance and towards a realistic appraisal of themselves and of their own abilities and potential abilities.

Assessing self-esteem

Once teachers are aware of the vital role in a child's life played by positive self-esteem, they can do much through simple observation and classroom conversations to build up a picture of how individual children see themselves. Taking Coopersmith's work as a model, the teacher can note whether children join in or not, whether they are unduly daunted by criticism, whether they have an unusual need for attention, whether they capitulate in the face of failure or rise to the challenge, whether they have a realistic view of their own abilities and of their future goals, whether they have in short a proper sense of their own worth and of their basic rights as people. But much can be done more formally. For example in lessons such as creative writing, children can be encouraged to put their feelings about themselves into words. One way of doing this is to invite them to write descriptions of themselves in the third person. Such descriptions can start with the words 'Do you know Janet Smith (or whatever the child's name happens to be) . . .?' or 'We like Janet Smith because . . . ' 'Janet Smith was very happy last week because . . . ' or in any other similar way that the teacher feels to be appropriate. Fine art and drama lessons can also help the child to communicate a view of self, and give the teacher clues as to the kind of help he or she may need to rebuild any aspects of this view which appear negative.

The only cautions required here, of course, are that the teacher should not invite children to reveal too much of their mental life before classmates who may scoff at them afterwards, and that the teacher should not read too much into any one thing that a child happens to say. Children have their ups and downs, and a child who is feeling badly at odds with him or herself one day may be much happier about things the next. Similarly, children may sometimes read themselves into a part and say what they think the teacher expects of them. Wise teachers place the events of any one lesson or any one day within the wider context of what they know of the child.

In addition, teachers can also use some of the more specific techniques mentioned earlier in the chapter. The semantic differential is a very straightforward test, and needs no special training in administration. The Q-sorting is only marginally more complicated. And although ideally the teacher should have attended appropriate workshops before using the repertory grid, there are many useful texts available which explain in detail how to proceed. Obviously, great care must be taken in interpreting the results of all tests of this kind. There is a danger if these results are taken too literally, or if too much is read into them. As used by the teacher, their function is simply to provide structured information which supplements what the teacher already knows about the child. In any case, all knowledge we have about children must be subjected to continual rescrutiny and reappraisal. It is all too easy to fall victim to the *halo effect* (because a child appears to do well at certain things we automatically overcredit his or her performance in other areas) or to its equally damaging opposite, the *demon effect*.

Further sources of information come from watching individual children with their peers. Are they confident and assured? Are they able to put forward their own views, to assert themselves where necessary, to show initiative and leadership? Do they tackle group tasks enthusiastically? Do other children listen to them when they speak? Do other children help them in case of need? Or do other children tease or victimize or ignore them? How do they stand in the eyes of others? All too often, people who are undervalued by their peers also undervalue themselves. The two kinds of undervaluation influence and feed each other.

Self-esteem and overassertion

Since low self-esteem can also go with delinquent and antisocial behaviour, it is also necessary to look out for children who are *overassertive* with others, or who make a general nuisance of themselves. Often their attempt to dominate, or to impress others comes from a need to boost their own self-esteem. Children who are naturally competitive may show similar traits, but the clue lies in the degree of exaggeration which this behaviour shows. Wherever children show a desire to force their attentions upon others which is out of proportion to the real needs of the moment, then teachers can suspect that they may have problems with their self-regard.

In any attempt to assess a child's self-esteem, and particularly if they are using techniques like the repertory grid, teachers are well-advised to discuss matters with the school psychologist. Educational psychologists will have extensive experience in applying and interpreting measures of self-evaluation, and are in a position to help the teacher focus upon the child's real problems and decide on appropriate remedies. No teacher should feel isolated in attempts to help children develop the positive self-regard that will enable them to experience their lives in a satisfying and rewarding way.

Self-maturity

In all discussions of the self we are concerned not just with people as they now are, but with people as they will one day become. The individual's notion of him or herself is undergoing constant change, particularly in childhood. Sometimes this change can be abrupt as, for example, when individuals achieve sudden success at a task that they have been trying to master for some considerable time, or when they experience equally sudden failure in an area in which they thought themselves competent. More usually, however, it takes place gradually, as individuals react with the environment and ponder over the lessons it has taught them. Obviously, teachers are particularly concerned with the nature of this change, and are anxious to see that is takes a positive and desirable form in the children for whom they are responsible.

One way in which we can discuss this change is to see it as a movement towards *self-maturity*: that is, towards self-concepts that are realistic and self-accepting, and that contain an assessment of the self broadly in line with the assessment that other people have of one (I shall have more to say about the definition of maturity shortly). There are various theories within psychology as to how the individual moves towards this self-maturity, but for the teacher one of the most helpful is that advanced by Erik Erikson (e.g. 1950). Erikson suggests that individuals are faced by a number of learning tasks as they go from infancy to old age, each of which should be completed satisfactorily before they tackle the next. If they fail in any of these tasks, then their later development is handicapped, and they will be faced one day with having to go back and rectify this failure if they are ever to become fully mature. These learning tasks, together with the approximate period of life associated with each, are given below. It will be noted that against each task Erikson suggests the consequences to the individual of failure. Thus if small infants do not learn trust they are left with mistrust; if older infants do not learn autonomy they are left with shame and doubt, and so on.

Erikson's eight stages and personal maturity

1. Early infancy: trust versus mistrust
2. Late infancy: autonomy versus shame and doubt
3. Early childhood: initiative versus guilt
4. Middle childhood: competence versus inferiority
5. Adolescence: identity versus role confusion
6. Early adulthood: intimacy versus isolation
7. Middle adulthood: generativity versus stagnation
8. Late adulthood: self-acceptance versus despair

It can be seen, therefore, that in terms of Erikson's theory, young infants need to learn that other people can be *trusted*, and be relied upon to satisfy their physical and emotional needs. This trust gives them a secure base from which they can reach out and explore the world with confidence. In later infancy, growing physical and psychological abilities bring with them the beginnings of *independence* from others, and older infants need increasing freedom to express their own wishes and to make choices for themselves. If they are confronted by adults who see this bid for autonomy as stubbornness, and turn everything into a battle of wills, then they feel doubtful and confused, and even ashamed of their own desire for greater independence. As mentioned earlier, this is particularly apparent in the third year of life, when children often go through what appears to be a very negative phase in which they respond with awkwardness and disagreement to the wishes of others. Far from indicating that they are becoming difficult, this negative phase is a healthy sign of the beginnings of autonomy, and should be met by understanding, sympathy, and patient firmness where such becomes necessary. Children then learn that their autonomy is welcome to those around them, but that at the same time there are reasonable limits which they must observe if they are not to restrict other people unduly in turn.

Children's ages and Erikson's stages

Erikson is not precise about the ages associated with these stages of personal maturity, and accepts that there are wide individual differences. However, late infancy probably includes the nursery school years in most cases, and by the early childhood stage the child is usually entering infant school. In terms of Erikson's theory, early childhood is characterized by the need to develop *initiative*, which is an extension of autonomy into more specific, focused activity, with the child able to take responsibility for inaugurating this activity where appropriate. As with autonomy, if initiative is thwarted and children are made to feel in some way unacceptable for wanting to make it a part of their behavioural repertoire, they are left with self-doubt and guilt, and the feeling that there is something seriously wrong with them for having such desires.

Having learnt the task of initiative, children are faced in middle childhood (approximately junior school age) with learning that of *competence*: that is, with learning to do things well and to develop the skills necessary for coping with immediate problems. If they fail in this task (and naturally it involves what goes on in the home as well as what goes on in school, and what goes on in social life as well as what goes on in academic life), then they show the symptoms of inferiority and low self-esteem that were discussed in the last section. The next stage, adolescence, brings with it the search for *identity* (which is so important that a separate section is devoted to it below), and this is followed in early adult life by the search for *intimacy* (close ties with another person or persons as in, for example, marriage), in middle adulthood by *generativity* (creative and self-fulfilling roles in the rearing of children, in one's profession, in the community at large), and in late adulthood by the *self-acceptance* that comes from knowing one has done one's best in life and made the maximum use of whatever opportunities and abilities have come one's way.

Self-maturity and the school

The work of psychologists like Erikson, Rogers and Maslow (1970) gives us a relatively clear picture of what the mature individual looks like. They have a range of qualities which make them well-balanced and effective human beings, aware of their own worth, able to empathize with others, and to relate to them warmly and openly instead of using them for selfish reasons or as instruments for satisfying their own inadequacies. This may suggest that maturity is only something acheved in later life, and that at school level all a teacher can do is to help children work towards this maturity. But in fact it is perfectly realistic to talk about maturity in children. Mature children are not individuals old before their time, but people who, commensurate with their years and experience, show the kind of qualities just listed. Many children have these qualities, just as many adults, however high their social or professional status, lack them.

The job of the teacher therefore is in many cases to encourage what is already there, rather than to try and develop it from scratch. And here the rule is that if children are to manifest their maturity, and to act responsibly towards themselves and towards others, they must be given the right kind of opportunities. It is no good demanding children show maturity, and then treating them most of the time as if they are not capable of taking the simplest decisions about their own lives. It is no good urging them to think in a mature way about the world, and their place in it, about personal relationships, and about life goals and ideals if no attention is paid when they try to put these thoughts into words, or, worse still, if the adults in their lives show clearly that they themselves are incapable of such thought. The involvement of children wherever feasible in classroom decisions and in the formulation of school policy helps them to see themselves as valued members of the school community, and to practise the behaviour that go with this valuation.

Helping children to practise co-operation with each other and with the community, and to practise the kind of social skills dealt with in Chapter 11, are also vital components of education for maturity. Indeed, together with self-exploration, self-expression, mutual respect between children and between children and adults, and a full understanding of school ethos and of necessary social restraints they are components not only of this education but of the wider education for 'being' referred to later in the chapter. Some psychologists still fight shy of the notion of 'being', since they see it as too vague to be of scientific use. From the point of view of each individual, however, 'being' is all-important, since it is the way in which we experience our lives. Most teachers are well aware of this, and look to psychologists amongst others to give them a lead in how to educate in this crucial area. Once teachers know how to do so, and are aware of the implications such education has for a child's present and future happiness in life, then ways of incorporating it into the curriculum become increasingly clear.

Defining the mature personality

Gordon Allport, whose work shows reciprocal influence with that of Erikson at a number of points, suggests that as individuals move through the various stages of personality development towards maturity so they become more integrated and consistent as people. In the early stages of this development Allport sees children as possessing a number of rather disparate personality traits (e.g. friendliness, honesty, bookishness) which they may use inconsistently in dealing with others (e.g. they may be honest with friends but not with teachers, bookish at home but not at school). As they grow older these coalesce into a smaller number of what Allport calls *selves* (e.g. the child may have one identifiable, consistent self within the school – both in terms of behaviour and self-concepts – and another within the home), which later become integrated into a single personality. To avoid confusion over terms, note that in this context Allport only uses the word 'personality' when the individual has reached self-maturity, and uses the word 'selves' to denote units that cohere to make up personality, while in this chapter I use the word 'self' to cover all the awareness and concepts that individuals have of themselves.

In terms of Allport's model, one sign that individuals have not yet reached self-maturity is that they behave inconsistently. They seem, in other words, to shape their behaviour to the circumstances in which they find themselves. Actions which they would regard as unthinkable in the context, say, of their family, church or golf club they may perform without a second thought when it comes for example to their business lives. People who meet such inconsistent individuals in these different circumstances therefore see quite different sides of them. Alternatively (though less usually) inconsistent individuals may show different selves within the same environment dependent upon moods, the state of their relationships that day with spouse and children, the difficulty of their journey to work and so on. Obviously, we all vary the details of our behaviour from one context to another (the informality of our behaviour with close friends might be out of place, for example at a business meeting), but if we are mature we are still identifiably the same person, with the same value system, the same self-concepts, the same attitudes and so on, no matter where we find ourselves.

In addition to this unified, consistent approach to their life circumstances, Allport (1961) sees mature people as possessing the following characteristics:

- an extended sense of self (the ability to identify with other people's concerns as well as with one's own; to offer sympathy and empathy)
- a warm, unselfish relationship with others
- emotional security
- self-insight (a realistic knowledge and appraisal of oneself
- a realistic orientation towards the world (the ability to exercise sound judgement and take necessary decisions)
- a unifying philosophy of life (some consistent, coherent view of the purpose and meaning of life, whether it be religious or humanistic, that helps resolve questions of value and helps to determine life goals).

We must not overlook the fact that temperamental factors may play some part in the development of this maturity in the sense that, for example, the 'easy' children in the Thomas, Chess and Birch study (see p. 167) might find warm unselfish relationships with others come more readily to them than they do to the 'difficult' children. But in the main, most of the qualities listed would appear to be heavily dependent upon learning. Even cognitive factors such as high intelligence, though they might be helpful in the development of, for instance, a realistic orientation towards the world, are no guarantee of maturity in the absence of the right kind of learning experiences.

Of course, Allport does not suggest that we must wait until we are adults before we can show some of the qualities associated with self-maturity. These qualities may be developed at different times (with a unifying philosophy of life perhaps always coming last) and to different degrees, with a ten-year-old child perhaps showing emotional security, unselfish relationships with others, and a certain degree of self-insight, and not manifesting any of the other qualities until rather later. Since we could well have an adult who showed none of these, it is perfectly feasible to maintain that some children show greater maturity than some of their elders.

Self-identity

This is the developmental stage associated particularly with adolescence and, as was indicated above, it is of sufficient importance to warrant a section to itself. Self-identity is really the sum total of the concepts individuals have about them-selves. Thus there is, of course, some sense of self-identity in early infancy and in all the tasks identified by Erikson as taking place before adolescence. But when we talk of self-identity we are really also inferring that these self-concepts should band together in a coherent way and give individuals some reasonably complete picture of the kind of people they are to become, and this kind of coherence usually begins to emerge at adolescence (Erikson, 1971). Note that this is not the same thing as saying that the personality becomes fixed at adolescence. Growth, change and development remain possi-ble (and desirable) throughout life, but adolescence marks the transition from the fluid personality of the child (i.e. from the traits and selves of which Allport talks) to the more constant one of the adult.

Adolescence also marks the emergence of more mature life goals. Up to this time individual children will have normally had few clear life goals, not only in terms of their future vocations but in terms of their ideal selves, the kind of people they would like to become. More will be said about these (and in particular about vocational goals) when educational and vocational guidance is discussed in Chapter 12, but it should be clear to the reader that life goals are closely linked to the sense of identity, to the sense that 'this is the person I am, these are my abilities and my values, and this is what I want to do with my life'.

The search for self-identity in adolescence is often accom-panied by a great deal of experimentation. The adolescent, as it were, tries out a number of different forms of behaviour, as if asking 'Which of these different kinds of people is really me?' To help this process, he or she will often adopt role models: older people (friends, pop stars, teachers, sportsmen and women) whose life styles and whose values are deemed worthy of imitation. Since identity is often expressed through the groups to which one belongs, the peer group also becomes very important, and adolescents may change their behaviour (clothes, speech and habits as well as values and opinions) in order to be accepted by it. Since acceptance by the opposite sex is also important, behaviour considered to make one sexually attractive may also be adopted.

Learning to be adult

All this may appear rather amusing (or tiresome, depending upon where one stands) to the adult, who has long left this stage behind and who in any case has to have some defence against being made to feel old or out of touch; but this is often to misinterpret what is really going on. In our complex, industrialized society we keep the young in a subservient role (i.e. still at school) long after they have reached physical maturity. We do this because there just seems to us to be so much to learn, but this places heavy potential strains upon the young themselves (and upon teachers too, sometimes). In addition, in spite of their physical maturity, and their strong sex drive and other emotional changes, adolescents are really given very little help on what it is like to be grown-up. They may be given adult reading matter and taken out to look at the community and at people at work, but useful as this is it does not give adolescents any real sense of natural transition from childhood to adulthood.

In less complex communities than ours children learn by working alongside their parents, and grow up with the knowledge of what it is like to be adult and of the rights and responsibilities that go with adult status. At some point in puberty this status is conferred upon them, often at a set ceremony or initiation, and from that time on they are recognized as full members of the community (Turnbull, 1984). Thus it is sometimes suggested that what we in advanced industrialized societies recognize as adolescence, with all the storms and stresses that often accompany this period, is essentially a cultural phenomenon, and that it is not the adolescent growth spurt and the physiological changes that go with it that create the rebellious teenager, but society itself with its artificial methods of relating to its young people.

Understanding the adolescent

It will be recalled from Chapter 3 (p. 48) that *cognitively* the adolescent has also usually achieved the stage of formal operations, and is therefore able to reason in abstract terms. As a consequence, many of the concepts associated with religion, politics, and social relationships begin to take on a deeper and more complex meaning, and adolescents often call into question the activities and policies of the adult generation in these important areas. Since they may find such activities and policies wanting, and wish to see them replaced by more equitable practices, adolescence is often described as a period of idealism, and this idealism may also be reflected in the kind of life goals that the adolescent chooses at this point. These goals may later have to be modified in the light of experience, but for the present the adolescent may feel passionately about them, and resent the apparent inability of elders to understand if not actively share this passion.

This breakdown of understanding between the adult and the adolescent is also sometimes apparent in our inability to recognize that in spite of their apparent assurance, adolescents are often prey to insecurity. While they search for identity, they are never sure that the people they are becoming will prove acceptable and successful in the adult world. They have learnt to cope with being children, but now they have to find out whether they can cope with being adults. Thus although they may seem unimpressed now by parents and teachers, the support and good opinion of such people is still vital to them. Teachers who work well with adolescents seem aware of this fact, and are often able to create a relationship with them that the latter will one day come to regard as amongst the most formative of their lives.

Such teachers seem able to understand and sympathize with adolescents' problems, to tolerate patiently their occasional outbursts and strange mannerisms, to excite their interest and involvement in the subject being studied, and perhaps above all to provide them with clear, consistent and reasonable guidelines to the kind of behaviour best suited to the adult world and to the achievement of long-term life goals. Of course the teacher must not compromise personal standards in the interests of making him or herself acceptable to the class. Where these standards concern values or opinions the teacher makes them available to the class while insisting that in the final instance these are matters of personal choice. Where they concern school rules or regulations the teacher stands firm on them, explains the reasoning behind them (and the correct machinery for attempting to change them if this is desired), and points out that few jobs and professions are without their rule books and codes of conduct. Where they concern the subject being taught the teacher insists on each individual aiming for the highest levels of which he or she is capable. Where they concern social behaviour, the teacher demonstrates through personal conduct the importance of an awareness of the feelings and rights of others as well as for those of oneself.

Role confusion

It will be seen from the list of Erikson's eight stages in the development of personal maturity that the consequence of failure to develop identity is *role confusion*. Role confusion implies that individuals have no clear idea of the kind of people they are or of the role that they should assume in life. They may show the several different *selves* mentioned by Allport, or the low self-esteem and insecurity of Coopersmith's boys, or even the uncertainty and the constant self-doubt and self-questioning that is a feature of some kinds of neurotic behaviour. Note, though, that Erikson does not suggest they will inevitably become failures in life. Many apparently successful people in business, politics and all walks of life show the symptoms of role confusion. Erikson would argue that this is amply born out by the high incidence of psychological problems that seem to beset the outwardly successful in our community as well as the apparently unsuccessful. It is estimated that one person in ten will at some point in their lives require in-patient help for these problems (in reality the figure is probably much higher, with many psychological problems disguised by more obvious physical symptoms), and although a failure to develop self-identity successfully is only one of the causal factors, it is nevertheless a major one. Erikson is arguing, therefore, that the development of a consistent identity and the various other qualities that go with self-maturity cannot be inferred simply from the material position that one has achieved in life. They show themselves instead in the much subtler areas of one's relationships with one's fellows and with oneself.

Knowing and being

The responsibility of the school for helping children work towards a valid sense of personal identity and an absence of role confusion brings me to my final point, namely that we can identify within all levels of education two major interrelated areas. We'll call them the *knowing area* and the *being area* respectively (Fontana, 1987). The knowing area has to do with the facts, techniques, strategies and patterns of thinking involved in mastering subject knowledge, while the being area has to do with the way in which individuals experience their own lives. The knowing area is the area sampled by examinations, and the area that leads to paper qualifications and to career opportunities. The being area is the area of the self, of feelings, and is the area that primarily leads to psychological health. Both areas are important, but formal education concentrates almost exclusively upon the knowing area, to the virtual exclusion of the being.

What this means in practical terms is that most schools do very little in any systematic or focused way to develop 'being' in children. Yet 'being' is the essence of our lives. We may be the most knowledgeable person under the sun, but this is of scant consolation to us if we experience ourselves in a confused or unhappy or unsatisfactory way. 'Knowing', ultimately, must feed 'being' if it is to be of real value to the individual. Without the necessary development of their 'being', individuals cannot acquire as they grow through life the balance, the personal adjustment, the creative independence and the rewarding relationships with others that make up psychological health and that lead to a proper understanding and acceptance of the self.

Through good teaching strategies and good teacher–child interactions, the school can play a major part in the development of this understanding and acceptance. In both arts and science subjects children can be prompted to explore and reflect upon themselves and upon the meaning their lives have for them. Much depends upon the ability of individual teachers to see the relevance of their subject to a child's personal growth, but in the absence of this relevance it is often fair to ask precisely why a particular subject is being taught in the first place. Techniques like Q-sorting, the semantic differential, and above all the repertory grid can be utilized to explore why children are becoming alienated from school, from particular subjects, and most of all from themselves. We live at a time when concern about vandalism, drug-taking, and a range of other antisocial and anti-self activities are causing ever-increasing concern. Frequently this concern is expressed in terms of criticisms of schools. Usually the criticism is unfair, but schools can go much of the way towards answering it by using all aspects of the curriculum as an aid towards the self-development which is vital if children are to mature into well-adjusted and socially constructive human beings.

References

Allport, G.W. (1961) *Pattern and Growth in Personality*. London: Holt, Rinehart & Winston.

Bannister, D. and Fransella, F. (1980) *Inquiring Man*, 2nd edn. Harmondsworth: Penguin.

Coopersmith, S. (1968) Studies in self-esteem. *Scientific American, February*.

Erikson, E.H. (1950) *Childhood and Society*. New York: Norton.

Erikson, E.H. (1971) *Identity: Youth and crisis*. London: Faber.

Fontana, D. (1987) Knowing about being. *Changes, April*.

Kelly, G.A. (1955) *The Psychology of Personal Constructs, Vols. I and II*. New York: Norton.

Maslow, A.H. (1970) *Motivation and Personality*. New York: Harper & Row.

Mead, G.H. (1925) The genesis of the self and social control. *International Journal of Ethics, 35*, 251–273.

Rogers, C.R. (1961) *On Becoming a Person*. Boston, Massachusetts: Houghton Mifflin.

Thomas, L. and Harri-Augstein (1985) *Self-organised Learning*. London: Routledge & Kegan Paul.

Turnbull, C. (1984) *The Human Cycle*. London: Jonathan Cape.

SOME QUESTIONS

1. Why is it difficult to put the concept 'myself' into words?

2. What part do our memories play in our sense of personal identity?

3. List the labels that most commonly become attached to people.

4. What effect do judgemental labels have upon individuals?

5. Where do individuals' pictures of themselves originate?

6. At what age do these pictures begin to emerge?

7. Why is it that some children develop a confused picture of themselves?

8. Why is self-knowledge described as 'the beginning of all wisdom'?

9. Why is the 'I and me' model of the self helpful?

10. What does Rogers mean by 'incongruence', and why is this concept important to our understanding of successful development of the self?

11. Explain the technique of Q-sorting. Why is this technique helpful in an exploration of the self?

12. What are 'personal constructs' as defined by Kelly? List as many different types of constructs as you can.

13. How would you go about constructing a repertory grid to explore individual children's concepts of themselves?

14. Can we unlearn our self-concepts?

15. Identify some of the factors which can be grouped respectively under the 'knowing' and 'being' areas in school. Which factors receive the greater attention in most schools? How can the balance be redressed?

16. What is 'self-actualization'? How can the individual be helped towards attaining it?

Additional Reading

Barron, F. (1979) *The Shaping of Personality: Conflict, choice, and growth.* New York: Harper & Row.
An excellent text that roams widely in the field of personality, and has a great deal of value to say about the self.

Bruno, F.J. (1983) *Adjustment and Personal Growth: Seven Pathways*, 2nd edn. New York: Wiley.
A comprehensive attempt to define psychological health and the major pathways towards its achievement.

Burns, R. (1982) *Self Concept Development and Education.* London: Holt Rinehart & Winston.
The fullest available survey of all aspects of the psychological approach to the self.

Coopersmith, S. (1967) *The Antecedents of Self-esteem.* San Francisco: Freeman.
Discusses his work fully. A classic text in the history of work on self-esteem.

Coopersmith, S. (1975) Self-concept, race and education. In G. Verma and C. Bagley (ed.) *Race and Education Across Cultures*. London: Heinemann.
A more recent survey by Coopersmith that also looks at ethnic differences in self-esteem.

Erikson, E.H. (1968) *Identity: Youth and crisis*. New York: Norton.
Those readers interested in Erikson's work will enjoy this. Especially good on adolescence.

Fransella, F. and Bannister, D. (1977) *A Manual for Repertory Grid Technique*. London: Academic Press.
An essential text for anyone wishing to undertake extensive use of repertory grids. Explains all aspects of the application and assessment of grids.

Jersild, A.T., Brook, J.S. and Brook, D.W. (1978) *The Psychology of Adolescence*, 3rd edn. London: Collier Macmillan.
A comprehensive book on all aspects of adolescence and of the challenges it poses to the self and the sense of identity.

Kasper, F.H. and Goldstein, A.P. (1986) (ed.) *Helping People Change: A textbook of methods*, 3rd edn. New York: Pergamon.
An alternative to Bruno's book. Even wider in scope but not so readable or humanistic.

Kegan, R. (1982) *The Evolving Self: Problems and process in human development*. Cambridge, Massachusetts: Harvard University Press.
A cognitive approach to the self, strongly influenced by Piagetian developmental theories. Recommended for the way in which it integrates thought and emotion in the total picture of the self.

Kelly, G.A. (1963) *A Theory of Personality*. New York: Norton.
Contains the first three chapters of Volume I of the classic The Psychology of Personal Constructs. *An excellent introduction.*

Kleinke, C.L. (1978) *Self-Perception: The psychology of personal awareness*. San Francisco: Freeman.
A good survey of the ways in which individuals comes to know and understand themselves.

Kotarba, J.S. and Fontana, A. (1984) *The Existential Self in Society*. Chicago: University of Chicago Press.
The joint author isn't a relative, so I can safely recommend this as a stimulating examination of psychological and sociological aspects of the self.

Maslow, A. (1962) *Towards a Psychology of Being*. London: Van Nostrand.
This has proved a very influential book over the years.

Radford, J. and Kirby, R. (1975) *The Person in Psychology*. London: Methuen.
A highly readable little book, dealing with broader aspects of the self.

Wells, B.W.P. (1983) *Body and Personality*. London: Longman.
Especially good on the links between self-esteem and body image, but a valuable introduction to the whole area of the body–personality link.

Part four

Social Interaction, Teacher–Child Relations and Teacher Personality

Introduction Much teaching and learning is done through social interaction, with the teacher interacting with the class both as individuals and as a group, and the children interacting with each other. Social behaviour, particularly within the classroom, but at all points where contact is made between people which renders learning outcomes possible, is therefore of great interest to teachers. The better they understand this behaviour, the better they are able to provide optimum learning environments for children.

Social behaviour, however, does not mean merely the formal interchanges between the teacher and the class, and the interchanges between children during group activities. Teacher and class form together a distinct social unit, and within that unit there exists a complex and fluid undercurrent of social relationships and social attitudes which shape individual and group responses in a range of subtle ways. Some children will emerge as leaders and trendsetters, others as followers or as isolates. Some children will pair off into close friendships, others will form larger subgroups with group membership based upon unspoken rules of behaviour or upon socio-economic status. The class may develop a kind of pecking order, with 'in-groups' who are generally admired and 'out-groups' who are generally ignored or even ridiculed. There will be rivalries and small feuds, sometimes teasing and perhaps bullying, sometimes co-operation and mutual help, sometimes a sense of common purpose, and at other times

257

social fragmentation and a movement towards anarchy.

Prompted by these forces the class will develop a distinct social 'character' of its own that will mark it off even from parallel classes of similar ability. This character will often manifest itself in particular class attitudes towards particular teachers: sometimes friendly, and at other times less so. Sometimes it will work to the benefit of class learning while at other times it will become a positive handicap. Sometimes hard work and academic success in class members will be the focus of general admiration, while at other times they may become the focus of banter and even of sneering. On occasions a small subgroup may develop with positive work-orientation, and have sufficient internal solidarity to function independently of the rest of the class, sustained by its own enthusiasms and interests and ready to ignore the censure of the rest. On other occasions a different kind of subgroup may develop, united perhaps by feelings of failure and inferiority, and intent on bolstering self-esteem by ridiculing the efforts of their more successful classmates.

The long-term survival of these subgroups is determined in part by the teacher's behaviour towards them, in part by the strength of response of the rest of the class, and in part by their own cohesion and motivation as groups. If they do manage to survive, then they may increasingly become trend-setters for the rest of the class, exerting a generally good or bad influence as the case may be. Sometimes, however, different teachers will experience the same class in quite different ways. One teacher may find them alert, interested, and co-operative, another may find them apathetic and unhelpful, while a third may find them downright difficult and unman-ageable. Where this happens, it becomes clear that it is individual teachers who have become the crucial variable, and that it is their social interactions with the class and with its subgroups that are determining the general response.

In the chapter that follows the varied field of social behav-iour is surveyed, providing a basic grammar of the subject that allows us to identify units of classroom interaction and to assess the relative importance of each one.

11

Social Behaviour and Social Skills

We live in a social world, yet there is little evidence that most of us know how to analyse social experiences and how to improve our social skills. Nor is there much evidence that formal education tries to teach us how to do so. Schools ideally should be places where both staff and children are very much aware of what is happening at each point of social interaction, and very much alert to the role this interaction plays in helping individuals formulate opinions about themselves and others. But in reality, social relationships are almost as much of a hit and miss business in schools as they are in society generally. Teachers receive little training in social behaviour, and beyond the routine enforcement of the rules of politeness they often have limited expertise in this behaviour to pass on to children.

Dyadic interactions

Let us start with two-person (or *dyadic*) social interactions. Two people meet and hold a conversation. During the course of the conversation, they communicate with each other through talking and listening. But they communicate by non-verbal signals as well, some intentional, some spontaneous, such as smiles, nods, frowns, raised eyebrows, grimaces. These non-verbal signals are called *communicative synchrony*, and they play an important part in conveying meaning in any dyadic interaction. Imagine how difficult it would be to hold a conversation with someone who stared at you without moving a muscle. Communicative synchrony indicates that the person to whom you are talking is listening and responding, and giving clues through these responses to what is going on in his or her mind.

Communicative synchrony seems to be an innate feature of human beings. There is no evidence it is present in animals, but from the early weeks of life onwards small babies can be observed moving muscles (initially the large muscles of the arms and legs but very soon facial muscles too) in response to the sounds adults make to them. This helps demonstrate to us that in human beings social interaction is by nature a two-way process. So attuned are we to this that even if individuals deliberately try to ignore us and refuse to show communicative synchrony their very cussedness still conveys a powerful message to us. They are indicating that they do not think much of us or of what we are trying to say, and that we would do much better to save our breath.

People meeting for the first time obviously react to each other very differently from people who are old friends. Meeting for the first time, many individuals feel a little unsure of themselves. They are anxious to give a good impression, while at the same time they are keen to sum up the person opposite them in their own turn. From what we know of personality it is probable that introverts on this first acquaintanceship will be more aware of themselves, while extraverts will be more aware of the other person. Neurotic introverts in particular may be very ill at ease and very preoccupied with their own behaviour, while stable extraverts may be particularly orientated towards the behaviour of the other person.

Social psychologists draw attention to variations in dyadic interactions dependent upon such factors as the age, sex and relative status of participants. Some examples should make this clear.

───────────────────Example 1───────────────────

Mrs Brown: "I've booked a hair appointment for tomorrow afternoon."

Mr Brown: "Fine. Just in nice time for the dinner party with our new clients tomorrow evening. I'll take you there in the car."

Office junior: "I've booked a hair appointment for tomorrow afternoon."

Mr Brown: "Out of the question. You'll just have to cancel it."

───────────────────Example 2───────────────────

Mr Brown:" What's the time?"

Mrs Brown: "Four o'clock dear."

Sally Brown: "What's the time?"

Mrs Brown: "It was a waste of money buying you a watch."

Example 3

Boyfriend: "Like your dress."

⬇

Sally Brown: "Why thanks. I wore it to please you."

Brother: "Like your dress."

⬇

Sally Brown: "What do you want to borrow?"

In each of the three examples we see that the same remark produces two quite different responses. The variable is not the form of words contained in this remark, but the relationship which the people concerned have with each other. This may appear too obvious to be worthy of comment, but in fact the implications of it go very deep and tell us a great deal about the use of language in social relationships. Socially, the precise meaning of individual words are often of less importance than the interpretation we put upon them. In talking to his wife in the first example, Mr Brown responds to the issue of physical appearance. If his wife has her hair done, this will enhance the good impression he hopes to make with his new clients. In the conversation with the office junior he is responding to the issue of office management. If the junior spends time at the hairdresser's during the afternoon this means there will be no one to do the office jobs.

Similarly in the second example the wife responds to her husband supportively. The only thing at issue is that he wants to know the time. When her daughter puts the same question to her, other issues get in the way. Why isn't the girl using her new watch? Has she lost it or broken it? In the third example the girl takes her boyfriend's remark as a compliment, but suspects her brother is using the same words to flatter her with a future favour in mind.

We could hardly expect both Mrs Brown and the office junior to respond to Mr Brown in the same way after his very different treatment of them. The same applies to father and daughter in the second example and to boyfriend and brother in the third one. Social interaction is very much a negotiated process, with the response of each person at each point influenced strongly by what has just been said by the other. Nowhere is this more true than at school level, a point fully appreciated by the good teacher, who uses words as an aid to mutual understanding rather than as a goad towards resentment and confrontation.

Social interaction between teacher and child

The points in the last paragraph can be understood more clearly by examining exactly what happens in the dyadic interaction between teacher and child. When the teacher talks to the child he or she receives a response which helps determine what is said next. The response may be verbal but may just as easily be non-verbal (e.g. facial expression, or shuffling feet). The thoughts and feelings it conveys may involve comprehension or incomprehension, interest, boredom, anxiety, hostility, amusement, or a host of other similar things, each of which influences the teacher's own thoughts and feelings in turn.

It is one thing to know that this is happening, of course, and quite another to be able to analyse it in detail and decide where and how to change one's own behaviour in order to help change that of the child. Socially inadequate people, and particularly socially inadequate children, are usually very bad conversationalists. This is mainly because their self-conscious preoccupation with their own feelings prevents them from viewing the conversation objectively and seeing the way in which each person is influencing the other. The examples given just demonstrate how profound this influence can be. By studying dyadic interactions in the classroom, the teacher can identify ways of helping children extend and develop their conversational interactions. For instance by using what social psychologists call a *proactive* conversational move (i.e. one which, by including a question, prompts a response from the other person), the teacher allows the conversation to continue into a further interchange. Failure to use a proactive move brings the conversation to a stop. Thus when answering a child's question the teacher can follow up with a question of his or her own ('I go to the seaside for my holidays; where do you go?'), instead of simply providing the answer ('I go to the seaside') and leaving it at that.

Similarly, in a more general interaction, perseverance by the teacher can be rewarded eventually by the desired response from the child. A teacher's first conversational move ('you ought to know how to read music') may produce an unsatisfactory response from the child ('oh'); the teacher then modifies his or her conversational move ('yes, it's a very handy skill') which now prompts the child to produce the desired response ('Why is that?'). Note that if the teacher had persisted with the first move (i.e. repeated the information or instruction in the same form), then the child might well have gone on replying unsatisfactorily, leading to mounting frustration and anxiety all round.

Social status   The examples on p. 260 also illustrate the way in which people assert their social status through the use of language. Mr Brown can speak abruptly and authoritatively to his office junior, without expecting her to answer him in kind. But with his wife it is a different matter. In the same way, Mrs Brown uses her parental status to imply a rebuke to Sally when the latter asks for the time, but treats a similar request from her husband co-operatively. Social psychologists gain great amusement (or sadness!) from observing the way in which people develop and use a myriad little strategies for signalling their status vis-à-vis those they see as their social inferiors. For example a 'superior' can place a friendly hand on the shoulder of an 'inferior', but not the other way around. If you doubt this, look at how some teachers react if pupils touch them in this way. Similarly a superior can call an inferior by his or her surname, but an inferior has to preface a superior's surname with a title. A superior can sit in the presence of an inferior, but an inferior sits only with a superior's permission (stated or implied). An inferior is expected to hold a door open for a superior, but not the other way around. An inferior is expected to give way in a conversation if the superior interrupts, to drop their eyes in a visual confrontation, to stand aside if in the superior's way, to laugh at the superior's jokes (while not telling a joke him or herself unless given the go-ahead), to answer questions while not necessarily expecting answers in turn, and to watch and obey any hints the superior might give that a conversation between them is now at an end.

All these subtle interpersonal strategies exist over and above any specific rules which the inferior is expected to obey, and over and above any direct commands which the superior may give. Notice how these strategies operate within the school, and in many ways cut across the true lessons of politeness which the school is trying to teach. Politeness has far more to do with thoughtfulness and respect towards others than with the dogmatic assertion of social status. So it is hard for a school to teach the values of politeness if staff consistently refuse to show any evidence of this virtue in their dealings with pupils.

Social psychologists also draw attention to the way in which individuals surrounded by higher-status workmates adopt strategies to enhance and protect their own standing. For example security guards, porters, caretakers or groundsmen can sometimes be deliberately awkward in their dealings with other colleagues, insisting on their right to impose petty restrictions upon the use of the facilities in their charge. Such restrictions are designed to bring home to people the degree of power (and therefore of implied status) contained in the role of the low-status workers concerned. Even high-status people who feel unsure of their standing or who consider that others are giving them insufficient recognition may resort to the same kind of awkwardness. For instance teachers who feel they have been passed over for promotion may do their best to frustrate colleagues' attempts to change the syllabus or school organization. Senior members of staff who feel their position is not respected may be intentionally abrupt and offhand to the newly-qualified teacher in order to emphasize professional disparities. All these strategies are signs that the individuals concerned feel themselves to be socially undervalued, and the remedy lies in convincing them that their roles are in fact recognized as an essential part of the organization, and that their attempts to draw attention to this fact are unnecessary.

When individuals of equal status try to assert their super-iority over the other, the situation becomes particularly com-plex. Two deputy heads or two heads of equal sized departments in school for example. Each will try to convince the other of their greater importance, adopting increasingly exaggerated techniques. Strategy will be capped by strategy, until in the end one of the contestants comes out victorious or both give up through sheer exhaustion. Stephen Potter (e.g. 1947), a comic writer with a wickedly accurate eye for social one-upmanship of this kind, gives an hilarious snippet of fictional dialogue between a prominent MP and an eminent medical consultant (both high-status occupations) in which each vies to outdo the other. The MP is initially at a disadvan-tage, in that he is submitting himself to medical examination by the consultant, but forges ahead by explaining that his symptoms occurred after a prestigious debate in the House of Commons. The consultant counters by brisk commands to the MP ('now take off that shirt or whatever it is you're wearing') while the MP fights back with increasing claims for his role in the Commons debate. In the end the consultant wins the day by the triumphant instruction: 'now open your mouth'. Deprived of speech, even an MP can do little!

Amusing as this piece of writing is, it nevertheless brings home to us just how petty people can become when fighting the status battle. In the course of the battle, the good of the endeavour or of the institution which both people are sup-posed to be serving often becomes forgotten, and all that counts is who comes away socially enhanced and who comes away socially diminished. Relating this sad state of affairs to my earlier examination of personality and of the self, it is probably fair to say that many of the people who fight unnecessarily for status are insecure not only about the nature of this status but about themselves. People with genuine self-acceptance and self-esteem have no need to go to extreme lengths to impress others or to enhance themselves at others' expense. They know who they are, have a realistic assessment of themselves and of their abilities (however high or however modest these happen to be), and see little point in boosting themselves through petty social posturing.

Social status and the school

The issue of status is present in all social institutions, particularly those which have a hierarchical structure, such as schools. In schools hierarchy ranges from the headteacher down through deputy heads, heads of departments, heads of year, class teachers, ancillary staff to children. Such a hierarchy is understandable and serves a useful purpose. So does the respect which each level of the hierarchy is expected to show towards the levels above. But there are two important points to be made. The first is that respect which is earned is of much more value than respect which is simply given because a person holds a particular office. Adults who claim that children show no respect towards them are often hoping to rely upon an automatic respect for their office or for their age or for their simple status as adults, rather than upon a respect for their behaviour and for the wisdom that lies behind it. If that automatic respect is not forthcoming, they are at a loss how to handle matters, and fall back upon an increasingly critical and authoritarian manner.

The second point is that it is unfortunate that children should automatically be seen as occupying the bottom place in the school hierarchy. In a sense there is no escape from this, since children necessarily carry least authority in the school set-up. But the school ultimately is there to serve its children. Without children, there would be no need for schools and no need for teachers. This is not an argument for suddenly treating children as if they have higher status than adults, but it is an argument for seeing that the school orders itself with the interests of the children and of their education uppermost in mind. Hierarchy and status are only of value if they make the school function more effectively as a facilitator of children's learning, in both the 'knowing' and the 'being' areas (see p. 252).

At the disciplinary level, it is also true that an exaggerated attempt by the teacher to stand upon status and dignity provides many children with just the challenge they relish. Teachers to whom status and dignity are of vital importance offer children the constant temptation to find ways of engineering their discomfort. Good teachers have the respect of the class because they represent an acceptable role model: they interest the class and have skills which the class would like to share, they act promptly and appropriately to deal with classroom difficulties, and they impress the class with their fairness and interpersonal qualities. They have no need to resort constantly to the status of their position in order to be effective in front of the class.

Unnecessary assertion of teacher status

It is useful for individual teachers, therefore, to look closely at the little strategies which they may have developed for unnecessarily asserting this status. The examples given earlier in the chapter show something of the flavour of these strategies. Ignoring a child's legitimate request for attention or information; assuming that children must 'put up with' inconveniences and discomforts that no adult would tolerate for a moment; treating a child's property contemptuously; interrupting children unnecessarily before they have finished speaking; refusing to listen to reasoned explanations and justifications; rude comments on children's written work; the use of demeaning names and expressions; sarcasm; discourtesy; lack of feeling and sympathy; deliberate unfairness – these and a host of other similar strategies are all signs of a teacher asserting status over a child. Whenever one individual treats another in a way that cannot be answered in kind, we must suspect that status is at work. On occasions, of course, status is perfectly justified. The teacher who tries to be on terms of total equality with children all the time will not last very long in most classrooms. But there is a big difference between a necessary and legitimate use of status and the kind of instances just given. The behaviour contained in these instances is intended primarily to boost teachers in their own eyes by deliberately humiliating children.

Similarly, it is useful for a school to look at its own management structures, and to see whether unnecessary hierarchy and status operate between members of the teaching staff, and between teachers and ancillary workers. With a sophisticated workforce like teachers, there is ample evidence that people do their best work where they feel their efforts are recognized and respected, and where they feel they have their due say in the running of the organization. Class teachers who consider they have no way of making their views on the running of the school known to those above them in the hierarchy, and who are working under conditions which are inappropriate and which could easily be changed if only superiors would listen to them, can hardly be expected to work with maximum efficiency and maximum enthusiasm.

Social conformity

Closely linked to status is the issue of conformity – the tendency to go along with the group. At school level, the concept is of major importance, since teachers expect a degree of conformity from the children they teach. Without this conformity schools would be impossible places to run. Such conformity may be of a formal kind (as in adherence to school rules and to the constraints of the curriculum) or it may be informal (as in adherence to the unwritten values and expectations of the school and of individual members of staff – the so-called 'hidden curriculum').

Staff also have to conform. Dependent upon the school, the system used to obtain this conformity may vary. In a democratically-run school, the staff meetings and the views of individual teachers will be a major factor. In other schools, the management team, or perhaps the headteacher alone, will have the more effective say. The local education authority (LEA) and school governors, the Department of Education and Science (DES) and inspectors will also play a part.

Schools differ in the way in which they handle non-conformist teachers. In a school which lays stress upon indivi-duality, a degree of non-conformity will be tolerated and perhaps even encouraged, provided it remains within certain implicit or explicit limits. In a sense, the non-conformist teacher has an informal contract with the headteacher and the rest of the staff. 'Keep your non-conformity within recognized bounds and we'll let you get on with it. We may even be rather proud of you, particularly if you work in an obviously 'creative' area [non-conformity is more likely to be allowed in an art teacher than in a science teacher – rightly or wrongly]. But step outside these bounds, and something will have to be done.'

When I say 'tolerated and perhaps even encouraged', I am talking about a specific kind of toleration or encouragement. A school may be happy enough to have a non-conformist in its midst, may even indicate to him or her that they are an asset to the school ('adds colour'; 'keeps us amused'). But when it comes to applying for promotion, the position may change abruptly. The non-conformist is all very well in his or her way, but 'can you really see them in charge of a depart-ment?'; 'Are they *sound* enough?'. So even tolerated non-conformists need to be clear where they stand professionally. It is one thing to be given the impression that people are happy having you around the way you are, and quite another to find they change the rules when you expect promotion.

Non-conformity

Social psychologists have done a great deal of work on non-conformity. In a classic series of experiments some years back Asch (1955) studied the way in which people are pre-pared to change their opinions in the face of group pressures. The subjects in his experiments were told that the researcher was exploring perception, and they were asked as a group to look at a series of variably-sized lines and then to nominate, in the hearing of the rest of the group, the line they judged to be identical in length to an additional line. Although it was clear which of the lines was identical, all members of the group bar one had been primed beforehand to give the wrong answer. The interests of the research focused upon the one member of the group who was not party to the conspiracy (the *naïve* subject). The experiment was tried with several different groups, and it was found that many naïve subjects, having heard everyone else give the same wrong answer, made the same error themselves. They were thus prepared to go against the evidence of their senses in order to conform.

The results of experiments such as Asch's suggest some 60 per cent of naïve subjects, even though drawn from intelligent student groups, may show this conformist behaviour. There is indeed safety in numbers! We do not, it seems, like to go against everyone else, even when deep down we are sure we are right. Another revealing set of experiments was carried out more recently by Milgram (1974). Milgram's subjects were told they were taking part in a learning experiment, and were paired off and separated from each other in adjoining rooms connected only by microphone. One member of the pair was required to pose a series of questions to the other. Each time the latter got an answer wrong, they were given an electric shock by the former. The shock was administered by pressing a button, and it was made clear that with each successive mistake the electric shock would become stronger, rising to high levels. At first all went well. Every time a wrong answer was given, the electric shock was mild, but as the experiment proceeded and the shock became stronger and stronger, the subject on the receiving end began to yelp with pain, then to plead to discontinue the experiment, then to bang on the wall and show increasing signs of serious distress, and finally to fall completely and ominously silent. Yet each time the subject administering the shock protested to the experimenter and requested to stop, they were simply told that the right answer had not been given from the other room and that they were 'please to continue'.

In actual fact the experiment was a fake. The subject receiving shocks was an actor hired to give a convincing performance, and the electrical apparatus was a dummy. There was in reality no shock and no danger. But the point of the experiment was that the subject administering the 'shock' did not know this. Milgram was interested to see how far an individual, on the instructions of an authority figure such as the white-coated experimenter, would go on inflicting pain and physical damage on another. The parallels with Nazi concentration camp guards and with others who have committed atrocities under orders were obvious. The results were disturbing. Most subjects, though expressing their reluctance, nevertheless went on under the promptings of the experimenter to administer 'shocks' right up to an apparently dangerous level, after the subject on the receiving end had apparently collapsed into silence.

It could be argued that since the experiments were being conducted in a prestigious university (Harvard) and under the direction of a qualified professional, the subjects asked to give the shocks were not really in the same position as concentration camp guards. Nevertheless, Milgram's results are profoundly disturbing. They show the readiness with which we are prepared to suspend our own judgement in the face of instructions from authority figures, and this has implications for our behaviour in all walks of life.

The peer group

An aspect of conformity, particularly evident at school level, is the pressure placed upon individuals by their peer groups. Especially in adolescence, but even in the junior and infant school, children are very influenced by what other children of their age are doing. The need to be accepted, to be a part of the group, is very strong, and often the group develops distinctive behaviour which must be followed as a badge of group membership. Some years ago, when selection at 11+ was still the rule throughout the UK, Hargreaves (1967) and Lacey (1970) independently examined social relationships in a secondary modern and a grammar school respectively. One of their findings was that in both schools definite 'A' and 'C' stream mentalities prevailed. The 'A' stream mentality was marked by conformity to the school and by a generally positive response to teachers and to what they were trying to do, while the 'C' stream mentality was the very opposite. In the 'A' stream, the outsider was the child who could not do the work or who went against the system, while in the 'C' stream it was the child who tried to work and who supported the system. The implications are that so strong are peer group pressures that children will allow them to mould their behaviour even in areas where their individual inclinations may be at odds with those of the group.

In looking at conformists and non-conformists, Crutchfield (1955, and see more recently Shaw, 1977) suggests that individuals who stand out against group pressures when they disagree with the group tend to be independently-minded, confident, and high in self-esteem. By contrast individuals who conform to these pressures tend to be less secure, with lower self-esteem, and often with a rigid and rather intolerant attitude. Conformists seem to need the 'certainty' provided by the group, and by the inflexible and clear-cut values and rules which it provides. Though note that when it is 'safe' to do so, as with for example within a tolerant and responsible adult group, some individuals who stand out against group decisions demonstrate attention-seeking behaviour. The group is far too humane to ostracize them, so they are able to get away with – and at the same time to feel significant because of –

269

their refusal to go along with even the most sensible and democratically-taken decisions. By disrupting the workings of the groups they are able to enjoy a sense of importance, of power, which for reasons of personal inadequacy they seem unable to gain in other more sensible ways.

The school and conformity

Clearly schools carry an important responsibility in the area of conformity. A line has to be steered — and is not easy — between instilling rigid conformist behaviour into children on the one hand, and allowing them to go entirely their own way on the other. Children need help in recognizing when conformity is called for and when it is not. Without such help they will find it difficult to exercise social judgement and to decide between social demands and inner convictions.

Some of the same considerations that apply to status apply to conformity. Children (and teachers) have to learn the lesson that social institutions cannot function unless each individual agrees to limit personal freedom and conform to the interests of the majority. But as the experiments of Asch and of Milgram show, there are dangers here. The best form of education allows the individual to see both the value of conformity and non-conformity, and to judge when one is appropriate and not the other. Originality and creativity also require judgement of this kind, a blend of discipline and of freedom. A rigid educational framework in which chidren are never allowed to think and choose for themselves, or to learn the procedures for responsibly questioning decisions and opening matters up for debate, is unlikely to produce individuals with this blend. Dependent upon temperament, it is far more likely to produce people who are equally inflexible and who are unable to think for themselves, or people who go to opposite extremes, and develop rebellious attitudes, refusing to accept any hint of conformity, no matter how reasoned and sensible it might be.

The lesson as a social encounter

Let us turn now from these more general issues to actual social processes in the classroom. It is useful first of all to look at the lesson itself, and see it as a set of social encounters between teacher and class, a set of encounters which follow a relatively clear-cut and consistent pattern. This pattern can be expressed as follows:

1. *Greeting.* The teacher enters the classroom and contact is made. Whether the greeting is formal (e.g. 'good morning children') or not, some social interaction takes place at this point as the teacher and class acknowledge each other's presence.

2. *Establishing a relationship.* The teacher talks to the class, tells them what is expected of them, listens to questions and so on.

3. *Tackling the lesson task.* The class gets down to work, whether verbal or written, and teacher–child interactions take place.

4. *Concluding the relationship.* The teacher focuses class attention upon him or herself once more as the lesson draws to an end, expresses feelings about the work that has been done and sets further work.

5. *Parting.* The teacher and the class take leave of each other.

Throughout this five-step episode sequence, teacher and class interact with each other socially in a number of ways, both verbally and non-verbally. Gaze is one example: the teacher looks at the class or at individuals within it pleasantly, sternly, questioningly, humorously and so on, while the class looks back alertly, dully, insolently, joyfully. Very often as much social information is conveyed through gaze as through speech. Teacher and class spend a great deal of time during the lesson looking at each other and registering their reactions, and much of the relationship between them is mediated and monitored in this way.

Gesture also plays a part. So does the way in which teachers carry themselves and go about classroom duties. They may be stiff and formal, nervous and jerky, relaxed and at ease, explosive and hasty, slow and uncertain, smooth and fluent, in command of their environment or dominated by it. Through watching teachers, the class picks up a great deal of information about them, and this information influences their own behaviour, which in turn feeds back into verbal and non-verbal signals apparent to teachers. *Social information* is also conveyed by a teacher's style of dress, of hair, and by the amount of books and papers and other bits of equipment he or she carries around from lesson to lesson. In the primary school, where the children are looking all day at the same teacher, there is often a particularly alert scrutiny even of such things as a new tie, a favourite jacket or blouse or pair of shoes.

Teacher awareness of social interaction

The effective teacher is usually aware of all these subtleties of social interaction, and is prepared to send out the right social signals. These involve not only signals of friendliness and welcome, but also of a measure of social unity. By the nature of their role teachers are always separate from the social group represented by the class, but if they are to work effectively with it this separation must not be too extreme.

271

Teachers who indicate by speech, by dress, by manner that they are alien to the social context of their children put themselves at a considerable disadvantage. It may even appear that, by emphasizing at every point their social aloofness from the class, they are passing judgement on its members. Inevitably this will invoke resentment and hostility, and lay teachers open to whatever reprisals the children can best engineer.

It must be emphasized of course that teachers who set out deliberately to ingratiate themselves socially into the classroom group, apeing the children's speech and fashions and trying all too obviously to close the gap of age or background which lies between teacher and child, are causing equal problems for themselves. Children easily see through this artificial performance, and find it hard to respect a teacher who wants simply to be like them. Children expect teachers to have something of their own to offer, to be confident in their own behaviour and standards, and are suspicious and scornful of adults who are so limited they have to take their cues exclusively from them. The correct course is to show that one understands and accepts the social context within which children live their lives, but that while being in communication with this context one does not abandon one's own social identity and pretend to be something one is not. Where children are dissatisfied with their own lifestyle, they will in any case be on the look-out for examples of other ways of doing things, and will look to the teacher to provide these examples.

It is clear, of course, that we cannot simply isolate the five-step episode sequence from the social interactions to which the children are subjected both before the lesson begins and after it ends. The children will be under the influence of what has happened in the previous lesson (or what has happened at home and on the way to school) on the one hand, and will be thinking about what is going to happen in the next lesson (or during break or lunchtime) on the other. These factors will inevitably influence the way in which children respond to what is on offer, especially when it comes to the greeting and the parting stages. Children coming from a lesson which emphasizes free informal expression (as in drama) or physical movement (as in sport), or who are going to such a lesson after the bell, will inevitably have their social responses during the current lesson coloured accordingly. So will they if (at secondary-school level) they are coming from or going to a lesson with a particularly strict or ineffectual teacher. The good teacher understands this, makes allowances for it, and does not automatically blame the children for the particular mood they happen to be in.

The five-step episode sequence

Let us now look at the five-step episode sequence in more detail, and see how each step interacts with the next. In the first step the teacher greets the class ('Good morning, children', 'Hello everyone', or – less desirably – 'Er, well now'). This greeting leads on to the second step, which consists of establishing a relationship. The teacher tells the class to listen carefully, or to look at the board, or to get out certain books, or to hand in their homework or simply to pay attention and stop looking round. The better the teacher knows and understands the class, and the more acceptable he or she is to them, the shorter this second step is likely to be. The lesson then moves on to the lesson task, which obviously consists of the material to be studied and the exercises to be carried out, and which will include several sub-tasks. When this is complete (or time runs out), the fourth step of concluding the relationship comes around, and the teacher will again address the whole class and tell them what he or she thought of their work and what is expected from them in the future, and then will dismiss them (pleasantly, gratefully or wearily as the case may be) and the fifth or parting step will be complete and the sequence terminated.

Looking at the five-step sequence in this way allows us to appreciate the extent to which each step influences the next. The way in which teachers greet the class influences the class's response to their attempts to establish a relationship, which in turn influences the success with which the lesson task is tackled, which in turn influences the attempt to conclude a relationship, and which in turn influences the parting. This completed cycle then influences the way in which teacher and class think about each other during the interval before the next lesson, which influences the way in which they greet each other when this lesson begins, which inevitably influences the whole of the next cycle and so on. The five-step sequence also helps us to appreciate what is really going on in terms of teacher–child interaction, and not merely what seems to be going on. The teacher might, for example, snap at the class to come in quietly as they enter the room, seeing this as nothing more than a routine rebuke whereas, for better or worse, the children see this as his or her greeting to them.

A greeting is not simply something that we decide to call 'a greeting' whenever it happens; it is the first interchange that takes place between people when they meet, and studies show that this interchange is of great importance in determining the nature of the relationship that follows. If the greeting is not a welcoming one, then you may have to work very hard in the following episodes to repair the damage. Similarly, the next step – that of establishing a relationship – is not just a convenient label. Research shows that after the greeting there is a definite stage in which the individuals concerned weigh each other up, make deductions as to each other's intentions and so on. Thus, although teachers may think they are simply giving the class the results of a test or handing back homework, what is actually happening is that they are moving into this second phase and providing the class with clues which help in the weighing-up process. The class decides whether the teacher is pleased or disappointed with them today, whether he or she is going to make more demands on them over the 40 minutes of the lesson than usual, whether they have reason to be anxious, whether the teacher has positive or negative concepts of them and their abilities, and even whether he or she is in the same mood as when they last met. These decisions help determine their own responses – enthusiastic, wary, friendly, hostile, co-operative, aggrieved and so on – which in turn influence the teacher's own behaviour and the way in which the whole class settles to the central task of the lesson.

The nature of communications

So far I have been using such general terms as 'welcoming', 'friendly', 'co-operative', and so on, but there are in fact much more precise categories that help us formalize our thinking. Communication can be *egocentric* (directed to the self) or, if *socially directed*, can consist of such categories as orders, questions, information, informal speech, expressed emotions, 'performative' utterances, social routines or latent messages. By studying these categories, and by then applying them to their own characteristic behaviour with children, individual teachers can gain valuable insights into their professional skills. Do the majority of their social interchanges with children take, for example, the form of orders and information rather than of questions? If so, does this mean that they are directing the class too frequently instead of prompting children to think, examine and deduce? Do they use informal speech where appropriate to encourage a relaxed and friendly atmosphere? If not, are they creating unnecessary barriers between themselves and the class which inhibit children from asking for help and guidance? On the other hand, do they perhaps overdo informal speech so that the children find it hard to recognize their authority when they wish to reassert it? Do they encourage the expression of emotion where this is helpful to children and learning (this means not just encouraging expressions of humour and pleasure but prompting the articulation of anxieties and disappointments: for instance, 'I can see you're upset about it; what's the trouble?'). Or do they dismiss emotions as inappropriate (for example 'Pull yourself together'; 'Don't be so silly')? Do they frequently express latent messages in their utterances, and are these often of the negative kind (for example 'I'm too busy for that now' might imply 'I'm just not interested in your problem')?

Interaction analysis

The task of analysing communications is helped if individual teachers look at one of the many systems now available for coding and classifying classroom interaction. Normally these systems are used by an observer, who sits at the back of the class and watches closely what happens each time the teacher communicates with the class or with individual members of it. Because of the demands made upon the observer, particularly in a busy classroom where several things seem to be happening at once, the categories employed in these systems tend to be somewhat condensed and simplified. The best-known of these systems is that of Flanders (1970), which is set out in Table 11.1. When using the Flanders system, the observer marks one of the ten categories every three seconds (which is about the top speed at which one can operate), and analysis of the data after the lesson gives the teacher a clear indication of the percentage of time taken up by each of the ten behaviours categorized, and also the extent to which he or she talked compared with the extent to which the children were stimulated into so doing.

Table 11.1. Flanders's categories for interaction analysis. Adapted from Flanders, N.A., (1970) *Analyzing Teaching Behavior.* Addison-Wesley Publishing Co. Inc. Reprinted by kind permission of the author.

TEACHER TALK
Response

1. *Accepts feelings*: accepts and clarifies the feeling tone of the students in a non-threatening manner; feelings may be positive or negative; predicting or recalling feelings are included.
2. *Praises or encourages*: praises or encourages student action or behavior; jokes that release tension (not at the expense of another individual), nodding head or saying 'um hm?' or 'go on' are included.
3. *Accepts or uses ideas of student*: clarifies, builds, or develops ideas suggested by a student. (As a teacher brings more of his ideas into play, shift to category 5.)
4. *Ask questions*: asks a question using own ideas about content or procedure with the intent that a student should answer.

Initiation

5. *Lectures*: gives facts or opinions about content or procedure; expresses own ideas, asks rhetorical questions.
6. *Gives directions*: gives directions, commands, or orders with which a student is expected to comply.

Table 11.1. *continued*

7. *Criticizes or justifies authority*: makes statements intended to change student behavior from non-acceptable to acceptable pattern: bawls someone out; states why the teacher is doing what he is doing; refers very often to self.

STUDENT
TALK
Response

8. *Response*: makes a predictable response to teacher; teacher initiates the contract or solicits student statement and sets limits to what the student says. (As student introduces own ideas shift to category 9.)

Initiation

9. *Initiation*: initiates talk; makes unpredictable statements in response to teacher.
10. *Silence or confusion*: pauses, short periods of silence and periods of confusion in which communication cannot be understood by the observer.

Over 100 of these interaction analysis systems are now in existence. Some are what is known as low-inferential, in that like Flanders's they simply allow the observer to record what happened. Others are high-inferential or evaluative, in that they allow the observer to record whether in his or her opinion the teacher was, for example, 'warm', 'enthusiastic' or 'stimulating'. In some systems the observer is able in addition to note the type of student with whom the teacher is interacting (e.g. 'high achiever', 'low achiever'). The choice as to which system to use depends to a large measure upon the kind of information required. If the aim is merely to record the percentage of time spent on the various categories of teacher and/or student talk respectively, then an instrument of the Flanders type is ideal. If, on the other hand, we want to know whether the teacher, say, behaves differently towards boys than towards girls, or uses non-verbal signals such as tone of voice or facial expression, then a more complex system with inferential categories would have to be employed.

If, as a third possibility, we wished to study a specific teacher skill, such as questioning, then we could use a system that concentrates on this aspect alone. Such an instrument would look at the type of question asked (seeking facts, opinions, emotional reactions), at the manner in which it is delivered (challenging, threatening, neutral, encouraging), and at the individual to whom the question is directed (boy or girl, high-, medium- or low-achiever). In its simplest form, such a specialist system is constructed as a matrix, with the type of question asked down the left-hand side and one other variable (e.g. manner in which delivered) across the top. Yet another possibility is for the observer to try and ascertain what the teacher expected from a particular item or interaction with a particular child, and what the child thought the teacher expected. This involves videotaping examples of classroom interaction, and then showing the tape as soon as possible afterwards independently to both teacher and child, and asking the teacher what was wanted from the child and whether or not it was considered to be forthcoming, and also asking the child for his or her version of events. Results sometimes indicate that teacher and child have quite different ideas about what was going on. The child may, for example, have thought the teacher was requesting opinion when in reality what was demanded was fact, or that the teacher was being serious when in reality they were trying to be humorous, or that censure was being offered when in reality it was an attempt at help. Similarly, if we reverse the procedure, the teacher might interpret child behaviour as being impertinent when it was not intended by the child as such, or as providing incorrect responses to a question when in fact the child was trying to convey something quite different and much nearer the truth.

ANALYSING THE RESULTS OF INTERACTION ANALYSIS. Whatever the system used, individual teachers can often be surprised to see how much of the lesson they spent lecturing (talking at the class), or how infrequently they offered praise or encouragement, or how often children had to seek direction on points that should have been made clear at the start. Alternatively, they may be heartened to see how often they asked questions or accepted feelings or stimulated the class to initiate their own ideas. Where a videotape has been used to keep a visual record of the interaction, then individual teachers may be surprised to notice not only the number of times they censured the class, but the ferocity of their expression as they did so or the number of mannerisms they appeared to have developed. (Or, again, they may be charmed at what a graceful and attractive picture they cut, though such a discovery is not, in itself, without dangers!) If teachers are analysing the results of a system designed to look at just one aspect of their work, such as motivation, they might be disturbed to see how often they employed the use of threats (e.g. 'Work quietly if you want to get out to play on time'; 'Pay attention if you want to get through the examination'; 'Work hard or else'). On the other hand, they might be pleased to realize how often they motivated through positive encouragement ('I know you'll be able to do this because you've been working so well'; 'I'm sure you'll find this fun').

277

In the light of the complexity of social behaviour, it is only to be expected that no system for measuring classroom interaction is going to be completely comprehensive. There are all kinds of subtle interactions that in any case we cannot yet score, and two identical score sheets for two different teachers (or even for the same teacher with two different classes) may cloak numerous important variations in social behaviour. And of course, children will respond to the teacher not just on the strength of what the latter says or does in the present lesson but (as pointed out when discussing episode sequences above) on their memories of the social interactions that took place on the previous occasions they were being taught by him or her: ('When Miss Jones looks like that it means she's in a bad mood'; 'Mr Wombat won't shout at you if you get it wrong'; 'We've never once had a good laugh in old Stoneface's lesson'). Nevertheless, interaction analysis systems provide one of the best practical ways for helping teachers to study their own professional strengths and weaknesses (to say nothing of the behaviour of children), and it is unfortunate that in the UK at least more use is not made of them both in initial training and in in-service work.

Social roles

The importance of a close study of teacher behaviour and, by implication, of the behavioural examples it sets for children, bring us to the subject of roles and role models. A role model is someone who exemplifies to others a set of behaviours within a specifically defined social position. People can act as desirable or undesirable role models. Drunken feckless parents for example are pretty unsatisfactory role models to their children of what parenthood should be. Caring, unselfish, clear-sighted parents on the other hand are good role models. Role models can be people who fill roles that we covet one day for ourselves or people in positions with which we simply come into frequent contact. Teachers are good examples of this latter kind of role model. Most children in the class will have no opportunity (and probably no wish!) to become teachers, yet their picture of what teachers are like is moulded for them by the specific examples to which they are exposed. Good teachers will set good examples and will give children role models that will leave them favourably disposed towards teachers and towards the whole concept of education while unsatisfactory teachers will do just the opposite. Teachers sometimes are unaware of just how influential they are (though a look at autobiographical literature should leave them in no doubt), and of how permanent an impression they often make upon the young.

But teachers are also examples of the first kind of role model (that is of individuals occupying a role to which children themselves aspire) in that they occupy the role of adults.

278

A good teacher ('good' in the social relationship and social behaviour sense as well as in the academic) provides children with an example of the kind of adult they might themselves one day become. This example does not stop just with the teacher–child relationship. Children are very much aware of how teachers relate to each other within the school, of how they relate to parents on open evenings and at social events, of how they respond to the headteacher and to the school rules, of the loyalty they show towards colleagues, of how they behave towards the opposite sex, and of how they react to triumphs and disasters, set-backs and disappointments, winning and losing. If children look at a teacher, and see there the kind of human being they themselves would like to be, then the teacher has given them a gift that rivals any of the formal teaching that has been taking place.

Role conflict

Within the role of teacher, there are a number of sub-roles. In one of these sub-roles teachers are academics charged with the business of helping formal learning. In another they are administrators, sometimes with a large department or with a year group to run. In another they are counsellors, responsible for the pastoral care of children. In another they are leaders of extra-curricular activities, and have school societies or sports teams (in which the children participate voluntarily) to organize. In another they are representatives of the authority of the school, with perhaps specific disciplinary functions (e.g. as head of lower or upper school) to fulfil. And at all times they have their own careers to think about, their own promotion prospects. Additionally, they have roles outside the school, for example as family men and women, which may interfere with the exercise of their role as teachers.

Not surprisingly these sub-roles can at times come into sharp conflict. This is dealt with further in Chapter 12 (p. 299), where the guidance/counselling role is discussed, but let me first take one or two obvious examples. In his or her role as responsible teacher, a teacher knows that they should stay to see a certain group of children through to their GCSE examinations next year, but a good job comes up in another school and in their career role they agonize over whether or not to apply for it. Or the children complain to a teacher with justification about certain school rules (pastoral role), which as a member of staff he or she must be seen to uphold unless and until the rules can be changed (authoritative role). Or the demands of running a busy department take a teacher out of the classroom frequently (administrative role), and interfere wih the preparation and marking of work (classteacher role). Or family commitments (parental role) prevent a teacher from going on a vital school trip during the school holidays or from staying behind after school to run one of the school societies (extra-curricular role).

ACCEPTING ROLE CONFLICT. Each of these role conflicts can often only be resolved by weighing up carefully the competing claims upon time and energies and loyalties. But all too often the result is a rather unsatisfactory compromise, or the abandoning of one or other role to the detriment of all concerned. In a multifaceted role like that of the school teacher there is no obvious way around this problem, but one essential is for the individual teacher (and preferably also the headteacher) to recognize its existence, and to acknowledge the fact that it can be a major source of teacher stress. The only way to avoid this stress is to be realistic in one's expectations. Teachers cannot themselves expect to fulfil each of their roles equally well and at all times. There must be a sense of priorities. And once having decided on these priorities and acted accordingly, there must not be an excess of guilt and self-accusations. Teachers *are* often superhuman people, but they cannot do everything. Better to do the more important roles really well at the expense of the less important than to do none of them adequately. And better to avoid the unnecessary ulcers and coronaries that will put an effective end to the performance of any roles at all!

In addition to role conflict at the personal level, it is also important for teachers to be aware of how their roles may lead to conflict within the perceptions which children have of them. In one role they may be friendly and informal towards children, in another brisk and remote. In one they may be sympathetic and understanding, in another arbitrary and dismissive. In one they may be thinking primarily of themselves, in another primarily of children. At times, a child may want to consult them in one of their roles while they remain firmly fixed in another, quite different one. Though teachers cannot avoid these varied roles, the important thing is that they remain fundamentally consistent across them. Thus for example their concern for children will show through, whether they are in the class teacher, the counsellor, or the authoritarian role. Children will appreciate a teacher's fairness, and see that vital human qualities are not superficialities to be picked up and discarded with each change of role.

Social learning and role models

In this way, the teacher conveys to children important lessons on how to relate appropriately to others. For no teacher can escape the responsibility of being a teacher of good social behaviour. This teaching occurs not only when we teach children to show understanding and respect for peers and adults, but on a more personal level when we encourage them to join in more, to speak up for themselves, and to value themselves at their true social worth. Such teaching will sometimes take place as part of a formal lesson (for instance in drama or in any of the humanities subjects), but will occur more frequently as part of the day-to-day contact between teacher and child, in science subjects as well as in arts, and in extra-curricular activities as well as within timetabled ones.

I have already indicated at a number of points throughout the book that this kind of teaching involves example as well as precept. It is not only what teachers tell children that is important, but the way in which teachers behave towards them. A formal lesson on the subject of politeness, for example, is likely to be completely wasted if at the end of it the teacher is seen to act with extreme discourtesy towards a member of the class (or perhaps towards a colleague). Using the correct technical term we say that teachers should *model* for children the kind of behaviour it is intended they acquire.

Bandura, one of the main exponents of what are called *social learning theories*, argues that we have tended to under-estimate the importance of modelling, particularly when it comes to the learning of social skills. Thus although Bandura agrees that reinforcement is important in many learning acts, he argues that it is not always essential. The child, he claims, has an innate propensity for imitating the behaviour of others, particularly when these others enjoy prestige or status. Such imitation is often unconscious in the sense that the child is not deliberately setting out to ape the model concerned. Where the imitation is on a large scale and relates specifically to one of the child's roles in life (e.g. to 'maleness' or 'femaleness') then the model becomes a role model. Children's earliest role models, as I said in Part i, are usually parents, but as they grow older teachers, elder brothers and sisters, prestigious friends and, later still, national figures such as sportsmen and women come to assume increasing importance.

EMOTIONS AND SOCIAL CONTACT. Bandura's theories are referred to as social learning theories not because they explain how the child comes to learn many social skills, but because they suggest that social contact in itself produces learning, whatever category of skills happens to be involved. Of particular relevance for present purposes, since obviously such expression is closely linked to social skills and social accepta-bility, Bandura has demonstrated (1973) that the expression of emotions seems to be strongly influenced by this social contact. He has made a particular study of aggression, and has demonstrated that children who witness adult aggression are subsequently much more likely to behave aggressively them-selves. This is not, it appears, because watching aggression in others makes them aggressive, but because seeing adults behave aggressively seems to sanction the expression of the aggressive feelings they already have. They take the adult as their role model, and appear to consider that if it is all right for him or her to behave in that way then it must be all right for them too. This is an important point to bear in mind when considering the influence of television and of the media generally upon children. Watching televised violence may not turn children into violent individuals, but it may seem to sanction any inclinations in that direction they already have, and to suggest to them specific ways in which these inclinations can be put into practice. The more prestigious the person perpetrating the televised violence (whether fictional or factual), the more likely this is to happen. However, if children already have a well-developed value system taken over from parents and teachers, then they will resist the temptation to adopt new role models that appear to contradict this system, and their behaviour will in consequence remain unchanged.

Copying role models

Variation in children's responses to the same role model is also indicated by the fact that dependent children appear to imitate prestigious figures of all kinds more readily than do those who are more independent. Similar research shows that timid or anxious children copy fearful responses in others more readily than do secure and confident ones, while socially helpful children imitate helpful responses more readily than do those who are less socially inclined. This seems to indicate that, once children's repertoires of social behaviour are beginning to show some consistency, they will imitate more readily those models who confirm what they are already doing than those who introduce them to less familiar behaviour. Research also shows that children who have learnt in the past to respond to particular role models (such as teachers) will be readier in the present to take them as models again than will individuals who have learnt to reject them. Thus children in this latter category who would be perfectly ready to accept a certain adult as a role model on the strength of his or her personal qualities may nevertheless reject the adult if they discover that he or she happens to be a schoolteacher in professional life. Finally, research shows that children are less likely to imitate behaviour of people whom they have seen to be unsuccessful in the past, even though they now appear in a quite new role, than people whom they have seen performing successfully.

Although social learning does not appear to depend upon reinforcement, it is nevertheless greatly strengthened by it. Thus children who take over courteous behaviour from a teacher will be more likely to persist in this behaviour if they find it brings about desirable ends. For example, they may find that other people respond more thoughtfully to them in turn, that they become generally better liked, or that things which were denied them on the strength of their previous behaviour become available now that they know how to ask for them in a socially acceptable way. On the other hand, if they come from a background in which courtesy is under-valued and brings no intrinsic reinforcement they may decide, however strong the role model in favour of courtesy may be, that after all it does not seem to pay and may as well be abandoned.

Friendship patterns in the classroom

Most groups of any size tend to divide up into smaller subgroups. The classroom group is no exception. And once formed, each subgroup develops its own norms, with membership of the subgroup dependent upon recognition of these norms. There is no simple answer to why and along what lines classroom subgroups are actually formed. But it seems that the subgroup gives its members a feeling of security, of belonging and of being socially accepted, thus satisfying a basic human need. Children who are rejected by the subgroups usually end up lonely and isolated, with a keen awareness of those social inadequacies which militate against their subgroup membership.

As to the lines along which subgroups divide, sex obviously is a frequent factor. In a coeducational class, boys and girls tend to form separate subgroups. Ability is also a frequent factor, with the more able children in a mixed-ability class tending to draw together on the one hand and the less able on the other. The same is true of social class. Useful as the comprehensive school has undoubtedly been in breaking down social barriers, children nevertheless still tend to draw their immediate social circle from those with similar backgrounds to themselves. Interests and attitudes are also factors. Children group together with those who share their own outlook on life.

All this is straightforward enough, but there are other more subtle factors at work. The membership of a particular subgroup may confer prestige upon individual children. Or it may provide support. Or it may help to give them goals and objectives as they try to emulate the other group members. So important can the group become to children that they will abandon cherished beliefs and behaviour in order to conform to group norms, and in their efforts to do so may become comparative strangers to parents and teachers and those who knew them in the past. This is particularly true during adolescence, when the child is seeking an adult identity and places particular reliance upon acceptance by the peer group. It also holds good with younger children, right from the time in fact

283

when they become first aware of the social presence of other children and of the power these children have over them.

Classroom subgroups

In view of the importance of the group to the individual, the good teacher is careful not to threaten unnecessarily individual children's status in the eyes of their peers. To humiliate children in this way is not only traumatic for them, but may also encourage more difficult behaviour in the future as they struggle to re-establish themselves in the eyes of the group by getting back at the teacher. Good teachers are also careful not to set the group against itself. Nothing unites a group more closely than a threat from outside, and if the group conceives the teacher as that threat, then the implications are obvious. So are the implications of gaining the support and acceptance of the group. As mentioned earlier, teachers are always separate from the classroom group and its various subgroups, but if liked by them, and accepted as good role models, then the group norm will be for co-operation. Any group member who deviates from this norm will find group pressures at work upon him or her to come back into line.

Of course at times whole subgroups may deviate from required behaviour, or there may be rivalry or antagonism between subgroups, with one group wanting to work and to support the teacher and another wanting to do just the opposite. Some success can be achieved by physically separating the members of deviant and uncooperative groups. Putting them to sit some distance away from each other serves to break up something of the group's cohesiveness, but this must be done carefully. There is always the risk that disgruntled group members will now spend their time disturbing other children and generally making a nuisance of themselves.

So before taking action of this kind, it is best to try and win the group over to more conformist behaviour. Children at the upper end of the ability range tend to work better in self-selected groups, where group cohesion is high (Lott and Lott, 1960). The same is probably true of lower-ability groups, provided that task difficulty does not reach a point at which children become discouraged and obtain more fun from distracting each other and playing about. So it follows that if children are allowed to sit near their friends they will be more favourably disposed towards their work and towards their teacher than if they are routinely split up and set to work with relative strangers. The successful teacher is able to operate this system with the class and its subgroups on an informal contract basis. The children can sit with and work with their friends provided they produce results, results moreover which are clearly defined in advance and which the children understand and accept as reasonable. The teacher now has the clear sanction that if children do not keep their side of the contract, then they can expect to be split up.

The same applies to pairs of friends. Research into friendship patterns (e.g. Griffith and Veitch, 1974) shows that proximity, similarity in status and background, and shared interests all play an important part in cementing friendships. Education is concerned with helping children relate to each other and form mutually enriching bonds, and the standard procedure adopted by some teachers of separating friends during the lesson is hard to justify. By working together in friendship pairs children potentially gain more enjoyment from school tasks and learn more rapidly. They also help to motivate each other and to keep each other focused upon the project in hand. In a busy crowded classroom the teacher has to insist that noise levels are kept to a reasonable minimum, but there is no evidence these levels are lower when children are working with partners they dislike than when they are working with their friends. It is also pertinent to remember that adults working together like to discuss what they are doing just as much as do children. Working silently in a social environment does not come naturally to any of us. Children have to learn a degree of self-control for obvious reasons, but it is unrealistic to expect too much of them. And it is misleading to give them the idea that social communication in itself is wrong or even necessarily counter-productive.

Unsuitable friendships and the friendless child

Most teachers at some point come up against children who pair (or who become subgroup members) in a way that gives cause for concern. Children may for example pair up with others who are clearly a bad influence upon them, or who dominate them excessively or take advantage of them. At an early age, some children seek clearly to gain power over their fellows, either subtly or through bullying. Other children seem readily to become victims (see p. 21 for a discussion on what makes some children natural 'victims'). Bullies are people who victimize those weaker than themselves, but bullying is also present at times within apparent friendships and certainly within subgroups. Many subgroups develop a hierarchy, with a dominant child or children at the top, and a pecking order stretching downwards to the unfortunate child at the bottom, who is the general butt of the group. This unfortunate child's very group membership depends upon a willingness to fill the role of butt. Much as the child may dislike this role, he or she consents to it either because group membership is important in giving a sense of identity and belonging, or because of fears that his or her fate at the hands of the group would be even worse as an outsider than it is as a victimized insider.

The teacher who recognizes that a child has formed an unsatisfactory friendship or is being bullied within a group naturally wants to intervene. But there are limits to what can be done. Any incidence of bullying must of course be referred immediately to the appropriate authority within the school, but teachers cannot form friendships for their children. In the primary school, and in arts and social studies lessons in the secondary, the nature of friendship and the mutual obligations which it carries should be a frequent subject for class discussions, and the teacher can work unobtrusively to keep unsuitable friends apart. But forbidding children to mix together is usually counter-productive. Few things strengthen friendships more than threats from outside. The best strategy is subtly to prompt children to see that they have little in common with each other, or that they may be getting a bad deal out of the bargain of friendship. The teacher can also work to strengthen the confidence and independence of children who are on the wrong end of this bargain, so that they will have more autonomy in their future choice of friends.

With such children, and with the friendless, isolated child, the teacher needs to keep in mind the fact that we make friends when it is seen by others that we have something to offer. Up to now, the victimized child may have been offering to others the sense of power which they derive from victimizing him or her, or the sense of superiority they feel from their more elevated position in the group pecking order. The friendless child may have been offering even less. In fact, because of his or her general unpopularity, to be seen with them may have a negative effect upon the status of other children. Such a sad state of affairs cannot be remedied overnight by the teacher. But by increasing children's sense of their own worth, and through the social skills training discussed later in this chapter, the teacher can do a very great deal to help in the longer term. The simple fact, signalled clearly to a particular child, that in the teacher's eyes they are valued as highly as everyone else in the class, is the indispensable first step.

The popular child

By contrast to the friendless child, some children seem to be generally popular with the whole class, even though they may appear to have little in common with some of its members. Such individuals appear to have several identifiable important qualities. They seem to show a concern for others as well as for themselves, to inspire confidence in some way, and to satisfy group needs. For example, they may be able to offer encouragement or support, or to 'liven things up' in dull lessons, to offer instances of expertise in certain prized areas (e.g. sport, musical skills), to stand up for classmates when threatened, or to set some kind of desirable standard (perhaps in matters of dress or life style). Such children often develop into unofficial group leaders, either for the whole class or for a particular subgroup within the class. Research shows that people likely to become leaders tend also to be able to *define* the group in some way: that is, to give it identity, to recognize and emphasize those things about it that other group members feel (consciously or unconsciously) to be important. In addition they seem to have some social quality (charisma, prestige) which enables those in receipt of their friendship or attention to feel they are having status conferred upon them. To complete the picture, they generally appear to be a little above the average intelligence of the group, to show a problem-solving orientation, and to be able to initiate problem-solving behaviour.

Sociometry

One way of identifying the leaders in a class of children is simply to ask people to vote on who they are. A widely used technique for doing this, known as *sociometry*, involves asking each child to write down the name of the classmate they would most like to see in charge of a group in which they are working. We can be more specific if we wish and specify the kind of group concerned (academic, social, sporting). Alternatively, we could ask the children who they would least like as their leader, and thus get some idea of those with low leadership qualities (though we must always have reservations about inviting children to make negative comments about each other). Such children would not necessarily be unpopular, but might simply be regarded as too prone to act the fool, or perhaps too lacking in the skills required by the group.

Stars and isolates. Sociometry is not, of course, confined to studies attempting to identify group leaders. It can be employed in any study designed to pick out individuals with particular social skills, and has perhaps been most widely used in studies of friendship patterns. In these studies each child is asked who they would like to be friends with, and the children receiving the highest number of choices are labelled *stars* while those receiving the least are labelled *isolates*. Results are sometimes plotted in the form of a *sociogram*, with each child's name entered on the gram with an arrow drawn pointing towards him or her from each child who has nominated them as a friend. The sociogram enables us to see at a glance not only who are the stars and who are the isolates within the class, but also what subgroups exist, since these often show up as clusters of children who tend to choose only each other.

Once these patterns have been identified, we can then study the set of circumstances that appear to mark children out as stars and isolates, or which go to help the formation of subgroups. This has already been discussed within the context of friendship, and much research has emerged from work with sociograms; but there may be other factors which help determine whether a child is a star or an isolate in addition to simple matters of friendship. A star might perhaps bathe in the reflected glory of a popular brother or sister higher up the school, or of a parent or relative with local or national prestige. An isolate might simply be marked off from the rest of the class by widely differing academic ability or socio-economic status, by social aggression, exceptional timidity, or by some other kind of personality problems which may need particular guidance and counselling.

Note that stars are not necessarily class leaders (though they often are), and that they, along with isolates and subgroups, are subject to fluctuating social fortunes. The class, like most other social groups, is a dynamic unit, subject to constant change and development, and this term's star may be less popular next (for any one of a variety of reasons), while today's isolate could be more generally acceptable at a later date. The sympathetic teacher, sensitive to the social relationships within the class, can do much to prevent the formation of undesirable subgroups simply by remembering that friendship depends largely upon frequency of interaction. Thus by seeing to it that all children within the class have opportunities to interact with each other as often as possible (e.g. by the way in which group and project work is organized), the teacher can ensure that certain children are not thrown together unduly. Similarly, a great deal can be done to prevent vulnerable individuals from becoming isolates by ensuring that children are not always left to choose their own partners or to define their own social environments within the class, though this must be done carefully so that the children are not robbed of social choice or made to feel that the teacher is trying consistently to force unwanted work-partners upon them.

Social skills

As mentioned in Chapter 10, we place more emphasis in formal education upon the 'knowing' area than upon the 'being'. Often we do little to help individual children grow in self-understanding and self-acceptance, or in the ability to experience their own lives in positive and successful terms. The development of social skills should be an essential part of this education of being. We get much of our picture of ourselves from the reactions of others to us, reactions which are very much influenced by our social performance. Much of our progress in life, whether at school or in the later world of employment, depends upon our ability to master and use the necessary social skills. So does a significant part of our success

288

in family relationships and in relationships with friends and colleagues.

Increasingly schools are endeavouring to include some social skills training in the formal curriculum, either as part of life skills or as part of drama and creative activities lessons. But perhaps because it lies outside the examinations syllabus the area is still a sadly neglected one. Many teachers have had no training in the relevant techniques themselves, and find it hard to know how to present them to children. This is unfortunate, because social psychologists and sociologists have done much to identify these techniques, and to indicate ways in which they can be presented to children.

In any social skills training programme, a useful starting point is to invite people to assess their social competence as it stands at present. Until we recognize that we are not currently very successful at something, we may not be strongly motivated to learn it. Nor may we recognize in which particular areas of it we are most deficient. The teacher can draw up a simple list of social situations, geared to the age and background of the children, and present them to the class along with a number of questions designed to assess how individuals would be able to handle them. Standard questionnaires, such as that by Trower, Bryant and Argyle (1978) exist for this specific purpose, and the teacher can use them as a guide in developing his or her own. Other similar tests contain useful supporting material, designed to help the teacher develop a social skills programme on the basis of questionnaire responses (e.g. Spence, 1980).

Assertiveness

Having collected questionnaire results and discussed them with the group, most social skills programmes now proceed to a definition of what is meant by social skills. One variable that usually surfaces almost at once is assertion. In a number of situations people feel their inability to assert themselves, to have their say, to stand up for their rights, to lodge the necessary complaints etc. This variable is then broken down into its constituent behaviours. What does the individual actually need to be able to do if he or she is to be assertive? Studies (e.g. Lazarus, 1973) show that these needs include the ability to:

- say 'no' when the occasion demands it
- make requests or ask for help or favours
- express both positive and negative feelings
- start, carry out and terminate conversations.

You perhaps notice something strange about these requirements. Each of them represents behaviour which is frequently discouraged in children. Whenever they deal with adults, and

289

particularly with adults in authority over them, children run the risk of disapproval for indulging in them. Dependent upon circumstances, such indulgence may be labelled impolite, thoughtless, uncontrolled, defiant or even downright insolent.

Children *cannot* be allowed to ignore approved social conventions. None of us can go around asserting ourselves whenever the mood takes us. But if we consider assertion to be of value in the right context, and an important aspect of independence, self-confidence, self-esteem and social effectiveness, then children must be allowed guidance on how to develop it and on how to make decisions on when it is appropriate to use it. If children are made to feel guilty even for wanting to assert themselves, they are left with the feeling they have no right to their own views or to their own social space. Small wonder they may develop an inability to stand up for themselves or, at a deeper level, to think well of themselves as individuals.

Having isolated social assertion as one of the important variables, and having identified the requirements that go with it, the next step in any social skills programme is usually to allow participants to practise the behaviour that meets these requirements (saying 'no', starting and terminating conversations etc.). And here an important misconception often crops up. Many people have the idea that social assertion involves being unpleasant to people, saying 'no' aggressively and terminating conversations rudely or abruptly. Quite the contrary. Effective social assertion involves clear decisions and quiet determination, but there is no reason why these qualities should be used to wound others. Apart from the personal harm it inflicts, wounding can be socially very counterproductive, goading the person with whom we are dealing into becoming equally determined and into hitting back in their own turn. In social skills training, the emphasis is upon *skill* and not upon force. By studying the reactions of others, by increasing our awareness of their legitimate rights and needs, and by learning the right techniques of communication, we are more likely to achieve our reasonable objectives than by blurting out an ill-considered attack.

Assessing and responding to social situations

A social skills programme – and particularly one involving children – needs therefore to offer guidance in how to sum up a social situation. Why is the other person reacting as he or she is? Is our own position a reasonable one? What has so far been done and said on both sides? Videotaped material is invaluable here, with the class looking at specific examples of social interaction and commenting upon what went wrong and why, and what could have been done to avoid it. The videotapes can be purpose-made, or they can be taken from snippets of popular television drama, particularly snippets which involve child–child or child–adult interactions. The next stage is how to remedy the situation. What would each child do next if he or she were in that situation? What form of words would they use? What tone of voice? What non-verbal signals?

Usually at this stage it is appropriate to ask individuals to act out their chosen response, with the rest of the group looking on, and ready to comment helpfully. This is followed by more extended role-playing exercises in pairs: individual participants are given a short script by the teacher that helps set the scene, and they are then allowed to take things from there. Such scripts can include situations like job interviews, returning faulty goods to a shop, complaining to a neighbour over some domestic matter, speaking up for someone who is underprivileged, approaching strangers at a party, explaining to teachers that they have marked work unfairly, talking about something you like. One problem with work of this kind is that it sometimes appears highly artificial to all concerned, but this is primarily due either to the fact that we are placing too much emphasis upon dramatic skills, thus making the children feel self-conscious and over-anxious to get it right, or to the fact that the situations we have chosen lie too far outside their experience. Obviously, looking back at the examples just given, job interviews would only be of direct relevance to children about to leave school, while complaining to a neighbour would only work if children came from an area in which there was a great deal of friction between householders. The rule is that if we are engaged in assertiveness training we are not trying to teach children to be assertive at some indefinable date in the future but to be assertive now; or if we are engaged in social warmth training we are not trying to teach children how to relate to people at the sort of mythical cocktail party dreamed up by television producers but how to relate to people at the local youth club or disco. Often this will mean that the teacher should have no preconceived notions about the detailed behaviour that goes with such relationships, but should study children carefully to see what problems these relationships present to them. Often the children's own comments, if offered in the right spirit, will be of more help in guiding each other in this behaviour than will anything teachers themselves say.

Through the use of the videotapes mentioned earlier, or through still pictures and audiotapes if videos are not available, children can be helped to identify the factors that distinguish the socially skilled individual from the unskilled. Eye contact, facial expression, body posture, the use of gesture, physical appearance, head movements and smiles, all follow a markedly different pattern in the skilled person than they do in the unskilled. So does the use of the voice. Clarity and rate of speech, hesitations and pauses, dysfluencies ('er-ring' and 'umming'), volume and tone, vary markedly from a socially assured to a socially gauche person. Similar varia-tions are apparent in speech content. Length and interest of utterances, repetitions and interruptions all play their part, as of course do the sympathy and attention with which one person is able to listen to the other.

Again through the use of visual material, children can be helped to recognize emotions through the body postures and physical expressions adopted by the people with whom they are interacting. As an extension, they can be prompted to look more closely at their own behaviour, and to recognize their own emotions and the extent to which they are appropriate to the social situation in hand. Then their conversational skills can be developed under such headings as asking a favour, greeting a stranger, explaining an error, apologizing, dealing with criticism, talking to a member of the opposite sex, ordering goods by telephone and so on. The whole exercise should be carried out in a relaxed, informal way, with the videotapes and role-play exercises supplemented by game-like material.

For example, children can be asked to think up and act out inappropriate responses (slouching, swearing, violence, cheeking, evasion, ignoring), followed by appropriate ones (calmness, politeness, truthfulness). Role-playing roulette, in which children draw numbers and then have to act out the role associated with that number adds to the fun (though only if the teacher can remain clearly in charge!) Asking children to act out teacher-prepared scripts in which the characters be-have in socially unskilled ways helps to sharpen children's critical awareness. The identification game, in which each child is given a slip of paper with a particular social skill or deficit marked on it, and then asked to act accordingly while the rest of the class try to identify the variable in question, is also popular and helpful.

The right atmosphere for social skills training

Let me stress again the need for a relaxed atmosphere in work of this kind though. It should never be seen as a 'test', which some children pass and others fail. This is the precise opposite of good social skills training. The idea is to build confidence, not to undermine it further. If children feel embarrassed or inadequate during a social skills lesson, then this lesson simply becomes something else which they cannot do. Behind the deceptively simple pattern of the lesson goes a great deal of teacher preparation and planning. The teacher needs to see to it that, unobtrusively, the socially hesitant children are given the less demanding tasks, and are publicly encouraged and praised in their performance. No child should feel he or she comes badly out of a social skills lesson, and the class generally should be prompted to support and help each other, rather than to denigrate or worse still ridicule.

It is important, also, that exercises of this kind should be designed to teach general lessons, and not be specific attempts to make child A more assertive or child B less so, or child C more socially graceful and child D less tongue-tied. By spotlighting individual problems in front of the class the teacher may make life difficult for the children concerned, if only because other children may become over-curious about their 'problems', or may see them as subjects of amusement. Individual social problems are best dealt with (in the context of the school at least) on an individual basis and in confidence.

Lessons learnt from role playing

Care should also be taken not to ask children to jump into role playing without sufficient preparation. Participants need to know that the object is not artificial slanging matches, but thoughtful realistic communication. What emerges will be a much clearer understanding of the nature and power of persuasion, of the right wording needed if a request is to succeed, of how others see us, of the importance of voice, of manner, of non-verbal signals, and of studying the person with whom we are interacting. Confident statements and requests, spoken not too quickly and not too slowly, are far more effective than garbled ones. A smile (provided it is natural) is of more use than a scowl. Eye contact gives a better impression than eye avoidance. Expectation of social success produces a more direct manner than expectation of social failure.

Role playing also allows participants to see that much social interaction takes the form of a kind of contract. If I approach someone pleasantly, there is a good chance they will be pleasant back. If I know what I want to say, and say it clearly and without confusing or boring them, they will be far more likely to hear me out. If I show my request takes their convenience and well-being into account as well as my own, they are far more likely to agree to it. If I can show I am ready to return the favour I am asking, I will be more likely to have it granted. If I can show I am ready to listen to other people's points of view, and allow them to express their feelings, then they are more likely to extend the same consideration to me. The list is a lengthy but not a difficult one. The scant attention we normally pay to social skills training is amply demonstrated by the speed at which people pick up skills once they are exposed to them. Their response is very much of the order of 'yes of course, now I see how to do it; I just hadn't realized before'.

The importance of social warmth

After social assertion, the second major variable in social skills training is *warmth*. Many people find it well-nigh impossible to show social warmth, whether it be in the form of affection, sympathy, or simply a shared joy of some kind. Again our early training plays a part. Children are often told it just is not 'done' to express any of these emotions. In any case, the embarrassed way in which adults respond to such expression quickly convinces children that it is better to hide feelings of warmth and openness, to stop being spontaneous, to avoid showing that they feel drawn towards someone, to hold back if they feel sorry for them and want to comfort them. This unnatural social reserve serves as a handicap within families, between friends and acquaintances, and ulti- mately in boy–girl relationships. It places unnecessary bar- riers between people, and contributes to the sense of social isolation and loneliness which many individuals feel through- out life.

Social skills training within the context of warmth follows similar procedures to those already outlined. Children need help in recognizing their own feelings and the feelings of others, in choosing the appropriate words and actions to convey these feelings, in recognizing and overcoming unneces- sary reactions of social uncertainty and embarrassment, and in deciding how to respond when they themselves are the objects of social warmth. In all social skills training, it is important that children accept that each person is an indivi- dual, and will have his or her characteristic way of relating socially. It is a mistake to think everyone should think and behave as we do, and to pass social judgements on them if they do not. People vary, probably innately, in their readiness to give and receive social warmth (research shows that from a very early age some babies are 'cuddlers' and others 'non- cuddlers'). But a good social skills programme allows each person to express naturally and openly his or her feelings of companionship and support towards fellow human beings.

The place of self-disclosure

The third major variable in social skills is *self-disclosure*. How much of ourselves, and of our inner life, are we prepared to share with others? How easily does self-disclosure make us feel vulnerable? Conversely, how ready are we to overdo self-disclosure, telling people things about ourselves that may bore or even antagonize them? It seems likely that extraverts are more inclined towards self-disclosure than introverts (see p. 175), since introverts are, for better or worse, more private people than extraverts. But a degree of self-disclosure shows a desirable openness towards others and an honesty and lack of defensiveness about ourselves. It also shows a readiness to trust others, and is an essential ingredient in social intimacy. A social skills programme directed towards self-disclosure helps individuals to decide what degree of disclosure is appropriate and in what circumstances. It helps them to examine the reasons behind their reluctance to self-disclose (guilt, fear of vulnerability, lack of trust, doubts as to their own worth). And it helps them appreciate that others have problems very similar to their own, and that sharing these problems can be a help to both parties.

Above all it helps people to be good listeners. If we want to self-disclose, we must give others equal freedom to disclose to us. There are far more talkers in the world than listeners, yet listening is every bit as important a part of social skills as talking. Once children can appreciate the need to listen, and to develop the genuine interest in others that goes with it, they are usually quick to acquire the art. And to appreciate that perhaps more than any other social skill it is being a good listener that helps make us liked. There is far more to successful social interaction than simply ensuring we know how to have our say every time!

References

Asch, S.E. (1955) Opinions and social pressure. *Scientific American, November.*

Bandura, A. (1973) *Aggression: A social learning analysis.* Englewood Cliffs, New Jersey: Prentice-Hall.

Crutchfield, R.S. (1955) Conformity and character. *American Psychologist 10.*

Flanders, N.A. (1970) *Analyzing Teacher Behavior.* Reading, Massachusetts: Addison-Wesley.

Griffith, W. and Veitch, R. (1974) Ten days in a fall-out shelter. *Sociometry, 37,* 63–173.

Hargreaves, D.(1967) *Social Relations in a Secondary School.* London: Routledge & Kegan Paul.

Lacey, C. (1970) *Hightown Grammar.* Manchester: Manchester University Press.

Lazarus, A.A. (1973) On assertive behaviour: a brief note. *Behaviour Therapy,* 4, 697–699.

Lott, A.J. and Lott, B.E. (1960) The formation of positive attitudes towards group membership. *Journal of Abnormal and Social Psychology, 61,* 297–300.

Milgram, S. (1974) *Obedience to Authority: An experimental overview.* London: Tavistock.

Potter, S. (1947) *Gamesmanship.* London: Rupert Hart Davis.

Spence, S. (1980) *Social Skills Training with Children and Adolescents.* Windsor, Berks.: NFER/Nelson.

Trower, P., Bryant, B. and Argyle, M. (1978) *Social Skills and Mental Health.* London: Methuen.

SOME
QUESTIONS

1. Why does formal teaching generally fail to improve children's social skills?

2. Study your social interaction with other people and note the non-verbal signals each of you uses.

3. What clues do you use when summing up a person you have just met for the first time?

4. Observe the strategies you use when trying to make a good impression upon others.

5. List some of the methods individuals (including teachers) use to emphasize their status over others.

6. List some of the methods people use to protect their status when in the presence of social equals or superiors.

7. How are the pressures towards conformity (in particular school rules) formulated and enforced in most school communities?

8. How do you think you would react in a social situation similar to that used in Asch's experiments?

9. What are the qualities that make respectively for conformist and independent social behaviours?

10. What are the implications of Milgram's findings for society in general?

11. What is the 5-step episode sequence which characterizes most lessons?

12. How would you handle the greeting episode in order to get the lesson off to a good start?

13. List some of the good 'social signals' teachers should send out to a class.

14. What is the nature of the role conflict often faced by the teacher? How can it best be resolved?

15. What are the main reasons for popularity and unpopularity in children?

16. Why is it generally inadvisable to threaten children's status in the eyes of their peers?

17. How can the school best deal with the problem of bullying?

18. Outline the major requirements of a good social skills training programme for use either in the junior or secondary school.

19. Write a short role-play exercise for use in a social skills programme. Identify the skills it is designed to teach.

20. Why do many children find it hard to display a) social warmth b) self-disclosure? How can the school help?

21. Why is it some people are better listeners than others?

Additional Reading

Argyle, M. (1983) *The Psychology of Interpersonal Behaviour*, 4th edn. Harmondsworth: Penguin.
Still one of the best introductions to the general field of social interactions.

Aronson, E. (1976) *The Social Animal*, 2nd edn. San Francisco: Freeman.
Very readable introduction to the whole field of social interaction.

Bennett N. and Desforges, C. (ed.) (1985) *Recent Advances in Classroom Research*. Edinburgh: Scottish Academic Press.
Not restricted to social aspects of classroom behaviour, but contains much useful material on interaction.

Brophy, J.E. and Good T.L. (1974) *Teacher–Student Relationships: Causes and consequences*. New York: Holt, Rinehart & Winston.
Looks in great detail at the practicalities and subtleties of teacher–child relationships. (Also recommended for Chapter 14.)

Chanan, G. and Delamont, S. (ed.) (1975) *Frontiers of Classroom Research*. Windsor: NFER-Nelson.
Readers interested in learning more about interaction analysis and classroom-based research generally will find this of great interest.

Delamont, S. (1983) *Interaction in the Classroom*, 2nd edn. London: Methuen.
One of the best short works on interaction analysis.

Delamont, S. (1984) The observation and classification of classroom behaviours. In D. Fontana (ed.) *Behaviourism and Learning Theory in Education*. Edinburgh: Scottish Academic Press.
A full survey of the development and current status of research into classroom interaction.

Duck, S. (1986) *Friends For Life: The psychology of close relationships*. Brighton: Harvester Press.
A penetrating and comprehensive look at the mechanics of friendship.

Gahagan, J. (1975) *Interpersonal and Group Behaviour*. London: Methuen.
A useful short survey, which gives guidance on sociometry and allied techniques.

Good, T. and Brophy, J.E. (1978) *Looking in Classrooms*, 2nd edn. New York: Harper & Row.

Very highly recommended for its survey of the ways in which classroom data can be collected (as well as for its examination of all aspects of classroom management). (Also recommended for Chapter 13.)

Hook, C. and Rosenshine, B. (1979) Accuracy of teacher reports of their classroom behaviour. *Review of Educational Research,* 49, 1–12.
The discrepancy between the teacher's ideas on what is going on in the classroom and the ideas held by the children is brought out fully in the research reviewed here.

Kleinke, C.L. (1986) *Meeting and Understanding People.* New York: W.H. Freeman.
A splendid, highly readable and eminently practical guide to assessing and relating to others.

Kutnick, P. (1983) *Relating to Learning: Towards a developmental social psychology of the primary school.* London: Allen & Unwin.
Deals with younger children, but a valuable introduction to the way in which social factors influence learning and development.

Shaw, M. (1977) *Group Dynamics: The Psychology of small group behaviour.* New Delhi: Tara McGraw Hill.
Covers every aspect of group behaviour. Scholarly and very thorough.

Simon, A. and Boyer, E. (1967) *Mirrors for Behaviour: An anthology of classroom observation instructions.* Philadelphia: Humanizing Learning Program, Research for Better Schools Inc.
A good review of over one hundred different instruments used to analyse teacher and child behaviour.

Spence, S. and Shepherd, G. (1983) *Developments in Social Skills Training.* London: Academic Press.
Practical and comprehensive survey of social skills strategies suitable for classroom use.

12

Educational Guidance and Counselling

Counselling in school

An examination of guidance and counselling must begin by insisting that just as every teacher is a teacher of social skills (see p. 288), so every teacher is an educational counsellor. By this I mean that part of each teacher's function is to help children deal with personal problems and to make decisions about the course that their lives should take. Since teachers are individuals they will inevitably vary in the degree of importance they attach to their counselling roles, and they will also vary in the extent to which children seem prepared to consult them about their difficulties. Some teachers tend to invite confidences more readily than others, and to be more sympathetic and patient in their relationships with children. Children feel they can talk to them, and can trust their reactions. It is in fact these two qualities, sympathy and trustworthiness, rather than any great familiarity with counselling techniques, that children appear to look for when deciding to whom they should turn when in need.

The second of these qualities, trustworthiness, sometimes seems to be compromised by the fact that teachers have a dual role. Primarily they represent the authority of the school, and only secondly do they represent the disinterested confidentiality of the counsellor. Thus, if a child wishes to discuss with the teacher some problem related to school, such as alleged unfair treatment by another member of staff, or theft of school equipment, or cheating in a school examination, he or she may feel unsure whether the teacher will consider it proper to report matters to a higher authority. Similarly, the teacher may feel the tug of divided loyalties and be worried as to where professional duty lies, and this may be one strong reason why some teachers appear to discourage the kind of confidences that would put them in this uncertain position.

One way of avoiding the problem is for the school to employ a member of staff whose duties extend only to counselling, and who does not carry a teaching or a disciplinary function at all. The reason why this practice is not more widespread is hard to say for sure, though some teachers express themselves to be uneasy at the presence of a specialist counsellor on the staff. They are concerned that they might be the subject of discussion between the counsellor and children, that by their very presence in the school counsellors are a threat to their own pastoral roles, and that if there are secrets which the counsellor is not prepared to divulge even to the headteacher, then the latter's authority must to some extent be undermined within the school. It is probable that financial considerations also play some part. An extensive survey (Antonouris, 1974) indicates that some years ago only around seven per cent of LEAs made counsellors extra to quota in secondary schools (i.e. allowed schools to appoint counsellors over and above their normal staff entitlement), and the position has deteriorated even further over the intervening years. Many LEAs claim that the decision on whether or not to have a specialist counsellor is left to individual headteachers, but one is bound to conclude that few heads will choose to avail themselves of this facility if it means depriving themselves of a subject specialist in order to do so. Antonouris would seem to be right when he suggests that LEAs are generally in favour of counselling but not in favour of counsellors.

It seems, therefore, that however much we may be in favour of specialist counsellors, it is probable that the counselling role will still largely be left to the ordinary teacher for the foreseeable future. Thus it is important for teachers to have at least a limited knowledge of the major variables involved. Some schools give heads of house or heads of year the responsibility for co-ordinating counselling activities and for advising new members of staff on what to do, while others appoint a head of pastoral care, but few of those involved have attended more than short local education authority or Department of Education and Science courses on counselling, and fewer still have actual formal qualifications in the subject. This again is unfortunate, since one of the best ways of disseminating counselling skills is for someone on the staff with specialist training to become responsible for handing this information on to others. Thus individual teachers can learn these skills within the practical context in which they have to apply them, and can seek a convenient source of expert advice whenever they feel unsure of themselves.

The problem of confidentiality

To go back to the beginning, it has been stressed that trust-worthiness and sympathy are the basic gifts that the good counsellor has to offer to the child. I have also said, however, that a major problem arises when the child brings to the counsellor's attention material that concerns disobedience to important school rules, or that threatens important values and standards. Should the counsellor maintain confidentiality, or betray the child's trust and go to the headmaster or to another member of the school hierarchy? Some writers suggest that the teacher should always warn children before they offer confidences that he or she may feel it necessary to break confidence, and this is good policy as far as it goes. The problem is that it may deter the child from seeking help, and encourage silence on matters that, in his or her own interest, should be brought out into the open. There is, too, always the chance that confidential material may come up during conversation when the counsellor is unprepared for it and has not had a chance to issue a formal warning. This is particularly true when ordinary teachers act as counsellors, since they do not have the benefit enjoyed by the specialist counsellor of the semi-formal counselling interview at which certain procedural guidelines can be agreed upon at the start by counsellor and child. In a sense, therefore, individual counsellors must consult their own consciences on what to do about confidentiality (though ideally they should be able to do this within the context of an agreed school policy worked out in consultation between headteacher and staff). The two basic rules that must always apply, however, are that (i) the child's permission should first be sought before any confidence is broken or, at the very least, he or she should be told in advance of any action the counsellor plans to take in this direction, and (ii) consideration should only be given to the breaking of confidence when it seems to be in the child's long-term interests to do so. On no occasion should a confidence be broken simply to get the child punished or to show the head what a zealous member of staff one happens to be.

Sometimes, of course, children may need a great deal of persuasion before they agree that the matter must be taken further. Here the job of the counsellor should be to help the child to see that even if there may be certain unpleasant immediate consequences, in the long term there will be gains both in the respect and understanding of others and in self-esteem. Some counsellors argue that this is being too *directive* (a term to which I return in due course below), and that the child should always be allowed to come to a personal decision, but this seems to be placing undue responsibility upon young children who may genuinely want guidance as to their best course of action. Where it is agreed that confidentiality must be broken (and I am not using the term 'broken' here in a pejorative sense: 'terminated' might be a more appropriate word), the child must be assured of the counsellor's continuing support, even to the extent of accompanying the child to the head or possibly to parents or whoever else is involved. Should the child refuse permission for confidentiality to be broken, once having asked for this permission, the counsellor must then abide by the child's decision. He or she may feel it necessary to indicate, however, that this limits the practical support and help that can be given, since there may be no clear alternative desirable course of action for the child to take.

The only exception to the course of action outlined above would seem to be if the actions the child is reporting to the counsellor involve risk (or potential risk) to self, other children or the community at large. This would apply, for example, if the confidences included information about drugs or involved threats of violence to another individual. The law in the UK rarely imposes a positive duty upon a person to reveal knowledge of a crime or a possible crime, provided that the person concerned is not involved in the crime in any way (though it could be difficult to prove lack of involvement if it is demonstrated subsequently that one possessed such knowledge), but the teacher's contract of employment often imposes clear duties in this direction which must be abided by. In any case, whether a duty exists or not, teachers have a moral responsibility to prevent harm, and this means they may have no option but to inform the relevant authorities if they fear that silence may allow such harm to take place. It is important also to remember that, even if one is employed as a specialist counsellor, it is unlikely that one's contract of employment will differ from that of the ordinary teacher, and therefore unlikely that it would be accepted that one's responsibilities for the safety and well-being of the whole school community, whether these responsibilities be legal or moral, would differ in any way from those of the rest of the staff. This means that confidences imparted in what we might call the formal counselling interview are legally no more sacred than those imparted in normal conversations between the ordinary teacher and the child.

Certainly it is a painful business deciding that one must not under any circumstances keep silent, but once the decision is made it must be acted upon at once. The only proviso is that the child must, as indicated above, be informed first, and then given all the support the counsellor can offer. The counsellor's reasons for taking the proposed course of action must also naturally be explained, and an attempt made to show how, in the long run, this course of action is likely to be in the child's own best interest as well.

The importance of sympathy

Turning now from trustworthiness to the other main quality demanded of the counsellor, namely sympathy, we find that fewer problems are raised. Sympathy means that individual children must at all times be left in no doubt that the teacher understands their position and wants to help. In conveying this guarantee of sympathy, attention must be given not only to what the teacher says but also to the non-verbal signs given (see p. 259). A smile is a better non-verbal signal of sympathy than a frown, an encouraging nod better than a disapproving shake of the head, steady eye contact better than a remote gaze out of the window. And in verbal exchanges themselves it is much better to hear children out, letting them put things in their own words, than to keep interrupting them or finishing sentences off for them. At all points, the teacher should be conveying to the child interest and patience: he or she is interested enough to want to hear what the child has to say, and patient enough to be prepared to do so, however long this may take. Above all, perhaps, sympathy is conveyed through action. The teacher and the child together identify the latter's problems, and the teacher then shows readiness to do something practical to help. This does not mean doing the things that are really the child's own responsibility. It means supplementing and supporting the child's actions by appropriate actions of one's own in those areas where the child has little power (e.g. one may have to talk to other members of staff on the child's behalf, obtain the information and perhaps supplementary learning materials the child needs, liaise with welfare authorities, see to it that the child is better integrated into the social life of the class, give parents guidance on how they can best help with learning problems, take up the child's case with the headteacher and so on).

The counselling process

I have already suggested that the counsellor should be characterized by trustworthiness and sympathy, and that these qualities should be apparent in conversations and interviews between the counsellor and the child. There are other important considerations to be borne in mind when discussing the counselling process, however, which are now examined.

Categorizing the child's problem

The first of these is to find some way of categorizing the child's problem. One way of doing this is to regard it as either *simple* or *complex*. A simple problem is one that can be regarded as essentially self-contained. The child has got into difficulties with a certain member of staff, or has been blamed unfairly for something serious, or is having trouble with classwork. Usually simple problems can be dealt with through a single course of action, agreed between teacher and child (though this action may inevitably take some time to implement fully). The job of the counsellor faced with a simple problem is to listen carefully to the child, ask questions on necessary points of detail, assure the child that it was right to ask for help, and then turn to the constructive business of working out what is to be done. There is little virtue in passing judgement on who is to blame for the child's predicament, or in spending time criticizing his or her actions. This

303

will only deter most children from asking for help in the future. On the other hand, there may be occasions when the teacher feels the child will benefit personally from thinking through how a situation arose, and deciding how it might be prevented from recurring.

A complex problem, by contrast, is one that appears to involve the wider issues of the child's own personality. The child may, for example, be excessively shy, or feel unduly prone to victimization and bullying by other people. He or she may be low in self-esteem, or be too impetuous, or too prone to making violent responses to others. There might also be long-standing problems at home, or difficulties with the opposite sex, or extreme feelings of guilt or anxiety. Note that sometimes a simple problem may cloak a complex one, either because it arises directly from it, or because the child comes to the teacher with a minor problem in the half-hope that while discussing it a more major one will be allowed to come into the open. Note also that because a child is aware of a problem this does not mean he or she is also aware of its cause. The problem may be, for example, that the child is generally unpopular with others, but is unaware that the cause may be personal rather than to do with the 'unfair' attitudes of classmates.

The role of the counsellor

Where complex problems exist, the first job of the counsellor is simply to encourage the child to talk, and to listen to the child in the atmosphere of trust and sympathy to which I have already made reference. Indeed, if the counsellor does no more than this then a valuable service will have been performed. But most counsellors will want to do more. Let me summarize now some of the other major points that they should bear in mind.

Directivity. In general the counsellor should try not to be too directive. A great deal has been written in recent years about the relative merits of so-called directive and non-directive counselling respectively, with the emphasis in the former being upon telling children what they ought to do and the emphasis in the latter being upon helping them find their own solutions. But the consensus now seems to be that, wherever feasible, children should at least play some part in deciding what their future course of action should be. If the counsellor decides for them, then this is the counsellor's decision and not the child's own. And for all their concern, counsellors cannot know the situation as well as the child since it is the child who lives with it and has to react to it. The counsellor's decision, though it may appear to contain a nice neat little solution, may not be appropriate for the child concerned. Clearly, if the problem involves moral issues, with obvious responsibilities towards others, then (particularly with young children) the counsellor may wish to nudge them towards what seems to be the right decision, but even here children's own moral and social backgrounds must be taken into account. To force them into taking decisions which are quite out of keeping with their backgrounds, and which do not feel right to them, may be only to invite failure, and perhaps in future an even stronger rebellion against the views of others.

The immediate aim of counselling is to help children set their problems within a proper context, and to recognize and understand the important variables associated with these problems. This will involve posing children questions designed to prompt them to reflect upon what has been happening and upon the views of the various other people who may also be involved (e.g. 'What do you think your mother/ father/friend thought about that?'; 'What do you think you might have done instead of what you actually did?'; 'How would you feel about it if someone said that to you?'; 'Why were you upset about that?'; 'Did you think it meant they didn't like you?'). It will also involve showing children that the counsellor understands and accepts their feelings, thus encouraging them to put these into words ('That made you feel fed up, did it?'; 'You felt pleased when that happened?'; 'So you went away and worried about it?'). By putting problems into context and by reflecting upon the variables associated with them, children are helped to gain insights into these problems and, of equal importance, into themselves, and generally gain confidence in their ability to be objective and resourceful.

Non-judgemental approach. Counsellors should strive to maintain a generally non-judgemental approach. In other words, they should not give the child the impression that they are only waiting for the latter to stop talking before delivering a weighty opinion on his or her actions and personal qualities. Many children who need the help of a counsellor are already feeling inadequate, with low self-esteem and perhaps a dismal history of failure. The last thing they need is for the counsellor to start delivering a vote of censure. If any judgement is required, far better that it should come from the child, and if the counsellor deems it to be too harsh the child can be encouraged to take a more balanced and self-accepting view.

Responsibility. At all times, children should be helped to take increasing responsibility for their own behaviour. One day they will leave school and gain the age of majority, and it will be up to them to decide what they want to make of themselves. In spite of some opinions to the contrary, it is not the job of the school to 'mould' the child's personality (even were such a thing possible in a democratic society), but to place children in the position to make wise and informed choices for themselves. By observing the points already made above, counsellors will go some way towards encouraging this responsibility, but they should in addition help the child to realize the nature of personal choice (i.e. to recognize what is involved in this choice, why it becomes necessary, and how the individual can best go about it). This again is better done by prompting children to think for themselves than by reading lectures, however worthy and well-meant, on the subject.

Focusing. Next counsellors should try always in their conversation with the child to keep the latter focused upon the real problem once this has been identified. The tendency is sometimes to digress from this painful topic once things really get under way. Prompts such as 'but you were telling me that . . .' or 'tell me more about . . .' are usually all that is needed, but a useful technique is to ask for some kind of clarification. This has the added advantage of showing the child that the counsellor needs assistance too, and that the problem is therefore something they are engaged on jointly. Wording such as 'if you could tell me more about . . . that would help me understand', or 'I need some help over this; could you tell me about . . .' usually proves to be suitable.

Non-intrusion. Finally counsellors should never intrude where they are not wanted. Children should be encouraged to be honest, but if after prompting they clearly do not wish to go into further details (for instance about their private lives or the relationship they have with parents) then they should not be pressed to do so. They may be worried by feelings of loyalty to the other people concerned, or by embarrassment of some kind. It is no good trying to get children to accept responsibility and make decisions if we do not consider them competent to decide what aspects of their personal lives they wish to keep to themselves. And the counsellor's very attempts to probe too deeply may deter children from giving the information voluntarily at a later date when their confidence in the counsellor has increased. These attempts may even stop children from coming back for another chat altogether, since they may feel that such chats are dangerous because you are forced to reveal more about yourself than you should, or are left feeling shy and embarrassed in the counsellor's presence.

Problems facing the counsellor

Readers wishing to know more about counselling are referred to the recommended reading at the end of the chapter, but one of the best strategies is to attend counselling workshops run by universities or colleges or LEAs. There is no substitute for seeing techniques actually demonstrated, and for trying them out under guidance and in simulated circumstances where one's mistakes can cause no harm. Such workshops also offer the opportunity of learning about other kinds of counselling which have great relevance to education but which the teacher cannot use, such as *family therapy*. Family therapy is a recognition of the fact that when we have a child with a problem we also usually have a family with a problem. The latter problem does not necessarily arise out of the former (though it may be exacerbated by it), and in fact could itself actually be the root cause of it.

The family therapist, who is usually a trained psychologist or psychiatrist, meets the whole nuclear family together and prompts them to bring into the open the complexes and behaviour that have led to family tensions and perhaps to the child's difficulties. This is skilled, delicate work, and must be left to the expert, since the family members must each be protected from potentially harmful revelations until they appear to have gained the strength to deal with them and use them constructively. But knowledge of the existence of family therapy, and of how to create opportunities to observe the whole family together where possible, is of great value to teachers because it helps them reflect on the way in which family problems arise, and confirms yet again that the problem child does not exist in isolation but at the centre of an intricate web of shifting tensions and pressures, many of which are responsible for creating and sustaining his or her difficulties.

Social forces and conflicts

This last point was emphasized by Lewin as long ago as 1936 when he wrote that 'the behavior of a person or of a group is due to the distribution of social forces in the situation as a whole, rather than to intrinsic properties of individuals'. This means that, for example, children with a particular kind of temperament or with a tendency towards aggression are not bound, *ipso facto*, to become problems. They will only develop into problems if placed in a particular kind of relationship with a particular kind of social environment. Elsewhere, Lewin argues also that many of the problems with which the counsellor is faced can only be fully understood if one views them within the context of this relationship. Briefly, he holds that the social space within which the individual functions can be divided into a number of areas or *valences*. In the case of the child these valences would be such things as home, school, youth club, scouts or guides, church, groups of friends and so on. Ideally, we should each be able to move from one valence in our lives to another (e.g. go from home to school or from school to youth club) without having to make undue changes in our social behaviour and in the standards and values that inform it. As Lewin puts it, the barriers between the valences should be low. Thus the individual is able to lead a relatively harmonious social life, without feeling the need to fragment his or her social personality in order to become acceptable to the people he or she meets in each of the valences. (The reader may care to speculate on how such fragmentation delays the growth of identity and personal maturity discussed in Chapter 8.)

Where the barriers between valences are high, and children are constantly being forced into changing their social behaviour if they are to be acceptable within each area, this sets up conflict and self-doubt (as in the home–school conflict discussed in Chapter 1). Individuals are unsure which of their various social *selves* is the real one, and are prone to feelings of guilt at the way the behaviour of one self (e.g. the self when out with friends) contradicts the behaviour of another (e.g. the self when in church). Lewin considers that the conflicts faced by such individuals tend to fall into one or more of three major categories, namely:

- **Type 1 conflict** (approach–approach conflict). This occurs when the child is faced with two valences of equal force (e.g. home and school) but with a high barrier between them. The conflict can only be resolved by either rejecting one of these valences altogether (e.g. rebelling against the home or ceasing to bother about school) or changing behaviour markedly as he or she moves from one valence to the other, thus creating the kind of self-doubt and guilt to which I have just made reference.

- **Type 2 conflict** (avoid–avoid conflict). This kind of conflict happens when children are faced by two valences which they desire equally to avoid. For example, a child may know that working hard at a certain school subject will result in promotion to a higher set but with an unpopular teacher. On the other hand, refusal to work hard will mean staying in a lower set and being bored by the simplicity of the work and troubled by the thought of lost opportunities. The conflict can only be properly resolved by changing one of the valences into a positive one (e.g. getting to like the teacher in the top set after all) or by rejecting both of them (e.g. by dropping the school subject altogether).

- **Type 3 conflict** (approach–avoid conflict). This conflict occurs when children are faced by positive and negative valences of equal force. For example, the child may wish to move into the positive valence of having passed an exam, but can only do this by accepting also the negative valence of having to lose friends and take up a more solitary social life in order to study. Type 3 conflicts can only be resolved by making a decision on whether the advantages of the positive valence are worth the disadvantages of the negative one. If they are not, then the positive valence must be abandoned and replaced by one at a lower and less demanding level.

The examples advanced in connection with the above conflicts only cover, of course, a small part of the range of problems that can be associated with them. The reader might like to think of other important examples for him or herself. The point to emphasize is that by thinking in terms of these conflicts counsellors can help themselves understand the difficulties that may be facing the child, and can also help the child to identify and analyse these difficulties, ultimately coming to an informed and sensible solution on how they might best be resolved. Children can also be helped to see that their behaviour up to the present has perhaps been due to their inappropriate attempts to solve conflicts for themselves. School refusal (truancy), for example, could be an attempt at resolving the home–school conflict (it could also be an attempt to escape the experiences of failure and of low self-esteem which school can bring for the less able child). Stealing or bullying could be an attempt to resolve a Type 3 conflict, with the child having to adopt 'tough' behaviour in order to become acceptable within the positive valence of friends, but at the expense of having to move into the negative valence of being regarded as antisocial by the school and by society in general.

It is important to stress that I am not pretending the child's behaviour is never 'wrong' and that direct action is never necessary to curb truancy or stealing or whatever. But this direct action is the responsibility of the school acting in its authoritative role. The role of the counsellor, on the other hand, is to help children get at the reasons and the implications of their behaviour and to develop strategies to amend and alter it that actually mean something in terms of the way in which they themselves view the situation. Ideally we want children to change because they see both the need and the possibility of change, and not simply to avoid punishment and censure. Change of this former kind is likely to be much more permanent than change of the latter kind, and is likely to lead to further opportunities for growth and development in the future.

Vocational guidance

I return to some of the above points in the next chapter when behaviour problems are discussed. For the moment we need to turn our attention to another kind of counselling, namely that associated with vocational guidance. In offering vocational guidance, the counsellor has two main questions to ask: first, what occupation appears most likely to appeal to the child; and, second, to which occupation does the child appear to be most suited? Ideally the answer to both questions should be the same, but sadly children often have ambitions which appear quite clearly to be beyond them. While no teacher wishes to prevent children from trying for something that really appeals to them (children often surprise us by what they can achieve when they really apply themselves), it is as well to remember that children go through various stages before they arrive at a final career choice, and some of these stages are characterized by a lack of realism in that children know neither what is actually involved in the job that appeals to them nor the qualifications and skills required by employers.

Developmental stages in career choice

Super (1957) put forward a model, based on earlier work by Ginzberg, that attempts to define these stages. Note that this model, sometimes referred to rather misleadingly as a model of 'vocational development', suggests the period of childhood that goes respectively with each stage, but some individuals pass through these stages much later than others, and it is quite possible for someone even in adolescence to be still primarily in the fantasy stage usually associated with early childhood. A summary of Super's model is given below.

Stage 1. Fantasy stage (early childhood): during this stage, which persists usually at least into the lower junior school, children imagine themselves as being anything that appeals to the imagination. Little thought is given to the realities surrounding the jobs concerned.

Stage 2. Interest stage (later childhood): by the time children reach the later junior school years interest is beginning to take over from fantasy. Children are now drawn towards those jobs that seem to embody the things which they find interesting. Thus whereas in the fantasy stage they might have wanted to be astronauts, this ambition might now be rejected as they find they are not really interested in astronomy or in rocket propulsion.

Stage 3. Capacity stage (middle teens): by the age of 14 or 15 or so capacity is becoming important to children, and they develop a tendency to reject possible careers that appear to fall above or below their ability levels.

Stage 4. Tentative choice stage (later teens): the later teens see children making tentative choices as they begin the process of putting in the first job applications and finding out more about the realities of working life.

The above stages are the ones with which the teacher is primarily concerned, but Super's model does cover the whole of life. The early twenties are seen as the *trial* stage, in which the individual is trying things out and may frequently change jobs, while the period of middle age is seen as the *specialization* stage, with the individual now usually committed to a particular calling. To complete the picture, the years from 60 onwards are seen as the *deceleration* stage, with the individual no longer usually concerned about promotion and getting further ahead, and the years from 65 onwards as the *retirement* stage.

It should be kept in mind that Super's model was originally devised at a time when most women did not pursue careers outside the home (hence his retirement age begins at 65, and not at 60). Super was also writing at a time, back in the 1950s, when people did not change their jobs frequently in middle life, and it may be that the specialization stage is less applicable now than it was then. Nevertheless, his model still serves as a useful guide for the teacher when thinking about vocational guidance. Adolescents who, with little chance of good results in the school leaving examination, confidently see themselves as airline pilots or as medical doctors are obviously still primarily in the fantasy stage, while more able children who see themselves one day as waiters or waitresses are still clearly in the interest stage, where hobbies or the enthusiasms of the moment are allowed to overrule all other more long-term considerations. (The choice of degree course by some university students, made without any thought to the eventual market value of the degree concerned, suggests that this interest stage may, for better or worse, be much more persistent than Super supposed.)

The role of the counsellor in vocational guidance

Obviously, it is the job of the vocational counsellor to encourage children to think carefully about what occupation most appeals to them, and then to make available to them all possible information on the skills and qualifications demanded by that occupation, and the kind of long-term prospects and opportunities it is likely to offer. Obviously, no counsellor should ever try to tell children what they ought to do (though of course the counsellor may want to suggest possibilities), but where individuals are genuinely unable to make up their minds there are several job categorization systems that might help to clarify their thinking. One such is proposed by Holland (1959), and involves dividing jobs up in terms of the occupational environments they provide. The system is exemplified below, together with instances of the kinds of job that fall into each category.

Occupational environment	Job examples
Motoric	labourer, machine operator, truck driver, mechanic
Intellectual	technician, scientist, university lecturer
Supportive	social worker, teacher, vocational counsellor
Persuasive	salesrep, politician, publicity officer
Aesthetic	musician, writer, poet, photographer

When they come to study this system, children who, for example, think they would perhaps like to work with people might decide that they are interested in working in a supportive or persuasive capacity, and would then go through the examples (plus others that the teacher might like to provide) until they find one that appears to suit their particular inclinations. They would then be provided with details of the qualifications needed and the availability of jobs. In each of the categories there are, of course, jobs suited to various different levels of ability. Thus, for example, the child interested in an intellectual or scientific job could go from nuclear physicist at one end of the range to laboratory technician at the other.

Children must be cautioned, however, that some jobs at the lower end of the ability range that require little talent and few qualifications (e.g. stage hand, assistant groundsman and, dare one say it, pop star?) are nevertheless very hard to come by, either because they are competed for by able people who see them as a stepping stone to something higher, or because they carry with them an apparently desirable life style and some kind of glamour. The counsellor must also urge children to take into account a number of other factors which could affect their chances of obtaining the job of their choice, such as their readiness to move away from home, their ability to impress at an interview, their physical strength, appearance, the quality of their voice, and their general conscientiousness and readiness to take responsibility.

There is obviously no virtue in pressing children to make up their minds too soon about their future careers, but it is essential that when children take subject options within the school curriculum, or when they unilaterally decide not to bother very much with certain subjects in order to do well at others, they be informed what career avenues they may be closing for themselves. Unless children are provided as a matter of top priority with this kind of information, they may very well find themselves tragically without the necessary examination qualifications in a certain essential subject when they eventually come to fill in a job application form, or apply for entry into some area of higher education (e.g. they might find themselves without mathematics when applying for primary teacher training, or without English language when applying for a job in the media).

Vocational guidance tests

In addition to the kind of structures provided by Super and Holland, there exist a number of vocational guidance tests which the teacher can use with older children. These tests are by no means infallible, and should only be used along with other forms of guidance, but they do help discover the child's inclinations and concerns and provide examples of the kinds of job for which these inclinations and concerns suit him or her. The most widely used of these are of the self-report type, in which individuals answer a number of relevant questions about themselves. On the strength of their answers, the Rosenberg Occupations and Values Test, for example, assigns them to the category of those interested in people, or to the category of those orientated towards extrinsic reward (money, status), or to those orientated towards intrinsic reward (creativity, self-expression). The Rothwell-Miller Interest Blank, an even more widely used test, assigns them to one of 12 general job categories such as outdoors, scientific, social service, mechanical, clerical, or medical, and then like the Holland system provides examples of a wide range of jobs which go under each category. Having found themselves assigned to one particular category, and if they agree it is appropriate, children can often then be helped to focus upon one of these jobs and to find out more about it.

Local education authorities provide careers advice services that visit schools and interview school leavers, but such services are normally badly over-stretched and can do little for many children on the strength of one or perhaps two short interviews. Far better for the school, which of course knows the child best, to provide detailed careers guidance that begins well before school leaving approaches, and that includes visits to the school by local employers, regular visits to local factories and places of work, and special help in obtaining necessary qualifications and interviewee skills. The sad fact is that without such help many children reach school-leaving age with only the haziest notion of what they want to do in life and of the qualifications they may require. Usually these children are at the lower end of the ability range, with no obvious avenues open to them in further and higher education.

They badly need the assurance that the school really cares about their future, and is prepared to go to the trouble of providing all possible practical help. They should see the school as orientated towards what they may one day become, and not simply towards the way they are at present, and should see careers guidance as an integral part of their school life and not as a somewhat haphazard last minute scramble carried out at a stage in their progress when many desirable avenues have already been closed to them.

References

Antonouris, G. (1974) Subsequent careers of teachers trained as counsellors. *British Journal of Guidance and Counselling*, 2, 160–170.

Holland, J.L. (1959) A theory of vocational choice. *Journal of Counselling Psychology*, 6, 35–43.

Lewin, K. (1936) *Principles of Topological Psychology*. New York: McGraw-Hill.

Super, D.E. (1957) *Vocational Development: A framework for research*. New York: Teachers College Press.

SOME
QUESTIONS

1. Discuss some of the problems that the dual role of teacher and counsellor can create.

2. What are the qualities a child is likely to look for in a counsellor?

3. Give the arguments for and against the presence of a specialist counsellor on the school staff.

4. What are the considerations the counsellor must bear in mind before terminating a confidence entrusted to him or her by a child?

5. How does the counsellor convey to children that he or she sympathizes with their problems?

6. One broad way of classifying children's problems is into those that are 'simple' and those that are 'complex'. What is meant by these terms in this context?

7. What is meant by 'directive' and by 'non-directive' counselling respectively? Can you think of some of the advantages and disadvantages that may attach to each?

8. The questions put by the counsellor to the child are of vital importance. What general form should these questions take, and what are they designed to do?

9. What is meant by a generally 'non-judgemental' approach on

the part of the counsellor? Why is such an approach important?

10. Discuss ways of helping individual children to stay focused on their real problem or problems during the counselling interview.

11. Lewin suggests that the social space we each inhabit can be divided into a number of 'valences'. What does he mean by this term and why is it important to the counsellor?

12. What are the three major types of conflict Lewin feels the individual has to face in his or her social space?

13. What are the two main questions the vocational counsellor has to ask when offering guidance to school leavers?

14. What are the four stages Super (1933) suggests that the child passes through on his or her way to the development of mature career orientations?

15. How can the kind of job categorization system advanced by Holland (1959) be used in helping children make up their minds about their future careers?

Additional Reading

Fullmer, D.W. (1978) *Counselling: Group theory and system*, 2nd edn. Cranston, Rhode Island: Carroll Press.
Recommended for more advanced students, anxious to know something of group counselling methods.

Fullmer, D.W. and Bernard, H.W. (1977) *Principles of Guidance*, 2nd edn. New York: TY Crowell.
Also of value as a general text.

Hopson, B. and Hayes, J. (1968) The Theory and Practice of Vocational Guidance. Oxford: Pergamon Press.
A good introduction to vocational guidance techniques.

Jersild, A.T. and Brook, D.W. (1978) *The Psychology of Adolescence*, 3rd edn. London: Collier Macmillan.
Contains a lengthy and excellent treatment of vocational ideas and career orientation in adolescence.

Kline, P. (1975) Psychology of Vocational Guidance. London: Batsford.
A good introduction to vocational guidance techniques.

Laufer, M. (1975) *Adolescent Disturbance and Breakdown*. Harmondsworth: Penguin.
Both Wolff (see below) and Laufer provide good surveys. Wolff of earlier and Laufer of later childhood.

Lewis, D.G. and Murgatroyd, S. (1976) The professionalisation of counselling

in education and its legal implications. *British Journal of Guidance and Couselling,* 4, 2–15.
Sets out the counsellor's legal position in England and Wales fully.

Murgatroyd, S. (ed.) (1980) *Helping the Troubled Child: Inter-professional case studies.* London: Harper & Row.
Deals comprehensively with methods of treatment.

Murgatroyd, S. (1985) *Counselling and Helping.* London: Methuen/ The British Psychological Society.
Practical and readable introduction to the counsellor's tasks.

Nelson-Jones, R. (1982) *The Theory and Practice of Counselling Psychology.* London: Holt Rinehart & Winston.
A major text reviewing the whole area of psychological counselling. Excellent.

Rogers, C. (1951) *Client Centred Therapy.* London: Constable.
One of the most valuable and influential books on counselling to appear since the war; the book could be said to have ushered in a new era in counselling, with the emphasis upon the part played by clients themselves in solving their own problems. The reader interested in counselling will enjoy the book, not only for the practical guidance it provides but for the humanity and sympathy that characterize it throughout.

Rutter, M. (1975) *Helping Troubled Children.* Harmondsworth: Penguin.
A good practical text on causes and treatment.

Ryle, A. (1973) *Adolescent Casualties.* Harmondsworth: Penguin.
A good alternative to Laufer.

School Council Working Paper, 40 (1971) *Careers Education in the 1970s.* London: Evans/Methuen.
One of the most helpful books available on vocation and careers guidance.

Williamson, N. (1987) Tripartism revisited: Young people, education and work in the 1980s. In D. Marsland (ed.) *Education and Youth.* London and Philadelphia: Falmer Press.
A first-class look at vocational issues with an excellent bibliography. The rest of the book also makes relevant reading.

Wolff, S. (1973) *Children under Stress.* Harmondsworth: Penguin.

The material produced by the Careers Education and Guidance Project mounted by the School Council (1971–1974) is also likely to give the teacher many useful practical ideas. Most LEAs also now produce a range of appropriate material.

13

Class Control and Management

Problem behaviour

Of all the professional anxieties that assail the teacher, those associated with class control often loom the largest. Children, singly or in groups, can present problems that even the most experienced teacher may find hard to handle, and there is no denying the misgivings that working with children, control of whom is slipping away from one, can bring. To make matters worse, many teachers suggest that in the final analysis all the teacher's authority is based upon a kind of bluff. There are strict limits to the sanctions that can be brought to bear upon children, and if children test these limits and find themselves unimpressed by them, then the teacher's bluff is called and there is little further that can be done.

As we shall see, this suggestion is somewhat over-pessimistic, but it does draw attention to the fact that teachers who rely upon repeated threats in order to control a class may find in the end that children in effect dare them to carry out even the most extreme of these threats, knowing that if teachers remain within correct professional limits they cannot really do harm, while if they overstep these limits they put their own careers at risk. Besides rendering themselves ineffectual in this way, teachers who adopt a constantly threatening manner also need to ask themselves whether they really want a relationship with children which depends upon attempted intimidation, and must inevitably lead to mutual dislike and lack of respect. There are better ways of working with children than this.

Defining problem behaviour

The question of class control is linked inextricably with that of problem behaviour. If children never exhibited problem behaviour then the need for class control would never arise. We can define problem behaviour as behaviour that proves unacceptable to the teacher. This definition, which might at first sight seem an over-simplification, is of value because it introduces us to the important fact that problem behaviour is only problem behaviour because it appears so to the teacher.

And since teachers are all individuals, what may appear a problem to one teacher may not appear so to another. One teacher, for example, may be happy to tolerate a certain amount of conversation between children while they are working, but another may demand complete silence. One teacher may put up with children calling out in class while another may insist they wait quietly with their hands up until asked. One teacher may be happy with a certain amount of familiarity in any relationship with children, and a certain amount of humour in class, while another may prefer formality and a serious approach. One teacher may allow a certain amount of day-dreaming in class while another may want attention always to be focused upon work; and so on.

The point about these examples and the many more that I could offer is that they show that problem behaviour, like beauty, is in a sense in the eye of the beholder. So the first step in dealing with this behaviour is for individual teachers to ask themselves why they see it as a problem in the first place. Is it a sign of their own insecurity that they regard a child's attempt at humour as a threat to their authority? Have they perhaps been over-reacting to the group who tend to chatter over their work? Have they been setting unrealistically high standards and then become frustrated and angry when they are not achieved? Do they vary sharply from colleagues in what they expect, so that children become confused and resentful in their lessons? Have they perhaps forgotten what it was like to be a child, and to be cooped up in a classroom several hours a day? Do they see every transgression in class as a deliberate threat to them personally, rather than perhaps as an attempt to liven things up or to amuse friends or to let off steam after a previous lesson? Questions of this kind indicate that teachers need to think carefully about their own behaviour, and to talk to colleagues to see how their expectations and experiences compare with those of others.

Having reviewed one's own behaviour (and I have more to say about this review in a different context shortly), the teacher may well come to the conclusion that it is this behaviour that has been at the root of the problem or problems. By taking offence where none was meant, by tending to nag children, by being over-serious or apparently unfair, by being over-dignified and pompous, by expecting too much, by being inconsistent, one may well have aroused resentment or confusion (or mirth) in the class, which in turn has prompted them into further unacceptable behaviour to which one has again over-reacted, and so the process has gone on. The first move in bringing this process to a halt, therefore, is to change one's own behaviour into a more appropriate pattern.

Behaviour modification techniques

Nevertheless, there will, of course, be occasions when the root cause of the problem does not appear to lie with the teacher. There may be a child (or a group of children) in class who causes problems throughout the school, whoever the teacher. There may be other children who consistently contravene perfectly reasonable standards of behaviour, or who make it clear they have decided not to like the subject or the teacher or the ways things are organized even before the first lesson has got properly under way. With such children a useful technique known as *behaviour modification* can be applied. Behaviour modification technique (or more correctly techniques, since there is a range of them available) has been operated successfully in special schools and in clinical psychology, and has obvious application to the normal classroom. While by no means a panacea for all ills, in spite of the extravagant claims sometimes made for it, behaviour modification has the advantages of allowing the teacher to analyse the child's behaviour carefully, to identify the various factors that seem to be responsible for sustaining this behaviour, to formulate strategies for changing it in desired directions, and to monitor these changes as they take place. It warrants our attention in some detail.

Behaviour modification techniques are based essentially upon the operant conditioning model of learning (see p. 127). That is, they work on the assumption that behaviour which is reinforced or rewarded is likely to be repeated, while behaviour which is not reinforced will tend to disappear. At classroom level this means that the particular items of problem behaviour identified by the teacher and seen to operate persistently are being reinforced in some way by the environment. It is this reinforcement that accounts for their persistence. Without it, they would gradually fade away. Conversely, the opposite behaviour that the teacher would like to see replace the problem behaviour may be receiving no positive reinforcement at all, which may account for its failure to become established.

When operating a behaviour modification technique, the teacher's first strategy is to compile a list of the items of behaviour which pose problems in a particular child. Against each of these items, which are known as *target behaviours*, the teacher writes down what his or her own response (or sometimes the response of the rest of the class) usually is. The list may end up looking something like this.

Target behaviour	Teacher response
Child comes in class noisily at start of lesson.	Teacher says 'I've told you before not to make that row.'

319

Child does not get out books when class is told to do so.	Teacher says 'Why can't you do as you're asked like everyone else?'
Child yawns loudly and shows obvious boredom.	Teacher comments sarcastically that of course child can't be expected to be interested.
Child makes facetious remarks.	Teacher stops lesson and casts doubts on what child has between ears.
Child calls out silly answer to a general class question.	Teacher tells child to put hand up first.
Child puts up hand and again calls out silly answer.	Teacher asks child to wait until asked before offering answer.
Child says 'But you never ask me'.	???

And so the list goes on. The important thing is that we put down in the left-hand column each of the specific behaviours to which we take objection. It is not enough simply to write 'disruptive behaviour' or 'insolence', we need to know precisely what constitutes this disruptive behaviour and this insolent behaviour. Of course, if the list is a long one we need not put down the exact remarks made by teacher and child, as in our example, since in any case these will vary from lesson to lesson, but we would nevertheless have to enter all the child's separate behaviours and against each one the teacher's usual kind of response. The list may stretch to 20 or 30 items, but it will not be endless, and often the teacher will be surprised at how short it is, with the child obviously going through the same repertoire of behaviours *ad nauseam* each lesson. We may be just as frequently surprised, when looking at the right-hand column, at how stereotyped the teacher's own responses appear to be. Though the language may differ somewhat each time, these responses may seem always to consist of interrupting the lesson and administering a reprimand (to which the child may usually reply with a grin or a guffaw or a glance round at the rest of the class).

The origins of undesirable target behaviours

Looked at in this way, it will probably become clear to the teacher that, far from being a punishment, his or her own responses are actually serving as reinforcement for the very behaviour they are designed to eliminate. What has hitherto been regarded by the teacher as a stern rebuke is seen by the child as nothing of the kind. To understand why this is the case, we need to think a little about disruptive children's possible backgrounds. They may come from a home where they learnt at an early age, through operant conditioning, that the only way to obtain any kind of attention from others was to make a nuisance of oneself. Adult attention seems necessary to children not only because it is through this attention that they obtain satisfaction for their physical needs, but because this attention makes them feel they count for something as people. It enables them to feel significant, and to develop some kind of self-esteem. Thus although the attention they obtain through disruptive behaviour may be angry attention, it is nevertheless more acceptable to them (and therefore more reinforcing) than being ignored altogether. Through such reinforcement, this disruptive behaviour then becomes an established part of their behavioural repertoires.

When such children start school, they may find that an apparent lack of ability means that they tend to receive less teacher approval and praise than children from more favoured homes (teachers are after all only human and it may take a lot to realize the desperate need that a difficult and awkward child may have for approval and acceptance), and may be further conditioned into believing that the only way they can get attention is by making life difficult for others. Note that this is not by any means necessarily a conscious process. Like all conditioning, it can take place without the individual concerned being actually aware of what is going on. The child's behaviour is therefore not necessarily a deliberate attempt to create problems for teachers and parents and other children, but a conditioned response associated with the need for attention. Such behaviour is called *attention-seeking behaviour*, and is recognized as one of the major causes of classroom problems.

The teacher may find, of course, that attention-seeking behaviour in some children takes a non-disruptive but nevertheless still troublesome form. A child may constantly come up to the teacher in class, or constantly ask for help when none is really needed, or bring the teacher little gifts, or lie in wait each morning to recount some item of gossip, or stay behind consistently after school to offer to do jobs around the classroom, or ask to be allowed to walk home with the teacher, or send the teacher little (sometimes anonymous) notes, often containing intimate messages of affection and admiration. These activities are a sign that children need help, but often the teacher finds that by rewarding their demands with extra attention they become more and more insistent until finally they reach a point where they are distracting the teacher from work with the rest of the class.

With other children the problem may take a different form

again in that the attention they seek is that of other children rather than that of the teacher. They may have found themselves to be rather unpopular in class, and to have discovered, once more by operant conditioning, that the way to get a measure of acceptance is to raise a laugh at the teacher's expense, or to show themselves to be 'tough' or 'daring' by disobeying the teacher or by offering insolence.

Identifying both sides of the problem

With all these problems, the initial procedure in a behaviour modification programme remains the same, namely for the teacher to list the individual behaviours that go to make up the problem, together with his or her own usual responses to these behaviours. The next step is to draw up a second list, this time of all the behaviours in the child or children concerned which should be encouraged, and again to enter beside each what his or her own response usually is on the odd occasions when these behaviours have occurred. An example of this second kind of list is given below. To simplify matters, the examples assume we are talking about the same child dealt with in my earlier example.

Behaviour	Teacher response
Child comes in room quietly at start of lesson.	Teacher breathes sigh of relief and turns to lesson notes in order to make a quick start.
Child gets book out with the rest of the class when asked.	Teacher starts lesson.
Child puts hand up to answer question without calling out.	Teacher ignores child and asks someone else for the answer, afraid that child will give a silly response and spoil what is so far a good lesson.
Child works quietly.	Teacher continues thankfully to let sleeping dogs lie.

Looking at this list, it can be seen that the teacher response to each of these desirable behaviours involves taking no notice of the child of any kind. Thus instead of 'good' behaviour producing reinforcement in the form of teacher attention (and better still of teacher attention in the form of praise of some kind), it receives the punishment of being ignored. Small

322

wonder that the child starts playing up once more next lesson, and that the whole wearisome cycle starts all over again.

Enough has been said to show that we cannot understand the child's behaviour (and work efficiently to change it) unless we study the teacher's behaviour as well, which brings us back to my earlier point. Problem behaviour does not exist in a vacuum. It is the centre of a matrix of forces that work to create and sustain it. If we wish to change it, then we must first make a change in these forces. In the case of the class teacher this means, at its simplest, reversing what we have been doing up to now and applying the first set of reinforcers to the second set of behaviours and vice versa. In other words, attention is withdrawn when the child is producing the problem target behaviours, and is offered when their desirable counterparts are produced. This means (to use the above examples again) that the child is ignored when coming into the classroom noisily but greeted in a friendly fashion when coming in quietly; that the teacher takes no notice of the child (and does not interrupt the lesson) when the latter makes facetious remarks or calls out in class but directs a question to him or her when they put up a hand; that the teacher ignores the child and starts the lesson if the latter fails to get out books, but takes some opportunity of directing an encouraging remark towards him or her when they co-operate; and so on.

Gradually, over a period of time, the child's behaviours may come to be turned round, with the desirable ones replacing the undesirable. There will, of course, be relapses, and sometimes the child will appear to come half way to meet the teacher and then spoil things. For example, if the child puts up a hand and is asked for an answer he or she might give way to the temptation of producing a facetious one as before. In this case the teacher simply ignores the child and asks someone else. Alternatively, if he or she offers a sensible answer, even if it is a wrong one, the teacher gives a smile and a word of encouragement before seeking the right answer elsewhere.

Objections to behaviour modification techniques

Three practical objections are often raised to behaviour modification techniques as follows.

First, although we may well be able to identify the unwanted target behaviours and work to eliminate these, the child may show none of the opposite, desired behaviours, making it impossible for us to start reinforcing them. This is true, but the answer lies in what is called *shaping*. Shaping means that we take the behaviour closest to that which we actually desire and reinforce that instead. Thus although, for example, the child may never come into the room quietly, he or she will nevertheless at times come in more quietly than at others, and it is these relatively quiet entries that we will watch for and reinforce. Research shows that gradually, through shaping, behaviours come to approximate more and more closely to those we specifically want.

Second, with the best will in the world there are some undesirable behaviours that we cannot just ignore, such as those behaviours which directly harm another child, or extreme insolence which might set a thoroughly bad example to other children. This is a valid and important point. The teacher has a duty to the rest of the class as well as to the problem child, and cannot let the latter's behaviour unduly affect everyone else. Nor does the teacher want the problem child to become a role model for more impressionable classmates. But the answer is that he or she will only become such a role model if their behaviour is seen to be effective. Thus if the teacher becomes visibly frustrated or upset or is made angry, the risks are far greater than if he or she is seen to carry serenely on with the work of the class, without apparently bothering in the least about the minor silliness of one isolated class member.

Should teachers feel, however, that a child's misdeeds are such that they cannot possibly be ignored, then the exponents of behaviour modification techniques suggest they employ what has come to be called *time out from positive reinforcement*. Without using such a grand title, teachers have, of course, been resorting to this strategy from time immemorial by sending children out of the classroom. Once a child is removed from the room, all opportunities for receiving positive reinforcement in the form of attention from teacher or classmates disappear. Since, as already seen, it is this very need for attention that has probably caused the problem in the first place, the child soon tires of being outside the room and wants to come back in, but is given to understand that this is only possible if he or she enters into a kind of contract to be of good behaviour (and this behaviour gives the teacher the desired opportunity to apply positive reinforcement). If the child breaks the contract, out he or she has to go again.

In general, sending children out of the room has been frowned on in schools for some time now, on the reasonable grounds that (i) the children are missing lessons, (ii) if the classroom has a glass door they will divert themselves and others within visual range by pulling faces through it, and (iii) they may simply just decamp and go home. Research indicates, however, that these objections can be overcome if the school has a special room (a so-called *time-out room*) to which children are sent or taken, and where they must sit quietly under the eye of a member of staff. Even in a large school there would normally be no more than one or two children in the room at any one time, and there will always be a member of staff with a free period who can be posted for supervision. Research suggests that children need only remain in the room for a maximum of ten minutes before being returned to their class, thus missing only a short amount of lesson time. If they misbehave again, they go back to the time-out room.

It is sometimes objected that many children will find it vastly diverting to spend their day shuttling back and forth from classroom to time-out room, but this does not appear to be the case. After the initial novelty, children find the process both boring and unproductive in that, as already said, it deprives them of most of their opportunities for attention. Of equal importance, the rest of the class usually find lessons to be more relaxed and interesting in their absence, and there are thus mounting pressures upon them from their classmates to behave sensibly when they return to the room. Naturally, if a time-out room is to be operated, this must be school policy supported by all members of staff and under the direct control of the headteacher or deputy heads.

Even with a time-out room, however, it is often objected that there are frequent items of bad behaviour that the teacher cannot just ignore. There are also items of unwanted behaviour from children who are normally well-behaved. What happens about these? The answer to both these questions is that teachers can arrange unwanted behaviours into a hierarchical order, ranging from those most easily to those least easily ignored. They then decide whereabouts on the list to start their ignoring behaviour. Possibly the only item they feel they can ignore is when a child comes into the classroom noisily. With all the other items they therefore carry on as before, checking the child verbally as necessary. But they stick to the plan of ignoring the noisy entry and taking due notice of any attempt to come in more quietly. At the same time, they also make a point of noticing and rewarding all the positive behaviours on the second list as they occur. This twin strategy of ignoring the noisy entry and rewarding all positive behaviours (the latter technique is sometimes called 'catching the child being good') begins to modify the child's actions, and when they feel it is appropriate to do so teachers can introduce ignoring responses to the second and subsequent items on the hierarchy. With items of unwanted behaviour from normally co-operative children, teachers simply respond as appropriate. Sometimes judicial ignoring is the best response, at other times a spoken rebuke or a quiet word with the child after the lesson is over. Again the teacher will operate the hierarchy, ignoring where it is clear the child is simply seeking attention, and responding where the child is being drawn into misbehaviour for other reasons.

The third objection to behaviour modification techniques is that there is something dehumanizing about them, with children's behaviour being 'manipulated' by those in authority instead of being under their own conscious control. Most teachers would understandably much prefer to be able to reason with children and get them to change their ways by convincing them that bad behaviour is ultimately negative and self-defeating. The problem is, as I said when discussing attitude change (see p. 207), that even when we can change children's attitudes by talking to them there is no guarantee that their *behaviour* will necessarily change as well. Extreme exponents of behaviour modification techniques would in fact tell us we are wasting our time by making appeals to children and by assuming that they have the freedom to change themselves at will. Whether we like it or not, they argue, children's bad behaviour results from the undesirable reinforcement schedules to which they have been subjected in life up to now, and if this behaviour is to be changed then we must do so by changing these schedules for something more appropriate.

The position of behaviour modification exponents is clarified by looking again at what was said about operant conditioning in Chapter 7. However most teachers prefer not to be drawn into a detailed debate over issues of this kind. Given their usual concern and sympathy for their children, they prefer for the most part to use reason and persuasion in the first instance, and resort to behaviour modification only if such reason and persuasion consistently fail to work. In most instances, of course, happily they do work. Behaviour modifiers will say that this is because most children come from satisfactory homes in which reinforcement schedules have been correctly applied and which leave them seeking not teacher attention as such (since they already receive ample adult attention at home) but teacher approval.

The token economy

Behaviour modification techniques are the basis for the so-called *token economy* that is employed to good effect in some special schools. Since it is usually only operated in closed communities, such as residential institutions and clinical units where the staff can exercise a measure of control over most of the inmates' lives, I need not spend too long discussing the token economy, but the teacher needs to have some knowledge of how it operates since it figures quite extensively in the educational literature and gives us some pointers for more limited strategies in normal schools. Under the token economy, children are awarded tokens (which can be actual discs or marks entered in a book or any other suitable arrangement) each time they evidence the desired behaviours, and lose tokens each time they evidence the undesired. At the end of an agreed period they trade in their tokens for a treat of some kind (e.g. a certain number of tokens might win extra television viewing time, twice that number might win extra sports facilities or a trip into town, and so on). Thus children have tangible evidence of the rewards their improved behaviour is bringing, and through operant conditioning this behaviour should become an established part of their repertoires.

The token economy is essentially a form of 'performance contract'. Children enter into a contract with teachers to produce certain kinds of behaviour in return for certain kinds of reward. If they break their part of the contract, they lose the rewards. Thus they may contract not to be aggressive towards others, and be given a token for, say, each half day in which they refrain from offering an aggressive act. Each time they do assault another child they lose a token. Performance contracts have also been shown to operate satisfactorily in normal schools. The report card is an example, where the child contracts to be of good behaviour in each lesson, has the card signed by the teacher at the end of the lesson, and is then able to exchange the card at the end of the week for a clean bill of health. The main problems with the report card are, first, that the reward at the end of the week is not sufficiently impressive for some children with severe behaviour problems, so that they seem quite prepared to be put on report week after week and, second, that it does not focus sufficiently on individual items of behaviour. As already seen, it is important that we isolate each separate item of a child's difficult behaviour and try to apply appropriate negative reinforcement to each one. A card that simply covers the whole of a child's behaviour during the whole of the lesson fails to do this.

Research indicates nevertheless that problem children can be helped by the performance contract in the normal school, particularly if we can enlist parents and the local community in general as a source of rewards. This time, instead of merely putting children on report, we contract with them to refrain from certain specific behaviours (e.g. failing to hand in work, insolence in class, aggression towards another child). If they have shown a number of these behaviours, then we concentrate on one at a time, and eliminate that before going on to the next. After the end of each lesson, if individual children have fulfilled their part of the contract, the teacher signs their record cards. At the end of the set period, the satisfactory record (or more properly contract) cards are exchanged for the treats agreed at the beginning of the contract. These could be outings or favourite meals or gifts supplied by parents, or a morning spent at the local garage or the local riding stables, or some privilege conferred by the school itself.

The immediate objection to the performance contract in the normal school is that one cannot go on with it indefinitely, and children may lapse when one day we have to stop. The answer here is that while on the contract children receive not only the agreed reward but all kinds of other incidental (i.e.

uncontrived) reinforcers. They will find that teachers generally respond more favourably now they are on better behaviour; that they begin to get higher marks now they are keeping up with the work; that parents are pleased with their improved progress; that other children become more friendly; that lessons are more interesting; that their self-esteem improves and so on. As their horizons broaden, it is these incidental reinforcers that will sustain their new behaviour after the contract has come to an end.

A second objection sometimes raised to the performance contract is that it is unfair on law-abiding children, who see trouble-makers getting reinforcers denied to them. It is sometimes even suggested that children will deliberately misbehave in order to be put on a contract. In the main, though, this objection is unfounded. Law-abiding children are usually already receiving the relevant reinforcers, because they come from good home backgrounds and enjoy relationships with the staff in school which together ensure that these reinforcers are given as a matter of course. This is, indeed, the crux of the whole matter. To date, problem children behave as they do because they have learnt that for them this is the only way to get the things they want. Our aim is to help them unlearn this lesson, and to discover instead that, as with the law-abiding child, socially acceptable behaviour can be a much better way of obtaining valued rewards.

General points on behaviour modification

Before we leave the general topic of behaviour modification techniques there are two further points to make. The first is that these techniques are not exclusively for use with disruptive children. The Underwood Report (1955) defines maladjustment as applying to the child who is 'developing in ways that have a bad effect on himself or his fellows', and this clearly covers the isolate child, the withdrawn child, just as much as it covers more obtrusive classmates. In the case of the isolate child, behaviour modifiers suggest that we often unwittingly reinforce isolation in the early school years, and thus help to make it an established part of behaviour, by constantly approaching the child and soliciting his or her participation in activities. As soon as we obtain this participation, we tend to move away to attend to other children who need help. Thus, unwittingly, what we are doing is positively reinforcing isolate behaviour (by an approach response) and punishing social behaviour (by withdrawing as soon as we have got the child working with others). We should in fact seek to reward with attention not when the child is solitary, but when he or she makes a move in the direction of others. When such a move is made we should draw the child into activities, and stay with him or her as long as possible, thus rewarding participation. True, we cannot always be with isolate children once we have got them socially involved, but again incidental reinforcers should soon start to operate (e.g. access to the interesting activities that are going on at the tables where the other children are, the feeling of being part of a group, the friendship of other individuals), and these should serve to strengthen and sustain their social behaviour.

The second general point that must be made is that extreme exponents of operant conditioning theories see behaviour modification as a kind of mechanical manipulation of children, with the latter having no real power voluntarily to change their own behaviour. This harks back to the third of the three objections to behaviour modification discussed earlier. There is, however, no need for teachers to accede to this view. They may prefer to see children as being well aware of what the teacher is doing, and as making conscious decisions to go along with it as a way of getting what they want from other people. This view sees the child as a free agent rather than simply as a unit acted upon by others. Such a view is perfectly legitimate, and need be no bar to the use of behaviour modification techniques. It does, however, presuppose a different and more optimistic (some would say nobler) concept of human beings, a concept which argues that they have free will and are not merely the victims of circumstance. This raises important philosophical issues that unfortunately we have not the space to pursue here. All that can be said is that it is impossible to prove whether we have free will or not using the limited and precise methods of science. The German philosopher Immanuel Kant proposed some two centuries ago that the important consideration was therefore the demonstrable fact that people behave 'as if' they have free will, and it is doubtful if even the strongest supporters of the mechanistic view advanced by operant conditioning theorists can dispute this. In any case, to most teachers, classroom problems seem to arise from a deal too much free will rather than from its absence!

Other aspects of class control and management

Often, of course, problems of class control and management stem not from individuals but from the class as a whole. Even the most conscientious and work-orientated class can be boisterous on occasions, or can be bent on testing out a new teacher and finding the limits to which he or she will allow them to go, or can become frustrated and angry with a particular teacher's methods. The best way of discussing these problems is to sketch out a number of general ground rules that have relevance in most classroom situations. These are given below, in no special order or importance, and are couched for convenience in the form of direct instructions to the teacher.

1. Interest the class: in general a class that is absorbed in its work will not want to cause problems. In addition, the class members will act disapprovingly towards any of their number who try to distract their attention.

2. Avoid personal mannerisms: the point was made in the discussion of interaction analysis in Chapter 11 that mannerisms of speech, dress or gesture on the part of the teacher can prove intensely irritating (or comic!) to children who have to sit and watch them, and may well lead to negative behaviour on the part of the class.

3. Be fair: real or imagined injustices can breed resentment and hostility in children. Fairness means ensuring that any loss of privileges, etc., is appropriate to the original misdeed (and is wherever possible related to it in some way, so that the child can see a causal link between the two); it means behaving towards children consistently so that they know what to expect, and it means keeping one's word. Interestingly, children of all ages rate 'fairness' as one of the most desirable qualities in a teacher.

4. Be humorous: this does not mean that teachers try to resemble a knock-about comedian, but simply that they are prepared to laugh with the class (though not when the joke is on some unfortunate individual member of it), and to introduce humour into teaching material where suitable. It also means that they are prepared to laugh at themselves at times, both in class and in private. We all inadvertently do things on occasions that strike others as amusing, and the ability to join in general laughter is a sign of security and realistic sense of self-worth. People who fly into a rage if others ever laugh at them suggest that they see this laughter as a threat to an already depressed sense of self-esteem. And, of course, teachers who are always standing on dignity with children are in a sense challenging the class to find ways of puncturing this dignity. It is sometimes said that all authority is faintly ridiculous, particularly where it verges on the pompous. A healthy sense of the realities of their position, helped along by memories of how they themselves felt about members of staff when children, is a great asset to class teachers. And remember that a sense of humour often ranks second only to fairness in a child's list of good teacher qualities.

5. Avoid unnecessary threats: I have already drawn attention to the undesirability of relying upon threats to control children. But on the occasions when threats are felt to be unavoidable, they should always both be suited to the misdemeanour and realistic. Wild threats to, say, bring the class back on Saturday morning are simply an invitation to children to carry on with the prohibited behaviour for the sheer pleasure of seeing how the beleaguered teacher gets out of putting them into practice. And where threats are uttered they must be carried out. Constant offers of 'one last chance' soon weaken the teacher's standing in the eyes of the class.

6. Be punctual: a teacher who arrives late for a class not only sets the children a bad example but also may have to quell a riot before the lesson can begin. Punctuality at the end of the lesson is of equal importance. Children soon resent being constantly late out for break or last in the lunch queue or late for the next lesson.

7. Avoid anger: teachers who lose their temper may say and do things in the heat of the moment that they come to regret later. Their loss of self-control will also be noted with interest by the class, and the experience committed to memory for general dissemination later through the school grapevine. Before long such teachers will find other classes, with the true instinct of research scientists, trying out various ways of getting them to mount repeat performances. Certainly all teachers on occasions will feel the need to speak sharply to children, but this is quite different from heated outbursts that do nothing either for the teacher's standing in the school or for the state of his or her physical health.

8. Avoid over-familiarity: the line between friendliness and over-familiarity can be a narrow one, but it is better to start off rather formally with a class and become more intimate as one gets to know them better; to behave, indeed, much as one does when making any new friends. Research shows that many weak teachers start off the other way around, and then desperately try to tighten up when they have already made an over-lax first impression. But too much familiarity at any time is rather confusing to children, who know that the teacher is not really one of them since he or she represents the authority of the school, and leads inevitably to the feeling that they have been deceived when the time comes for the teacher to assert this authority.

9. Offer opportunities for responsibility: if all responsibility rests with the teacher, then it is not surprising that children behave irresponsibly when not under direct supervision. Offering children responsibility not only shows them they have the teacher's confidence, it also leads them to realize that what happens in the class is their concern just as much as it is the teacher's.

10. Focus attention: general appeals for quiet or order in a classroom are of much less value than calling out the name of the child or children most directly involved, and thus focusing the attention of the class. In the silence that follows, the teacher can then issue further instructions. One is much better able to focus attention in this way if one quickly learns the names of all class members. A seating plan is of help here (together with instructions that children must occupy the same seats in the room until told otherwise!) Getting to know children's names quickly also clearly demonstrates one's interest in them as individuals.

11. Avoid humiliating children: quite apart from the potential psychological damage to the child or children concerned, humiliation attacks a child's status in the eyes of the rest of the class, and he or she may well use various strategies, all aimed at the teacher's authority, in order to re-establish it. Note here that children often find sarcasm humiliating, and it has the added disadvantage of inviting an equally flippant reply. The teacher who reprimands a boy for looking out of the window by asking him if he is watching for Little Bo Peep can hardly grumble if the child answers that yes, he is, because he missed her on her last visit.

12. Be alert: an important characteristic of teachers with good class control is that they appear to know at all times exactly what is going on in the classroom. This impression that they have eyes in the back of their heads comes from the fact that they not only have keen eyesight and good powers of concentration but are physically mobile. They move frequently around the room, and insist children wait in their places when they have difficulties with their work rather than besieging the teacher who, like an inexperienced general, becomes isolated from the main action by a detachment of hand-waving children.

13. Use positive language: the emphasis should always be upon what we want children to do rather than upon what they must refrain from doing. Thus we say 'Come in quietly' rather than 'Don't make so much noise', 'Look at your books' rather than 'Stop turning around', and so on. Negative language suggests activities to children that previously might not have entered their heads, and thus focuses the attention of even the law-abiding class members in the wrong direction.

14. Be confident: the writer recalls that the only piece of advice he was given on class control when receiving post-graduate teacher training was that the teacher always gets what he or she expects from the class. He thought at the time that this advice was a little on the thin side (and said as much to all who were prepared to listen), but in fact if one has to be restricted to a single useful tip this is perhaps as good as any. Teachers who go into a class with a hesitant, tentative manner suggest to children that they are expecting trouble and are probably accustomed to being disobeyed. Very well, the class think to themselves, the teacher will not be disappointed. If, on the other hand, teachers are able to give the impression they are used to getting on well with children, then once again the children will be inclined to take this at face value and offer co-operation. So even if the teacher is feeling inexperienced and apprehensive, the moral is not to show it.

15. Be well-organized: a well-organized lesson, with adequate material carefully prepared and with all equipment to hand and in good working order, is far less likely to be disrupted by misbehaviour than one that even the teacher concedes bears a certain resemblance to a shambles. The shock to the teacher's own nervous system, when working with a potentially difficult class, of finding that the tape-recorder has the wrong mains plug, or that there are no pencils, or that a vital page is missing from his or her lesson notes, is in any case something to be avoided by all but the most masochistic amongst us! Good organization also means making clear to children exactly what is expected of them in the way of getting out or putting away apparatus and equipment *before* they start to do it, and while the teacher has everybody's attention. It also means only releasing them in carefully controlled groups to carry out these chores, rather than letting them all rush at once and then shouting vainly for order.

Good classroom organization also means that children know where things are kept and that they each have clear duties and responsibilities, both to deal with the normal running of the classroom and the sudden emergencies when things get spilt or broken. It also means planning lessons carefully so that the practical activities are within the scope and the competence of both teacher and class and never threaten to get out of hand. Many practical activities which seem such a good idea in prospect appear in retrospect little short of disastrous. If in doubt try them out first on a modest scale with a co-operative class. And finally it means keeping the theoretical side of the lesson within bounds too, and making sure it gives way to practical work before it has gone on too long. As mentioned earlier in the book, a rough rule-of-thumb is that the teacher should restrict the theory part of any lesson to about a minute or a minute-and-a-half (depending upon subject matter and the children's abilities) for each year of the children's age. Thus 10–15 minutes is ample for ten year olds, while with a sixth form one could go up to 25 minutes or so.

16. Show that one likes children: many people, recalling their schooldays, have favourite stories of ogres of whom they went in awe, and of kindly, well-meaning souls whose lives they made a torment, but these stories are only remembered because they are unusual. For the most part, teachers who relate satisfactorily to children have the gift of conveying to them sympathy, understanding, and a personal delight in the job of teaching. They indicate to the class that they want children to succeed not because this demonstrates their own competence but because success is important to children. Once the class is convinced they have the teacher's support, they will respond, as in any relationship, with co-operation and esteem.

No excuse is offered if the above 16 points appear in format (though not, let us hope, in substance) rather like the hints and tips for teachers that used to appear in pedagogical manuals between the wars. It is often said nowadays that inexperienced teachers should not be given guidance of this kind, but should be allowed to develop their own teaching styles in response to the particular groups of children with whom they work. One does not hear it said, however, by headteachers or by others faced with the problem of helping new members of staff over the first hurdles of their profes- sional lives. Certainly there is no denying that teachers must be equipped to act as researchers, able to ask themselves as indicated throughout this chapter why children behave as they do and what strategies appear most suited to their problems. But teachers should also be equipped with the kind of generalizations, based upon psychological theory and upon the results of classroom-based research studies in the United Kingdom and the USA, presented in these 16 points. As teachers grow in experience so they find there are others, and with experience they become able to work out what is best for themselves and for their particular school and pupils. But at the beginning they require a knowledge of these generaliza- tions if they are to make a sound start in the profession and provide effective learning opportunities for their pupils.

The application of punishment

While on the subject of class control some reference must be made to the use of punishment (perhaps 'sanctions' would be a less emotive term) in the classroom. In general, any punish- ment carries with it certain risks of which the teacher should beware, namely:

- the use of punishment of any kind may damage the relationship the child has with the teacher, perhaps per- manently. This is particularly true if the punishment is seen as unfair (see point 3 above) or designed to humiliate (see point 11);

- the child may develop strategies, such as untruthfulness, to avoid punishment. This is not only potentially bad for the child's long-term personality development, but it also threatens the existence of any trust between teacher and child;

- punishment teaches the child the undesirable lesson that it is acceptable for the strong to impose penalties upon those weaker than themselves.

Effective sanctions

Nevertheless, it would be unrealistic to pretend that sanctions of a limited kind are not seen as necessary by many teachers, and questions are often asked as to what is effective and what is not. I have already indicated in the discussion of behaviour modification techniques that the careful use of positive reinforcement, together with some sanctions, is often enough to produce the desired turn-around in behaviour by most children, but it would be incorrect to think that the teacher would class these techniques as punishment. By punishment, the teacher usually means some kind of imposition or some loss or privileges placed upon the child, usually as a deterrent to breaking school rules or as a prompt response to some particularly unacceptable piece of classroom behaviour.

The most frequently used item of punishment, and often the most effective with co-operative children, is the verbal rebuke. The teacher rebukes the child, the child accepts the rebuke, and the matter is finished with there and then. The reason why it is so effective is that children appear to have a need (Carl Rogers, 1951, regards it as an innate need) for adult approval. Granted that they are already receiving adequate adult attention, they now require it to be approving attention. This is probably linked in with their need for social acceptance (see the discussion of Maslow's work in Chapter 8) and their need for self-esteem (see Chapter 10). Thus children feel uncomfortable and alienated from the social group if the teacher withholds approval from them, particularly if the teacher is liked and respected by the class. Children also, since such teachers are usually regarded by them as sound judges, suffer doubts as to their own worth, and are anxious to remove such doubts by producing the desired behaviour and quickly moving back to good terms with the teacher.

Where stricter sanctions are thought necessary, a number of studies show that informing the parents of this lack of approval is very effective, since children now feel that if they continue with their misbehaviour they will encounter increasing disapproval at home as well. One strategy operated with an apparently high rate of success is for the headteacher to prepare a letter for the parents, and then summon the child and read it over to him or her. The child is then given the option of eliminating the unwanted behaviour or allowing the letter to be sent. Not surprisingly, the child usually chooses the former alternative. The letter is then placed upon the file, and sent only if the child fails to keep his or her part in what is a form of performance contract. It is important that, as with behaviour modification techniques, the letter spells out in precise detail the form of behaviour to which the school takes objection, and the child is left in no doubt as to the way in which it must be remedied.

Schools use a variant of this strategy every year (or sometimes every term) when school reports are sent out, and it is surprising that some teachers fail to recognize the impact that such reports can have upon a child's relationship with parents. The problem with the school report, however, is that usually it is not specific enough in stating exactly where the child has gone wrong in work or general conduct, and does not give clear directions on how these problems can be put right. Vague phrases such as 'could do better' (couldn't we all?) or 'has done little work this term' (which may be as much the teacher's fault as the child's) succeed only in upsetting the parents and confusing the child. What is needed instead is practical guidance which the child can put into effect and of which he or she can be reminded from time to time by parents. If the parents can also be enlisted into giving the child more specific help within the home, so much the better. Some teachers, for reasons that are not always clear or particularly defensible, are rather reluctant to draw parents into co-operating in their children's formal education. This is unfortunate because a few minutes of parental time every evening (e.g. spent hearing the child read, checking homework is done and the right books taken to school) bring enormous benefits to the child. Most parents are only too happy to co-operate, provided they know exactly what it is they are supposed to be doing and can speak to the teacher from time to time to make sure that all is going well.

Parents' evenings are also of great value here, though whether the knowledge that their teachers are going to report unfavourably on them orally, when the interchange may be softened by the natural sympathies created by face-to-face contact, carries quite the same impact with children as seeing things recorded in writing is not clear. One frequently voiced objection to both parents' evenings (see p. 17) and to school reports is that the parents one most wants to reach do not seem to care. This objection is true, but only for a very limited number of cases. Most parents are deeply involved with their children, whether they normally show it or not. This is (ideally) because they love them, but there are other complex forces frequently at work too. They may want their children to be a credit to them or to do as well as the children next door. Or they may feel that their children's failure, academically or socially, reflects back on them, or that there is a danger they will get into trouble with the police or cause damage that will have to be paid for, or that they will be unemployable when they leave school and so on. Each of these reasons, for better or worse, helps to ensure that for the vast majority of parents the progress of their children is of a great deal more than passing interest.

The law of natural consequences

Another sanction often used effectively in schools is what Rousseau called *the law of natural consequences*. Like behaviour modification this fits in with the operant conditioning model, but it differs from behaviour modification in that the consequences stem from the environment rather than from the teacher. Susan Isaacs, in her work at the Malting House School back in the 1930s, demonstrated the effectiveness of natural consequences, particularly with very young children. If children carried on playing with toys, for example, when called to lunch then they were allowed to remain where they were, but discovered when they did come to the table either that the food was cold or the second helpings had all gone. If a child was careless or destructive and broke something then he or she had to do without it for a certain interval of time. Obviously there are numerous occasions, particularly where physical safety is involved, when a child has to be protected from the natural consequences of his or her actions, but in general the law of natural consequences is of value because it allows children to see the causal link between their own actions and the undesirable results sometimes associated with them. In young children such an association is only likely to be set up if action and result occur close together in time (see the discussion of operant conditioning in Chapter 7), but as children grow older they become able to reason out the association for themselves. Essentially, the law of natural consequences suggests that if children commit misdemeanours they will learn more rapidly if, instead of being punished by the imposition of some arbitrary penalty, they are allowed actually to experience the consequences of their misdemeanours. They then come to understand the very good reasons why these misdemeanours are regarded as such, and thus grow in knowledge and in sense of responsibility.

The only caution here (apart from the one of physical safety) is that children should not experience the natural consequences for too long. Thus if, as an act of thoughtlessness or vandalism, a piece of school equipment (say, a television set) is broken, the children are told clearly that they will be without it for a definite time (say two weeks), since members of staff are too busy to see to its repair straight away. If they are without it for much longer than this, then they will get used to the deprivation and, when they think about it at all, will by degrees come to see it as a deliberate act of revenge against them by the staff. Thus the impact of the lesson will be lost.

Discussion of the law of natural consequences leads on to the point that missing breaktime or games or being in detention are not very effective in stopping specific problem behaviours because there is often a long interval of time between the behaviours and the penalties, and the two are in no way linked through natural consequences. Such penalties would work best if the children had brought them on themselves by, say, taking too long to clear up at the end of a previous lesson. Punishing children by putting them into detention and stopping their games for offences which have no obvious link with these punishments will certainly infuriate the games master or mistress, but will do nothing to help the child learn why his offences are unacceptable.

Group behaviour problems

Sometimes problems of class control stem more from the behaviour of certain groups within the class than from the behaviour of individuals. Each of the children, on their own, may seem amenable and friendly enough, but put them in the group and they appear to become different people. When this happens, again the teacher's first task is to list the problem behaviours. As with individual behaviour modification programmes, it may well be the teacher's own responses that are sustaining these behaviours or perhaps creating the preconditions for them, for example by poor organization (see point 15 of the list on general aspects of class control), or by over-familiarity (point 8) or by unpunctuality (point 6) or by standing too much on dignity or losing self-control (points 4 and 7 respectively). If this does prove to be the case, then the remedy lies at least in part with a change in the teacher's own behaviour, as it does indeed if the children are simply bored (point 1 on the list) or are perhaps defending themselves against feelings of failure either in that specific lesson or in school generally (see the discussion of such matters at various points in Part III).

Whatever the causes of the group's behaviour, and whatever the methods the teacher uses to remedy it, there are some additional general strategies that prove helpful.

- As an early priority, identify the most influential member or members of the group. Leaders and stars were discussed earlier, on p. 287, and the points made then will be relevant to this exercise. Once these individuals (the *gatekeepers*, as Lewin terms them) are picked out, the teacher is able to concentrate particularly upon them (using, for example, individual behaviour modification techniques) in the knowledge that once they are won over the rest of the group is likely to follow.

- Where possible, divide up a badly-behaved group. This means directing them to sit apart from each other in class, involving them in different class and homework projects and so on. I have already stressed in Chapter 11 the part played by frequency of interaction between children in establishing friendships; by reducing the proximity between group members the teacher tends to break up the cohesion within the group and to encourage group members to form friendships outside it. Ideally, of course, the children should not be made directly aware that this is the teacher's policy.

- Interact with the children as much as possible as individuals. Each child is therefore helped to form a personal relationship with the teacher, which again serves to break up group cohesion in that it destroys the corporate image of the teacher that the group has hitherto maintained.

- See as much of the children as possible, again as individuals, outside the context of the classroom; for example, in out-of-school activities. This weakens their tendency to associate the teacher exclusively with the classroom.

- Where possible avoid direct conflict with group members in front of the rest of the group. The need to maintain prestige and status in the eyes of the rest of the group will make each group member far more difficult to deal with than when on his or her own. This means doing one's best to defuse the situation at the time and to deal with it later. Assuming one is not using carefully formulated behaviour modification techniques with the child concerned one might, if the child for example attempts insolence in class, say pleasantly that one can see he or she is upset about something and can come and give the details after the lesson. Failure to do homework, which could be a simple ploy to 'see what the teacher will do about it', would be met in the same way by an invitation to come and talk about it at the end of the lesson, together with the strong hint that the class has better things to do with its time than to listen to explanations now. Homework, after all, is done for the child's own benefit and not for that of the teacher (who has to spend many patient hours each week marking it), and children should not be allowed to feel they are somehow 'getting at' the teacher when they fail to produce it. If the teacher prefers not to be constantly heard inviting children to see him or her after the lesson (this can become a ritual, with class members vying with each other on the number of times they can be kept back afterwards!) the child can simply be called to one side as they leave the room with the rest of the class when the bell goes.

Physical confrontation

Occasionally, the teacher may have to break up a physical confrontation between two children in the class. This raises special problems (particularly when the children are somewhat bigger than the teacher!) but the secret lies in quick, decisive physical action. With a confidence he or she may not feel, the teacher strides across the room and parts the children, holding on firmly to the one who appears to be the aggressor. Verbal appeals for *détente* before making this intervention are usually little use, but once the appropriate child is under restraint the teacher talks calmly to both children, using again the formula that he or she can see they are upset (or angry) about something, and would like to hear about it when everyone has calmed down. Behaving in an angry manner oneself is inappropriate. Unless you outscore both children in terms of muscle-power by at least 100 per cent your own anger is only likely to inflame matters further, and you may end up looking rather foolish as the children hurl you contemptuously aside, the better to get on with their business. Calmness, and a hint of humour, are far more appropriate. Above all, no threats of dire punishments awaiting both protagonists should be voiced. Not unreasonably, they may feel that if they are to be punished anyway for fighting, then they might as well get the fight over and done with first. Once you feel the tension relaxing, your grip on the child being held is released. And your promise to hear both sides of the story, sympathetically and patiently, either then or when the children have had time to calm down further, is meticulously kept.

School refusal

One further important item of problem behaviour remains to be discussed, namely school refusal. Children who consistently absent themselves from school for no good reason are signalling clearly that the consequences of not going to school are outweighed by the consequences of going. Again, as with all the problems discussed so far, the first question each time must be why should this be the case? The answer usually takes the form of one or more of the following.

- The child may be the victim of bullying by other children.

- The child may go in fear of a particular member of staff or of punishment of some kind.

- The child may associate school so strongly with failure that school refusal is a way of protecting self-esteem.

- There might be problems at home keeping the child away. He or she might have to look after a younger brother or sister, or help in some kind of family business. Or the child could be afraid of physical violence between parents or that one or other of them might desert if he or she is not continually on hand.

- The child's parents may feel they are working off some

kind of obscure grudge against society by preventing the child from attending school.

- The child might be sniffing glue, or taking alcohol or other drugs and be in no fit state to attend school (this is more likely to affect afternoon than morning classes).

- The child might be involved in some sort of delinquent activity.

- The child might just be plain bored, and be looking for something more exciting to do.

Note that again, as has been said in connection with other problems, school refusal is therefore not exclusively the child's own difficulty. Other children, parents, teachers, school organization or delinquent peer groups can all be involved. And, of course, once children start staying away they fall further and further behind in their work (making school seem even less attractive), and become ever more enmeshed in a web of lies and deceit (making it difficult ever to confide in people and ask for help).

Once we have identified the probable cause of school refusal (often no easy task in view of these lies) then we can take appropriate remedial action. Usually punishing children is unjustified, because as we have just seen the problem is often not of their own making. Worse, punishment can be actually counter-productive in that children come to associate school even more closely with unpleasant experiences, thus making them more inclined to stay away than ever and to lie in order to cover their tracks. Getting children to attend should not be seen as a battle between them and the school which the latter must win at all costs. Rather they should be prompted to see that the school is there to understand and sympathize with the fears and the anxieties that they may be feeling over the problems in their own lives, and is there to help. Even where children appear to be staying away out of sheer boredom there is little to be gained by meeting them in head-on conflict. Usually, if children are determined enough and care nothing for the school or its sanctions, and have parents who care even less, then they will win in the end and just stay away for good. A more appropriate strategy is to try to work out with children why school bores them to such an extent and seems so irrelevant to their needs. Schools that take the trouble to lay on special courses for less able school leavers (and it is in this group that school refusal is most apparent) usually succeed in reducing the problem to relatively insignificant proportions.

It must be emphasized that school refusal is definitely not a candidate for treatment by the more obvious behaviour modification techniques. It might be tempting to believe that if we ignore children's absence they will realize they have failed to draw attention to themselves and will start attending again, but there is little evidence that this happens very often in practice! Occasionally, certainly, children may stay away because they want to be noticed, but usually even here there are other more important reasons (quite apart from the question of why should they have to go to these lengths to be noticed?), and the school must take vigorous and resourceful action, long before things get too bad, to find out what these are. Once these have been established and steps taken to deal with them, some form of performance contract can be entered into, of course, and this is often a useful additional strategy, particularly in very intractable cases. But perhaps the over-riding consideration to keep in mind is that schools are there for the benefit of children, and if they choose not to avail themselves of this benefit we must look not only at children themselves but at the way in which this benefit is being packaged.

References

Isaacs, S. (1930) *Intellectual Growth in Young Children*. London: Routledge & Kegan Paul.

Isaacs, S. (1933) *Social Development in Young Children*. London: Routledge & Kegan Paul.

Rogers, C. (1951) *Client Centered Therapy*. Boston: Houghton-Mifflin.

Underwood Report (1955) *Report of the Committee on Maladjusted Children*. London: HMSO.

SOME QUESTIONS

1. Why is it inadvisable to rely upon threats in order to keep class control?

2. Why is problem behaviour, in a sense, in the eye of the beholder?

3. Why should teachers first examine their own behaviour when considering the causes of problem behaviour in children?

4. What is the reason suggested by operant conditioning theorists for the persistence of unwanted behaviour in children?

5. Describe the teacher's first strategy when compiling a behaviour modification programme.

6. What is 'attention-seeking behaviour' and why is an understanding of this behaviour important for the teacher?

7. What forms does attention-seeking behaviour take in the classroom?

8. What do we mean when we say teachers should reverse their

behaviour and withhold reinforcement from unwanted child behaviours and apply it to those that are wanted?

9. Define the term 'shaping' as applied to behaviour modification programmes.

10. Discuss the meaning of 'time out from positive reinforcement'.

11. What are the principles underlying the operation of the 'token economy' and the 'performance contract'?

12. What are 'incidental reinforcers' and why are they important in sustaining desirable changes in child behaviour?

13. Is the concept of the child as a free agent still tenable within the context of behaviour modification theory?

14. Suggest why a sense of humour appears to be an important quality in the teacher.

15. Why is it important to get to know the names of one's children as quickly as possible?

16. List the risks occasioned by the use of punishment with children.

17. Have school reports a value?

18. Give some of the reasons why parents are likely to be concerned about their children's progress and behaviour in school.

19. What is the 'law of natural consequences'?

20. Why is it important where possible to avoid direct conflict with group members in front of the group?

21. Give some of the considerations to be kept in mind when stopping physical conflict between children.

22. List some of the reasons for school refusal.

23. What do we mean when we say that school refusal 'is not exclusively the child's own problem'?

24. Why is punishment often counter-productive when dealing with school refusal?

25. Can performance contracts usefully be used in remedying school refusal?

Additional Reading

Fontana, D. (ed.) (1984) *Behaviourism and Learning Theory in Education.* Edinburgh: Scottish Academic Press.
Contains some highly relevant material on behaviour modification in both normal and special schools. (Also recommended for Chapter 7.)

Fontana, D. (1985) *Classroom Control: Understanding and guiding classroom behaviour*. London: Methuen/The British Psychological Society.
A close look at all aspects of class control problems and their management by the teacher.

Good, T.L. and Brophy, J.E. (1978) *Looking in Classrooms*, 2nd edn. New York: Harper & Row.
An excellent book, dealing practically and sensibly with all aspects of classroom behaviour. (Also recommended for Chapter 11.)

Laslett, R. and Smith, C. (1984) *Effective Classroom Management*. London: Croom Helm.
Sensible and informative text on how to organize and manage the successful classroom.

Leach, D.J. and Raybould, E.C. (1977) *Learning and Behaviour Difficulties in School*. London: Open Books.
Specifically concerned with the causes of behaviour problems in children, and strongly recommended. Also deals with the treatment of behaviour problems.

Rutter, M. *et al.* (1979) *Fifteen Thousand Hours: Secondary schools and their effects on children*. London: Open Books.
Geared more specifically towards the comprehensive school, it contains much useful information.

Upton, G. and Gobell, A. (ed.) (1980) *Behaviour Problems in the Comprehensive School*. Cardiff: Faculty of Education, University College Cardiff.
This has the advantage that many of the contributors are experienced practising teachers, able to discuss a number of strategies that have actually been demonstrated to work within their schools.

Walker, J.E. and Shea, T.M. (1980) *Behaviour Modification: A practical approach for educators*, 2nd edn. St Louis, Missouri: Mosby.
Probably the best practical text on behaviour modification techniques for teachers.

Wheldall, K. and Merrett, F. (1984) *Positive Teaching: The behavioural approach*. London: Croom Helm.
Good practical text from the behaviourist angle.

Wragg, E.C. (1984) *Classroom Teaching Skills*. London: Croom Helm.
Multi-disciplinary approach to classroom skills. Based on the research findings of the DES-funded Teacher Education Research Project.

14

Teacher Personality and Characteristics

A major emphasis throughout this book is that if we wish to understand child behaviour, we must consider not only children themselves but the various influences that are brought to bear upon them. Within the context of school, the most important of these is usually the teacher. Research into teacher personality, and by this I mean the whole range of personal characteristics that may affect the way in which teachers go about their tasks, has not been as systematic as research into child characteristics, but nevertheless there are a number of valuable inferences that can be drawn.

Teacher effectiveness

Before we look at these, I should say that any discussion of teacher characteristics merges into a discussion on teacher effectiveness in general, which in turn raises the question of what we mean by the 'good' teacher. The present writer pointed out some years ago (Fontana, 1972) that even experienced teacher educators are by no means agreed amongst themselves on the answers to this question, and the situation is little better today. Is a 'good' teacher a person who helps children's socio-emotional development, or who helps their cognitive development, or who teaches them subject knowledge or who gets them through examinations? And how, apart from the last named, do we measure whether a teacher is doing these things to our satisfaction or not? Just as we cannot understand the child's behaviour to the full without taking the teacher's behaviour into account, so we cannot understand the teacher's without taking into account that of the child. Some teachers may be very successful at, for example, fostering socio-emotional development with a particular group of children, but may be less good with another group where the problems, though no more extreme, are of a different kind. And the simple presence of one very disruptive child in a class may materially affect the teacher's performance with everyone else. So how and with what particular

345

group of children do we attempt to assess teacher competence?

Teacher educators, faced with the difficult task of deciding who should enter the teaching profession and who should not, use the teaching practice as a formal examination, and attempt to assess students in a variety of teaching situations. A number of rating scales and systems have been devised to help them, and careful note is also taken of the recommendations of the headteacher and of the staff in the school in which the practice takes place. But even here there is a wide margin of error, and the correlation between teaching practice success, and success and happiness in the profession five years later, has been shown by a number of studies to be disappointingly low. It seems probable that interaction analysis (see p. 275) with careful records kept over the years of precisely what teacher behaviour seems to go with what kind of responses in children, will do a great deal in the future to help us devise profiles of the successful teacher, but it must be pointed out that all teachers, and all children and all groups of children, exist as individuals, and we can never be certain that generalizations about success will hold good in all instances. Thus it seems unlikely that, in spite of arguments to the contrary, we will ever have a precise 'science' of teaching, which allows us to predict accurately in all cases whether individuals will become good teachers or not.

Assessing teacher characteristics

With this caution in mind, we can now look at the evidence currently available. One of the most extensive investigations into teacher personality and its relationship to teacher effectiveness was carried out some years ago by Ryans (1960) in the USA. Ryans constructed a special *Teacher Characteristics Rating Scale*, and found that the successful teacher tends to be warm, understanding, friendly, responsible, systematic, imaginative and enthusiastic (a somewhat daunting catalogue of excellence), but that the importance of these qualities seems to decrease with the age of the children being taught. In other words, secondary school children seem able to accommodate better to teachers low in these qualities than do those in primary schools. This makes sense, because normally the older children become, the better able are they to take responsibility for their own work, and the more resilient are they in relationships with adults. These findings, which have been generally supported by more recent work (see e.g. Fontana, 1985), are of great importance when it comes to refuting the argument that it is 'easier' to teach young children than older ones, but we should remember in fairness that Ryans was not looking into the importance of specialist subject knowledge, which might play a larger part in overall teacher success with secondary school children than with those in the primary school (though primary teachers can reasonably counter that they have to know more about a wider range of subjects than their secondary colleagues).

In spite of the extensive nature of Ryans's research, correlations between the qualities indicated and teacher success were not very high, however, That means that even in primary school some teachers without high scores on these qualities nevertheless produced satisfactory results. This could be, to hark back to the points already made, because they had particularly well-motivated or particularly resilient children, or it could be (and this again indicates the difficulty of research in this area) that the adverse aspects of their influence upon children take time to show through, and that in consequence they are not apparent until these children have become the responsibility of another teacher. Or it could be that there are other qualities, not measured by Ryans, that tend to compensate in some cases for the absence of those which he did manage to identify. Research by Rosenshine (1970) and others into both parent–child and teacher–child relationships suggests that a reasonably uncritical approach to children's work may be one of them. We have said enough about self-esteem and about the devastating effects of constant failure upon children to indicate why this may be. Children who are frequently criticized by a teacher, especially if they are already inclined to be low in self-esteem, will lose confidence in their own ability and will tend in consequence to under-achieve. Thus a conscientious teacher who believes in pressurizing children to come up to a certain standard could conceivably do more long-term harm to the progress of particularly vulnerable children than a teacher who seems less conscientious and more inclined to let children find what is sometimes described as 'their own level'.

Research also indicates (e.g. Bennett's discussion of teacher styles, 1976) that successful teachers are more likely to prepare their lessons well than are those who are less successful, to spend more time on out-of-school activities, and to show more interest in their children as individuals. Note, however, that this last quality does not mean that they become emotionally involved with their children. Teachers who rely upon their relationship with children to compensate for emotional deprivations in their personal out-of-school lives are being unfair both to themselves and to the children concerned. It makes it difficult for the former always to behave with professional objectivity, while the latter may feel they are having demands made upon them which embarrass and confuse. The teacher should certainly feel liking and affection towards children, but this must go hand-in-hand with a professional detachment and sense of responsibility.

Emotional security in the teacher

What this implies, in effect, is that another quality of success-ful teachers is that they are themselves emotionally mature. This means not only showing the behaviours advocated in the above paragraph, but also not being drawn into petty feuds and squabbles with children individually or in groups. Harder still, it means not being upset by the behaviour of children even when, as sometimes happens, there appears to be reason-able cause for such upset. Children can at times be very thoughtless in their dealings with teachers, particularly teach-ers who are inexperienced or who have the reputation of being unable to keep order. Indeed 'thoughtless' might be considered by some as a euphemism, but it is doubtful if stronger language is really justified since children are not experienced enough to be able fully to empathize with what such teachers are going through. Anyway, be this as it may, the fact that individual teachers show themselves to be upset only makes matters worse, with children now deliberately picking on them with a kind of awful glee. Teachers, on the other hand, who show themselves quite unmoved by even the most Machiavellian strategies mounted against them soon find these strategies lose their appeal for children, and they are able to deal quickly and effectively with any subsequent sporadic fresh outbreaks.

Emotional security of this kind is linked to what in psychol-ogy is called *ego-strength*. Ego-strength is a compound of realistically high levels of self-esteem and self-confidence, and an underlying composure that allows problems to be tackled calmly and objectively. This applies, in the case of the teacher, not only to day-to-day classroom problems but to the many other challenges of professional life, such as relationships with children's parents and with colleagues, decisions on career and promotion matters, sudden crises (whether they be accidents in the playground or visits of advisers and inspec-tors), and dealings with the headteacher and with school governors. Further, ego-strength allows teachers to rise above the failures and disappointments that, along with the achieve-ments and the successes, are an inescapable part of school life. It allows them to analyse and learn from the former without punishing themselves with feelings of guilt and inadequacy, and allows them to take delight in the latter without relin-quishing a sense of proportion.

Turning to standardized tests of personality, we find that there is no consistent evidence to show that successful teach-ing correlates with either significant levels of extraversion or significant levels of introversion. Common sense would sug-gest that extreme introverts would not do well in the class-room, since they would find the social demands made upon them unacceptable, but it is doubtful if such people would be attracted to teaching (at least to school teaching) in the first place. As pointed out in Chapter 8, however, the personalities of children must also be taken into account at this point, with extraverted children perhaps relating better to an extraverted teacher, and introverted children perhaps relating better to a teacher who tends towards introversion.

Teacher attitudes

In addition to the various aspects of teacher personality discussed above, there is some evidence that successful teachers have what are often referred to as 'desirable professional attitudes'. This means that they have positive attitudes towards responsibility and hard work, that they conceive of their role as extending beyond the business of simply teaching children subject matter and beyond the narrow hours of 9 a.m. to 4 p.m., and that they have a positive attitude towards the subjects in which they specialize and towards the place of the teacher in society.

A number of scales exist to measure the more obvious aspects of teacher attitudes, and in particular, of course, their attitudes towards children. One of the most widely used of these in the UK is that devised by Oliver and Butcher (1968), which scores teachers on three dimensions, namely naturalism, radicalism, and tender-mindedness. Student teachers interestingly tend to increase their scores on all three of these dimensions during the years of their training, and then to reduce their scores once they take up their first posts. This suggests that the realities of professional life serve to make teachers generally less child-centred, more conservative, and more tough-minded. This does not necessarily mean that teachers lose their idealism, but simply that they may find themselves working in less than ideal conditions, conditions in fact that at times may seem to render some form of compromise unavoidable. They may, for example, not only be battling against adverse environmental conditions (inadequate accommodation and facilities, over-large groups, problem children who really need specialist help), but may also find themselves working with colleagues whose philosophies and methods are somewhat different from their own.

This ability to compromise, however much we may regret its necessity, may be an important quality in the successful teacher. Cortis (1973 and 1985), in a longitudinal study of teachers during their first two decades in the profession, found that those who show most career satisfaction and seem to be making the best professional progress appear able to put school before self and to submerge minor differences with colleagues in the interests of establishing within the school those coherent, consistent policies that enable children to feel secure and confident. By contrast, Cortis found unsuccessful teachers tend to be more self-orientated and to be more dominant, suspicious and aggressive.

Teacher styles

Another fruitful line of research is to look at teachers' preferred teaching techniques (i.e. at their 'teaching styles'). At a time when the debate about formal and informal teaching methods and their respective influences upon children's learning has not yet been resolved, such an exercise is particularly relevant. In the main, *formal* methods imply an emphasis upon the subject to be taught, with the teacher's task being to initiate children into those aspects of the subject deemed essential, while *informal* methods imply an emphasis upon children, with the teacher's task being to identify their needs and to make available learning experiences appropriate to these needs. Formal methods usually involve a relatively high level of teacher talk and of individual work on the part of the children, while informal methods rely more upon project and group work, and give the child wider opportunities for choice and responsibility.

This kind of distinction is, of course, something of an over-simplification. Some teachers may employ a mixture of both approaches, while as Bruner (1976) points out, one can have formal lesson objectives, with the skills and techniques that one wishes the child to acquire clearly identified, but can work to achieve them by informal methods. This would involve, for example, providing children with the necessary apparatus and equipment and setting them certain problems, whose discovery would lead them towards the kind of learning that one has carefully specified in advance. These and other related points are fully discussed in Chapter 7, and are raised here only to indicate that the terms 'formal' and 'informal' may, in fact, not be specific enough for our purposes. An alternative is to drop these terms altogether and to use instead the indirectness measures developed by Flanders in connection with his classroom interaction analysis instrument. An *'indirect'* teacher is described by Flanders as one who accepts children's feelings, uses praise and encouragement, and uses pupils' ideas. The *'direct'* teacher, by contrast, is described as one who tends to lecture, to give directions, and to criticize pupils. A number of studies (see Bennett, 1976, for a good survey, and more recently Bennett *et al.*, 1984) show indirectness to be positively related to pupil achievement gains and to positive pupil attitudes, particularly in the case of more able pupils. Note, however, that indirectness does not necessarily imply a low level of teacher talk (one of the supposed features of the informal classroom), and indeed some studies suggest that a higher frequency of teacher talk is related to enhanced growth of non-verbal creativity in children.

The value of teacher talk

This last finding is of some importance, since it indicates the extent to which some children are stimulated by listening to an adult. In recent years, particularly in the primary school, there has been a tendency to discourage teacher talk *per se* and to emphasize the importance of children's own activity. Teacher talk, as indicated in Chapter 13, should never go on for too long, but rather than classifying it as good or bad in itself we should place emphasis upon what the teacher actually *says*. Teachers who can talk interestingly and relevantly, and who can stimulate children's imagination and thinking, are a far better aid to learning than any amount of misguided and rather desultory project work. They also have the advantage, possessed by no other teaching aid, of being almost infinitely flexible. They can respond to questions, introduce a whole new topic because children show a sudden interest in it, express humour, excitement, encouragement, awe and any other human emotion. True, they can do this with individuals as they move round the class and need not do it in the more formal 'teacher talk' situation with everyone listening, but this means that they cannot disseminate ideas quickly, and cannot use the question posed by one child as a learning opportunity for the whole class.

Perhaps, therefore, we should add another attibute to the list of those already used in this chapter to describe successful teachers: namely, that they should be good talkers. In the classroom context, being a good talker means being a disciplined thinker, with a mind that can concentrate creatively upon one group of relevant ideas and not keep darting off at a tangent. It means knowing when to provide an answer and when to leave the answer incomplete, so that the children are stimulated to make their own enquiries. It means using the voice expressively and fluently, and couching one's spoken thoughts in a form appropriate to the level of the children with whom one is working. And it means above all knowing when to stop, so that the children are directed to their practical work at a point when they would still like to hear more. Thus they never tire of teacher talk, but instead experience a pleasurable anticipation each time it is introduced into a lesson.

To be good at teacher talk may seem a tall order, since it is not the same thing at all as simply being a talker. Rather quiet teachers, who find ideas do not come to them very fluently when on their feet, may even find this talk something of a strain, and may prefer to keep it to the absolute minimum.

But if some teachers never acquire the art of good teacher talk there is no reason why they should not acquire the art of good listening. Every teacher must be able to encourage children to talk, and to hear them out with patience and interest, prompting only where necessary, and showing children that their ideas are entitled to a hearing. Even when those children who would monopolize classroom debate, either through natural forcefulness or through a desire for attention, have to have their remarks brought to a close, the good teacher is able to do this in a way that protects the child's self-esteem and leaves him or her ready to make a contribution again next time.

Introducing variety into teaching methods

What I am saying, therefore, to go back to the debate about formal and informal teaching methods, is that teachers can be non-directive, and good talkers and good listeners whatever methods they are using. There is also no reason why teachers should not vary their methods depending upon the subject being taught. Bennett (1976) produces impressive evidence to show that, in the primary school at least, progress in reading, mathematics and English (the so-called basic subjects) seems in the main to be more rapid where formal methods are used, but Haddon and Lytton (1968, 1971) show that general creativity (at least as measured by divergent thinking tests, which are by no means infallible (see p. 114) tends to be more marked in informal than in formal primary schools, and that the differences are maintained after transfer to secondary schools. This suggests that although work in the core curriculum might benefit from being subject-centred, with the teacher offering children clear standards which they must attain before they can be said to be literate and numerate, in other subjects the work can be more open-ended and less judgmental, with the emphasis upon each child making a more personal, subjective response.

Note that I am not saying that such core subjects as English and mathematics should cease to be enjoyable, while everything else in the curriculum should be seen as 'fun'. There is no reason at all why more formal methods, related carefully to the children's level of ability and understanding, and employing relevant and imaginatively used material, should not prove as acceptable as less structured methods. Interestingly, we have very little evidence of what teacher styles children themselves actually prefer in the long term. We do know, however, that they grow weary of situations in which they are unsure what is expected of them and in which their work is constantly being interrupted by the activities of others, and this can certainly happen more readily in an informal than in a formal environment.

Flexibility

The above arguments make clear that there is another teacher quality to which we must draw attention, namely that of flexibility, the ability to suit one's methods to the subject and to the children one is teaching. If teachers are too rigid, or have a doctrinaire belief that their methods are right and those of anyone who disagrees with them are wrong, then they will be depriving children of a range of possible learning experiences, to everyone's disadvantage. Most teachers never stop learning, and are always ready to consider new ideas and new techniques on their merits. If these new ideas often look suspiciously like the resurrection of old ones discarded years ago, then the teacher is still prepared to give them a fair hearing. In education, as in human psychology itself, no one has a monopoly of the truth, and people who close their ears to informed debate and to alternative views are the poorer for it.

Teacher stress

Stress in human beings has been defined in a number of different ways, but essentially it is a physiological response to undue external pressures. The body tries to adapt to these pressures, may cope for a while, but if the stress is prolonged a breakdown of some kind in this response occurs. Typically, this process of adaptation and breakdown involves three stages:

1. an alarm reaction followed by shock and lowered resistance, followed in turn by the mobilization of defence mechanisms and a resurgence of resistance.

2. a stage of resistance marked by varying degrees of adaptation;

3. a stage of exhaustion, followed by collapse of the adaptive response and physical or psychological breakdown.

If the level of stress is mild, or if the person concerned has high natural resistance or is skilled at adaptation, the third stage may never be reached. Some individuals cope successfully with stress for long periods, and even claim to thrive on it (though in this case, we probably would not describe it as stress; one person's stress is another's exciting challenge). But stress does take its toll, and it is important to know as much about it as possible if we are to be able to avoid it where we can, and handle it successfully where we cannot. And it is important to recognize the early stages of stress (stages 1 and 2) and to take remedial action before things get worse. Insomnia, panic attacks, abrupt changes in established life patterns, increased drinking, restlessness, depression, irritability are all signs of mounting stress and should be heeded before things get worse.

By its nature, teaching is a stressful occupation. The reasons are not hard to seek. Teachers have a constant range of demands made upon them, by children and by staff, many of them conflicting and many of them almost impossible to meet. Teachers have the continual challenge of maintaining class-room control. They have no clear limits to the hours needed to cover their work. Much of this work they take home with them, making it hard to switch off at the end of the day. They are open to criticism by government inspectors, parents, school governors, the media, and local and national politi-cians. They are short of resources and of opportunities for regular and extended re-training. They are expected to keep up to date with new syllabuses and with developments in their teaching subject(s). They may (dependent upon the head-teacher) have little say in school management and decision making. They are affected emotionally by the successes and failures of their pupils. And perhaps above all they have their own sense of professional standards, and suffer the frustra-tions that come from falling short of them.

Faced with these stressors, the teacher struggles on, often with little or no opportunities of support from outside. Working all day with children and in isolation from other adults, the teacher has limited scope to seek advice or discuss difficulties with colleagues. It may sound strange, but in many ways teaching is a rather lonely profession, with each teacher closeted alone with their problems from one end of the lesson to the other. Mutual support and encouragement from people involved in the same task and with an understanding of each other's difficulties can go a long way towards helping indivi-duals adapt to stress. So can help from experts specially trained to advise on specific issues (educational psychologists, LEA advisors and advisory teachers). If nothing else, such support and advice helps the individual feel less abandoned, less exposed. But in the case of the teaching profession, scarce resources mean that the great majority of people have to fend for themselves the great majority of the time.

It often comes as a surprise to learn that the stress-prone teacher is less the nervous individual or the one low in self-confidence than the hard-driving character who is over-dedicated to work and who takes things too seriously (Kyria-cou, 1982). This is not because over-dedication or seriousness are bad in themselves, but because these two qualities are often symptomatic of the demanding, determined state of mind which becomes frustrated by opposition or delays (a syndrome of behaviour referred to in the medical literature as the *Type A* personality, and linked at least in some research studies with physical breakdowns such as coronary heart disease). Individuals with this approach to life are often in conflict with themselves and with others, and pay a high emotional price for it. In a job such as teaching, where issues are seldom clear cut and where the speed of progress is often decided by factors outside our immediate control, they are often particularly at risk.

How to handle stress

The first piece of advice on handling stress is therefore to see whether you fall into this hard-driving category. If you do, it is not a matter of cutting down on dedication and workload. It is a matter of being more realistic in your expectations and in your judgement of what is possible and what is impossible in any given situation. And of equal importance, it is a matter of being able to laugh, particularly at yourself, when things go wrong. A sense of humour is not only a great help in reducing tension, it also seems to be linked to self-acceptance. People who can chuckle at themselves without embarrassment or self-rejection show they know and value themselves (see Fontana, 1985). They are free of the inner conflict that comes from a vast gap between who one is and who one likes to think one is. Such people often show the same degree of realism and acceptance when it comes to the outer world. They are not constantly wishing things were otherwise, and angry and frustrated when things are not. Certainly they try to change things in desirable directions where change is possible. But they start by first getting to know things as they are, and then working sensibly within the opportunities and the limitations thus offered.

The second piece of advice is to examine one's own reactions. In any stress reduction programme one of the first exercises is to look carefully at *why* certain things make us tense or upset or irritated. A teacher says, reasonably enough on the face of it, 'Class 3C you make me so angry', or 'Binks you make me lose all patience' or 'my colleagues make me feel inadequate'. But if we think about it, we can see none of these statements is actually true. There is no magic button on our foreheads labelled 'anger' or 'impatience' or 'inadequacy' which 3C or Binks or our colleagues can come up and press. There is no real sense in which they *make* us react as we do. Our reactions are our own affair. We may find it very hard to deal with them, but nevertheless, in the final analysis, we cannot automatically blame them on other people. It is up to us to look at them and to decide why they are as they are.

So what is it in me that prompts my anger at 3C or my impatience at the luckless Binks or my inadequacy when I see colleagues outperforming me? Do I feel my professional pride is taking a knock? Do I feel I am being diminished in my own eyes? Do I feel my picture of the world and of how quickly children should learn and of how I should compare with my colleagues is under threat? Whatever the reason, if I can identify it in myself I am a long way towards understanding myself that much better, and towards taking my reactions into my own hands. If my professional pride or my sense of my own worth leads me so easily into a negative emotional state then I have to question their value. These things should be there to help me, not make life more difficult. In any case, if my pride and my sense of worth are that easily dented they're pretty fragile things, and since fragility in such matters often suggests unreality, it may be that I've got a quite mistaken notion of what real professional pride or real self-worth actually are. I may simply have constructed a false picture of the good teacher (one who always has a docile obedient class, who always produces high-flyers, who always has an imma-culate classroom, who never looks undignified and so on) and a false picture of my ideal self (someone who wins every argument, who outshines everyone else around, who knows every answer, who attracts admiration wherever he or she goes). If I have, then herein lies the root of much of my problem. I've created a set of artificial models, and I'm now defending them like mad, getting angry or frustrated or upset when other people don't co-operate with me in treating my models as if they're real.

The third piece of advice is to study other people that little bit more closely, and be a little less eager to attribute motives to them. Class 3C are probably proving difficult not because they have anything particularly against me, but because they are generally bored with school and with lessons that seem irrelevant to them. Binks is probably a slow learner not in order to frustrate me but because no one has presented material to him or her in a form which they can quickly grasp. And my colleagues are outperforming me not in order to make me feel useless but because they are more experienced than I am or have learnt to make better use of their skills and abilities. Once I realize that people are not aiming things directly at *me* all the time, I'm able to be much more objective in my approach. And on those few occasions where perhaps they are aiming at me, I can deny them the satisfaction (and reinforcement) of hitting home.

Notice that the second and third pieces of advice apply even if your stress is not the result of a hard-driving personality. Although this personality seems particularly prone to the adverse effects of stress, other personalities are by no means immune. The tense, nervous personality is certainly at risk. So is the individual who is low on self-esteem and self-confidence. So is the peaceful soul who hates ever to be at odds with anyone else. Temperamentally some people are more easily upset than others and feel fear and anxiety more readily, and some people are more quick to anger. But in all cases a more realistic approach to life and a greater degree of self-knowledge and a greater knowledge of others are vital components in stress reduction. Simple relaxation techniques, with an awareness of bodily tensions and of how to release them, also play an important part. Meditation techniques, in which mind and body both become calm, are equally valuable. Relaxation and meditation produce an equanimity which allows one to contemplate stressful situations without alarm, and which then carries over into coping behaviours when faced with the actual situations themselves.

Finally, no one should feel helpless in the face of stress. Enough has been said in this section to show that there are strategies for dealing with it. Some of these strategies teachers can use on their own, others (like relaxation and meditation) can be learnt through the yoga or similar classes which are now freely available in most places. Nor should anyone feel that stress must be kept to oneself. Talking the problem over with colleagues and headteachers, and alerting others to the testing time one is having, are vital. Stress is a serious condition, which should be treated supportively and sympathetically by colleagues and friends.

References

Bennett, N. (1976). *Teaching Styles and Pupil Progress*. London: Open Books.

Bennett, N., Desforges, C., Cockburn, A. and Wilkinson, B. (1984) *The Quality of Pupil Learning Experiences*. London and New Jersey: Lawrence Erlbaum.

Bruner, J.S. (1976) The styles of teaching. *New Society, April*.

Cortis, G.A. (1973) The assessment of a group of teachers in relation to earlier career experience. *Educational Review, 25*, 112–123.

Cortis, G.A. (1985) Eighteen years on: how far can you go? *Educational Review, 37*.

Fontana, D. (1972) What do we mean by a good teacher? In G. Chanan (ed.) *Research Forum on Teacher Education*. London: NFER.

Fontana, D. (1985) *Teaching and Personality*. Oxford: Basil Blackwell.

Haddon, F.H. and Lytton, H. (1968) Teaching approach and the development of divergent thinking abilities in primary school children. *British Journal of Educational Psychology, 38*, 171–180.

Haddon, F.H. and Lytton, H. (1971) Primary education and divergent thinking abilities – four years on. *British Journal of Educational Psychology, 41*, 136–147.

Kyriacou, C. (1982) Reducing teacher stress. *Education Section Review, 6, 1*, 13–15.

SOME
QUESTIONS

1. Why is it difficult to define and assess the 'good' teacher?

2. List some of the qualities of the 'good' teacher identified by research.

3. What does 'emotional maturity' mean in the teacher, and why is it an important characteristic?

4. Give examples of what you take to be desirable professional attitudes.

5. How would you distinguish between so-called 'formal' and 'informal' teaching styles?

6. Is 'teacher talk' a good or a bad thing?

7. What are the qualities of a good listener?

8. Why is it important that the teacher should be able to show flexibility in professional life?

9. What factors do you think will prove most stressful to you in your professional life? How do you plan to cope with them?

Additional Reading

Bennett, N. (1976) *Teaching Styles and Pupil Progress*. London: Open Books.
This book contains relevant information on the issues in both teachers and pupils which lead to successful learning. Bennett et al. (1984) which also appears in the references is equally valuable in this context.

Brophy, J.E. and Good, T.L. (1974) *Teacher-Student Relationships: Causes and consequences*. New York: Holt, Rinehart & Winston.
Also recommended for Chapter 11.

Fontana, D. (1986) *Teaching and Personality*. Oxford: Basil Blackwell.
Contains a more extensive examination of teacher personality, together with an examination of all aspects of personality development in children. (Also recommended for Chapters 7 and 8.)

Simon, B. and Galton, M. (1980) *Progress and Performance in the Primary Classroom*. London: Routledge & Kegan Paul.
Presents the research-based finding that it is the teachers who spend most time on class teaching and who ask the most open-ended thought-provoking questions whose pupils make best progress in mathematics, reading and language. Makes interesting reading for all teachers.

Solomon, D. and Kendall, A. (1979) *Children in Classrooms: An investigation of person environment interaction*. New York: Praeger.
Good on the interaction between teacher and child personalities.

Wragg, E.C. (ed.) (1984) *Classroom Teaching Skills*. London: Croom Helm and New York: Nichols.
A research-based investigation of the skills teachers actually need in the classroom.

INDEX